Right-Wing Populism in Europe

Right-Wing Populism in Europe

Politics and Discourse

Edited by
Ruth Wodak
Majid KhosraviNik
Brigitte Mral

B L O O M S B U R Y
LONDON • NEW DELHI • NEW YORK • SYDNEY

Bloomsbury Academic

An imprint of Bloomsbury Publishing Plc

50 Bedford Square	175 Fifth Avenue
London	New York
WC1B 3DP	NY 10010
UK	USA

www.bloomsbury.com

First published 2013

British Library Cataloguing-in-Publication Data
A catalogue record for this book is available from the British Library.

ISBN: HB: 978-1-78093-232-3
PB: 978-1-78093-245-3
ePub: 978-1-78093-344-3
ePDF: 978-1-78093-343-6

Library of Congress Cataloging-in-Publication Data
A catalog record for this book is available from the Library of Congress.

Typeset by NewGen Imaging Systems Pvt. Ltd, Chennai, India
Printed and bound in Great Britain

Contents

List of Illustrations

Acknowledgements

Most of the contributions to this volume stem from a very stimulating, cross-disciplinary and international conference held in Loka Brunn, Sweden, in June 2010. We were very grateful for such a unique possibility to meet and discuss the complex and threatening phenomenon of 'old-new' radical right-wing populist movements across Europe for several days. We are also very grateful for having been funded by money related to the Kerstin Hesselgren Chair of the Swedish Parliament which was awarded to Ruth Wodak in 2008.

Moreover, we would like to thank the Department of Media and Rhetoric at Örebro University for supporting this conference, especially Agneta Klintenäs who oversaw all the difficult administrative and organizational issues so that this very special event could take place. We were very pleased that Bloomsbury Publishers immediately took an interest in this volume, specifically Caroline Wintersgill who gave us excellent feedback and support, from the very first proposal and throughout the production process. Finally, we would like to express our immense gratitude to Gerard Hearne, MA, who copy-edited the manuscript, revised the English of non-native writers and took care of the many details which we could not attend to.

Notes on Contributors

Editors

Ruth Wodak is Distinguished Professor of Discourse Studies at Lancaster University since 2004 and has remained affiliated to the University of Vienna where she became a full Professor of Applied Linguistics in 1991. Besides various other prizes, she was awarded the Wittgenstein Prize for Elite Researchers in 1996. She is a Past-President of the *Societas Linguistica Europea* (2011) and a Member of the Academia Europaea since 2010.

Her research interests focus on discourse studies, gender studies, language and/ in politics, prejudice and discrimination and ethnographic methods of linguistic fieldwork. She is on the editorial board of a number of linguistic journals and is co-editor of several peer-review journals such as *Discourse & Society*, *Critical Discourse Studies* and *The Journal of Language and Politics*; she is also co-editor of the book series *Discourse Approaches to Politics, Society and Culture* (DAPSAC).

She has held visiting professorships at Uppsala, Stanford University, University of Minnesota, University of East Anglia and Georgetown University. In 2008, she was awarded the Kerstin Hesselgren Chair of the Swedish Parliament (at the University of Örebrö, where she also received an honorary doctorate in 2010).

Recent book publications include: *Ist Österreich ein 'deutsches' Land?* (with R. de Cillia 2006), *Qualitative Discourse Analysis in the Social Sciences* (with M. Krzyżanowski 2008), *Migration, Identity and Belonging* (with G. Delanty and P. Jones 2008; 2nd rev. edn 2011), *The Discursive Construction of History. Remembering the Wehrmacht's War of Annihilation* (with H. Heer, W. Manoschek and A. Pollak 2008), *The Politics of Exclusion* (with M. Krzyżanowski 2009), *Gedenken im Gedankenjahr* (with R. de Cillia 2009) and *The discourse of politics in action: 'Politics as Usual'* (2009, 2nd rev. edn 2011). See: www.ling.lancs.ac.uk/profiles/265 for more information about ongoing research projects and recent publications.

Majid KhosraviNik, PhD, is a Lecturer in Critical Discourse Analysis (CDA) and Mass Communication at Northumbria University in Newcastle, United Kingdom. His research interests include the theory and application of critical discourse analysis, discourse and Identity politics and dynamics of discourse and society in the (mass/ new) media. Prior to Northumbria Majid held research and teaching positions at Lancaster University where he received his PhD in Discourse Studies. At Lancaster University, Majid was part of the RASIM (Refugees, Asylum Seekers and Immigrants) project researching the representation of immigrants in the British press. Among other publications, he has authored a number of papers on discourse and immigration and methods of CDA in *Discourse & Society*, *Critical Discourse Studies* and *Journal of Language and Politics*. Majid is the review editor for *Critical Discourse Studies* and a co-founder of the Newcastle & Northumbria Critical Discourse Group (N&NCDG).

He is working on a monograph about the representation of Iran's nuclear programme in the Iranian and British press. More info at: www.northumbria.ac.uk/sd/academic/sass/about/media/staff/khosraviNik

Brigitte Mral is Professor of Rhetoric, former Professor of Media and Communication Studies, at Örebro University, Sweden. She has published numerous books and articles concerning rhetoric in historical and contemporary situations, including *Talande kvinnor. Kvinnliga retoriker från Aspasia till Ellen Key* (Women Speakers. Women Rhetorics from Aspasia to Ellen Key) (1999), '*We're a Peaceful Nation*'. War Rhetoric After September 11 (2003), *Women's Rhetoric. Argumentative Strategies of Women in Public Life: Sweden & South Africa* (with Nicole Borg & Philippe Joseph Salazar, 2009) and *Bildens retorik i journalistiken* (Visual Rhetoric in Journalism) (with Henrik Olinder, 2011). She is currently leading a research project on 'Rhetorical Aspects of Crisis Communication' and is head of the recently founded Center for Crisis Communication, at Örebro University.

Chapter Contributors

Christoph Andersson is a journalist working for the Documentary Department at public Swedish radio, Sveriges Radio, P1. Since 2005 he has specialized in covering right-wing parties and groups. He has produced several radio documentaries on the subject and is now working on a programme about the ideas underlying Anders Behring Breivik's bomb attack and killings in Norway. His documentaries have also been published in the Swedish book *Från gatan in i parlamenten – om extremhögerns väg mot politisk makt* (From the Streets into the Parliaments – How the Extreme Right wants to Gain Political Power) (Norstedts Publishing Co., Stockholm, 2010). He also teaches investigative journalism at the University of Södertörn and the Stockholm Academy of Dramatic Arts (SADA). As a journalist he has mainly worked for radio, but also for union magazines. For some years he worked as an ombudsman at the Swedish Union of Journalists, handling issues on press ethics.

Daunis Auers, PhD (London) is Associate Professor of Comparative Politics in the Department of Political Science, University of Latvia, visiting Professor on the Executive MBA programme at the Stockholm School of Economics in Riga and Senior Researcher in the Advanced Social and Political Research Centre at the University of Latvia. He was a Fulbright Scholar at the University of California-Berkeley in the academic year 2005–6. He was the first managing editor of the *Baltic Journal of Economics* in 2002, and later served as Vice-President for Professional Development at the Association for the Advancement of Baltic Studies. His most recent published research has focused on studies of the Latvian Green Party (articles in the *Journal of Baltic Studies* and *Environmental Politics*), direct democracy (referendums and citizens' initiatives) as well as radical-right populist parties and movements in the Baltic States.

Laura Balbo has been Professor of Sociology at several universities in Italy (Milano, Ferrara, Padova) and President of the Italian Sociological Association, 1998–2001. She has been visiting professor at the University of California, Berkeley and Santa Cruz, and at the University of Sydney. She has taken part in many research projects and activities organized at the European Union (EU) level. She has been a Member of the Italian Parliament, from 1984 to 1993, and Minister of Equal Opportunities, from 1998 to 2000; she has developed upon Pierre Bourdieu's suggestion to 'think politics sociologically' and published a book (2002) and several essays from this perspective. She is currently President of the International Association for the Study of Racism and of Italia/Razzismo. She has written extensively on issues of racism and racialization. Among her books are *I razzismi possibili* (with L. Manconi, Milano Feltrinelli, 1990), *I razzismi reali* (Milano: Feltrinelli, 1992) and *'In che razza di società vivremo? L'Europa, i razzismi, il futuro'* (Milano: Bruno Mondadori, 2006).

Brigitte Beauzamy holds a PhD in Sociology from the École des hautes études en sciences sociales (EHESS), Paris, and was a lecturer in Political Science at the University of Paris 13 until 2009. She is currently a Marie Curie Advanced Research Fellow at the Centre for the Study of Globalization and Regionalization (CSGR), in the Department of Politics and International Studies (PAIS) at the University of Warwick. Her research interests deal primarily with the transnational agency of social movements, and she is currently focusing on a case study of French-Jewish peace movements in the Israel/Palestine conflict and their impact both on the conflict and on French society. Among her most recent publications is: *La créativité altermondialiste: discours, organisation, action directe* (Lille: Presses Universitaires du Septentrion, in press). She is also Security Editor of the openSecurity section of the www.openDemocracy.net website.

Heidi Beirich leads one of the most highly regarded non-governmental operations monitoring hate groups and extremism in the world today, the Southern Poverty Law Center's (SPLC) Intelligence Project. She oversees the production of SPLC's award-winning quarterly investigative journal, *Intelligence Report*, its Hatewatch blog and its annual hate-group list. An expert on white nationalism, nativism and the racist neo-Confederate movement, Beirich also acts as a key SPLC spokeswoman for issues involving extremism. She has appeared on numerous television news programmes and is regularly quoted by journalists and scholars in both the United States and abroad. She has been with the Center since 1999, joining its staff after earning a PhD in Political Science from Purdue University. Beirich was also a co-editor of *Neo-Confederacy: A Critical Introduction*, published by the University of Texas Press in 2008.

Hans-Georg Betz is an Adjunct Professor of Political Science at University of Zurich. He is also author of several books and articles on the populist right in Western Europe.

Kristina Boréus is professor of Political Science at Stockholm University. She has researched and published on ideology and ideological change – including the turn to the right of Swedish public debate that took place as part of the global ideological change in the 1970s and 1980s – and on ethnic and other kinds of discrimination. Her work on discrimination includes how it is expressed in argumentation and language use as well as in non-linguistic practices, for example in the social practices of workplaces. Her research also includes the study of ideas, textual analysis and discourse analysis as methods and theory. Recent research projects include a comparative study of populist-right parties and discrimination against immigrants in Austria, Denmark and Sweden, and a study of the inequalities between women and men, immigrants and natives, in Swedish workplaces.

Benjamin de Cleen received his doctorate at the Department of Communication Studies of the Free University of Brussels (VUB) in 2012. His doctoral dissertation presents a discourse-theoretical analysis of the rhetoric of the Flemish populist radical-right party Vlaams Blok/Belang. It focuses on a number of key moments of the discursive struggle between Vlaams Blok/Belang and other voices in which cultural performances and artists played a central role. Earlier publications include Popular Music Against Extreme Right Populism: 'The Vlaams Belang and the 0110 Concerts in Belgium', *International Journal of Cultural Studies* 12(6); 'Contesting the Populist Claim on "the People" Through Popular Culture: the 0110 Concerts versus the Vlaams Belang', *Social Semiotics* 20(2) (with Nico Carpentier); 'Bringing Discourse Theory into Media Studies', *Journal of Language and Politics* 6(2) (with Nico Carpentier). Benjamin is chair of the Young Scholars' Network of the European Communication Research and Education Association (YECREA).

Björn Fryklund is Professor in (Political) Sociology and Director for the Research Institute Malmö Institute for Studies of Migration, Diversity and Welfare (MIM) at Malmö University in Sweden. His main research interests are studies on populism, xenophobia and migration, and how these phenomena relate to each other. Other research interests are migration, health and care; migration, diversity and multiculturalism; migration, democracy and human rights.

Björn Fryklund is currently investigating different immigration countries, especially European, in a comparative way, while examining how populism relates to the problems and possibilities of multicultural democracy. His most important publications are *Populism and Parties of Discontent in the Nordic Countries – Studies of Petty Bourgeois Class Activity,* (Lund: Arkiv, 1981); '*Us against them' – the Double Estrangement in Sjöbo,* (Lund: Lund University Press, 1989) '*Until the Lamb of God Appears. . .' – The 1991 Parliamentary Election: Sweden Chooses a New Political System,* (Lund: Lund University Press, 1994) *Populism and a Mistrust of Foreigners – Sweden in Europe,* (Norrköping: Elander, 2007) and *A Changed Sweden: Migration and its Consequences,* (Malmö: Liber, 2008).

Aristotle Kallis is Professor of Modern and Contemporary History at Lancaster University. His main research interests lie in the fields of interwar fascism and the post-war/contemporary far right in Europe, as well as in mass violence and totalitarian propaganda. He has also conducted research on the diffusion of taboo ideas and practices in a number of fields, ranging from the diffusion of fascism and dictatorship in 1930s Europe to the spreading of eliminationist violence during the Second World War, and the 'demonstration effect' of revolutionary movements. He is the author of *Genocide and Fascism* (London: Routledge, 2009), *National Socialist Propaganda in the Second World War* (Basingstoke: Palgrave, 2005), *The Fascism Reader* (London: Routledge, 2003) and *Fascist Ideology: Territory and Expansionism in Italy and Germany, 1922–1945* (London: Routledge, 2000).

Andres Kasekamp is Professor of Baltic Politics in the Institute of Government and Politics at the University of Tartu, Estonia, and Director of the Estonian Foreign Policy Institute. He is a graduate of the University of Toronto and gained his PhD in modern history from the School of Slavonic and East European Studies, London University, in 1996. He is a member of the European Consortium for the Political Research Standing Group on Extremism and Democracy, and is currently Vice-President for Professional Development at the Association for the Advancement of Baltic Studies. In the past, he has served as Chairman of the Board of the Open Estonia Foundation and Editor of the *Journal of Baltic Studies*. He is the author of *The Radical Right in Interwar Estonia* (Basingstoke: Palgrave Macmillan, 2000) and *A History of the Baltic States* (Basingstoke: Palgrave Macmillan, 2010), which won the 2011 Baltic Assembly Science Prize.

András Kovács is Professor at Central European University, Budapest, and Senior researcher in the Centre of Social Research at the Hungarian Academy of Sciences.

Previous appointments and research stays are at Paderborn University, École des Hautes Études en Sciences Sociales, New York University, TH Twente, Salomon Steinheim Institut für Deutsch-Jüdische Geschichte, Institut für die Wissenschaften vom Menschen, Vienna, Moses Mendelssohn Zentrum für Jüdische Studien, Potsdam, Internationales Forschungszentrum Kulturwissenschaften, Vienna and Zentrum für Antisemitismusforschung, TU Berlin.

His research subjects are Jewish identity and anti-Semitism in post-war Europe, memory and identity and post-communist extreme right.

Selected publications include 'Jewish groups and identity strategies in post-communist Hungary', in Zvi Gitelman, Barry Kosmin and András Kovács (eds), *New Jewish Identities* (Central European University Press: Budapest, New York, 2003). 'Hungarian Jewish politics from the end of the second world war until the collapse of communism', in Ezra Mendelsohn (ed.), *Jews and the State. Studies in Contemporary Jewry, XIX*, (Oxford: Oxford University Press, 2004), 'Two sides of the coin: Clean break and usable history. The case of Hungary', in Ruth Wodak and Gertraud Auer-Boreo (eds), *Justice and Memory. Confronting Traumatic Pasts* (Vienna: Passagen Verlag, 2009); *The Stranger at Hand. Antisemitic Prejudices in Post-communist Hungary* (Leiden-Boston: Brill, 2010).

Dr Michał Krzyżanowski works at the University of Aberdeen in Scotland where he came in 2012 after holding posts at Lancaster University (UK), University of Vienna (Austria) and Adam Mickiewicz University, Poznan (Poland). In 2011 he was also a Visiting Professor in Media and Communication Studies, Örebro University (Sweden). He is specialised in Critical Discourse Analysis and has done much research on political as well as media communication and the public sphere. Michał is the author, co-author and editor of several monographs and anthologies as well as journal articles in the field of critical discourse studies of media and political discourse. He is Associate Editor of the *Journal of Language and Politics* and serves on editorial boards of such journals as, *Critical Discourse Studies* or *Qualitative Sociology Review*.

Magnus Engen Marsdal is an author and journalist based in Oslo, Norway. One of Marsdal's best-selling books is *Frp-koden* (*The Frp Code*), which is a study in political sociology based in part on in-depth interviews with working-class voters supporting the Norwegian Progress Party (Frp). *The Frp Code* generated massive media attention when published in 2007, and won an award from The Norwegian Sociologial Association. It has since been translated into Swedish. Marsdal is also a well-known analyst and commentator on current affairs in the Norwegian public media. He has worked as a news editor and journalist for several years and published his first book, *Tredje venstre, for en radikal individualisme* (*Third Left: In Defence of Radical Individualism*), in 2004. Marsdal is currently the chairman of the Manifest Centre for Societal Analysis in Oslo.

Stig A. Nohrstedt is Professor of Media and Communication Studies in the Department of Humanities, Education and Social Sciences at Örebro University and a Guest Professor in Journalism at Linneaus University, Sweden. He has a PhD in Political Science from Uppsala University and a Docent title (Assistant Professor) in Journalism and Mass Communication at Göteborg University. His primary research interests include war and conflict journalism, journalistic ethics, risk and crisis communication as well as media and structural discrimination. His recent publication is Stig A. Nohrstedt (ed.) *Communicating Risks – Towards the Threat Society?* (Stockholm: Nordicom, 2011).

Simon Oja is a PhD student in the Department of Rhetoric, Örebro University, and is working on a dissertation with the title 'The Sweden Democrats 2002–10: A rhetorical study of public debate and argumentation'.

Merijn Oudenampsen studied Political Science and Sociology at the University of Amsterdam. He was a researcher at the Post-Academic Art Institute Jan van Eyck in Maastricht in a multi-disciplinary research project on populist aesthetics. In 2010 he edited the Dutch art theory magazine *Open*, which investigated the populist imagination. From 2011 he began PhD research at Tilburg University on political populism and the swing to the Right in Dutch politics, combining contemporary political theory and insights gleaned from cultural studies, media studies and nationalism research.

Anton Pelinka is Professor of Nationalism Studies and Political Science, Central European University, Budapest, since 2006. He was Professor of Political Science, University of Innsbruck, 1975–2006, Visiting Professor at Jawaharlal Nehru University (JNU), New Delhi (1977), University of New Orleans (1981), Harvard University (Schumpeter Fellow, 1990–1), Stanford University (Austrian Chair, 1997) and the University of Michigan (2001–2).

Research and publications are located in the following fields: Democratic Theory (e.g. *Dynamische Demokratie* (Stuttgart: Kohlhammer, 1974); *Politics of the Lesser Evil* (New Brunswick: Transaction Press, 1999)); Comparative Politics (e.g. *Social Democratic Parties in Europe* (New York: Praeger, 1983); *Democracy Indian Style* (New Brunswick: Transaction Press, 2003)); Austrian Politics (e.g. *Austria: Out of the Shadow of the Past* (Boulder: Westview, 1998); *The Haider Phenomenon in Austria*, co-edited with Ruth Wodak (New Brunswick: Transaction Press, 2002)).

John E. Richardson is a Senior Lecturer in the Department of Social Sciences, Loughborough University. He is Editor of the international peer-review journal *Critical*

Discourse Studies and is on the editorial boards of *Discourse & Society, Social Semiotics, the Journal of Language and Politics* and *CADAAD*, among other journals. His research interests include structured social inequalities, British fascism, racism in journalism, critical discourse studies and argumentation. His publications include books: *Language and Journalism* (2009, London: Routledge), *(Mis)Representing Islam: The Racism and Rhetoric of British Broadsheet Newspapers* (paperback edition 2009, Amsterdam: John Benjamins), *Analysing Newspapers: An Approach from Critical Discourse Analysis* (2007, Basingstoke: Palgrave), *Analysing Media Discourses* (2011, London: Routledge, co-edited with Joseph Burridge) and *Analysing Fascist Discourse: European Fascism in Talk and Text* (2012, London: Routledge, co-edited with Ruth Wodak); and academic articles on critical discourse studies, newspaper representations of Muslims, balance and impartiality in BBC reports of Israel/Palestine, argumentation in readers' letters, political communications and party political leaflets. He is currently co-editing a book on *Cultures of Post-War British Fascism* (London: Routledge, forthcoming).

Carlo Ruzza, MA SUNY, PhD Harvard, is Professor of Political Sociology at the University of Trento, Italy and at the University of Leicester, UK. He has previously taught at the Universities of Essex and Surrey. His research interests focus upon civil society, social movements and right-wing parties. His book publications include: *Migrants in the Health Care System* (with Christiane Falge and Oliver Schmidtke; London: Ashgate, 2012); *Reinventing the Italian Right: Populism, Post-Fascism and Territorial Identity* (with Stefano Fella; London: Routledge, 2009), and *Europe and Civil Society: Movement Coalitions and European Governance* (Manchester: Manchester University Press, 2007). His journal publications include articles in the *Journal of European Integration, West European Politics, Acta Politica, International Journal of Sociology, European Political Science*, and *Journal of Contemporary European Studies and Policy and Society*. His edited books include *Conflict Citizenship and Civil Society* (with P. Baert, S. Koniordos and G. Procacci; London: Routledge, 2009), *Governance and Civil Society: Policy Perspectives and Europe* and *Civil Society: Normative Dimensions* (both co-edited with Vincent Della Sala; Manchester: Manchester University Press, 2007); *Anti-racist movements in the European Union: between Europeanisation and National Trajectories,* London: Palgrave (with Stefano Fella, 2012). He has also edited volumes on environmental issues.

Britta Schellenberg is a research analyst at the *Center for Applied Policy Research* and a lecturer in the Faculty of Political Sciences at the *Ludwig-Maximilians University,* Munich. After study visits in Heidelberg, Jerusalem, London, New York, and Berlin she coordinated several projects on the extreme right at Munich University, for instance in cooperation with the Bertelsmann Foundation. Her research focuses on the radical right and strategies against right-wing radicalism. Britta Schellenberg is the author of a wide range of publications, including: *Rechtsextremismus und Fremdenfeindlichkeit im öffentlichen Diskurs der Bundesrepublik Deutschland. Die Debatte über den Fall Mügeln* (Right-wing extremism and xenophobia in the public discourse of the Federal Republic of Germany. The debate about the case Mügeln), PhD thesis, TU Berlin, 2012; *Is Europe on the 'Right Path'? Right-wing Extremism and Populism in Europe*, Berlin: Friedrich-Ebert Foundation, 2011(with Nora Langenbacher); *Strategies for Combating*

Right-Wing Extremism in Europe, Gütersloh: Bertelsmann Foundation, 2007 (with Orkan Kösemen).

Anton Shekhovtsov is a Junior Visiting Fellow at the Institute for Human Sciences, Vienna, Austria, and European Fellow of the Radicalism and New Media Research Group at the University of Northampton, UK. He specializes in the study of radical right-wing parties and far-right music. He has published several articles and chapters in this area in English, Russian and Ukrainian. In 2009, he co-authored a book on radical Russian nationalism, and in 2011 he published a monograph of new radical right-wing parties in European democracies. He is General Editor of the *Explorations of the Far Right* book series at *ibidem*-Verlag, Germany, and is on the Editorial Board of *Fascism. Journal of Comparative Fascist Studies*.

John Solomos is Professor of Sociology at City University, London. Before that he was Professor of Sociology at South Bank University, Professor of Sociology and Social Policy at the University of Southampton and has worked at the Economic and Social Research Council (ESRC) Centre for Research in Ethnic Relations, University of Aston and Warwick and at the Department of Politics and Sociology, Birkbeck College, University of London. He has researched and written widely on the history and contemporary forms of race and ethnic relations in Britain, theories of race and racism, the politics of race, equal opportunity policies, multiculturalism and social policy, race and football and racist movements and ideas. His most recent book is: *Transnational Families: Ethnicities, Identities and Social Capital* (co-author with Harry Goulbourne, Tracey Reynolds and Elisabetta Zontini; London: Routledge 2009). He has also recently edited *The Sage Handbook of Race and Ethnic Studies* (co-editor with Patricia Hill Collins; London: Sage, 2010); *Race and Ethnicity in the 21st Century* (co-editor with Alice Bloch; Basingstoke: Palgrave Macmillan, 2010); *Theories of Race and Racism:* A Reader 2nd edn (co-editor with Les Back; London: Routledge, 2009). He is joint-Editor of the international journal *Ethnic and Racial Studies*, which is a monthly scholarly journal published by Routledge.

Dynamics of Discourse and Politics in Right-wing Populism in Europe and Beyond: An Introduction

Ruth Wodak and Majid KhosraviNik

Much research in the social sciences provides ample evidence for the current rise of right-wing populist movements and related political parties in most European Union (EU) member states and beyond (Wilson & Hainsworth 2012). On the one hand, neo-Nazi movements are to be observed in the form of extreme far-right parties; on the other, a salient shift is occurring in the forms and styles of political rhetoric of right-wing populist parties which could be labelled the *Haiderization* of politics.[1] This volume attempts to explain why this transformation is currently taking place from an interdisciplinary perspective; moreover, various strategies of combating such movements will also be briefly discussed.

Right-wing extremism and right-wing populism are not new phenomena. Ever since the end of the Second World War, revisionist ideologies have circulated and been taken on board by neo-Nazi or right-wing extremist parties such as the Freiheitliche Partei Österreichs/ Austrian Freedom Party (FPÖ), the French National Front/ Le Front National (FN) and the British National Party (BNP). While resemblances to older, well-known ideologies can be traced in many of the 'new' right-wing discourses (Mammone 2009), it has been argued that right-wing populism differs from those other trends as it does not convey a coherent ideology but rather proposes a mixed bag of beliefs, stereotypes, attitudes and related programmes which aim to address and mobilize a range of equally contradictory segments of the electorate.

Moreover, we are witnessing the development of a 'media-democracy' across Europe and beyond, in which the individual, media-savvy performance of politics seems to become more important than the political process (Grande 2000). Accordingly, politics becomes simplified and dumped down to a few slogans apparently comprehensible to the broad public at large. As argued by Ellinas (2009), the media communication and appropriation employed in the recent success of populist-right parties cannot be overlooked. Furthermore, the disproportionate success of some of these parties, Ellinas claims, could be explained by the excessive exposure that these parties receive in the media, despite their lacking the required organizational and political structures (ibid.) (see chapters by Anderssen (Ch. 22), Krzyżanowski (Ch. 9), Nohrstedt (Ch. 21) and Oja and Mral (Ch. 19) in this volume).

---

[1] See Pelinka and Wodak 2002, Wodak and Pelinka 2002, Rydgren 2005, Gingrich and Banks 2006, Ellinas 2009, Krzyżanowski and Wodak 2009, Bruter and Harrison 2011, Delanty et al. 2011, Steinmetz 2011, Wodak and Richardson 2012 and Wodak forthcoming; see also the chapter by Pelinka (Ch. 1) in this volume for a typology of right-wing populist parties.

Hence, we argue, far-right extremism is overtly reliant on charismatic personalities and media-savvy populism. This is particularly relevant with respect to the growing apathy of the general public to mainstream politics as populist extremist discourses seem to fill the gap created by the public's disenchantment with (mainstream) politics (Hay 2007, Wodak 2011a, b). In this same vein, Judt (2010) notes that what the 'baby-boomer politicians' have in common is 'the enthusiasm that they fail to inspire in the electors of their respective countries'. He is even more concerned that politicians like Sarah Palin 'can only benefit from rising confusion and anxiety in the face of apparently unmanageable change' (ibid.: 48). If one studies recent opinion polls (such as *Eurobarometer*), it becomes apparent that trust in mainstream politicians and governing parties has dropped significantly across Europe. Indeed only 29 per cent of European citizens trust their national governments as opposed to 34 per cent in 2007; in 2009, the numbers dropped even more: only 13 per cent of British citizens, for example, trusted their politicians, and 82 per cent believed that politicians were not telling the truth.[2] In 2011, on average, 16 per cent trusted their national political parties, and the level of trust in several major EU countries (including the United Kingdom and France) did not exceed 10 per cent. Researchers point to two parallel phenomena that may help explain this change:

- The so-called *Berlusconisation* of Europe (Ash et al. 2010). The latter is defined as 'a happy-clappy populism mixing feel-good consumerism, ethno-nationalist sentiment and shallow hedonism with lamentable actions against immigrants, minorities, and the vulnerable in general' (ibid.: 1).
- The so-called *Haiderization* of Europe, a label drawing on the name of the former leader of the FPÖ, Jörg Haider, indicates the rise of right-wing populist parties in several EU member states (such as Austria, Belgium, Hungary, etc.) since the end of the twentieth century. These parties, which claim to speak for 'the people' and to oppose those in power, frequently endorse chauvinist and nativist ideologies which may lead to an overall 'politics of fear' (see also Richardson & Wodak 2009a, b, Wodak & Richardson 2012).

Indeed, the results of the most recent elections to the European Parliament, in June 2009, manifest a significant growth in right-wing extremist (and right-wing populist) parties, and thus related MEPs, for example, the British BNP, the Austrian FPÖ, the Dutch Party for Freedom/ Partij voor de Vrijheid (PVV), the Hungarian Jobbik (The Movement for a Better Hungary/ Jobbik Magyarországért Mozgalom) and the Danish Dansk Folkeparti (Danish People's Party) have all won over 10 per cent of national votes. These election campaigns were accompanied by – sometimes indirect, usually quite explicit – xenophobic, racist and antisemitic propaganda in the respective nation-states. In some countries, like Hungary, violence against Hungarian minorities, such

---

[2] See <www.guardian.co.uk/politics/2009/sep/27/trust-politicians-all-time-low> (accessed 25 April 2012).

as Roma and Jews, has become part of everyday experience (Iordachi 2009, 2010; see chapter by Kovács (Ch. 15) in this volume). In some other cases, such as Estonia and Latvia, extremist parties have not had much success simply because the mainstream parties have to some extent accommodated the radical rhetoric of the extreme-right movements and parties (Auers & Kasekamp 2009; see chapter by Auer and Kasekamp (Ch. 16) in this volume).

Various sociopolitical, socio-economic, ideological and structural factors contribute to such a general swing to, and success of, these extreme/populist right-wing parties, all of which endorse exclusionary chauvinistic and nativist ideologies within national and/or regional domains. There exist some case studies on various countries across Europe: For example, Bakic (2009) argues, on the one hand, that the attractiveness of the Serbian Radical Party to the lower social strata lies within the party's populist appeal and, on the other, attributes the party's appeal to an extreme lack of credibility of the 'Left' in post-communist Serbia. Ellinas (2009) focuses on the FN and investigates the function of media communication in its success (see chapter by Beauzamy (Ch. 12) in this volume). On a wider regional level, Bustikova (2009) studies extreme-right discourses and related parties in Eastern Europe, especially in the new EU member states. She states that contextual sociopolitical features, such as widespread corruption and an absence of political accountability, might play an important role in the popularity of extreme rhetoric, as these parties thrive on the back of a weak (or absent) rule of law (ibid.).

Other studies have looked at the cannons of inspiration for extreme-right parties. Bar-on (2008), for example, discusses the role of the Nouvelle Droite in national and pan-European identity politics since its birth in 1968 (see also Bar-on 2012). Peunova (2008) analyses the ideas of Aleksandre Panarin and his notion of Russian-nationalist Eurasianism, which has fostered several European extreme-right conceptualizations, for example of Nouvelle Droite intellectuals. Thus, Panarin should or could be considered a spokesperson for the European new right wing in Russia, along with the transnational nature of the extreme right (ibid.).

While general trends in European politics towards the Right are visible across the continent, the specific characteristics of various European countries, that is, their history, and political and social imaginaries, also play a significant role in each case. Hence, the rightist populist parties in Europe can be classified into some general categories (see chapters by Pelinka (Ch. 1) and Kallis (Ch. 4) in this volume): First, there are the rightist parties within the context of Western and post-communist Europe which, despite other crucial differences, share a clear past history of fascism; next are parties without a history of populist or revisionist roots; and finally come parties which seem to cut across traditional left- and right-wing politics and target a combined electorate (see chapter by Marsdal (Ch. 3) in this volume). Regardless of these differences, issues of race, immigration, national identity, welfare and social inequality are central to most of these parties, to varying degrees (see KhosraviNik 2009, 2010, KhosraviNik et al. 2012).

To understand the nature of right-wing populism from a scholarly point of view requires a critical look at the concepts of 'populism' and 'right-wing politics'. Some studies argue that populism can be viewed as an aspect of the political persuasive rhetoric and ideology of parties on both the Right and the Left (Azmanova 2012). Nevertheless, right-wing populism is distinguished from other types of populism by its explicit or implicit sharp dichotomization of the social into an 'Us identity' constructed along national, regional, religious and ethnic lines versus 'Them' in various (and sometimes contradictory) ways. Mammone (2009) challenges the appropriateness of labelling the recent rise of a 'new' phenomenon and argues that populism is not the main and foremost feature of certain extremist parties. He maintains that the use of labels like populism should be avoided, as this may serve as an indirect and unintended form of democratic legitimation.

There are also ethical-philosophical/practical issues regarding whether or not such far-right parties should in any way be restricted by law beyond the electoral mechanisms (see chapter by Ruzza and Balbo (Ch. 11) in this volume). The problem with such measures would be that – on the one hand – the outlawing of such parties might be viewed as unfair intervention in the democratic process and – on the other – the efficiency of such measures could be challenged, as banning a party from official participation in the public sphere would not necessarily result in the abolition of its attractiveness, discourse and policies in society. However, there is also a philosophical dilemma, as in whether or not a party with inherently undemocratic, discriminatory and exclusionary policies can/should be seen as a legitimate entity in Western democracies. In other words, should such a party be allowed to assume power through democratic means? This is, we believe, a salient point whereby important aspects of (the efficiency, effectiveness and power of) civil-society movements across European countries should be re-examined.

This volume accounts for the most recent trends in European politics towards right-wing populism. Adopting an interdisciplinary approach to the analysis of modern extremist discourses – rather than relying on the methods of political science (see Mammone 2009) – it investigates the origins and different manifestations of these parties and movements across the EU and beyond from a comparative perspective (see also chapters by Beirich (Ch. 6), Boréus (Ch. 20) and Shekhovtsov (Ch. 17) in this volume). In this way, we bring together insights from political science, rhetoric and discourse-analysis, anthropology and media studies and attempt to explain the emergence and rise of this exceptionally complex phenomenon. Thus, the book adopts both a general European perspective from which the issues and developments are viewed and accounted for across EU member states, as well as providing a set of case studies and accounts of individual political developments by focusing on specific sociopolitical and historical contexts. Furthermore, this book integrates theoretical discussions on politics and European studies, such as the conceptualization of populism, fascism, racism, ethno-nationalism, risk society and neoliberal populism, with empirical in-depth case studies by analysing data from mainstream media, electoral campaigns, party propaganda and structured interviews. The appropriation of pop culture, new hybrid genres and new media in the recent political campaigns of populist parties are also analysed and illustrated in detail (see chapters by Betz (Ch. 5), de Cleen (Ch. 14), Krzyżanowski (Ch. 9) and Wodak (Ch. 2) in this volume).

In addition to the theoretical discussions and conceptualizations, the book analyses the unique nature of these parties in various contexts, apart from their assumed similarities across Europe: how they have developed and/or been reinvented, how they have (re)organized themselves and what changes there have been in their rhetoric, perspectives and discursive strategies. The book also seeks to answer the questions of why and under what conditions these parties have managed to become successful on both national and European levels; moreover, special attention is paid to the interplay between the rhetorical/discursive aspects of these parties and the countries' socio-economic, sociopolitical, historical and structural contexts. The role of the media in promoting right-wing populism as well as the commodification of politics are addressed in much detail in relation to the apparent success of these parties (e.g. the British BNP, the Austrian FPÖ, The Dutch PVV, the Hungarian Jobbik and the Danish Dansk Folkeparti) (see specifically Oudenampsen (Ch. 13) and Kovács (Ch. 15) in this volume).

Outline of the book

This book provides an overall picture of the dynamics and development of, and conditions for, right-wing populist discourses (and parties) across Europe and beyond, including the very nature of the many meanings and notions of 'populism'. Such an enterprise, however, would not be complete without specific detailed case studies at local, countrywide and regional levels. This is to avoid making sweeping assumptions about similarities in the sociopolitical dynamics of countries/regions in Europe and to accentuate the specificities of their differences in context, including past collective experiences and economic conditions/visions, as well as current international and national affairs. Having this general perspective in mind the book is divided into four sections.

The first section of the book consists of (more) theoretical accounts and conceptualizations regarding the 'nature' of populism, the development of right-wing populist movements in the twentieth and twenty-first centuries, and their relation to past histories, as well as the rhetorical mechanisms and orientation of their discourses. This section also considers issues on the EU scale and beyond, including the United States of America.

Anton Pelinka's opening chapter provides a rich theoretical account of the concept of right-wing populism and how it relates to other political perspectives and movements. It problematizes the notion of 'people' (*demos*) in the way it is exploited in populist discourses. Populism is theoretically characterized as an approach in politics which can be upheld by both Left and Right of the political spectrum. Pelinka explicitly defines what are to be considered right-wing populist parties/groups, as opposed to mainstream conservative political groups, and illustrates how their beliefs, programmes and discourses are entangled with anti-foreigner tendencies – in addition to the constructed 'enemy within' for opposing parties – in their inherently populist cycle of self and other categorizations. In the process of dichotomization of self and other, these parties draw on a vast array of real and constructed 'differences', functionalizing other religions, ethnic groups and liberal-minded parties/groups to international-level institutions, that is, the EU and global-level 'financial capital'. Pelinka also provides a typology of five tendencies in European right-wing populist groups and parties in terms of their past histories and revisionist agendas coming from Western or post-communist Europe, the nature of their traditional electorates and their economic interests.

Ruth Wodak's chapter on the Haiderization of Europe argues that the strategies and model of political communication which supported the rise of Jörg Haider in Austria are now at work throughout Europe. She maintains that, in addition to material practices and social dynamics which have contributed to the rise of right-wing populist groups, certain models of textual and visual rhetoric have also been 'successfully' adopted by various right-wing populist parties across Europe. Wodak emphasizes the changes in norms, practices and functions of political performance which are employed to construct, convey and recontextualize discrimination and exclusion across Europe through an array of meanings in all kinds of modes and genres of communication.

Thus, she illustrates how the new wave of right-wing populist parties exploits the ubiquity of 'celebrity culture' as part of globalized culture and resonates more with younger generations. Moreover, she states that a multi-methodical and interdisciplinary approach is necessary in order to investigate the apparent success of such parties in propagating their xenophobic, chauvinistic and antisemitic messages in a differentiated way. While drawing on comparative EU and national research, this chapter focuses on the similarities of rhetorical patterns and on the manipulative agenda-setting techniques in keeping with the various exclusionary discourses at work in a range of settings.

Magnus E. Marsdal's chapter systematizes the dynamics of Left and Right in a 'third way social democracy'. It focuses on the inroads that the Norwegian right-wing populist party – The Progress Party – has recently made and illustrates how and why a large proportion of the working-class electorate has decided to vote for this party. He categorizes the factors involved in voting decisions into 'value politics' (immigration, crime and foreign aid) versus 'class politics' (income distribution, employee power and taxation of the rich), in addition to voters' leftist or rightist dispositions. Hence, he argues that right-wing parties can break through among previously leftist/working-class electorates when the consensus on economic policies obfuscates traditional notions of class politics. The groups with a propensity to move to the right are of course targeted in right-wing populist discourses.

Aristotle Kallis' chapter elaborates on how the broad political spectrum has shifted to the right via the popularization of certain contentious debates on the role and consequences of Islam in Europe. Such a shift is substantiated when characteristics of 'extreme' right-wing discourses are incorporated into what is ordinarily considered the centre-right. He maintains that even though the shadow of 'fascism' has dominated the debates of the right-wing populist parties, usage of the term 'fascism' per se is unhelpful and misleading. Kallis explains that many radical populist right-wing parties have managed to distance themselves rhetorically from this symbolic notion and (re)construct themselves as mainstream political parties.

Meanwhile, there is a deeper connection between fascism and contemporary right-wing populism in terms of a strong concern with the perceived inefficiency of the modern political system and aspirations to glorify a constructed racial/national identity. In similar ways, the obsession with a powerful 'total' sovereign community resembles the fascist agenda which, in turn, is used to justify aggressive exclusion and even violent discrimination against the constructed 'Other'. Kallis's chapter focuses on two case studies – the Lega Nord (LN) in Italy and the Greek Laikos Orthodoxos Synagermos (LAOS) – as two examples of parties which label themselves 'post-fascist'.

Hans-Georg Betz's chapter attends to the role of Islam across Europe and its identity politics. He argues that confrontation with Islam has become a central issue for the political mobilization of various right-wing parties. Through a series of widely popularized controversies over the symbolic presence of Islam in public spaces in Europe, for example minarets, burqas and mosques, along with other high-profile Muslim-related global events, Muslims are constructed as the threatening 'Other'. Moreover, right-wing popular parties also invest heavily in casting themselves as defenders of the 'Christian West', and its liberal democracy and respect for human rights, against the perceived totalitarian ideology of Islam. Betz concentrates on the Swiss ban on minarets controversy as a case in point and elaborates on the range of communicative strategies employed by the right-wing populist parties to incite collective fear among the public for their own political gain.

Heidi Beirich takes the debate beyond Europe – to the United States of America – and looks at transatlantic connections between radical right-wing groups, figures and parties. She illustrates that, despite differences, for example, the size and extent of participation of radical groups in national or local electoral politics in Europe, the rise in radical right-wing politics on both sides of the Atlantic has been triggered by similar causes (i.e. real or perceived rapid demographic changes through immigration and the pressures of a sour economy). She explores the links and close cooperation between some American and European extremist figures and groups through meetings, invited lecturers and tours, as well as how these are facilitated by their computers. With all the debates and discourses surrounding European identity, such links and overlaps are becoming more relevant as Western radical groups are increasingly emphasizing a common bloc identity rather than a strictly national one. Radical populism in Europe taps into such a common identity based on an opposition to Islam, while a glorified identity in the United States is mainly fostered by the opposition to Latin-American immigration.

The second section of the book includes case studies of several 'Western' European countries in which populist right-wing parties have recently made some remarkable inroads. Case studies attend to the specific contexts of these countries as well as to particular historical developments, changes and the (re)emergence of populist right-wing rhetoric and discourses.

John Richardson and John Solomos attend to the nature and development of right-wing populist discourses in Great Britain. Richardson's chapter accounts for the ways in which the BNP has been representing itself via party-related texts. He throws light on the duplicity and dishonesty of BNP discourse. While being ideologically coherent in its content, BNP discourse is duplicitous in terms of the contradictory claims it makes as well as in its surface messages vis-à-vis its ideological commitment. Richardson shows how a discourse approach to analysing party-produced 'texts' can reveal their internal paradoxes and radical commitments. This involves close analysis of layers of meanings in party texts (guidelines, speeches, policy documents, etc.) in relation to their audiences (insiders and outsiders, potential voters and party initiates). Richardson maintains that the BNP still draws strength from the racist fascist doctrine of Leese which involves, at its core, a racial-purification agenda.

John Solomos captures the historical development and transformation of right-wing populist parties in Britain. He draws attention to the changing forms of extreme-right mobilization in contemporary British society, for example, the BNP and the English Defence League (EDL), and discusses some of the challenges that these new forms of racist and populist moblizations pose for anti-racist strategies. He argues that since the 1970s, and particularly in relation to the National Front in Britain, racist populist mobilizations have succeeded in presenting themselves as a social and political force, albeit on the margins. Solomos accentuates the ways in which ethno-populist discourses and practices are heading and argues for the necessity to raise awareness of these strategies, this being the best way to challenge the racist populist movements in the United Kingdom.

Michał Krzyżanowski concentrates on Austria. His chapter elaborates on the discourses of the Austrian right-wing populist party, the FPÖ, over the last decade. He accounts for significant changes in their discourses by analysing two specific periods: the late 1990s/early 2000s – when the party was in the government and under the patronage of Jörg Haider – and the mid-/late 2000s: when the FPÖ returned to opposition, under its new leader H.-C. Strache. In tracing such continuities, Krzyżanowski argues that the FPÖ has departed from an Austrian-specific imagery to a set of more internationalized arguments, for example, Islamophobia and strong Eurocentricism, in line with many other right-wing populist parties in Europe.

Britta Schellenberg focuses on Germany and elaborates on how the radical right wing has been repositioning itself in the German public space, considering the existence of strong fascist and anti-fascist discourses. Schellenberg accounts for the major orientations of these populist-right discourses, from National-Socialist oriented groups to élitist racist and xenophobic anti-Muslim groups, while also discussing possible future trends and the transformation of the country.

Carlo Ruzza and Laura Balbo analyse the situation in Italy, and focus on Berlusconi and Bossi. They problematize the notion of 'populism' in Italy by examining these two charismatic leaders and how they relate to their constructed '*popolo*'. They maintain that anti-immigration xenophobic attitudes and language are openly part of, and fully legitimized by, their policy proposals and public discourses. Their narratives and constructed 'publics' are very different. Ruzza and Balbo also consider the impact of the current economic crisis on public opinion.

Brigitte Beauzamy's chapter classifies various explanations towards what is perceived as the sudden success of right-wing populism in France and the rise of the FN. The chapter covers many approaches in deciphering the phenomenon, from biographical studies of Jean-Marie Le Pen's leadership to sociological studies of the FN's electorate. These explanations also include socio-economic explanations of the perceived French fear of globalization and Europeanization which may have paved the way for the rise of populist discourses. Beauzamy's main argument, however, is that these various dimensions of explanations – environmental/structural, organizational, discursive, etc. – need to be brought together, into a comprehensive framework, in order to understand the success of parties such as the French FN.

Merijn Oudenampsen's chapter considers various approaches to explaining the rise of Dutch right-wing populism. The chapter adopts a theoretical view to explain the Dutch swing to the right. The author outlines the shortcomings of the reflective approach by detailing aspects of the 'mass culture debate' and 'behavioural tradition'. He argues that a constructivist approach to the interpretation of Dutch populism – which considers questions like how populism helps constitute the very identities that it represents – can offer a deeper and more fruitful understanding of the swing.

Benjamin de Cleen's chapter analyses the rhetoric of the Flemish radical party, Vlaams Blok/ Vlaams Belang (VB), in Belgium. He focuses on the debate between the party and Flemish city theatres which have acted as strong voices against the VB. The chapter adopts a discourse theoretical methodology to examine how the VB represented those theatres, between 2005 and 2006, by investigating external communication texts as well as instances of what was reported in the mainstream media. De Cleen elaborates on the details of the main discourses used by the VB to criticize the city theatres' discourses of 'nationalism', 'conservatism' and 'populism', and how they overlap and reinforce each other.

The third section of the book involves case studies from the former Communist European countries in which populist right-wing parties have recently become successful. This section draws attention to the fact that post-communist contexts and issues of transition, for example, the viability, reality, usefulness, nature, etc. of the 'new' order, play a crucial role in the formation, development and (re)emergence of right-wing populist groups. It could be argued that more room for 'populism' in the political spaces of these countries has existed since the monolithic authoritarian communist veil was lifted.

András Kovács' chapter focuses on the recently formed Jobbik party in Hungary and its success in parliamentary and European elections. Kovács provides information on the specific sociopolitical context of the country and maintains that among the main reasons for Jobbik's success are electoral volatility, the widening gap between political institutions and society and the decreasing authority of these institutions. Jobbik's main discourse is built upon questioning the validity and usefulness of the 'new democratic order' advocated by left and centrist parties and groups. As such, the party specifically accuses the political élites of adhering to an authoritarian cliquey politics. Analysis of Jobbik's electorate indicates that while in the prosperous regions the 'losers' (in the new order) constitute the major electorate, in poorer areas with large Roma populations a relatively well-educated and economically better-off group constitutes Jobbik's core voters.

Daunis Auers and Andres Kasekamp's chapter accounts for Estonia and Latvia. They point to several crucial contextual issues and map out the network of right-wing populist movements and parties and their electoral achievements. The chapter discusses three key radical right-populist dimensions: nativism, authoritarianism and populism; it also accentuates the role of language and rhetoric in the rise of the National Alliance. This is positioned in a long-standing political communication norm where explicit utterances of extreme radical propositions are freely expressed without the stigma ordinarily attached to such rhetoric elsewhere in Europe. The chapter concludes by presenting an explanation of why radical right-wing discourses are more prevalent in Latvia than in Estonia by looking at societal, institutional and political differences.

Anton Shekhovtsov's case study is about the Ukraine. He points to the differences in political public spaces in the industrial and former socialist states and maintains that, in general, the electoral participation expression of populist right-wing parties and tendencies has only become viable with the collapse of the former structure. As such, the presence of the radical right in the electoral system of Ukraine could be regarded as both a sign of democratization as well as a threat to it. Shekhovtsov accounts for the nature, rise and development of the All-Ukrainian Union 'Freedom' (Svoboda) party and elaborates on its organizational and ideological fabric, leading to its rise in popular support.

The last section of the book comprises five chapters which analyse the rise of right-wing populism in Scandinavia. Fryklund captures some aspects of the development of populist parties in the region; Oja and Mral provide a country-specific case study of Sweden; and Boréus and Nohrstedt take a comparative perspective to consider the media's role in this. Andersson's contribution is a case study of how journalists might manage to perform their professional duties when dealing with radical right-wing groups.

Björn Fryklund's contribution provides information on the development of and changes in right-wing populist parties and groups in Nordic countries from a historical perspective. He argues that various sociopolitical issues and debates have contributed to the 'successes' of such parties in different periods. While in the 1970s the focus was on taxation issues, since the early 1980s the populist discourse has revolved around immigration issues. Fryklund argues that regardless of what the core contentious issues might be – for example, taxation or immigration – there are similarities through which a populist discourse may gain more visibility and/or popularity.

Simon Oja and Brigitte Mral focus on the Sverigedemokraterna (SD) (Sweden Democrats), a nationalist-populist party in Sweden. They trace the party's upward trajectory in the electoral process from 1988 to 2010 when the party won 5.7 per cent of the vote, exceeding the threshold needed to gain representation in Parliament. It is argued that the party did not emerge from criticism of high taxes or bureaucracy, rather its historical heritage lies in racism and neo-Nazism, and the party has links to fascist and Nazi ideology through individuals and personal relationships. The SD has moved away from this complex background over the past few years and has, in many respects, become a different and 'cleaner' party, compared to when it was first founded. Oja and Mral elaborate on the arguments *pro et contra* allowing the SD into the media by specifically focusing on the debate about whether or not the SD should be allowed to buy advertising space in newspapers and on TV.

Kristina Boréus contributes a comparative analysis of nationalism and discriminatory discourses in Austria, Denmark and Sweden. She accounts for the interconnectedness of discourses of nationalism and discrimination and focuses on discursive aspects of discrimination. The chapter reports a discourse analytical study of election-campaign texts in the three countries. She concludes that discursive discrimination seems to be stronger – more overt – in the rhetoric of these parties in Austria as compared to Danish or Swedish campaigns. The author also links her findings to other scholarly literature on Swedish nationalism and argues that there is a higher degree of implicitness in the Swedish radical-right rhetoric as a communicative culture.

Stig Arne Nohrstedt focuses on the high-profile cases involving the publication of the Muhammad cartoons in Denmark and Sweden and the way they contributed to threat spirals, which could be exploited by right-wing populist groups. He sees these cases as key indicators of a new phase of modern society that might be called the 'threat society'. Mediated speculation regarding fears and dangers have created a culture of fear and thus a feeding ground for the rise of new right-wing populism. By focusing on these cases involving the (re)publication of the cartoons, the author suggests that the editorial decisions to publish the cartoons cannot be explained simply by the ideological profiles of the newspapers, but rather by a combined effect of the superficial journalistic scrutiny of the threat images promoted by the artists and the political context of an emerging threat society. Nohrstedt argues that a thorough study of the media's role in disseminating threat perceptions is a long-overdue necessity in order to counteract populist discourses which exploit real or constructed social uncertainties and fears.

The last chapter of the book is Christoph Andersson's contribution, which throws light on the difficulties and risks involved for journalists reporting on right-wing populist groups. As an experienced journalist, Andersson discusses the strategies that journalists should employ to fulfil their job to the highest professional standards, even though their personal beliefs and ethics may stand in stark contrast to the participants of such events. He emphasizes the role of good reporting and journalism when it comes to right-wing populists and suggests an innovative model to minimize threats and provocations.

References

Auers, D. and Kasekamp, A. (2009), 'Explaining the Electoral Failure of Extreme-Right Parties in Estonia and Latvia', *Journal of Contemporary European Studies*, 17(2): 241–54.

Azmanova, A. (2012), *The Scandal of Reason*, Princeton: Princeton University Press.

Bakic, J. (2009), 'Extreme-Right Ideology, Practice and Supporters: Case Study of the Serbian Radical Party', *Journal of Contemporary European Studies*, 17(2): 193–207.

Bar-on, T. (2008), Fascism to the Nouvelle Droite: The Dream of Pan-European Empire', *Journal of Contemporary European Studies*, 16(3): 327–45.

— (2012), 'Italian Post-War Neo-Fascism: Three Paths, One Mission?', in R. Wodak and J. Richardson (eds), *Fascism in Text and Talk*, London: Routledge (in press).

Bruter, M. and Harrison, S. (2011), *Mapping Extreme Right Ideology*, Basingstoke: Palgrave.

Bustikova, L. (2009), 'The Extreme Right in Eastern Europe: EU Accession and the Quality of Governance', *Journal of Contemporary European Studies*, 17(2): 223–39.

Delanty, G., Wodak, R. and Jones, P. (eds) (2008), *Migration, Identity and Belonging*, Liverpool: Liverpool University Press.

Ellinas, A. (2009), 'Chaotic but Popular? Extreme-Right Organisation and Performance in the Age of Media Communication', *Journal of Contemporary European Studies*, 17: 209–21.

Gingrich, A. and Banks, M. (eds) (2006), *Neo-nationalism in Europe and Beyond: Perspectives from Social Anthropology*, Berghahn Books.

Grande, E. (2000), 'Charisma und Komplexität: Verhandlungsdemokratie, Mediendemokratie und der Funktionswandel politischer Eliten', *Leviathan*, 28(1): 122–41.

Hay, C. (2007), *Why we Hate Politics*, Cambridge: Polity.

Iordachi, C. (2010), 'Introduction: Fascism in Interwar East Central and Southeastern Europe: Toward a New Transnational Research Agenda', *East Central Europe*, 37: 161–213.

Iordachi, C. (ed.) (2009), *Comparative Fascist Studies*, London: Routledge.

Judt, T. (2010), *Ill Fares the Land*, London: Penguin.

KhosraviNik, M. (2009), 'The Representation of Refugees, Asylum Seekers and Immigrants in British Newspapers During the Balkan Conflict (1999) and the British General Election (2005)', *Discourse & Society*, 20(4): 477–98.

— (2010), 'The Representation of Refugees, Asylum Seekers and Immigrants in British Newspapers: A Critical Discourse Analysis', *Journal of Language and Politics*, 9(1): 1–28.

KhosraviNik, M., Krzyżanowski, M. and Wodak, R. (2012), 'Dynamics of Discursive Representations of Refugees and Asylum Seekers in the British Press 1996–2006', in M. Messer, R. Schroeder and R. Wodak (eds), *Migrations: Interdisciplinary Perspectives*, Springer-Verlag (in press).

Krzyżanowski, M. and Wodak, R. (2009), *The Politics of Exclusion: Debating Migration in Austria*, New Brunswick, NJ: Transaction Press.

Mammone, A. (2009), 'The Eternal Return? Faux Populism and Contemporarization of Neo-Fascism across Britain, France and Italy', *Journal of Contemporary European Studies*, 17(2): 171–94.

Pelinka, A. and Wodak, R. (2002), *Dreck am Stecken. Diskurs der Ausgrenzung*, Vienna: Czernin.

Peunova, M. (2008), 'An Eastern Incarnation of the European New Right: Aleksandr Panarin and New Eurasianist Discourse in Contemporary Russia', *Journal of Contemporary European Studies*, 16(3): 407–19.

Richardson, J. E. and Wodak, R. (2009a), 'The Impact of Visual Racism: Visual Arguments in Political Leaflets of Austrian and British Far-right Parties', *Controversia*, 2: 45–77.

— (2009b), 'Recontextualising Fascist Ideologies of the Past: Right-Wing Discourses on Employment and Nativism in Austria and the United Kingdom', *Critical Discourse Studies*, 6(4): 251–67.

Rydgren, J. (2005), *Movements of Exclusion*, New York: Nova.

Steinmetz, W. (ed.) (2011), *Language in the Age of Extremes*, Oxford: Oxford University Press.

Wilson, R. and Hainsworth, P. (2012), 'Far-right Parties and Discourse in Europe: A Challenge for our Times', *European Network Against Racism*, Brussels.

Wodak, R. (2011a), *The Discourse of Politics in Action: Politics as Usual*, Basingstoke: Palgrave.

— (2011b), Old and new demagoguery. The Rhetoric of Exclusion. <www.opendemocracy.net/ruth-wodak/old-and-new-demagoguery-rhetoric-of-exclusion> [published online, 5 May 2011].

— (forthcoming), *Politics of Fear. Rhetoric of Rightwing Populism*, London: Sage.

Wodak, R. and Pelinka, A. (2002), 'From Waldheim to Haider: An introduction', in R. Wodak and A. Pelinka (eds), *The Haider Phenomenon in Austria*, New Brunswick: Transaction Press, pp. vii–xxvii.

Wodak, R. and Richardson, J. (eds) (2012), *Analyzing Fascist Discourse. Fascism in Talk and Text*, London: Routledge.

Section I

Theories and Comparative Approaches

1

Right-Wing Populism: Concept and Typology

Anton Pelinka

Historical roots, theoretical implications

Populism is a general protest against the checks and balances introduced to prevent 'the people's' direct rule. The beginning of modern populism was a radical understanding of democracy as government by the people, beyond the distinction between majority and minority, beyond limitations 'the people' are told to respect. Populism also tends to neglect the problem of inclusion and exclusion: Who belongs to 'the people' – and who does not? What are the criteria to be part of the 'Demos'? (Dahl 1989: 119–31).

As a concept, populism is a rather vague understanding of democracy, emphasizing plebiscitary direct democratic elements over a representative indirect democratic structure. Populism is based on Abraham Lincoln's famous definition of democracy as 'government of the people, for the people, and by the people'. In other words: 'the people' should govern themselves. Intermediary actors like parliaments and political parties are secondary instruments at best, and potential obstacles for 'true democracy' at worst.

The conceptual weakness and political impetus of populism are responsible for significant contradictions. Populism starts from an understanding of 'the people' as a given factor. The weakness is the lack of a clear understanding of 'the people': who is part of it – and who is not? Were Native Americans and African Slaves part of the people when, in 1776, some Americans declared and spoke on behalf of 'We, the People of the United States'? Is everybody who lives in a given territory – independent of their roots – part of 'the people'? The principally radical consequences of populist democracy are based on an extremely ambiguous precondition – the self-evidence of 'the people'.

Populist democracy as a theoretical construct of political order goes way back to the first known discourses about democracy. As a way to define the sovereignty of a political system, 'the people', the 'Demos', were seen as the final source of power – an alternative to kings, tyrants or experts like Plato's philosophers. At the beginning of democracy was the construction of the 'Demos' – as the logical opponent of any kind of monarchical or aristocratic order (Müller 2011: 7–48).

The people 'is never a primary datum but a construct' (Laclau 2005: 48). The 'Demos' has to be represented. The reality of representative democracy creates frustration among those segments of society that do not feel represented by that which has always been a rather élitist establishment. The frustration and anger of members of the 'Demos', directed against the official and legal representatives, are the sources of contemporary populist movements and populist parties.

In modern times, populism is the antithesis to 'Madisonian Democracy' (Dahl 1970). 'Madisonian Democracy' – especially articulated in the theoretical mainstream underlying the American constitution – is based on the understanding that 'the people' should have a role in politics; but the people's power must be limited by the prerogatives of the minority, and through safeguards give an enlightened upper class the possibility to prevent a takeover by 'the mob'. 'Madisonian Democracy' represents élitist scepticism regarding majority rule – a scepticism expressed in the separation of power and the system of 'checks and balances'.

The shaping of the US constitution provides for an excellent introduction to the history of 'populism'. In the Constitutional Convention (1787), the basic competing ideas on how to form a representative government were articulated. On the one side, there was Alexander Hamilton's deep scepticism about democracy. He argued against 'popular passions' and displayed a strong revulsion at the 'amazing violence and turbulence of the democratic spirit' (Beeman 2010: 168f.). The constitution, strongly influenced by James Madison, was the product of a compromise between the idea of democracy as such and (in the view of the 'founding fathers') the necessary control over 'the people' by an enlightened élite.

Populism is the consequence of an optimistic understanding of majority rule. The populist creed is that 'the people' are entitled to govern – without restrictions. The problem – of course – is the definition of 'the people'; the problem is that any understanding of the 'Demos' makes inclusions and exclusions necessary: who does and who does not belong to 'the people'? This is not a problem any kind of democratic understanding can avoid. The history of modern democracy is the history of permanent debate about the necessary inclusion of excluded people – like the 'lower classes', women and (former) slaves. Populism tends to differ from other approaches to democracy by assuming a kind of self-evidence for the inclusion in as well as for the exclusion from 'the people'.

Populism, as a modern phenomenon with an impact on politics, can be observed in different forms, beginning from the nineteenth century. Populism has been the term to characterize protest movements expressing disillusionment and disappointment with established systems. Populist movements in the Americas – in the United States as well as in Latin America – have opposed an existing order for being insufficiently democratic. The different movements – from Agrarian populism in the North American West to Peronism in Argentina (Barros 2005: 254–63) – aimed for a better 'real' democracy.

Robert Dahl's analysis of the development of democratic theory shows the beginning of 'populist democracy' as an antithesis to Aristotle's pattern of 'mixed government': As any unchecked government in Aristotle's understanding tends to develop negative qualities, giving all the power to 'the people' would create plebeian chaos (1970). Democracy should be combined with elements of monarchy and aristocracy. The same approach defined the beginning of the modern concept of the separation of power and of 'checks and balances' – reflected in the writing of John Locke, Charles Montesquieu and others and enshrined especially in the constitution of the United States: 'the people' has power – but only within certain limits, watched over by an independent judiciary and checked by an élitist Senate and a strong executive.

Modern democracy in Europe and America began with guarantees against the 'tyranny of the majority'. This is expressed, by different power-sharing arrangements, as the necessity for cooperation between different institutions (like the US presidency and the US Congress) and different societal segments – like the formula for Swiss democracy, which consists of a permanent coalition arrangement between the representatives of different religious and linguistic identities.

Modern democracy, as enshrined in the US constitution and the Swiss consociational democracy (Lijphart 1977: 21–52), has been a phenomenon full of ambiguities from the very beginning: on one side, democracy claimed to give all the power 'to the people'; on the other, democracy took care to channel the people's power through the institution of a system of representations.

In the nineteenth century, populism began as a protest against the overwhelming power of élites: economic élites like the 'trusts' in the United States; social élites like the dominant aristocracies; political élites like elected representatives who did not seem to care enough for the interests of 'the people'. Robert Michels' 'Iron Law of Oligarchy' and the key terms 'Democratic Aristocracy' and 'Aristocratic Democracy' described and explained the self-interest of democratic representatives – élitist interests contradicting the populist doctrine of democracy (1962: 43–51).

Robert Michels' criticism, published at the beginning of the twentieth century, exemplifies the ambivalence of the (seemingly) radical democratic approach of populism. On the one side, Michels can be used to make Leninism understandable: the very idea of rotating élites and the inbuilt possibilities of democratic recall stood at the beginning of the Union of Socialist Soviet Republics (USSR), even if it soon became clear that the soviet system petrified élites beyond the élitism known from 'bourgeois' democracies. On the other side, Michels' criticism has been used by Fascism and Nazism: if (liberal 'bourgeois') democracy is nothing more than a scheme to protect the existing élites, fascist élitism must be seen as the better alternative, as an openly declared honest élitism.

Carl Schmitt and others argued that the 'Führer'-state represented the 'people's will' more efficiently and more truthfully than the liberal parliamentarianism of Weimar or Westminster. The 'Führer' or the 'Duce' – united with 'the people' in a rather mystic way – acted on behalf of 'the people'. 'The people' were reduced to the function of legitimizing the leader. In practice, this meant that the people were allowed to applaud the actions of the leader (2007: esp. 80–96).

The intellectual and analytical weakness of populist democracy is rooted in the assumption that 'the people' do exist, and exist in a homogeneous way. This creates the 'ambiguities and paradoxes' of populism (Laclau 2007: 3–20): who is included in and who is excluded from 'the people' is not seen as the result of social and cultural developments but as a simplistic dogma, by ignoring social fragmentations. National and race identities are constructed to create the illusion of 'natural' borders between 'us' and 'them'. The differences within 'the people' tend to be overlooked. 'The people' exist above the diversities of class and religion or gender and generation.

The whole concept of 'the people' is an antithesis to the reality of cleavages as developed by authors like Seymour Martin Lipset and Stein Rokkan (Lipset 1981, Rokkan & Flora 2000). Considering the reality of intra-societal conflicts, the very idea of a uniform nation ignores the existing differences – and the long-term existing lines of conflict as the result of varieties of social, economic, ethnic and religious identities. In reality, the people – any people – consist of different identities, creating contradicting interests. If the term 'people' no longer means the historical opposition to the monarchy, and if it is not an abstraction for the whole of humankind, then the term people is not a concept which can be used for any serious analysis of contemporary politics and society.

The ambivalence of the concept can be exemplified by asking a question of the 'defining other': who is not part of 'the people'? At the beginning of modern democracy, the defining other was the ancient regime, the pre-revolutionary power of monarchs and aristocrats. When, in 1776, in Philadelphia, Americans declared 'We, the People of the United States', the defining other was the British king and a political order designed on the other side of the Atlantic. This moment was anti-aristocratic and, in its historical context, revolutionary.

Excluded from 'the people' in 1776 were not only the king and the British aristocracy but, implicitly, native Americans and African-Americans. The concept of 'the people' had, from the very beginning, an ethno-national aspect. When – more than two centuries later – the revolutionary movement in the German Democratic Republic (GDR) had to define the people it was speaking for, the choice was between 'We are the people' and 'We are one people'. The first slogan was purely anti-élitist, directed against the rule of the communist one-party state. The second slogan had a distinct ethno-national meaning: the people were 'the Germans'. African students or Vietnamese workers, who may have demonstrated in Leipzig under the first slogan, must have felt excluded under the second: they ceased to be part of 'us', they became part of 'them'.

The consequences of conceptual ambivalence

As long as democracy was identified with revolutionary movements, directed against the rule of princes, there was no need to confront potential contradictions and ambiguities, like the question of inclusion and exclusion, of minority rights and checks and balances. Democracy's historical success made it necessary to reflect on the people's power and this power's limitations, on the need to interpret democracy as a representative form of government. When the rule of the kings ended and the political systems all over Europe and in most of the world became republics or parliamentary monarchies, the historic 'defining other' of democracy and populism lost its meaning. On the one side, one could declare 'mission accomplished': as soon as democracy had become self-evident, populism had reached its final goal. In Fukuyama's interpretation, not only did the victory of democracy mean an 'end of history', as democracy enjoys a monopoly no longer challenged by an alternative concept (1992), it could also imply an end to the populist drive. Populism, one could argue, had become the victim of self-elimination by success. Do not 'the people' govern everywhere?

But populism survived – as a tendency to criticize existing democracies for not being sufficiently democratic, to ask for more direct power for 'the people' – and less for the people's representatives, to protest against the self-interest of politicians, parties and parliaments who tend to forget their democratic mandate. Populism survived – not within the mainstream of democratic activities but as an element outside this mainstream. But to survive, populism needed a new 'defining other': who was to be seen to be the decisive opponent of 'the people'?

As there is no democracy without significant misgivings, there has never been a deficit of potential opponents of 'the people'. Corrupt élites have always been on the radar of critical democrats. Arrogant economic or intellectual power brokers have given enough reason to see them as a significant problem for democracy. And, other 'people' offered themselves as defining others: people defined as 'alien', as foreign due to birth, citizenship, religion, culture or 'race'.

Depending on the definition of the people's defining other, the different contemporary populist phenomena can be categorized in different ways. But any kind of populism directed against an ethnically and/or nationally and/or religiously defined 'other' can be seen as 'right wing'. Left-wing populism does exist. But by definition it is not ethically exclusive. Political parties with an agenda aiming primarily at the exclusion of or discrimination against (sub-)societies or different social groups follow a narrow ethno-nationalistic and potentially racist agenda claiming to speak on behalf of 'the people' – but the people they are speaking for are defined by the exclusion of others.

This narrowness does not contradict the anti-élitist agenda. Ethno-nationalist populism at the beginning of the twenty-first century challenges élites whose positions are based on higher education and individual achievement. By criticizing élites in this way, right-wing populism is using rhetoric traditionally associated with left-wingers. It is a socialist (or quasi-socialist) rhetoric directed against profiteers, especially in the context of globalization. But it is a leftist rhetoric, always suspiciously missing one element of traditional socialism: the international dimension. Any sign of solidarity with the fate or misery of those who are excluded from 'us' is missing. The anti-élitism of the right-wing populist may be called socialist. But it is a narrow national socialism that the right-wing parties in contemporary Europe are expressing.

The anti-élitism of the populist right is the most significant difference from the traditional right of the mainstream: the nineteenth century defenders of the 'ancient regime'; the reactionary romantics who fantasized about an ideal pre-revolutionary life; the conservative sceptics of democracy; the stalwarts of the Church's dominance over politics – these are not what contemporary right-wing populism is about. There may be some tendencies to use religious loyalties against religiously defined 'others', or some sentimental perception of pre-modern times, but the essence of right-wing populism is a democratic claim: right-wing populism today can easily identify with 'we, the people' of the bourgeois revolutions – as long as 'the people' are seen to be distinctly different from other peoples.

The development and stabilization of (liberal 'Western') democracy in Europe had a significant impact on the definition of 'the other'. The 'enemy' against whom populist movements and parties mobilized is no longer a one-party regime and is not the traditional feudal regime of the past. There are aspects of an anti-élitism directed against economic élites and/or intellectuals, but the most important populist energy today is directed against the enemy who is considered to be foreign – ethnically, culturally and religiously foreign. Contemporary populism does not so much mobilize against the (perceived) enemy above but more against the (perceived) enemy from abroad. Populism has become more and more ethno-nationalistic.

Populist anti-élitism today is directed against those who seem to be responsible for Europeanization and globalization, and especially for mass migration, against élites who have opened the doors to foreign influence and to foreigners. Of course, the basic assumption of this perception does not reflect a realistic picture of the past, which has always been characterized by migration. And, of course, the tendency to see individuals (politicians – the 'classe politica', or intellectuals – 'the chattering classes') as responsible for modernizing trends is beyond any realistic and empirically sound analysis of the trend which tends to put an end to the nation state.

Populism simplifies complex developments by looking for a culprit. As the enemy – the foreigner, the foreign culture – has already succeeded in breaking into the fortress of the nation state, someone must be responsible. The élites are the secondary 'defining others', responsible for the liberal democratic policies of accepting cultural diversity. The populist answer to the complexities of a more and more pluralistic society is not multiculturalism. Will Kymlicka's 'liberal multiculturalism' is not on the agenda of ethno-nationalist populists – despite the evidence of multicultural realities he and others are providing (2009: 61–86). On the contrary, right-wing populism sees multiculturalism as a recipe to denationalize one's (own) nation, to deconstruct one's (own) people.

Of course, there is a great deal of easily recognizable naiveté in the populist assumption that there are pure nations and homogeneous 'peoples' in today's world. Populism constructs a non-existent ethno-national purity to defend it against those who seem to jeopardize such fictitious purity. But as long as there is a tendency to believe in the non-existent homogeneity of 'us', there is enough energy to defend 'us' against 'them'.

Contemporary populism is very much a phenomenon of the Far Right. But it is also to be seen in the actions of mainstream parties and of parties of the Left. Right-centre and left-centre parties tend to simplify their political message – like the French Union pour *un Mouvement Populaire* (UMP) under Nicolas Sarkozy, the German Social Democratic Party (SPD) under Gerhard Schröder or the British Labour Party under Tony Blair. Mainstream parties are tempted to play down the complexities and contradictions of their policies to claim they are speaking on behalf of 'the people'.

There has always been and still is the populism of the Left: the German Left Party is using some anti-immigration, and especially anti-EU-rhetoric, in a verbally milder but substantially not so different way. And in the European Parliament, the positions of the party grouping of the 'United European Left' – an alliance of some unreformed communist parties and left-socialist or left greens from Scandinavia – do not differ very much from the Far Right in their attitudes towards European integration (Bartolini 2007: 313f.).

But it is the Far Right which is using the mobilizing keywords and topics which are dominating some of the political discourses: migration, multiculturalism and the end of the nation state. In the United States, Ross Perot's campaign of 1992 can be considered to be populism of the centre. Centrist populism has been replaced in the United States by the populism of the Tea Party, a kind of libertarian anti-government movement playing the patriotic (jingoistic) card of 'American Exceptionalism' (Lipset 1997). There has been significant anti-élitism in the American varieties of populism – directed especially against the academic élites from the élite universities. But all in all, the most dominant character of the contemporary US populism is no longer the radical farmers' movement of the nineteenth and early twentieth centuries, but a distinct nationalistic agenda, based on the assumption of a very specific role the United States has to play, an assumption – and this is a significant difference from the European variations of the Populist Right – which is based on strong religious Christian-fundamentalist beliefs.

Contemporary populists have some strong anti-government tendencies – for example, mobilization against 'Washington' in the US case. The defining other may be a treacherous government but the core message is nationalistic (or, in the US case, 'patriotic'): we have to defend 'us' from the aggression of foreigners, of foreign thinking, of foreign agents, of foreign ways of life. Contemporary populism is distinctly anti-cosmopolitan – anti-internationalist.

Populism and party typology

Until the late twentieth century, populist parties were not considered a specific prototype for a party. The basic literature – like that of Giovanni Sartori (2005) – did not see 'populism' as a defining agenda for a 'party family', like liberalism, conservatism, socialism, fascism, communism or Christian democracy. Sarah Harrison and Michael Bruter see populism as one of four pillars (together with the xenophobia, reactionary and repressive positions of contemporary extreme right parties but not responsible for defining a party family of its own) (Harrison & Bruter 2011: 207–9). Populism is seen as responsible for a specific strategy and a specific behaviour – but not for a specific programmatic outlook. Populism was a distinct method of mobilization used by very different parties. The Russian Bolsheviks used populist techniques in 1917, as did the Italian Fascists in 1922. Franklin D. Roosevelt's 'fireside chats' during his presidency had a distinct populist flavour, like Harry Truman's re-election campaign in 1948. Populism as a technique – not as an ethnically exclusive programme – played an important role in the beginning for the European green parties. Populism was (and still is) an instrument open to anybody, any politician, any political party.

Populism's anti-élitist character makes it easier for parties outside the mainstream to make use of populist elements. But even presidential parties in the United States have been able to behave like a 'populist' 'us' against an élitist 'them', a 'defining other' within the political system ('Washington') or outside the system – like economic élites.

It was development in prosperous Europe that became responsible for the rise of a specific type of populist party. Herbert Kitschelt was among the first to describe and analyse the phenomenon of a 'new radical or extreme right' (2006: 286–8). Kitschelt sees a distinct agenda, partially different from that of the traditional extreme right: the 'new' extreme right is different because it does not have 'movement support' like traditional fascism. A small formal membership and the absence of an organized rank-and-file activism are behind the volatility and fluidity of contemporary right-wing populism. The parties' electoral bases are lower-middle-class and blue-collar voters. The programmatic agenda in some cases (like Denmark) is a protest against taxation, but especially and generally strong opposition to immigration and European integration.

A not so new phenomenon is the decisive role of a central 'charismatic' figure. Personalization tends to overshadow the issues. The most significant example is Pim Fortuyn's party – its success and decline. The party's dramatic upswing in 2002 was followed by an equally dramatic fall. Without its murdered leader, the party lost its orientation and appeal (ibid.: 287). Pim Fortuyn's case is important for understanding the differences and similarities between right-wing populism and traditional far-right extremism: Pim Fortuyn stood for certain aspects of cultural tolerance which were unthinkable for the traditional far right of the past – like tolerance of feminism and same-sex orientation. Pim Fortuyn and his party did not claim to destroy 'the system' – as did the traditional fascist parties in the past. He claimed to defend the liberal values of Western democracy against the intruders from elsewhere, against immigrants and Muslims in particular.

The 'new' far right in (Western) Europe is not characterized by a strong structure, an organized movement, a dense party organization or semi-military militias. The 'new' far right is very much single-issue oriented. It is not the specific concept of a 'new state' beyond the rules of liberal democracy that right-wing populism has its focus on. It is not any kind of (superficially) 'revolutionary' agenda that right-wing populist parties are using to maximize their electorate. They have a very defensive agenda, the preservation of the status quo – or the status quo ante – as it was before mass migration, Europeanization and globalization started to challenge the nation state. Their ideal is the homogeneous, democratic nation state.

There is a social parallel between contemporary right-wing populism and the traditional extreme right: their appeal has been (or is) especially successful among the lower-middle-classes, among those voters who believe that the socio-economic trend is directed against their status, among 'modernization losers'. But it is not the 'small bourgeoisie' and farmers of the past – so significant for the rise of fascist parties in the first half of the twentieth century – it is a new kind of modernization losers who are over-proportionally backing the 'new' far right. It is the 'working class', defined as blue-collar voters, which is, to a significant degree, responsible for the successes of right-wing populist parties (Beyme 2011: 58–65).

In Austria, the FPÖ became the party with the highest number of blue-collar voters among Austrian parties in the 1990s. In France, the decline of the French Parti Communiste and the rise of the FN are interdependent phenomena: the 'working class' has become a decisive part of the far right's electorate. Together with the 'gender bias' – the far right attracts an over-proportionate number of male voters – the trend of the 'modernization losers' towards the far right has become a significant quality of the right-wing populist electorate (Mudde 2007: 135f., 297f.).

The swing of the blue-collar vote from the left to the far right is the consequence of two long-term developments:

> Blue-collar voters in Europe have much more to lose than (as Karl Marx and Engels put it) 'their chains': they have a significant network of social security and (modest) individual prosperity. As the (national) welfare state is less and less able to guarantee security and prosperity, the blue-collar electorate has responded in a similar way to that of the 'small bourgeoisie' decades ago.
>
> Blue-collar voters in Europe are no longer the (quantitative) winners of modernization. The numbers in the industrial work force are shrinking all over Europe. The winners of modernization are white-collar voters – and the work force outside the European sphere, in eastern, southern and South-East Asia in particular.

Contemporary right-wing populist parties articulate an empirically arguable fear: the fear of today's less-privileged segments of European societies. As it enjoys certain advantages that the development of welfare systems within an increasingly prosperous Europe has guaranteed, the contemporary 'small bourgeoisie' – the proletariat – protests at the decline of its social status. The traditional leftist parties, for most of the twentieth century the parties of the proletariat, seem to be paralyzed between the growing segments of better educated, culturally liberal and socially progressive voters and their declining traditional blue-collar electorate. The European proletariat has lost its political anchor. The right-wing parties – to a certain degree newly designed – are offering, to the victims of modernization, the opportunity to articulate their anger. Voters lacking higher education and in traditional blue-collar jobs, who feel threatened by globalization and the loss of national sovereignty, are tempted more than others to vote for the populist far right.

To win the blue-collar vote, the far right had to realign itself. The old fascist recipe – based on strict authoritarian or totalitarian tendencies plus traditional nationalism – would not have been successful for a blue-collar strategy today. The post-1945 history of the far right in Western Europe demonstrates the inability of post-fascist and post-Nazi parties to become a significant factor in Europe. The far right needed a strategy without the traditional nationalistic agenda, without the replaying of French-German or other ethnic conflicts. And the far right had to dissociate itself from any direct link to its fascist/Nazi past. The Italian post-Fascists had to play down their links with the Mussolini regime, as had the Austrian FPÖ with respect to its historical Nazi links.

Right-wing parties in Europe – at least in Western Europe – have become parties without a history. By avoiding any discourse about fascism or Nazism, by claiming to represent a completely new agenda, right-wing populism tries to avoid a debate which could jeopardize its rise – a debate about Mussolini or Hitler, Franco or Pétain. If the contemporary far-right parties in Western Europe are using historical memories, it is about events centuries ago – like Joan of Arc or the invasion of the Ottoman armies. In some cases, far-right parties dissociate themselves from a non-democratic past more convincingly than others, which still satisfy an anti-democratic revisionism like the Austrian FPÖ. But the Austrian far right is, to a certain extent, less part of the contemporary Western European tendency as represented by Gert Wilders and more that of the strongly revisionist contemporary Central and Eastern European far-right parties.

The contemporary success of the far right is based on its ability to become populist. The old extreme right had been openly anti-democratic, following the script of totalitarian personalization. The new far right argues from a democratic perspective. In France and in Sweden, in the Netherlands and in Austria, the populist far-right parties do not oppose the rules of the democratic constitutions. They argue for change – within the frameworks of the constitutions. They do not present an alternative to the political system as it is; they present an alternative to specific policies – like migration and European integration.

Gert Wilders, very much in the tradition of Pim Fortuyn, does not oppose the concept of human rights – like the traditional far right did in the past. Gert Wilders claims to defend basic human rights against Islam. His party speaks not against liberal democracy, but on behalf of it. It tries to be seen as the protector of liberal democracy against the enemy from the outside – against the 'cartel of traditional parties and social partners' (van Praag 2008: 178f.).

This populist agenda enables the populist far right to slip into the role of defender of the national welfare state. The democratic, social and welfare state, the product of a broad post-1945 consensus between the mainstream parties and between business and labour, is hijacked by the far right. The difficulties national welfare systems have had to face since the 1980s all over Western Europe make it possible for the far right to portray itself as a protective shield for the welfare state. This is the main element of the far right's successful blue-collar electoral strategy. This is the reason small extremist parties, traditionally backed by bourgeois and agricultural voters, became the representatives of significant segments of the European proletariat.

A typology of contemporary right-wing parties

In Europe, there are several differences within the group of right-wing parties. The parties of the far right can be distinguished between traditional far-right parties and right-wing populist parties. For some authors – like Hans-Georg Betz – radical right populism is a rather new phenomenon, linked to the traditional extreme right in only a limited way (Betz 1994); others, like Sarah Harrison and Michael Bruter, stress the parallels between the old and the new (populist) far right (Harrison & Bruter 2011). The general debate accepts a significant overlapping between the old, (neo-)fascist or (neo-)Nazi far right and the newly emerged populist far right. The different opinions are about the extent of continuity between the old and the populist far right.

Rightist populist parties with or without pre-populist roots

The Austrian FPÖ is perhaps the best example for right-wing populism based on a pre-populist past. The FPÖ is the successor of the Pan-German 'camp' in Austria's history, responsible for the strong 'Anschluss' movement during the first decades of the twentieth century. When Austrian Pan-Germanism became part of the rising Nazi movement, Austrian Pan-Germanism became as populist as was the NationalSozialistische Deutsche ArbeiterPartei (NSDAP). But this did not completely eliminate the pre-populist social roots of Austrian Pan-Germanism, represented by 'honourable' citizens – lawyers and pharmacists, doctors and farmers – especially in the provinces. The FPÖ with its new beginning in 1955 seemed to fall back on its roots. But locked into the status of a small party, it started to become populist in the 1980s – making the party into a model case of successful populist xenophobia (Wodak & Pelinka 2002).

The model for a right-wing populist party without pre-populist roots is the Dutch Freedom Party. Based on the short but spectacular success of Pim Fortuyn, the Freedom Party succeeded as a single-issue party: anti-immigration and anti-Islam are the all-dominating topics the party is using. As the party is – differently from the FPÖ – free from an anti-democratic fascist past, it does not have the burden of a quotable history of traditional racism and especially anti-Semitism; but neither does it have a traditional milieu (Mudde 2007: 84–6).

A different example is the Swiss People's Party (SVP), which does not have any continuity with an anti-democratic past. The focus of the Swiss far-right populist agenda is on immigration – especially on Muslim immigrants. But differently from the Dutch radical populist right, the SVP has been a member of the Swiss government – within the four-party coalition – for decades (Kriesi & Trechsel 2008: 94–8).

Rightist populist parties with or without a national revisionist agenda

Revisionism – understood as opposition to the outcome of the Second World War – is a distinct quality of many of the extreme right parties. The nostalgia for Hitler and Mussolini, Pavelic and Franco, and other fascist, semi-fascist and/or Nazi dictators has been, for decades, the driving force behind the extreme right in Europe. Revisionism had its focus on the territorial design of post-1918 Europe – like the German-Polish or Italian-Slovene borders. In some cases – like in the case of Hungarian revisionism – territorial nostalgia is still directed against the post-First World War borders.

The second element of revisionism is focused on liberal democracy, and especially against the concept of universal human rights. This is the link between a more general xenophobic or racist attitude and a specific direction: the anger of the far right has been, and still is, directed against social groups defined as 'foreign', be they migrants (like the Turks in Germany) or not (like the Roma in Central and South-Eastern Europe). It is especially the second revisionist orientation which is manifested in a populist manner. But the two sides of the European far right are interwoven – and it is not an 'either or', but a 'more or less', which distinguishes the parties of the European far right.

A good example of the relationship between populism and revisionism is the Italian case. The first post-fascist Italian elections took place in 1946. At that time, the country was ruled by a broad coalition of anti-fascists from the left and the centre. The elections more or less confirmed a 'grand coalition' of Christian democrats, communists, socialists and some minor centrist parties. The only principle opposition against the governing alliance came from a seeming newcomer – the 'Fronte dell' Uomo Qualunque' ('The Common Man's Front'). The party combined the protest votes of (former) fascists and regional discontent. At the beginning, the 'Qualunquists' successfully played the card of the 'man of the street', who is overwhelmed by the dictates of the political élite – and the (Western) allies who were still present in Italy at that time (Ginsborg 2003: 99–105).

When the coalition between the Christian Democrats and the Communists ended, in 1947, the Qualunquists soon started to decline – to be replaced by an openly revisionist party, the neo-fascist 'Movimente Sociale Italiana' (MSI). The more general right-wing populism of the Qualunquists was replaced by the open revisionism of a traditional (neo-)fascist party.

The implosion of the Italian party system in the 1990s brought a realignment of the Italian far right. A new party became influential on the far right – the Lega Nord. The Lega 'emerged as a result of the un-freezing of political cleavages . . .' (Bulli & Tronconi 2011: 51). The Lega is not concerned with defending Italy's fascist past but with protesting Roman centralism – in that respect distinctly not following the fascist tradition and mobilizing anti-immigration sentiments. The Lega represents the third stage of post-1945 Italian right-wing extremism: from populism to revisionism of a neo-fascist kind and back to a new version of populism – with a specific revisionist agenda directed against the central Italian state.

Rightist populist parties of Western and post-communist Europe

A special case is the rise of far-right populist parties in the Nordic countries. Scandinavia, for a long time considered to be the safe haven of liberal tolerance, has become a hotbed of anti-immigration activism, especially directed against migrants from Muslim societies. The Danish People's Party, rooted in a broad protest movement of the 1970s directed against taxation, has been the trendsetter. Other Nordic parties followed. The parties – the Danish People's Party, the Sweden Democrats, the True Finns and the Norwegian Progressive Party – are not the products of any revisionist agendas. Neither the national conflicts of the past nor a visible nostalgia for Nordic fascism play any role in the performance of the Nordic far-right parties. They are parties with an extremely narrow outlook – they are against immigration; and they oppose the deepening process of integration within the EU. The anti-immigration topic played a role in the Norwegian mass murder of July 2011: the perpetrator's 1,500-page manifesto praised the Nordic rightist parties (Living with the far right 2011).

Different from contemporary right-wing populism in Western (and especially Northern) Europe, the far right in post-communist Europe follows a revivalist strategy. The old cleavages and prejudices are identical to the agenda of parties like the Greater Romanian Party, the Hungarian Jobbik, the Slovak Slovenská Národná Strana (SNS) or the Bulgarian Attaka. Open anti-Semitism and ethno-nationalism – directed especially against minorities (like the Turks in Bulgaria or the Roma in all these countries) – are combined with the renaissance of an aggressive attitude when one of the nationalisms is dealing with another – as can be seen, for example, in the clashes between Slovakian and Hungarian nationalists. The same can be said about the post-Yugoslav situation: the war after 1991 can be considered to be the latest of the Balkan wars between those with nationalist aspirations (Glenny 2000, Ismayr 2010).

The collapse of the communist systems created a specific political environment. As 'nationalism' was – officially – anathema under communist rule, the political freedom created by the transformation of 1990 and 1991 was seen as a new freedom for the suppressed nationalistic sentiments of the past. In Western Europe, nationalism was – with the exception of openly anti-democratic parties and movements – never suppressed and had not become a 'victim'. In Central-Eastern Europe, different kinds of nationalism could take the victim's role after transformation.

Rightist populist parties with a libertarian economic agenda and rightist populist parties with a kind of (national) socialist agenda

Today's US populism is in many respects – not in all – different from the European phenomenon of the populist far right. One difference is the clientele: the Tea Party represents the older white middle class with 'somewhat higher incomes than typical Americans' – distinctly not proletarian voters (Williamson et al. 2011: 27). US populism usually has a strong religious-Christian fundamentalist agenda.

Contemporary European populism disproportionally represents the lower classes, especially blue-collar voters; Tea Party followers are from the economically rather prosperous segments of US society. Right-wing populism in Europe articulates the fears of the modernization losers; the Tea Party speaks on behalf of a significant religious interpretation of politics, especially concerning the attitudes of Evangelical Protestants. The European populists are using religion (Christianity) only as a vehicle to construct a cultural war against 'Islam'. The populist electorate is – with the exception of the Polish PiS (Law and Justice Party) – rather secular. The Tea Party is not a party but a pressure group, one more or less linked to one of the two traditional US parties, the Republicans; the European populist parties are competing for votes with all the others, especially the mainstream parties. The Tea Party is a movement with the intention of influencing the Republican Party – with some significant impact on electoral results (Karpowitz et al. 2011); the European populist right-wing parties are not – at least not primarily – movements. They are political parties.

There are some parallels – the focus on immigration and variations of nationalism: in the US case the patriotic interpretation of 'American Exceptionalism'; in the European case either more traditional forms of exclusive ethno-nationalism (especially in Central-Eastern Europe) or a kind of post-nationalist nationalism, directed against newcomers who are constructed as 'foreigners'. All the variations, on both sides of the Atlantic, are potentially racist – like the anti-Semitism and the anti-Roma sentiments of the Hungarian Jobbik or the Islam-bashing of the Dutch Freedom Party, as are emotions directed against Hispanic immigrants in the United States.

But the biggest difference is the anti-state, anti-government orientation of the Tea Party, an orientation not to be found within the European populist parties. European right-wing populism tends to be pro-state, tends to criticize the absence of a strong role of government in the realm of the economy, tends to lament the decline of the national welfare state. The tentative anarchism, so typical of the US Tea Party, is nothing the European far right could endorse. European populist far-right parties represent 'nativist economics' (Mudde 2007: 122), based on an understanding of state intervention in the economy.

Of course, there are variations. The Danish Progress Party, predecessor of the contemporary Danish People's Party, represented a strong anti-taxation sentiment – not so different from the Tea Party's libertarianism. But the general agenda of Europe's contemporary far right is to ask that the State play a significantly stronger role in economic matters. In that respect, Europe's right-wing populism is more socialist than (neo-)liberal. But in the national variety of socialism, the far right represents a brand of socialism lacking a systematic agenda of international solidarity.

All the different variations of Europe's far right are in the process of developing a common identity by constructing common enemies. The specific common enemy of the Polish PiS, the Hungarian Jobbik, the Danish People's Party and the Norwegian Progressive party is globalization. Defined as the lifting of economic and cultural and political borders, the far right defends 'identity' – first and foremost national identity, but more and more European identity in the sense of Western 'Christian' civilization, the 'Abendland'. For the far right, the Europe they are defending is not the Europe of the EU. On the contrary, the EU is seen as responsible for the dangers national identities have to face. The mobility (and modernity) that the EU stands for is anathema to the parties of the far right.

In combination with other traditional enemies – 'America' or the 'Jewish Conspiracy', merged in the code word 'East Coast' – today's far right calls for a Europe different from the rational federation-building that the EU can be identified with. If the traditional nationalistic contradictions between nationalism and nationalism can be replaced by an all-European agenda, and directed against globalization and immigration, America and 'Brussels', the populist far right could become Europeanized; it could be transformed into a European party family of post-ethno-nationalist populist parties translating the ethno-nationalist agenda into an agenda of exclusion, with Europe confronting the 'defining others', like Islam or America, 'multiculturalism' or 'political correctness'.

This could be seen as a final triumph for the concept of European integration: the arch-enemies of European unification, traditionally divided by the nationalistic conflicts of the past, could develop into a European party family and a European party within the EU – no longer so different from the Europeanized mainstream parties such as the conservatives or social democrats, liberals or greens. Thanks to populism and its not necessarily nationalist agenda, yesterday's extreme right could transform itself into an all-European populist party. If the West European, post-nationalistic and post-revisionist trend defines the future of Europe's far right more and the Central and Eastern European, traditionally nationalistic and revisionist tendencies less, the contradictions between the different brands of nationalism will not stand any longer in the way of a unified European far right. The present anti-European or at least anti-EU agenda of the far right could be replaced by a fight for a post-nationalistic, but strictly exclusive Europe – for 'Fortress Europe'.

It is especially the Austrian FPÖ which is trying to bridge the gap between the post-nationalistic far-right parties like the Dutch Freedom Party and traditional nationalism as represented, for example, by the Hungarian Jobbik. The purpose of these not yet successful attempts is to establish a far-right party group in the European Parliament (Schiedel 2011: 91–6) This would make the European far right an all-European factor beyond the EU member states.

How to deal with right-wing populism?

The established European democracies have developed different kinds of policies regarding the rise of right-wing populist parties:

- *Delegitimizing* the right wing due to its incompatibility with democratic values, enshrined in constitutions; excluding the right wing from the electoral process.
- *Isolating* the right wing by excluding it from electoral or executive alliances.
- *Embracing* right-wing parties in the hope that populism in power will demonstrate its professional inability and the impossibility to fulfil the expectations of its voters as a governing party.

The first option is based especially on the German model of militant or defensive democracy ('Wehrhafte Democratie'). The theoretical justification for the instrument of outlawing an extremist political party is based on the understanding that democratic freedoms should not be guaranteed to the enemies of democratic freedom. This leads to delegitimization and, in particular cases, to the outlawing of extremist parties. With respect to openly neo-Nazi parties this has a clear impact: parties like the German NPD (National Democratic Party of Germany), always threatened by the possibility of becoming outlawed by Germany's Federal Constitutional Court, have been kept on the fringes of the political system.

As the populist far right claims to represent a 'true' form of democracy better than the mainstream parties, the instrument of delegitimizing and repressing the populist far right is seen as an implausible instrument. This is the reason why the legal existence of parties like the Dutch Freedom Party, the French FN, the Austrian FPÖ, the Danish People's Party or the Italian Lega Nord is not threatened. The populist far right – different from traditional fascism – is anxious to prove its democratic credentials. The populist far right tries to demonstrate its legitimate existence within the framework of representative democracy. Following the arguments of the populist far right, the mainstream parties have a problem with accepting democracy. From its viewpoint, it is the populist far right which has to defend democracy – against the 'political class', against the 'power cartel' of the traditional mainstream parties. Any threat to the rule of law – such as a ruling by the German Constitutional Court to outlaw such a far-right party – is considered to be too crude an instrument, not sophisticated enough to deal successfully with the populist far right.

For that reason, most of the European political systems tend to live with extreme right-wing parties. Even the German government has been more than hesitant in using the constitutional instrument of outlawing the NPD: The argument is that it may be better to confront the enemies of the democratic consensus in the public arena of Parliament and electoral campaigns.

Parties without an obvious link to an anti-democratic past or anti-democratic intentions cannot be confronted by the instruments of the judicial system. A possible consequence is the isolation of the party, preventing it from becoming a power broker within the party system. This is the intention of the French and Belgian 'cordon sanitaire'. The French FN and the Belgian (Flemish) Vlaams Belang are challenged by the negative consensus of the other parties, a common understanding of the other actors not to permit the far right any role in coalition-building. A policy of 'cordon sanitaire' means that the other parties – from the moderate (conservative) Right to the Left – agree to avoid any kind of alliance with the far right. This policy of isolating the far right is not designed to succeed as an electoral strategy – the far right may become more attractive as the only opposition to a perceived cartel of the political establishment. Jean Marie Le Pen's success in the French presidential elections of 2002 is evidence to such an effect. But a 'cordon sanitaire' prevents any such party winning executive power: neither the FN nor Vlaams Belang has yet been able to transform electoral success into executive power (Mudde 2007: 197, 289).

The obvious precondition for the success of such a 'cordon sanitaire' is the existence of a stable majority which does not accept the far right as a legitimate partner. As coalition governments are the rule in European democracies, the 'cordon sanitaire' reduces the possibility of forming a coalition. It is a permanent temptation for mainstream parties to use the far right, either as a bargaining instrument to get better coalition agreements with other mainstream parties or, if necessary, to violate the 'cordon sanitaire' and bring a far-right party into a coalition cabinet.

This leads to the other option: mainstream parties have to compete with the far right, a policy of embracing. The principal argument for this kind of strategy is that by bringing far-right populist parties into government positions, the populists will fail – due to the incompatibility of their populist agendas, which may succeed as long as a party is in opposition without the responsibility of government. It is argued that far-right parties in government cannot deliver what they promised while in opposition.

This temptation can be felt by parties of the (mainstream) Right and by parties of the Left. The case of Austria 2000, when a conservative mainstream party (the Austrian People's Party ÖVP) accepted the far-right FPÖ as a coalition partner to force the (mainstream) Left into opposition, is a source of possible temptation for the centre-right. The case of Slovakia 2006, when a leftist mainstream party (the social democratic Smer) welcomed two smaller far-right parties (SNS – National Party, HZDS – Movement for a democratic Slovakia) is a source of temptation for the centre-left: Confronted by the choice to govern in a coalition with the far right or to go into opposition, mainstream parties may opt to bring the far right into a coalition government.

In both cases, we can observe the consequences of such a policy of embracing. In the short term, the losers have been the far-right parties: the ÖVP's as well as Smer's two far-right coalition partners declined significantly after the first period of their respective coalitions: the FPÖ in 2002, HZDS and SNS in 2010. The mainstream party which had invited the far right into a governing alliance benefited, especially the ÖVP, but Smer did also win a higher share of votes than they had before the arrangement with the far right. But, in the long run, the conclusion may be very different: after the FPÖ split in 2005 and went into opposition in 2006, the Austrian far right successfully repositioned itself to where it had been in 2000, a party of about the same strength as the two mainstream parties of the centre-left (SPÖ) and centre-right (ÖVP). Embracing the far right and including it in a coalition alliance may be a recipe for domesticating right-wing populism in the short term, but not for a longer-term perspective (Swoboda & Wiersma 2008).

The case of the Swiss People's Party (SVP) provides further experience. The SVP has been part of the Swiss party coalition for decades. The SVP was considered to be a conservative voice for German-speaking Protestants. However, in the 1980s, the party started to change its attitude: it behaved like a populist opposition party, using immigration (and especially Islam) and the EU as the defining elements of its agenda. Among the extreme-right parties in Europe, the SVP must be ranked as the most successful: in 2007, the party received 28.9 per cent of the vote (Harrison & Bruter 2011: 7).

The SVP has no fascist past – it has become a very successful right-wing populist party despite being in power. Chantal Mouffe's observation that the appeal of far-right populist parties 'diminishes once they become part of the government, and they seem able to strive only when on opposition' (Mouffe 2005: 70) is correct with respect to the Austrian and Slovak cases, but the example of the Swiss People's Party demonstrates that there are no iron rules regarding the ups and downs of the far right; and there is no fixed recipe for dealing with right-wing populism.

Of course, the most convincing long-term strategy would be to extinguish the preconditions of contemporary populism by satisfying the needs and fulfilling the demands of those who are the potential electorate of the Far Right: the dissatisfied, frustrated, angry voters. As they are, to a significant degree, articulating socio-economic interests, it would be the responsibility of social and economic policies to eradicate some or perhaps most of the conditions on which the success of rightist populism is based: by improving or at least guaranteeing the standard of living and especially the social security of the populist electorate.

However, the traditional European welfare state, which has been so successful in integrating different segments of European societies by increasing social equality, is now a shambles. For some decades now, European societies have been characterized by increasing social inequality. The European labour market is in extremely bad shape – and not only due to the global financial crisis of the last three or four years. The gap between a generation that had become used to a comparatively high standard of social security after 1945 and a generation which has reason to believe it will not enjoy a similar standard is becoming deeper and more visible.

Of course, voting for parties like the Dutch Freedom Party or the French FN is escapism. Neither of these far-right populist parties can demonstrate any credbility to reconstruct the leaking networks of social security. The populist far right complains about globalization and the end of national sovereignty. But there is no conclusive agenda for re-establishing the nation state and its protective role. The rightist populist electorate votes first and foremost *against* the 'old' parties of the mainstream – and only secondly *for* the far-right parties. But the motivation – of a contemporary European,

20 years old, without higher education and threatened by unemployment and a general decrease in his (her) quality of life – to protest against the decline of his/her status quo by voting for a populist party is not, per se, irrational: He/she has reason to believe that the post-1945 systems of social security – the British or the Swedish or even the communist systems of Eastern Europe, systems which brought a degree of security – seem to be lost for good.

As the mainstream parties cannot credibly claim to be able to reinstate yesterday's level of national welfare – how can the preconditions of far-right populism be extinguished? Europe has to live with the phenomenon of far-right populism – because there is no visible policy to change the attitudes of the modernization losers: The losers are realizing that they have lost. They have lost the level of security and predictability established in Europe after 1945.

The perspective of a 20-year-old European without higher education is the perspective of a loser. At the beginning of the twenty-first century, an undereducated European had reason to fear a deterioration in his or her chances in the near future. Compared with the expectations of one generation earlier, this undereducated European has to face mass unemployment as well as a decline in the quality of social security provided by the nation state. To eradicate these conditions, the reconstruction of the nation state and its sovereignty – or a transfer of the functions of social and economic intervention from the nation state to the European level – must be possible. The first option seems no longer to exist and the second does not exist yet.

In the foreseeable future, the social and economic preconditions favourable to the rise of right-wing populism will become stronger. To deal with the far right by re-establishing the good old post-1945 welfare state is not a realistic option. But if it is not possible to extinguish the socio-economic conditions of the contemporary far right, it might be possible to reverse the acceptance of extremist parties on the fringes of the political mainstream.

This possibility is demonstrated by Germany: the German party system permits the existence of some rather small far-right parties, but there is no equivalent of the French FN or the Austrian FPÖ. The crisis in the German welfare state is no different from the crises in the Netherlands or Denmark, but the response to rising unemployment and the general decline of social guarantees is different in Germany. It is plausible that this is – to a certain degree – a consequence of the post-1945 re-education. As a consequence of the shock German society had to face when the realities of the Nazi crimes could no longer be repressed, voting for an extreme rightist party has become socially, morally and ethically unacceptable. No other European democracy is as successful as Germany when it comes to minimizing the possibilities for the political far right.

Europe will have to live with radical populist parties. The different political strategies a democracy can employ to deal with the far right differ from case to case (Bertelsmann 2009). No general recommendations are possible. There is no simple recipe. But the German case demonstrates that a moral 'cordon sanitaire' can have a significant impact – not so different from the French and Belgian strategic 'cordon sanitaire'.

No strategy can succeed without changes in the electorate. As long as significant segments of society can be tempted by populist simplifications, by xenophobic rhetoric, by prejudices creating scapegoats, right-wing populism will play a significant role in democratic politics – independently from the situation in the labour market and the ups and downs of the economy. The decisive answer to the challenge of the populist far right has to come from 'the people' – from the citizens, from the voters.

References

Barros, B. (2005), 'The discursive continuities of the menemist rupture', in Francisco Panizza (ed.), *Populism and the Mirror of Democracy*, London: Verso, pp. 250–74.

Bartolini, S. (2007), *Restructuring Europe. Centre Formation, System Building and Political Structuring between the Nation State and the European Union*, Oxford: Oxford University Press.

Beeman, R. (2010), *Plain, Honest Men. The Making of the American Constitution*, New York: Random House.

Bertelsmann, S. (ed.) (2009), *Strategies for Combating Right-Wing Extremism in Europe*, Gütersloh: Bertelsmann Stiftung.

Betz, H.-G. (1994), *Radical Right-Wing Populism in Western Europe*, Basingstoke: Macmillan.

Beyme, K. von (2011), 'Representative democracy and the populist temptation', in Alonso, S., Keane, J. and Merkel, W. (eds), *The Future of Representative Democracy*, Cambridge: Cambridge University Press, pp. 50–73.

Bulli, G. and Tronconi, F. (2011), 'The Lega Nord', in Elias, A. and Tronconi, F. (eds), *From Protest to Power. Autonomist Parties and the Challenge of Representation*, Vienna: Braumüller, pp. 51–74.

Dahl, R. A. (1970), *A Preface to Democratic Theory. How does Popular Sovereignty Function in America?* Chicago: University of Chicago.

— (1989), *Democracy and Its Critics*, New Haven: Yale University Press.

Fukuyama, F. (1992), *The End of History and the Last Man*, New York: The Free Press.

Ginsborg, P. (2003), *A History of Contemporary Italy. Society and Politics 1943–1988*, London: Penguin.

Glenny, M. (2000), *The Balkans 1804–1999. Nationalism, War and the Great Powers*, London: Granta Books.

Harrison, S. and Bruter, M. (2011), *Mapping the Extreme Right. An Empirical Geography of the European Extreme Right*, Houndmills: Palgrave Macmillan.

Ismayr, I. (ed.) (2010), *Die politischen Systeme Osteuropas*, 3rd edn, Wiesbaden: VS Verlag für Sozialwissenschaften.

Karpowitz, C. F., Monson, J. Q., Patterson, K. D. and Pope, J. C. (2011), 'Tea time in America? The impact of the tea party movement on the 2010 midterm elections', *PS – Political Science and Politics*, 44 (April): 303–9.

Kitschelt, H. (2006), 'Movement parties', in Katz, R. S. and Crotty, W. (eds), *Handbook of Party Politics*, London: Sage, pp. 278–90.

Kriesi, H. and Trechsel, A. H. (2008), *The Politics of Switzerland. Continuity and Change in a Consensus Democracy*, Cambridge: Cambridge University Press.

Kymlicka, W. (2009), *Multicultural Odysseys. Navigating the New International Politics of Diversity*, Oxford: Oxford University Press.

Laclau, E. (2005), 'Populism: What's in a name?', in Francisco Panizza (ed.), *Populism and the Mirror of Democracy*, London: Verso, pp. 32–49.

— (2007), *On Populist Reason*, London: Verso.

Lijphart, A. (1977), *Democracy in Plural Societies. A Comparative Exploration*, New Haven: Yale University.

Lipset, Seymour Martin (1981), *Political Man. The Social Bases of Politics*, Baltimore: Johns Hopkins University.

— (1997), *American Exceptionalism. A Double-Edged Sword*, New York: Norton.

'The Sweden Democrats, Living with the far right. The fringe tries to go mainstream', in *The Economist*, 10 September 2011, 32f.

Michels, R. (1962), *Political Parties: A Sociological Study of the Oligarchical Tendencies of Modern Democracy*, With an Introduction by Seymour Martin Lipset, New York: Collier.

Mouffe, C. (2005), 'The "end of politics" and the challenge of right-wing populism', in Francisco Panizza (ed.), *Populism and the Mirror of Democracy*. London: Verso, pp. 50–71.

Mudde, C. (2007), *Populist Radical Right Parties in Europe*, Cambridge: Cambridge University Press.

Müller, J.-W. (2011), *Contesting Democracy. Political Ideas in Twentieth-Century Europe*, Newhaven: Yale University Press.

Rokkan, S. and Flora, P. (2000), *Staat, Nation und Demokratie in Europa. Die Theorie Stein Rokkans*, Frankfurt am Main: Suhrkamp.

Sartori, G. (2005), *Parties and Party Systems. A Framework for Analysis*, Colchester: ECPR.

Schiedel, H. (2011), *Extreme Rechte in Europa*, Vienna: Edition Steinbauer.

Schmitt, C. (2007), *The Concept of the Political: Expanded Edition*, With a Foreword by T. B. Strong and Notes by L. Strauss, Chicago: University of Chicago Press.

Swoboda, H. and Wiersma, J. M. (eds) (2008), *Populism and Minority Rights*, Brussels: PSE – Socialist Group in the European Parliament.

van Praag, P. (2008), 'Démocratie Consociative et Cartellisation. Le cas des Pays-Bas', in Aucante, Y. and Dézé, A. (eds), *Les systèmes des partis dans les démocraties occidentals. Le modèle du parti-cartel en question*, Paris: Presses de la Fondation nationale des sciences politiques, pp. 171–94.

Williamson, V., Skocpol, T. and Coggin, J. (2011), 'The Tea Party and the Remaking of Republican Conservatism', *American Political Science Association, Perspective on Politics*, 9 (March): 700–10.

Wodak, R. and Pelinka, A. (eds) (2002), *The Haider Phenomenon in Austria*, New Brunswick: Transaction.

2

'Anything Goes!' – The Haiderization of Europe

Ruth Wodak

In case of doubt *we* have put a limit on the presumptuousness of the powerful and have strengthened *the back of citizens*. Although the ruling class has never forgiven *us* for this, *the people* have thanked *us* for this by supporting *us*. *Our* politics has thus been condescendingly denounced for being populist. But whatever!

> Jörg Haider, Speech 'On the State of the Republic and the
> Situation of the FPÖ', 12 November 1999, emphasis added

'We' and 'the people'

On 21 February 1848, *The Communist Manifesto*, written by Karl Marx and Friedrich Engels, was published in London. The *Manifesto* starts with a phrase which soon became, and has remained, very famous: 'A spectre is haunting Europe, the spectre of communism'. In the meantime, this prominent phrase has been recontextualized many times: to indicate the 'democracy deficit and loss of trust in the European Union',[1] or the alleged and perceived 'threat of migrant workers from Eastern Europe who might take the jobs away from German workers',[2] or to point to manifestations of racism across Europe.[3] In all these cases, what seems to be meant and described points to something unknown or strange, a vague, only partially visible and blurred phenomenon (a 'spectre'), which has thus not become distinct, nor attributable to a traditional and recognizable category. Moreover, this vague phenomenon is seen as potentially powerful, threatening to 'overwhelm' an entire continent, or impinge on abstract concepts, such as employment or democracy, related to this continent, namely Europe. Semantically, the meaning of this phrase also entails dynamicity and change.

---

[1] <www.euractiv.de/europa-2020-und-reformen/artikel/eu-vertrauenskrise-ein-gespenst-geht-um-in-europa-005084> [accessed 15 November 2011].
[2] Ibid.
[3] <http://minderheiten.at/stat/stimme/stimme25c.htm> [accessed 15 November 2011].

In this way, this famous and so frequently re- and misused phrase seems to fit the phenomenon under investigation in this chapter (and volume) well: the 'spectre which is haunting Europe', some 60 years after the end of the Second World War and the official abolishment of the Third Reich and its national-socialist ideology, is the 'spectre of radical right-wing populism' (see also Judt 2008, 2010). To date, although many books, book chapters and articles[4] have attempted to understand and propose theories about these 'new' social movements, we are still confronted with a range of puzzles and unexplained aspects: Are these movements really new and in what ways? Why have these social movements become so successful in such historically different national and sociopolitical contexts as, for example, France, Austria, Greece, Hungary, Sweden and Switzerland? Whom do they address and how, and what kinds of rhetoric, slogans and argumentation schema do they usually employ? Do they 'perform politics' in the same way, that is, like more traditional mainstream politicians in a globalized world where politics and media are related to each other in such intricate ways (Wodak 2010a, b, 2011a, b, c, Higgins 2009)?

If one reads the above-quoted utterance by Jörg Haider, the infamous former leader of the *Austrian Freedom party* (FPÖ) from 1986 until 2005, and then of the FPÖ's splinter group *Bündnis Zukunft Österreich* (BZÖ) until 2008,[5] the identification with *the people* is striking. Who are '*THE*' people? The use of the *argumentum ad populum* in an overgeneralizing manner to define one's own identity is certainly a constitutive feature of radical right-wing populist parties. *Argumentum ad populum* is integrated with the *fallacy of hasty generalization*, which implies that: first, Haider does represent *THE* people; secondly, that all individuals who make up this vague group have the *same* beliefs, hence projecting his own beliefs onto the entire group of Austrians; and thirdly, that nation states actually consist of *homogenous* groups, of people. An important related rhetorical trope comes to mind: *metonymy*. In this way, Haider sees himself as standing for the people: 'Haider = Austria' is the underlying metonymic meaning.[6]

But not only identification is noticeable, a sense of achievement is also explicitly visible – Haider seems proud of having already succeeded in stopping the implied exploitation of 'normal' citizens by the powerful: the FPÖ thus supports the people *against those up there*. And thirdly, there is Haider's positive self-presentation as courageous and defiant: 'even if the others are angry and will not forgive us [the FPÖ], it does not matter!' Haider is the authentic representative of 'THE people', 'one of us',

---

[4] See inter alia: Butterwege 1996, Pelinka and Wodak 2002, Wodak and Pelinka 2002, Rydgren 2005, Ignazi 2006, Hainsworth 2008, Mudde 2009, Krzyżanowski and Wodak 2009, Kovács 2010, Harrison and Bruter 2011, and Globisch and Pufelska 2011.

[5] On 8 October 2010, Haider – totally drunk – was speeding and crashed his Porsche in a small Carinthian village in the middle of the night, and subsequently died.

[6] See Reisigl and Wodak (2001), van Eeemeren (2010) and Reisigl (2007) for detailed definitions of specific argumentative schemes and moves. In this chapter, I rely on the Discourse-Historical Approach (Reisigl & Wodak 2009, Wodak 2001, 2011a) when analysing radical right-wing populist rhetoric in some of its current manifestations. Due to space restrictions, I cannot present this framework in any detail in this chapter; however, I will define and explain specific concepts whenever I apply them in the analysis of concrete examples.

chosen to protect and defend 'us' like *Robin Hood*, courageous and brave, saying things which others would like to say but do not dare. I will come back to these typical features of radical right-wing populist rhetoric below.

Of course, similar rhetoric can be observed in many European countries and beyond. Thus, not only in Austria but across Europe, the *extreme right* have carefully refined their electoral programmes under the rubric of nationalist-populist and chauvinistic slogans, and have subsequently adopted more subtle (i.e. *coded*) forms of exclusion and racism.[7] The move away from overt neo-fascist discourse has in fact allowed some parties to expand their electoral support as *populist nationalist parties*, focusing on the protection of – seemingly homogenous – national identities or a 'mythical' homeland (*Heimat*).[8] This has led to an increase in discriminatory and exclusionary language use, not its decline, since racism often now takes more pervasive diffuse forms on board, except for some Eastern and South European countries (such as Hungary, Poland, Romania, Russia, Greece, and the Baltic States; see, for example: Wodak & Richardson (2012), chapters by Kovács (Ch. 15), Auer & Kasekamp (Ch. 16), and Shekhovstov (Ch. 17) in this volume) where explicit racist, xenophobic and antisemitic utterances remain part and parcel of respective political cultures. Indeed Holz (2011) suggests that in the former Stalinist-communist European countries, anti-Semitism has a specific unifying transnational function:

> Der nationale Antisemitismus ist aufgrund der ihm inhärenten Figur des Dritten genuin transnational und im gleichen Atemzug und aus dem gleichen Grund heraus national. Er ist transnational, weil er die Juden als *Welt*feind der Nationen und der nationalen Ordnung imaginiert. Beides zusammen aber bedeutet, die Welt aus Sicht der eigenen Wir-Gruppe zu beschreiben, also von einer Mehrzahl an Völkern auszugehen, und diese nationale Ordnung der Welt – und nicht nur der eigenen Existenz der eigenen Gruppe – im Juden bedroht zu sehen . . . Ein solcher gemeinsamer Feind verbindet. Der gemeinsame Antisemitismus lässt keineswegs alle Grenzziehungen zwischen den europäischen Nationen verschwinden. Gerade die extremen Rechten sind in aller Regel extreme Nationalisten und Feinde all dessen, was sie für fremd halten. (200–1)

> National anti-Semitism is genuinely transnational because of the inherent figure of 'the Third/Other'; simultaneously, anti-Semitism is national because of the same reason. It (anti-Semitism) is transnational because it views Jews as the enemy of the entire *world* and also of all national order. Taken together, this means that the world – seen from the perspective of a 'we-group' and not only from the view of one's own existence in one's own group – feels threatened by 'the Jew'. Such a common enemy unites. The common anti-Semitism does not make all borders between European nations disappear. However, precisely the extreme Right are extreme nationalists and enemies of everything which they perceive as strange/ foreign (translation by RW).

[7] See Krzyżanowski and Wodak 2009, Mammone 2009, Richardson and Wodak 2009a, b, Wodak 2007, 2011b, c, Harrison and Bruter 2011 and Delanty et al. 2011.

[8] See Billig 2006, Gingrich and Banks 2006, and Wodak and Köhler 2010.

Holz is certainly right in stating that a typical kind of traditional, national and simultaneously transnational anti-Semitism continues to unify radical right-wing populist parties, in spite of seeming to be paradoxical. However, as Holz argues very plausibly, the alleged transnational influence presupposes the old stereotype of the so-called world conspiracy, whereas on a national level, Jews are perceived as foreigners and thus as threatening the alleged homogenous national identity. Moreover, the patterns of antisemitic prejudice are recontextualized – as a kind of archetype of hatred and prejudice – onto other ethnic and marginalized groups, such as Roma, Muslims and so forth. In some countries, anti-Muslim prejudice and stereotypes seem to have replaced, or at least backgrounded, antisemitic rhetoric (e.g. in the United Kingdom and in Germany); in other countries, both traditional antisemitic and anti-Muslim attitudes are explicitly combined (e.g. in Austria); and in the Eastern European countries, both sets of prejudices are vibrant but do not always occur simultaneously. Of course, there are more and other possible combinations, such as in Sweden[9] and in France (see the chapter by Beauzamy (Ch. 12) in this volume).

Currently, in all European countries, there is considerable evidence of a *normalization* of – even explicit – 'othering' in political discourse in the public sphere, and there is much to indicate that this is occurring at all levels of society, ranging from the media, political parties and institutions to everyday life interactions (KhosraviNik 2009, 2010, Krzyżanowski & Wodak 2012).

Extensive research illustrates that radical right-wing populist parties across Europe and beyond draw on different *political imaginaries*[10] and different traditions, evoke (and construct) different nationalist pasts in the form of *identity narratives* and emphasize a range of different issues in everyday politics (Bar-on 2008, Peunova 2008, Bustikova 2009): some parties gain support via an ambivalent relationship with *fascist* and *Nazi* pasts (e.g. in Austria, Hungary, Italy, Romania and France); some parties, on the other hand, focus primarily on a *perceived threat from Islam* (e.g. in the Netherlands, Denmark, Poland, Sweden and Switzerland); some parties restrict their propaganda to a *perceived danger to their national identities* from ethnic minorities (e.g. in Hungary, Greece, Italy and the United Kingdom); and some parties primarily endorse a *traditional Christian (fundamentalist) conservative-reactionary agenda* (e.g. in the United States). Of course, most parties integrate several features at once, depending on the specific audience and context; thus the above-mentioned distinctions are, of course, primarily analytical (see also Wodak, forthcoming):

1. All of these parties instrumentalize some kind of ethnic/religious/linguistic/ political minority as a *scapegoat* for all current woes and subsequently construe

---

[9] In Sweden, for example, many antisemitic incidents are reported in some big cities, such as Malmö, which seem to be reactions to Israeli governmental politics but directed against Swedish Jews. The Sweden Democrats, however, are not openly antisemitic but are publicly more focused on their anti-immigrant rhetoric (see also the chapter by Oja and Mral (Ch. 19) in this volume).

[10] *Political imaginaries* are defined as being in a 'landscape of power as a space of political action signified in visual and iconographic practices and objects as well as in the literary-textual field that depicts the political scene, its structure, and its stakes' (Bob Jessop, personal communication, 10 February 2010).

the latter as dangerous and a threat 'to us'; this phenomenon manifests itself as 'discourses of fear'.

2. All of these parties seem to endorse – what I label as – the 'arrogance of ignorance'; appeals to common-sense and anti-intellectualism mark a return to pre-modernist or pre-Enlightenment thinking.

Current right-wing populist rhetoric manifests common characteristics, which may be combined with different content to achieve distinctive context-dependent discourses, genres and texts (oral, written and visual, that is, semiosis). These resonate with their respective national audiences, thus reducing instances of seemingly incomprehensible complexity in typically simplistic and seductive ways.

In this chapter, I will first present some typical characteristics and rhetorical patterns of right-wing populist parties in a range of national contexts. Here, I will also focus on their habitus and performance as acceptable mainstream media-savvy politicians. Secondly, I will illustrate two salient rhetorical and persuasive strategies: 'calculated ambivalence' and the strategy of 'systematic provocation' (see also: Engel & Wodak 2009, 2012, Köhler & Wodak 2012) which such parties employ extensively and successfully in their attempts to dominate the political agenda and media reporting.

Constructing a 'politics of fear'

Below, I briefly list nine features which are, I claim, common to all or most radical right-wing populist parties (see also Wodak, forthcoming).

First, it is important to emphasize that right-wing populism[11] (RWP) is a political style which can relate to various ideologies, not just to one (Taguieff 2003: 8). Overall, we find left-wing and right-wing populist parties; the difference relates to the political imaginaries which they put forward as well as to the structures of the parties and their recruitment patterns. Secondly, RWP cuts across the traditional left-right cleavage and constructs new social cleavages, frequently related to many, often legitimate and justified, fears about globalization and the subsequent rise of nationalism/chauvinism, the failure of current mainstream parties to address acute social problems, like the financial crisis, and so forth (Azmanova 2009, Judt 2010).

Thirdly, RWP parties' success also depends on performance strategies in modern media democracies (Wodak 2011a). This implies extensive use of the media (press and TV, new media such as comics, homepages, websites, Facebook, Twitter and so forth). Moreover, RWP politicians are usually well-trained as media personalities, and have frequently transformed a 'thug-like' appearance to that of a quite 'slick' mainstream politician's appearance: they exhibit youth, they are handsome, fit, well dressed. In short, they assume the habitus of serious statesmen and stateswomen.[12]

---

[11] I prefer the term right-wing populism to both radical and extreme right-wing populism, as these superlatives/attributes are a question of relative scale and perception.

[12] See, for example, <www.hcstrache.at> [accessed 2 May 2011].

Fourthly, the *personalization* and *commodification* of current politics and politicians leads to a focus on 'charismatic' leaders; RWP parties usually have a hierarchical structure with (male) leaders who exploit modern trends of the political profession to perfection.[13] Recently, female leaders have also come to the fore (in France, Denmark, Norway and the United States).

Moreover, fifthly, leading populist politicians employ *front-stage performance* techniques which are also linked to popular *celebrity culture* (well-known from the tabloids and sensationalist media reporting): they oscillate between self-presentations as *Robin Hood* (i.e. saviour of 'the man and woman in the street') and self-presentations as 'rich, famous and/or attractive' (i.e. an 'idol'), frequently leading to a 'softer' image, adapted to mainstream values, but only on the front stage. As Gingrich (2002) states, such leaders can dress and behave like 'a man/woman for all seasons'. Hence, such politicians carefully prepare their *appearance/performances* for different audiences; their rhetoric and programmatic proposals are heavily *context-dependent*. This implies a specific selection of meeting places (beer tents, pubs, stages, market places, discos, and the so-called tea-parties in the United States), the clothes they wear (from suits to casual leather jackets, t-shirts or folklore dress), their selection of spin-doctors and accompanying 'performers' on stage, the music, posters and logos on display, and so forth (Goffman 1959, Wodak 2011a).

Sixthly, RWP usually correlates with strong *anti-intellectualism* and, as a result, with the aforementioned *arrogance of ignorance* (Wodak, forthcoming). Appeals to common-sense and traditional (conservative) values linked to aggressive exclusionary rhetoric are, for example, particularly apparent in some parts of the US *tea party* movement, performed and instrumentalized almost 'perfectly' by Sarah Palin or Michelle Bachman. Seventhly, linked to anti-Muslim rhetoric and campaigns, RWP parties currently seem to endorse pseudo-emancipatory *gender policies* which, on second view, are extremely contradictory; in this vein, the US Republicans claim, for example, to support a so-called right-wing feminism which supports feminist values linked to traditional family values and campaign against pro-choice movements.[14] Thus, on the one hand, traditional family values are emphasized (which position women primarily as mothers, caring for children and their families); on the other hand, though 'freedom for women' is proposed, this refers solely to Muslim women, who are depicted as wearing headscarves or being veiled. In this way, gender becomes instrumentalized in very specific ways (see Pedwell 2007) and linked to a rhetoric of exclusion, for example, to the exclusion of Turkish migrants who form the third largest ethnic minority in the city of Vienna. Moreover, the 'freedom' of women is contrasted with fundamentalist Islam, implying that every woman wearing a headscarf is potentially dangerous. In this way, the theme of security is linked to the so-called freedom of women.

---

[13] Silvio Berlusconi is/was, of course, an obvious case in point, due to his ownership of almost all the relevant Italian media.

[14] See, for example, <http://dailycaller.com/2012/02/16/what-are-women-for/> or <www.msnbc.msn.com/id/21134540/vp/46523668#46523668> [both accessed 26 February 2012].

Eighthly, there is a distinct difference between populist styles and rhetoric in *opposition* and in *government*. Few right-wing populist parties survive if elected into government because they lack the necessary programmes, strategies and skills (Grande 2000). This is why many scholars suggest that the coalition government between conservatives and RWP failed in Austria in 2006 (Reisigl 2007). Thus, it is also not surprising that the FPÖ managed to grow very quickly again after 2006, as a party in opposition. In the Netherlands, the extreme right also lost once they formed part of the second chamber in the Dutch government (2002–6) after the assassination of Pim Fortuyn on 6 May 2002.

Finally, I claim that RWP is based on a generalized and salient claim to represent '*THE (homogenous) people*' (based on nativist ideologies). The construction of these groups is thus contingent on many historical, national and sociopolitical factors. Their claims are accompanied by a *revisionist view of history* (see above; Engel & Wodak 2009). In this way, the rhetoric of exclusion has become part and parcel of a much more general discourse about migrants and migration, with the overall motto: '*We*' (i.e. the Occident or Europe) have to defend '*Ourselves*' against '*Them*' (i.e. the 'Orient': Roma, Jews, Muslims). RWP movements are – as already indicated above – based on a specific understanding of the '*demos*/people': the complexity within a society is denied. These parties continuously position and discursively construct themselves as the 'saviours of the Occident', who defend the man/woman on the street against 'those up there' and 'the Turks/Barbarians' who might take away 'British (Dutch, Belgian, Italian) jobs from British (Dutch, Belgian, Italian) workers' and who 'do not want to integrate and adapt to "our" culture', or similar.

RWP parties are thus primarily defined by the construction of common enemies: 'They' are foreigners, defined by 'race', religion or language. 'They' are élites not only within the country but also on the European ('Brussels') and global level ('Financial Capital'). Cleavages within a society are neglected, such as class, caste, religion, gender and so forth, or are interpreted as the result of 'élitist conspiracies'. The discursive strategies of 'victim-perpetrator reversal', 'scapegoating' and the 'construction of conspiracy theories' thus belong to the necessary toolkit of RWP rhetoric (Wodak 2010b, 2011b). Two brief examples, below, illustrate typical applications.

The Austrian press and a European 'crisis'

Exclusionary discursive strategies become obvious if one follows the debates in spring 2011 about Tunisian refugees trying to reach the Italian coast by boat. The then Italian Berlusconi government decided to issue Schengen visas to the refugees so that they could cross the borders into other European countries – a measure supported by the European Union (EU) Commissioner Cecilia Malmström. The then Italian minister for Interior Affairs, Roberto Maroni, officially requested support and solidarity from neighbouring EU member states. The latter, however, did not want to comply: in a press conference on 26 April 2011, the then French President Nicholas Sarkozy and former Italian Prime Minister Silvio Berlusconi emphasized that the Schengen borders should be closed again, even though this would contradict EU policy. Many national media supported this campaign for 'Fortress Europe'.

On 11 April 2011, for example, the conservative Austrian broadsheet *Die Presse* stated in bold letters: 'Italy washes its hands [of Tunisian refugees]' (*Italien putzt sich ab*). Below this headline, the then Minister of Interior Affairs from the conservative People's Party (ÖVP), Maria Fekter, claimed that these Schengen visas would have an 'enormous vacuum effect' (*Staubsaugereffekt*). Austria should thus also consider closing its borders again.[15] Such headlines and utterances are characteristic of – a relatively coded and metaphorical – exclusionary rhetoric in several ways: first, refugees are *indirectly* depicted as being dirty, relating to the metaphorical meaning of 'cleaning up'. Attributing 'dirt' to specific groups immediately evokes a very old stereotype, traditionally ascribed to Roma or Jews. Dirty people are not civilized, and thus not welcome and expendable. Secondly, the Tunisian refugees are dehumanized, that is, they are not talked about as human beings but only referred to metonymically via the documents they might carry (Schengen visas). Thirdly, the metaphorical use of 'vacuum' implies that large numbers of refugees will inevitably be expected; thus it is further implied that other countries (like Austria) will have to *defend themselves* against this quasi-causal 'effect' by necessarily and legitimately closing their borders.

Nowhere do we read about the plight of these refugees; we are also not informed about the reasons why they have fled their home country; and no concrete numbers are mentioned which might substantiate the *implied threat* for EU countries. Moreover, the distinction between migrants and refugees is neglected: in the third paragraph of this article, the minister claims that 'this is new illegal migration . . .; although our [Austrian] asylum system is stable in relation to its level [in numbers], illegal migration presents a mega-problem'. Hence, the Tunisians fleeing conflict suddenly mutate into *illegal migrants*, that is, people who have left their country voluntarily and who pose a *mega*-problem. Conflating two categories into one, namely 'migrants' and 'refugees' into 'illegal migrants', allows the construction of one threatening 'other': in this way, the different legal statuses of asylum seekers and migrants is not accounted for. The overall implied meaning becomes apparent: any foreigner entering the EU from Africa is, per se, illegal. No evidence seems necessary for this claim (see Baker et al. 2008, KhosraviNik 2008, 2010, KhosraviNik et al. 2012).

Further, below, other politicians are quoted as stating that 'illegal streams of refugees [*Flüchtlingsströme*] will cost Europe even more'. Here, another typical rhetorical device is employed: exaggeration. Europe is thus confronted with a '*mega*-problem'; not only will 'streams' flow into Europe, but 'masses of floods' will also, a metaphor indicating a natural catastrophe defying control. The article concludes by quoting the German and Swiss Interior Ministers, Simonetta Sommaruga and Hans-Peter Friedrich, who agree with the papers' overall assessment of this 'mega-problem'.

This example illustrates how mainstream politics and politicians have increasingly appropriated arguments, metaphors, idioms, symbols and images from the far right. They believe, quite wrongly, that by implementing proposals from the extreme right wing that they will be able to win new voters, or at least keep their existing voters.

---

[15] <http://diepresse.com/home/panorama/welt/649385/Fluechtlinge_Italien-putzt-sich-ab> [accessed 15 April 2011].

'Strangers' and 'barbarians'

Leaders of right-wing populist parties tend to express exclusionary ideology far more directly and explicitly: For example, on 25 March 2011, the Dutch populist right-wing politician Geert Wilders delivered a speech, in Rome, in which he claimed that 'The failure to defend our own culture has turned immigration into the most dangerous threat that can be used against the West. Multiculturalism has made us so tolerant that we tolerate the intolerant'.[16]

He then refers to the end of the Roman Empire, thus drawing a very tenuous analogy to current immigration flows from North Africa (Tunisia), Turkey and the Middle East:

> Rome did not fall overnight. Rome fell gradually. The Romans scarcely noticed what was happening. They did not perceive the immigration of the Barbarians as a threat until it was too late.... People came to find a better life which their own culture could not provide. But then, on December 31st in the year 406, the Rhine froze and tens of thousands of Germanic Barbarians crossed the river, flooded the Empire and went on a rampage, destroying every city they passed. In 410, Rome was sacked.

Wilders emphatically presents the fall of the Roman Empire as an unavoidable consequence of the mass migration of barbarians to Roman provinces. In fact, as the historian Walter Pohl has indicated, it is highly unlikely that systematically keeping the Germanic tribes (i.e. the so-called barbarians) from crossing the frontiers could have prevented the defeat of Rome in 406–7.

Due to space restrictions, I cannot demonstrate in detail why Wilders' historical argument does not work (see Pohl & Wodak 2012, Pohl forthcoming for details). This speech illustrates that many debates on migration explicitly or implicitly rely on historical arguments (*topos of history*, condensing the warrant: 'if X happened in the past, Y will happen now (again or in a smilar way)').[17] Moreover, metaphors of fluidity are a familiar part of it; migrants first trickle in, then turn into streams and finally flood a peaceful country and drown it in mayhem and general destruction. Unlike the 'parasite metaphor', liquidity does not even belong to the realm of living beings. Thus, Wilders would need to explain why peaceful migration would necessarily lead to violent destruction. Yet, there is no historical evidence for this, just a well-worn

---

[16] <www.pi-news.org/2011/03/speech-geert-wilders-rome-25-march-2011> [accessed 22 April 2011].

[17] Within argumentation theory, '*topoi*' can be described as parts of argumentation, which belong to the required premises. They are the formal or content-related *warrants* or 'conclusion rules', which connect the argument(s) with the conclusion, the claim (Manfred Kienpointner 1996: 194). The warrant can always be made explicitly conditional, such as 'if x, then y' or 'y, because x'. There are, of course, many meanings associated with the concept of *topos* (see van Eeemeren 2010, Wodak 2011a). Moreover, the distinction between topos and fallacy is also frequently blurred; as Reisigl and Wodak (2009: 102) admit, it is not always easy to distinguish precisely, without contextual knowledge, whether an argumentation scheme has been employed as reasonable topos or as fallacy.

stereotype. The historical disciplines have done much in recent decades to deconstruct these old ideologically charged images. But even liberal quality media still reproduce the old stereotypes, as our research suggests (Baker et al. 2008).

Be that as it may, it becomes apparent that both mainstream and right-wing populist politicians endorse similar concerns and objectives, albeit with different discursive strategies and levels of explicitness: to keep 'them' out of Europe! In debates about immigration and religious difference, or in media reporting, speakers/writers will often employ arguments of 'culture', depicting it as an essentially bounded entity whose integrity is threatened by the presence of residents supposedly belonging to a different 'culture', and thus not willing to learn and adopt 'our' conventions and norms, that is, to assimilate; in these argumentative sequences, deictic elements acquire salience.

Calculated ambivalence and discursive provocation

The rise of right-wing populist movements in recent years would not have been possible without massive media support. This does not, of course, imply that all newspapers share the same positions, although some tabloids, of course, do. For example, the former leader of the FPÖ, Jörg Haider, frequently appeared on the cover of weekly magazines such as *News* or *Profil*, thereby ensuring higher sales for these publications and adding to his visibility in the public sphere. The Austrian tabloid *Neue Kronenzeitung*, similar to the *Sun* or the *Daily Mail* but with a larger reach in relation to the country's population (approx. three million weekend readers in a country of eight million), campaigned explicitly and implicitly for Haider: headlines, editorials, images and letters to the editor were all streamlined to provide support. Leading populist politicians also have to be media savvy: they undergo rhetorical training (such as neurolinguistic programming, NLP), employ qualified spin-doctors and are educated in performance techniques which lead to a 'softer' image, adapted to mainstream values (but, of course, only on the front stage).

On the other hand, they intentionally provoke the media by violating publicly accepted norms (Engel & Wodak 2009, 2012, Köhler & Wodak 2012). In this way, the media are forced into a 'no-win' situation; if they do not report a scandalous racist remark, such as the FPÖ's slogan, as part of the 2010 Viennese election campaign: 'More courage for "Viennese Blood". Too much foreignness is not good for anybody!' (*Mehr Mut für Wiener Blut. Zuviel Fremdheit tut niemandem gut*) they might be perceived as endorsing it. If they do write about this, they explicitly reproduce the xenophobic utterance, thereby further disseminating it. A predictable dynamic is triggered which allows right-wing populist parties to set the agenda and distract the media from other important news. This dynamic consists of several stages which can only be briefly summarized at this point and which I label as 'The Right-wing Populist *Perpetuum Mobile*'.

The right-wing populist perpetuum mobile also serves as example for the overall claim of my chapter: 'Anything goes' implies that RWP parties and politicians have developed discursive and rhetorical strategies which combine incompatible phenomena, make false claims sound innocent, allow denying the obvious, say the 'unsayable' and transcend the limits of the permissible. Usually they get away without being sanctioned and, even if they have to apologize, they do so in a calculated and ambivalent way (see below). Rarely do they have to resign, and even if they have to, some of them seem to 'bounce back' quite quickly (see Wodak & Pelinka 2002 for detailed examples). Below, I briefly elaborate the dynamic of the right-wing perpetuum mobile.

First, *scandal* (e.g. the posting of the racist slogan: 'More Courage for "Viennese Blood"!'; see Figure 2.1) is intentionally provoked by the FPÖ.[18] Once some evidence for the inherently racist meaning is produced by the opposition, the offensive meaning of the slogan is immediately denied; then the scandal is redefined and equated with entirely different phenomena (by redefining and reformulating the meaning of concepts or by employing analogies and metaphors, or by constructing contrasts or arguing via *topoi of* history); in this case, the FPÖ claimed that they were only quoting the title of a well-known Viennese operetta, '*Wiener Blut*', whose libretto had been written by an Austrian-Jewish author in the nineteenth century. By invoking a Jewish authority, the FPÖ believed that they had established innocence (*topos of authority:* if a Jewish person has said or written X, then X cannot be wrong' which is, of course, fallacious as being Jewish certainly does not guarantee that this person will necessarily be saying/doing/writing/endorsing the right and politically correct view). The FPÖ, however, claimed, that they were thus certainly not referring to any racist/ nativist meanings.

In this way, the FPÖ employed the discursive strategy of *calculated ambivalence* and succeeded in conveying a *double-message* – readers could either understand the literal meaning (the operetta whose libretto had been written by a Jewish (sic!) author) or associate the name of the operetta with the insinuated and implied meaning of 'Viennese blood'. In any case, the FPÖ was – they further stated – not responsible for readers' interpretations. Both readings are, of course, possible. The strategy of calculated ambivalence allows multi-addressing while at the same time providing the speaker/writer with an exit strategy via quasi-innocent denial: The FPÖ could claim that they had never considered the second dimension of meaning.

This allows, as a further step, to claim *victimhood* by the respective politician and so the event is *dramatized and exaggerated*, that is, the FPÖ claim to have been wrongly accused of having posted a racist slogan. They also emphasize the right of freedom of speech for themselves, as a *justificatory strategy*: 'Why can one not utter critique?' or 'One must be permitted to criticize Turks, Roma, Muslims, Jews . . .!' or '*We* dare say what everybody thinks', and so forth. Such utterances, of course, immediately trigger another debate – unrelated to the original scandal – about freedom of speech and political correctness, and thus serve as a distraction and allow evasion of the primary scandalous issue.

Moreover, the accusation is instrumentalized for the construction of a *conspiracy*: somebody must be 'pulling the strings' against the original culprit of the scandal and

---

[18] See Köhler and Wodak 2012 for a detailed analysis of this poster.

Figure 2.1 Poster used by the FPÖ in the Vienna election campaign of 2010: 'More courage for our "Viennese Blood". Too much foreignness is not good for anybody' (translation by the author). © Helge Fahrnberger.

scapegoats (foreigners, liberal intellectuals and so forth) are quickly discovered. Once, the accused finally have a chance to present substantial counter-evidence, a *new scandal* is launched. A '*quasi-apology*' might follow in case 'misunderstandings' might have occurred and the entire process begins afresh with a new scandalous utterance, again an instance of calculated ambivalence.

This dynamic implies that right-wing populist parties cleverly manage to frame media debates; other political parties and politicians as well as the media are, in turn, forced to react and respond continuously to ever-new scandals. Few opportunities remain to present other frames, values and counterarguments, or another relevant agenda. As a consequence, mainstream politics moves more and more to the right and the public becomes disillusioned, de-politicized and 'tired' of ever-new scandals; hence, RWP rhetoric becomes more explicit and extreme and continuously attracts further attention.

References

Azmanova, A. (2009), '1989 and the European Social Model. Transition without Emancipation?', *Philosophy and Social Criticism*, 35(9): 1019–37.

Baker, P., Gabrielatos, C., KhosraviNik, M., Krzyżanowski, M., McEnery, A. and Wodak, R. (2008), 'A Useful Methodological Synergy? Combining Critical Discourse Analysis and

Corpus Linguistics to Examine Discourses of Refugees and Asylum Seekers in the UK Press', *Discourse & Society*, 19(3): 273–306.

Bar-on, T. (2008), 'Fascism to the Nouvelle Droite: The Dream of Pan-European Empire', *Journal of Contemporary European Studies*, 16(3): 327–45.

Billig, M. (2006), 'Discourse and Discrimination', in K. Brown (ed.), *Second Edition Elsevier Encyclopedia of Language and Linguistics*, Oxford: Elsevier, pp. 697–99.

Bustikova, L. (2009), 'The Extreme Right in Eastern Europe: EU Accession and the Quality of Governance', *Journal of Contemporary European Studies*, 17(2): 223–39.

Butterwege, C. (1996), *Rechtsextremismus, Rassismus und Gewalt*, Darmstadt: Primus Verlag.

Delanty, G., Wodak, R. and Jones, P. R. (eds) (2011), *Identity, Migration and Belonging*, 2nd rev. edn, Liverpool: Liverpool University Press.

Engel, J. and Wodak, R. (2009), 'Kalkulierte Ambivalenz, "Störungen" und das "Gedankenjahr": Die Causen Siegfried Kampl und John Gudenus', in R. de Cillia and R. Wodak (eds), *Gedenken im "Gedankenjahr": Zur diskursiven Konstruktion österreichischer Identitäten im Jubiläumsjahr*, Innsbruck, Studienverlag, pp. 79–100.

— (2012), 'Calculated ambivalence and Holocaust denial in Austria' in Wodak, R. and J. E. Richardson (eds), *Analyzing Fascist Discourse: Fascism in Talk and Text*, London: Routledge, pp. 73–96.

Gingrich, A. (2002), 'Haider – A Man for all Seasons', in Wodak, R. and Pelinka, A. (eds), *The Haider Phenomenon in Austria*, New Brunswick, NJ: Transaction Press, pp. 67–94.

Gingrich, A. and Banks, M. (eds) (2006), *Neo-nationalism in Western Europe and Beyond: Perspectives from Social Anthropology*, New York: Berghahn Books.

Globisch, C., Pufelska, A. and Weiss, V. (eds) (2011), *Die Dynamik der europäischen Rechten*, Wiesbaden: VS Verlag.

Goffman, E. (1959), *The Presentation of Self in Everyday Life*, New York: Doubleday.

Grande, E. (2000), 'Charisma und Komplexität: Verhandlungsdemokratie, Mediendemokratie und der Funktionswandel politischer Eliten', *Leviathan*, 28(1): 122–41.

Hainsworth, P. (2008), *The Extreme Right in Western Europe*, London: Routledge.

Harrison, S. and Bruter, M. (2011), *Mapping Extreme Right Ideology*, Basingstoke: Palgrave.

Higgins, M. (2009), 'Populism and security in political speechmaking: the 2008 US presidential campaign', in L. Marsden and H. Savigny (eds), *Media, Religion and Conflict*, Farnham, Surrey: Ashgate, pp. 153–68.

Holz, K. (2011), 'Die antisemitische Verbrüderung der europäischen Rechten', in C. Globisch, A. Pufelska and V. Weiss (eds), *Die Dynamik der europäischen Rechten*, Wiesbaden: VS Verlag, pp. 187–202.

Ignazi, P. (2006), *Extreme Right Parties in Western Europe*, Oxford: Oxford University Press.

Judt, T. (2008), *Postwar*, London: Penguin.

— (2010), *Ill fares the Land*, London: Penguin.

KhosraviNik, M. (2008), 'The British Newspapers and the Representation of Refugees, Asylum Seekers and Immigrants between 1996 and 2006', *Centre for Language in Social Life*, Lancaster University.

— (2009), 'The representation of refugees, asylum seekers and immigrants in British newspapers during the Balkan conflict (1999) and the British general election (2005)', *Discourse & Society*, 20(4): 477–98.

— (2010), 'The Representation of Refugees, Asylum Seekers and Immigrants in the British Newspapers: A Critical Discourse Analysis', *Journal of Language and Politics*, 8(3): 1–29.

KhosraviNik, M., Krzyżanowski, M. and Wodak, R. (2012), 'Dynamics of Representation in Discourse: Immigrants in the British Press', in M. Messer, R. Schroeder and R. Wodak (eds), *Migrations. Interdisciplinary Perspectives*, Berlin: Springer, pp. 283–296.

Kienpointner, M. (1996), *Vernünftig argumentieren. Regeln und Techniken der Diskussion*, Hamburg: Fischer.

Kovács, A. (2010), *The Stranger Within*, Leuven: Brill.

Köhler, K. and Wodak, R. (2012), 'Mitbürger, Fremde und "echte Wiener"' – Ein- und Ausgrenzungen über SpracheDiskursive Konstruktion von Macht und Ungleichheit am Beispiel des Wiener Wahlkampfes 2010, *Deutschunterricht*, 63(6): 64–74.

Krzyżanowski, M. and Wodak, R. (2009), *The Politics of Exclusion. Debating Migration in Austria*, New Brunswick, NJ: Transaction Publishers.

Mammone, A. (2009). 'The Eternal Return? Faux Populism and Contemporarization of Neo-Fascism across Britain, France, and Italy', *Journal of Contemporary European Studies*, 17(2): 171–94.

Mudde, C. (2009), *Populist Radical Right Parties in Europe*, Cambridge: Cambridge University Press.

Pedwell, C. (2007), 'Tracing the "Anorexic" and the "Veiled Woman": Towards a relational Approach', *New Working Papers Series*, 20, Newcastle.

Pelinka, A. and Wodak, R. (eds) (2002), '*Dreck am Stecken*'. *Politik der Ausgrenzung*, Vienna: Czernin.

Peunova, M. (2008), 'An Eastern Incarnation of the European New Right: Aleksandr Panarin and New Eurasianist Discourse in Contemporary Russia', *Journal of Contemporary European Studies*, 16(3): 407–19.

Pohl W. (forthcoming), *The Barbarian Challenge*, Turnhout.

Pohl, W. and Wodak, R. (2012), 'Debating Migration', in M. Messer, R. Schroeder and R. Wodak (eds), *Migrations. Interdisciplinary Perspectives*, Berlin: Springer, pp. 205–13.

Reisigl, M. (2007), 'The Dynamics of Right-wing Populist Argumentation in Austria', in F. Van Eemeren (ed.), *Argumentation*, Norwood, NJ: Ablex, pp. 1127–34.

Reisigl, M. and Wodak, R. (2001), *Discourse and Discrimination. The Rhetorics of Racism and Antisemitism*, London: Routledge.

— (2009), 'The discourse-historical approach (DHA)', in R. Wodak and M. Meyer (eds), *Methods of Critical Discourse Analysis*, London: Sage, pp. 87–121.

Richardson, J. and Wodak, R. (2009a), 'Recontextualising Fascist Ideologies of the Past: Right-wing Discourses on Employment and Nativism in Austria and the United Kingdom', *Critical Discourse Studies*, 6(4): 251–67.

— (2009b), 'The Impact of Visual Racism. Visual Arguments in Political Leaflets of Austrian and British Far-right parties', *Controversia*, 2: 45–77.

Rydgren, J. (ed.) (2005), *Movements of Exclusion. Radical Right-Wing Populism in the Western World*, New York: Nova Science.

Taguieff, P. (2003), *Illusione Populista*, Milano: Bruno Mondatori.

van Eemeren, F. (2010), *Strategic Manoeuvring in Discourse*, Amsterdam: Benjamins.

Wodak, R. (2001), 'The discourse-historical approach', in R. Wodak and M. Meyer (eds), *Methods of Critical Discourse Analysis*, London: Sage, pp. 63–95.

— (2007), 'Pragmatics and Critical Discourse Analysis', *Pragmatics & Cognition*, 15(1): 203–25.

— (2010a), 'The Politics of Exclusion: The Haiderisation of Europe', in A. Landwehr (ed.), *Diskursiver Wandel*, Frankfurt: VS Verlag, pp. 355–76.

— (2010b), 'The Glocalisation of Politics in Television: Fiction or Reality?', *European Journal of Cultural Studies*, 13(1): 43–62.

— (2011a), *The Discourse of Politics in Action: Politics as Usual*, 2nd rev. edn, Basingstoke: Palgrave.

— (2011b), 'Old and new demagoguery. The Rhetoric of Exclusion'. <www.opendemocracy.net/ruth-wodak/old-and-new-demagoguery-rhetoric-of-exclusion> [accessed 5 May 2011].

— (2011c), 'Suppression of the Nazi past, coded languages, and discourses of silence: applying the discourse-historical approach to post-war antisemitism in Austria', in W. Steinmetz (ed.), *Political Languages in the Age of Extremes*, Oxford: Oxford University Press, pp. 351–79.

— (forthcoming), *The Politics of Fear: Analysing the Rhetoric of Radical Rightwing Populist Politics*, London: Sage.

Wodak, R. and Köhler, K. (2010), 'Wer oder was ist "fremd"? Diskurshistorische Analyse fremdenfeindlicher Rhetorik in Österreich', *Sozialwissenschaftliche Studien*, 50(1): 33–55.

Wodak, R. and Pelinka, A. (eds) (2002), *The Haider Phenomenon in Austria*, New Brunswick, NJ: Transaction Press.

Wodak, R. and Richardson, J. E. (eds) (2012), *Analyzing Fascist Discourse: Fascism in Talk and Text*, London: Routledge.

3

Loud Values, Muffled Interests:
Third Way Social Democracy and Right-Wing Populism

Magnus E. Marsdal

The Progress Party (Frp), established in 1973, has become, at times, Norway's leading opposition party, with support reaching as high as 37 per cent according to some polls in 2006. In the last two parliamentary elections, the Frp scored 22 per cent. It does exceptionally well among unskilled workers, especially the non-unionized, although it also attracts better-off people (private sector types without 'old money'). The main focus of this chapter is the Frp; however, the results should be relevant to the analysis of right-wing populism in other countries as well.

The most interesting aspect of the Frp's rise to popularity is probably its ability to attract an impressive proportion of working-class votes. In a predominantly social-democratic country such as Norway, this is something of a paradox in view of the policies of the Frp in areas such as economic redistribution, workers' rights and trade-union power. The economic policies of the Frp are drawn from the chilliest wells of American *laissez-faire* and Thatcherism, although these have been tempered by more than 30 years of ideological accommodation to Scandinavian welfare-state traditions. While paying considerable lip service to these traditions, the Frp retains a more radical programme on privatization and tax cuts than any other political party in Norway. It is still the Norwegian party that is most hostile to trade unions. The Frp's programme is opposed (in principle) to nationwide tariff agreements, which are seen by many as the *sine qua non* of the trade union movement in Norway. Still, many workers favour this party at the ballot box. Even unionized workers now vote in large numbers for the Frp (Marsdal 2007: 18).

Adding these votes to those usually obtained by the more traditional right-wing parties could prove crucial to the establishment of lasting right-wing hegemony in the Norwegian Parliament (this was the situation in Denmark, where the Danish People's Party made an important contribution to the undisturbed reign of the centre-right coalition from 2001 to 2011). The Frp's emergence as the 'new labour party' could be the most serious threat faced by the Norwegian left parties since the battle with the radical right during the 1940s.

In my 2007 book *Frp-koden* ('The Frp Code'), I set out to explore the reasons why the Frp has gained such considerable support among working-class voters. In this chapter, I will present some of my findings. My investigation, consisting of qualitative interviews with 13 Progress Party voters (in their homes, at their workplaces, during leisure activities and on vacation on the Spanish Costa Blanca), drew on extensive sociological data of voters and their opinions, and on comparisons with accounts (from political science, sociology and journalism) of similar voters and parties in other countries (primarily Denmark, France and the United States). The aim of this chapter is not to set out a coherent theory or comprehensive account of the success of right-wing populism among working-class voters, but merely to convey some elements that make up the analyses put forth in *Frp-koden*. One controversial topic to be discussed is what relation, if any, we can find between 'Third Way' social democracy (especially its accommodation to neo-liberal economic policies) and the emergence of right-wing populism as such a strong political current in large sections of the working-class electorate in many European countries (Rydgren 2005).

The position of Frp voters in a two-dimensional social space

In order to explore the political sociology of these voters, it makes sense to use a two-dimensional map of Norway's 'social space of occupational groups' distributed according to the weight of economic capital and cultural capital held by members of

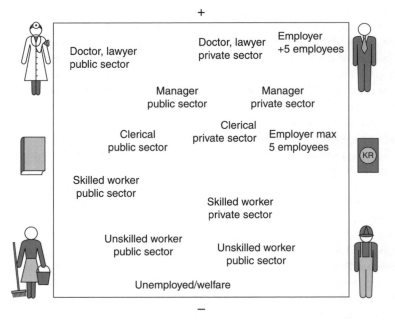

Diagram 3.1 The social space of occupational groups

these groups. The data presented in Diagram 3.1 are drawn from the market analysis firm TNS Gallup's Norwegian survey 'Forbruker & Media', with a representative sample of 10,000 respondents, and processed with the Norwegian statistics tool *Sosioraster*. The concept of 'capital' used here is in the tradition of the French sociologist Pierre Bourdieu (1986: 241–58). 'Cultural capital' is defined here by parameters such as level of education and father's level of education. Annual income and different forms of accumulated wealth define 'economic capital'.

Along the vertical axis, groups of respondents are distributed (using the statistical method of correspondence analysis) according to their *overall volume of capital* ('have-nots' at the bottom and 'have-lots' at the top). Along the horizontal axis, the groups are distributed according to a different principle, the *composition of capital*. Respondents on the right have more money (symbolized in the diagram by the Norwegian unit of currency 'Krone' (KR)) than education (symbolized in the diagram by a book); on the left, the composition is the opposite. In the middle, we find respondents with a balance of the two forms of capital.

How is the propensity to vote for the Frp distributed in the social space thus constructed? In order to map this out, the respondents can be separated vertically into three 'classes' (Élite, Middle, Lower). These are then divided horizontally into three 'class fractions' (Cultural, Balanced, Economic) within each class. This produces a total of nine class fractions of equal size (same number of respondents in each), as shown in Diagram 3.2.

Respondents are distributed along the vertical axis according to their total volume of capital, and along the horizontal axis according to the composition of their capital, with cultural capital (primarily education) to the left and economic capital to the right. Respondents are divided into nine equal size groups, as shown.

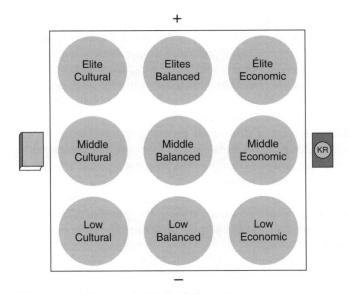

Diagram 3.2 The population divided into nine groups

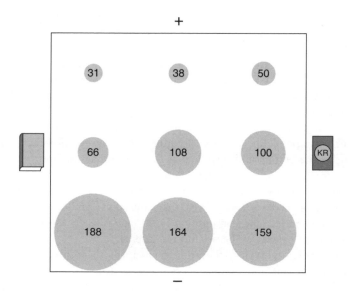

Diagram 3.3 Smokes roll-your-owns

It is now possible to show social patterns of opinion or taste by measuring the average propensity of respondents within each of the nine class fractions. As an example, consider the pattern of propensity for smoking 'roll-your-owns', illustrated in Diagram 3.3 above.

If a group of respondents shows exactly the same propensity as the average for the whole sample, it is set to 100 (as the middle-class economic fraction in Diagram 3.3). Those with a score higher than 100 show over-propensity, those with a score lower than 100 show under-propensity. (Please note that this diagram says nothing about the overall prevalence of the measured preference, neither within each group nor in the total sample; it merely indicates in which regions of social space we find *over-representation* (or the opposite) of this preference. Also, be aware that the geometrical increase in the size of these circles overstates the differences, due to a methodical error in the statistics tool *Sosioraster* (the numbers are, nevertheless, correct).)

The diagram reveals a clear social pattern in the preference for roll-your-own cigarettes. The largest difference observed is the one between those at the top and those at the bottom. This indicates that the most powerful *principle of social differentiation* in this case is the *overall volume of capital*. The smoking or non-smoking of such cigarettes is thus 'a class issue', that is, if, by 'class', we refer to differences pertaining to the vertical axis in the constructed social space, as opposed to differences pertaining to the horizontal axis. Now let us look at the propensity for voting for the Frp, as shown in Diagram 3.4.

This party is more popular on the right-hand side than it is on the left. This indicates that the *composition of capital* is an active principle of differentiation for this issue: The Frp is more strongly favoured by those who have 'more money than education'

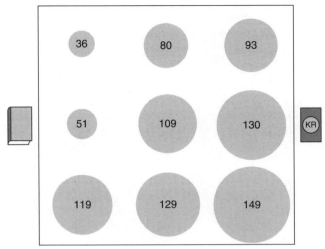

Diagram 3.4 Votes for the Frp

(which, to a certain extent, translates to 'the private sector', which again, to some extent, translates to 'men'). However, the *volume of capital* is clearly also relevant: The Frp is more strongly favoured by those placed at the bottom of the diagram than by the élites found at the top. Hence, the Frp is a 'popular' party with a stronghold in the male-dominated private sector. In *The Frp Code* (as mentioned in this chapter), the object of analysis is not the Frp supporters found higher-up in this social space, but the 'working-class' voters of the party (which, for the purposes of analysis in my book, I define, somewhat arbitrarily, as *those 60 per cent of the Frp voters who have the lowest annual income*).

The most striking feature of this chart is perhaps the exceptional dislike of the Frp expressed by 'the educated', especially in the public sector (the élite-class cultural fraction and the middle-class cultural fraction). To shed light on the meaning of this relation, we may compare the distribution of the propensity for voting for the Frp with that of voting for the Socialist Left Party (SV), currently a junior partner to Labour in the coalition government and the most radical of the leftist parties in the Norwegian Parliament (its support ranging from 4.1 to 12.5 per cent in the last four national elections). The two groups who dislike the Frp the most are strongholds of the SV, as presented in Diagram 3.5.

In light of the SV's programmatic references to the political importance of 'the working class', it is interesting to note that the most powerful principle of differentiation in this diagram is clearly the *composition of capital* (which, to some extent, translates into the opposition between the public and private sectors). The SV is clearly not a 'class' party; it is a sector party. It is the party of, one might say, those with more education than money, and who are a little on the privileged side (Marsdal 2007: 220–35).

The Frp is quite the opposite – it is the party of those with more money than education, but who are a bit on the underprivileged side (ibid.: 234–5). Historically, these are both *middle-class parties* ('middle class' in a modern sense, not the more

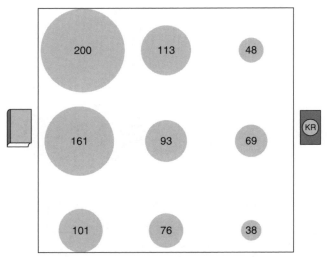

Diagram 3.5 Votes for the Socialist Left Party

aristocratic English sense where 'middle class' often means 'the bourgeoisie'). The SV was formed in the 1970s, by the *educational middle class*. The Frp was formed around the same time, by the *business middle class*. This sociopolitical development, spurred by opposing fractions within 'the middle class', is observed in several countries in post-Second World War Europe. Whereas previously the most explosive ideological show in town *used* to be the confrontation between capital and organized labour – a bottom-top opposition, as it were – we now witness a 'horizontal' polarization between the 'socialism' of the growing educated middle class and the right-wing 'populism' of the striving and often discontented business middle class. This confrontation is described by Bourdieu as the opposition 'between the primary school teachers and the small shopkeepers, which in post-war France has been expressed as a political opposition between left and right' (Bourdieu 1995: 35–6).

Both the SV and the Frp have made efforts to appeal to working-class voters. Whereas the socialists have mainly 'talked the talk' (with programmatic references to 'the working class'), the right-wing populists seem to have 'walked the walk', making remarkable electoral progress among exactly those social groups which the radical left is trying to win. In 2005, the Frp was for the first time the most popular party among unskilled workers (receiving 36 per cent of the votes among this group), thus achieving a narrow victory over the social-democratic Labour Party within this group of voters (Marsdal 2007: 18).

Confusing patterns of political attitudes?

A quantitative study was performed by exploring the Norwegian dataset *Forbruker & Media*, number 1/2006 produced by TNS Gallup, through surveys of 10,000 respondents. From my own studies of the Frp and also European research on right-wing populism (Rydgren 2005), I knew that the heterogeneous electoral base of the party could be divided into one 'working class' segment and one more 'petit bourgeois' segment (small-business owners, shopkeepers, etc.). I was more concerned with the former. My crude construction of the Frp's 'working class' voters was achieved by removing the top 40 per cent income earners among their voters in the TNS Gallup dataset. The remaining 60 per cent were the object of the quantitative study, in the book these are referred to as the Frp's 'common folk' voters.

From the quantitative data, as well as through qualitative interviews, I found that these voters share a set of thoroughly *conservative* or *right-wing* attitudes on issues including the following:

- Immigration;
- Crime/punishment;
- Foreign aid to developing countries;
- Environmentalism (and especially environmentalists);
- Feminism (and especially feminists).

On these issues, the Frp's working-class voters are very well aligned with the party leadership. However, the same voters also share a set of *leftist* attitudes on issues including the following:

- Reduction in economic inequality in society;
- State responsibility for providing welfare services to all citizens;
- Increased workers' power/influence in the workplace.

On these issues, the Frp's working-class voters (here defined as the 60% of Frp voters with the lowest incomes) are not at all aligned with the party leadership, which is positioned far to the right of these voters. For instance, according to the Frp programme, the party wants to abolish the taxation of wealth and discard all inheritance tax. These are the demands of the rich and wealthy, not of the Norwegian workers who would have to shoulder a higher proportion of total national taxation if the rich received these tax cuts from the Frp.

In fact, the Frp's working-class voters are very similar to the Labour Party's working-class voters (here, defined by education as the lowest 60% of Labour's voters) on these issues: Both groups hold traditional working-class views, so much so in fact that the *Frp's working class voters stand alongside or to the left of Labour's élite voters* (here, defined by education as the 15% of Labour voters with at least four years of higher education) on issues such as increased workers' power or economic redistribution through the tax system. While 34 per cent of the Frp's working-class voters 'fully agree' that 'Employees should have a much greater influence in the workplace', only 18 per cent of élite Labour voters 'fully agree' with the same proposition. Among the Frp's working-class voters, 50 per cent 'fully agree' that there should be higher taxes on higher incomes, whereas the figure among élite Labour voters is 47 per cent (Marsdal 2007: 187–91).

The Frp's working-class voters are right wing/conservative on some important issues and left wing/socialist on other political issues. This makes it challenging to position them on a simple left-to-right political axis. In order to plot the coordinates of these voters, we need to make use of two *different* right-to-left political axes simultaneously. These are the traditional left-right axis (the 'class' axis) and the axis of value politics, as given in Diagram 3.6.

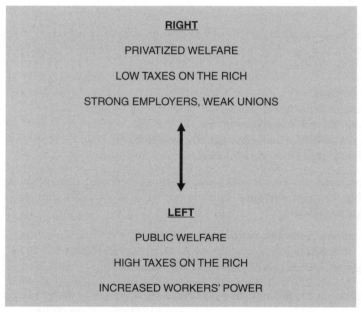

Diagram 3.6 The traditional left-right axis

On this axis, working class Frp voters are on the left, while the party leadership is on the right. However, as mentioned above, we need one more axis to plot the coordinates of these voters, as shown in Diagram 3.7.

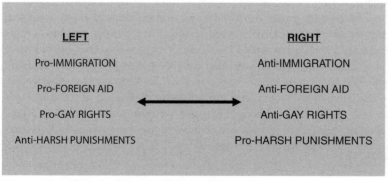

Diagram 3.7 The left-right axis of value politics

On this axis, the Frp's working-class voters are placed on the right. Thus, their approximate coordinates can be drawn as illustrated in Diagram 3.8.

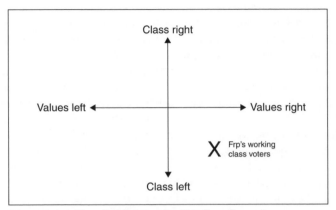

Diagram 3.8 Two dimensions of political confrontation

The conflicts which define the traditional axis are characterized by the fact that they stem from the oppositions between rich and poor, capital and labour, the powerful few and the organized many. As such, they are true 'class conflicts'. The issues that define the horizontal axis of so-called value politics do *not* spring from such class oppositions. They may be equally important or salient, but they are not 'class issues'.

This difference is of relevance to the political strategies of the left. While the issues defining the vertical axis tend to unite working-class voters politically, the issues defining the horizontal axis tend to divide them. The left-wing political mobilization of majorities used to be interest-based and built around class issues that united workers. In Scandinavia (and elsewhere), this strategy successfully promoted workers' movements to positions of political power (such as parliamentary majorities), via which the movements' parties *also* implemented progressive policies on so-called value issues. The sociopolitical *basis* of the political mobilization, however, remained 'class' issues relating to welfare, power and economic distribution (ibid.: 44–52).

A new top-level consensus in party politics

Many of the Frp voters I encountered during my investigation were unionized workers who had previously voted for Labour. One of these, a 67-year-old pensioner, told me that she now voted for Frp in the local elections, but was sticking with Labour in the national elections. She was clearly considering moving over to the Frp camp for good, like her son had done some seven years previously. This woman had been a worker and unionized throughout her adult life. Her father was a radical and active organizer in the construction workers' union from the 1940s through to the 1970s, and her late husband was a unionized worker. The whole family was proud of their history as staunch trade unionists. She also held very clear left-wing social democratic views on growing inequalities, the need for more union activism, the rich being too powerful, etc.

So I asked her: 'Eli, you have all these clear views about equality and inequality, which the Frp does not share. Shouldn't you be voting with the left?' She looked at me and said: 'Well, does it make a difference? It seems to me that whoever is in power, it's always the same. They all come straight out of school and go into politics, they know nothing about ordinary workers' lives, and still they go about passing all kinds of laws and regulations and impose them on us. No one listens to people like me.' In short, when asked why she would not stand by the left anymore, she answered: 'We've already tried that'.

This does not explain why the Frp has a strong appeal among voters like her, a question which is explored further in my book. However, it does give us a clue as to why a social democrat such as her has – over time – opened up to the *possibility* of voting for a right-wing political party. It seemed to me that she, and several others I met, could not really see the difference between Right and Left anymore, and so the fact that the populist Frp had always been a right-wing party did not matter very much to them, even though they would never identify themselves as being 'right wing'. I wondered: Has the left-right political compass of these workers really been broken?

I went on to explore what had actually happened in top-level party politics over the last three decades. I found a clear pattern of convergence around market-oriented policies: Policies, which up until the 1970s had been considered right-wing/conservative/economic liberalism and thus the opposite of what the labour movement stood for, had gradually become the favoured policies of the social-democratic leadership – and hence the new orthodoxy in Parliament was more or less unchallenged. This was the case for a number of important and previously hotly contested areas of public policy. Under the new consensus, the outcome was the following, *regardless of who was in power:*

- Reduced taxation on capital, wage-earners should shoulder a larger proportion of the cost;
- Increasing economic inequalities;
- Privatization of major public companies (Statoil, Telenor);
- Deregulation of the electricity market (Norway introducing the world's most marketized system in 1991);
- Abolition of social-housing policies;
- 'Free trade' policy restrictions dictated by the European Union's (EU) internal market and the World Trade Organization;
- Pension cuts;
- More power and influence to the deregulated private financial sector.

The old woman had a point: It can certainly be hard to tell the difference between one government and another, these days. While election campaigns tend to make voters believe that by changing the government they can actually turn the political steering wheel of society, the reality for three decades has been that voters are only able to get their hand on the gear stick – by changing the government they are only changing the *pace* of political transformation towards increased inequalities and weakened public welfare provision, and not the overall direction of socio-economic development.

At the ideological level, this course of events was justified most vigorously, within social democracy, by proponents of the 'Third Way' – such as Anthony Giddens and Tony Blair. They saw the submission to neo-liberal policies not as retreat, but as the necessary modernization of the Left in an era of 'globalization' and 'individualization' in which economic policy-making had moved 'beyond left and right' (Giddens 1994). This ideological current has held a strong position among social democratic élites, especially in the 1990s, including the Jospin government in France, the Schröder government in Germany, the Prodi governments in Italy, Nyrup Rasmussen in Denmark and Stoltenberg's first government (2000–1) in Norway. The interesting question here is not whether one agrees with the 'Third Way' accommodation to the neo-liberal orthodoxy of economic policy or not. Rather, it is how this unprecedented right-wing convergence in the field of economic policy might affect our object of investigation: right-wing populism's potential voters among the working class.

The salience of value politics on Election Day

'Earthquake', shouted the front page of the French daily newspaper *Le Monde*. It was the morning after the *Front National*'s Jean-Marie Le Pen beat the Socialist Party's Prime Minister Lionel Jospin in the first round of the 2002 presidential election. For the Left this spelled catastrophe. The sociologist Loïc Wacquant was quick to pass the blame:

> The rise of the extreme right, starting in the early 1980s, coincided with the jettisoning by the French left of its working-class tradition and ambition. As the Socialist Party switched its doctrine and policies to appeal to the educated middle classes and dragged the Communist Party alongside it (and into government), the *Front National* became the top vote-getter among workers and the unemployed.
>
> The French socialists have even theorized this betrayal. Dominique Strauss-Kahn, Jospin's spokesman and likely prime minister had Jospin become president, has explained that, in spite of three million unemployed and four million officially living under the poverty line, even as the stock market booms, French *'society considers that it has reached its limits in matters of redistribution'*.
>
> Jospin even became the first left-wing prime minister in French history to reduce income tax rates for the rich. In September 1999, he explained: '*I don't believe that one can administer the economy any more. One does not regulate the economy through the law, through texts. Everyone admits* [the rule] *of the market'*.
>
> So long as the Socialists of France, and of the rest of Europe, continue to ignore the growing social insecurity spawned by welfare retrenchment and economic deregulation, they will continue, stone by stone, to pave the road toward fascism. (Wacquant & Halimi 2002)

In his polemical account, Wacquant claims that there is some kind of causal relation between 'Third Way' (neo-liberal) social democracy and the rising tide of right-wing populism among the working class. In *The Frp Code*, I investigate whether such a relation indeed exists.

Some interesting pieces of evidence from political science emerged in the aftermath of the landslide victory of the right in Denmark's 2001 general election. In Denmark, both the xenophobic Danish People's Party (Dansk Folkeparti) and the more mainstream Liberal Party (Venstre) have exploited the anti-élitist rhetoric of right-wing populism in recent election campaigns, with strong emphasis on immigration issues and on the 'culture war' waged by bearers of so-called common sense against the stuck-up *besserwissers* of the universities, the official cultural committees and the intellectuals of the Left in general.

During this period, the Danish Social Democrats have subscribed, in Third Way fashion, to the new orthodoxy of economic policy, often to the disappointment of many among their voters. One example is how the Social Democrats government in 1998 enacted controversial pension cuts, despite having promised in the election campaign that same year to safeguard people's pensions. Eighty-two per cent of Danes at this point were of the opinion that the Social Democrats had broken their promise (Goul Andersen & Borre 2003: 49). While the Social Democrats pushed through policies of the new orthodoxy, the Liberal Party adjusted its rhetoric towards the centre, praising the virtues of Scandinavian welfare-state accomplishments. Ideological lines were blurred.

The landslide victory of 2001 ushered in a stable decade-long right-wing hegemony in Danish politics. In the 2001 election, the Social Democrats suffered a terrible blow in their traditional stronghold constituencies – among the workers. The political scientists leading the Danish Election Project pointed out that there was 'a complete breakdown of the collective mobilization within the working class . . . a near extinction of the workers' parties among the younger part of the working class . . . especially among skilled workers' (ibid.: 2007–11).

So what happened in 2001? The Danish Election Project, led by Jørgen Goul Anderssen at the University of Aalborg, provides some interesting information:

- Workers and white-collar occupation groups switched places on Election Day: On average, workers who used to vote to the left of the non-manual groups now voted to the right of them.
- Workers had, however, *not* moved to the Right on welfare policies: They are traditionally to the left of white-collar voters on issues such as economic redistribution and public welfare, and they remained so in 2001 (on some issues even *further* to the left of the white-collar workers than they were in 1979).
- Voters in general had *not* moved to the Right on welfare and economic policies.
- Voters in general had *not* moved to the Right on issues such as immigration and other 'value politics'.
- Voters in general did not even report that they were *emphasizing* 'value politics' over welfare issues. From voters' answers to the question 'Which problems do you see as most important today, that politicians should deal with?', welfare issues received a 51 per cent score, economy (unemployment, taxes) 13 per cent and immigration 20 per cent.

So what had changed? On one particular question, the political scientists registered a significant change among the electorate. This was on how they replied to the question of *what issues determined their choice of political party* on Election Day.

2001 saw the first Danish election (registered by researchers) in which the axis of value politics was more salient to voters in determining party choice than the axis of economic policy. The 'value politics' axis is defined here by issues of immigration, environmental protection, foreign aid and the punishment of criminals (harsher punishment or not). The 'economic' axis is defined by issues of maintaining the level of welfare-state provision, decreasing inequalities in wages, the democratic regulation of business life and increased taxation of high incomes (ibid.: 171–3).

Taken together, welfare policies and economics were still by far the most important issues for voters. But they no longer made such a big difference on Election Day. Though there was much anger among many voters when the great pensions reform was pushed through in 1998, come Election Day in 2001, there was in fact no (significant) correlation between voters' opinions on this huge political issue and whether they voted for the Right or for the Left. This is perhaps no wonder, as the traditional party of the workers – the Social Democrats – was the government party behind the pension cuts and in this regard indiscernible from the right-wing parties.

The neo-liberal consensus on economic policies widely affects the course of election campaigns and media coverage. In Denmark, the parliamentary consensus turned the pension reform into a 'dead' political issue, even though it affected the huge majority of voters. When an issue is 'left for dead' like this, the effect is usually enhanced by the mass media. Political journalists cover conflict, not consensus. Thus, when political journalism is reduced to covering political parties (which it most often is), an élite consensus in Parliament means that there is nothing to report. This *depoliticizing of economics* leads to the politicizing of everything else. With nothing to report on pensions or inequalities, journalists move on to cover those topics that *are* still perceivable as being controversial under the new consensus, namely 'value politics'. In Denmark this means, above all, immigration and immigrants. In the Danish state television's news coverage of the 2001 election campaign, 66 per cent of the stories were about 'foreigners', 14 per cent were about 'welfare' and 12 per cent were about 'the economy' – almost an inversion of voters' priorities (ibid.: 121–2).

All in all, the neo-liberal élite consensus in the field of economics ensures that economic and welfare policies – issues which once were the basis of successful majority mobilization by the left – are 'taken off the table' before voters have their say. The effect on the relation between the two dimensions of political confrontation amounts to something like Diagram 3.9.

Class issues are shoved into the background and value issues come to the fore. Tensions over economic distribution and fairness are *demobilized*. This takes place, however, at the top level of party politics, and *not* in society. In society, economic and social inequalities and tensions have been rising over the last decades, not only in Denmark, but also all over Europe. The political demobilizing of class conflicts does not take place because most voters have come to emphasize value issues more than class issues, which they have not, but rather because, under the neo-liberal élite consensus on class issues, confrontation on moral and cultural issues ('values') has become the

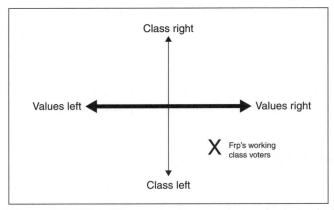

Diagram 3.9 Effect of the new consensus on the two dimensions' salience for party choice

only available means of party-political and ideological demarcation. Welfare issues and the economy may still be a high priority in election campaigns (party slogans, etc.), but they are rarely the disputed terrain of *demarcation* and *confrontation*. To many voters, all party leaders sound the same on these issues. Economic policy debates are dull and grey. Then, someone says something about the Muslim veil and media hell breaks loose.

This modus operandi of the political system has proved fortunate for right-wing populists such as the Frp. Whereas the party has *much in common* with its potential working-class voters on the axis of value politics, it is *opposed* to those same voters on 'class' issues of power and economic equality. On this axis, it retains a Thatcherite agenda (although these days Frp politicians seldom broadcast this to a wide audience). So the more a strongly neo-liberal orthodoxy enforces its élite consensus in the field of economic policy, the more space is created for confrontation along the conflict lines of value politics – and the more the Frp stands to gain from working-class voters. And this seems to be exactly what has happened over the last three decades, not only in Norway but also in many other countries. Among those mentioned in 'The Frp Code' are Denmark (People's Party), France (Front National), Austria (Haider's movement/ FPÖ), Belgium (Vlaams Blok/Vlaams Belang), Italy (Fini and Berlusconi), Switzerland (People's Party) and the United States, where the Republicans exploited the new consensus of neo-liberal orthodoxy within economics to attract a substantial number of working-class voters from previous Democrat strongholds through 'culture wars' waged against the educated élites (Frank 2004).

The Third Way and right-wing populism

So, what of the Third Way and its relation to right-wing populism? Within the party political left, Third Way leaders have represented the ideological current most eager to deregulate financial markets, introduce market mechanisms to the provision of public services and enforce 'flexibilization' of labour laws. In other words, they have been eager to blur or altogether eliminate the political opposition between Left and Right on key issues of economic and welfare policy. The question is whether, by promoting this strategy of depoliticizing the economy, they run the risk of promoting a politicizing and a polarization of 'value' issues, which is a development most conducive to the success of right-wing populist mobilization among workers. If this is the case, one might hypothesise, from the strategic viewpoint of a right-wing populist party, that the preferred leadership of the political Left must be the Third Way type of social democrat.

For the Left, the opposite might be true, at least as far as winning over or securing working-class votes that are within the reach of right-wing populism is concerned. If we look at where the Frp's working-class voters are located in Diagram 3.8, a feasible strategy for a leftist party trying to win them over, would be connecting with them through policies firmly located around the left pole on the 'class' axis. This strategy would necessarily include a redistribution of power and income, shifting away from a neo-liberal process of increasing financial domination towards a more democratic and egalitarian development, which was what happened during the construction of the welfare state in the heyday of popular social democracy. Such a confrontation with the interests of the wealthy few seems all the more relevant in the current state of financial, state and welfare crisis, seen by many to have been brought about by three decades of neo-liberal redistribution to the top.

With rising unemployment in the aftermath of the great financial crisis, the 2011 election campaign in Denmark saw economic issues at the top of the agenda. The Left's narrow victory in September of that year was, however, no thanks to progress by the Social Democrats. In spite of the economic crisis and the centre-right government's growing unpopularity after ten years in power, the social democratic party of Helle Thorning-Schmidt actually lost one seat, compared to the result of the 2007 election. The 2011 victory was secured by Thorning-Schmidt's centre-left coalition partners, along with parliamentary support from by far the most radical leftist party in Denmark, Enhedslisten, which won eight new seats in 2011. Notably, the Danish People Party's progress was reversed, as it lost three seats in this election. As a supporter of the centre-right coalition, it had been made responsible for unpopular welfare cuts, especially concerning early retirement pensions. This was eagerly pointed out by the trade unions in a national campaign to expose the right-wing character of the Danish People's Party on economic issues.

There is, however, no sign of any renewed strategy among social-democratic party leaders. In Greece, they have sided with the banks and the International Monetary Fund, imposing harsh austerity measures with dramatic consequences for large parts of the population, rather than siding with the trade unions struggling for increased equality and reduced financial power. As head of the EU presidency, Helle Thorning-Schmidt might have been expected, as a social-democratic leader, to voice political alternatives to the austerity policies drawn up by German Chancellor Angela Merkel and other conservatives in the EU; but while the debate over the austerity pact ran high in other quarters, Thorning-Schmidt retained a pose so depoliticized that one commentator at a major Danish daily was inclined to ask whether 'there is any Government present in Denmark at all' (Mogensen 2011).

With the neo-liberal model in deep crisis, it could have been the mission of the political Left to confront the powers of financial capital and turn the tide of increasing inequality. For Third Way social democrats, such a strategy might appear not only difficult but outright unthinkable given that they claim to have moved 'beyond Left and Right' on economic policy. From my studies of the Norwegian Progress Party's success among working-class voters, I draw the conclusion that this Third Way strategy seems bound to reproduce, in the political field, that *opus operatum* of muffled interests and loud values which has proved so favourable to the growth of right-wing populism.

References

Bourdieu, P. (1986), 'The forms of capital', in J. E. Richardson (ed.), *Handbook of Theory of Research for the Sociology of Education*, New York: Greenwood Press, pp. 241–58.
— (1995), *Distinksjonen, En sosiologisk kritikk av dømmekraften*, Oslo: Pax Forlag.
Frank, T. (2004), *What's the Matter with America? The Resistable Rise of the American Right*, London: Secker & Wartburg.
Giddens, A. (1994), *Beyond Left and Right, The Future of Radical Politics*, London: Polity Press.
Goul Andersen, J. and Borre, O. (eds) (2003), *Politisk forandring, Værdipolitik og nye skillelinjer ved folketingsvalget 2001*, Aarhus: Systime Academic.
Marsdal, M. E. (2007), *Frp-koden. Hemmeligheten bak Fremskrittspartiets suksess*, Oslo: Forlaget Manifest.
Mogensen, L. T., 'Ingen Helle i kampen om Europa', *Politiken*, 16 December 2011. <http://politiken.dk/debat/signatur/ECE1481160/ingen-helle-i-kampen-om-europa/> [accessed 16 March 2012].
Rydgren, J. (2005), 'Is Extreme Right-wing Populism Contagious? Explaining the Emergence of a New Party Family', *European Journal of Political Research*, 44: 413–37.
Wacquant, L. and Halimi, S. (2002), 'Jospin pays for the class betrayal of the Socialists', *Guardian*, 25 April 2002.

4

Breaking Taboos and 'Mainstreaming the Extreme': The Debates on Restricting Islamic Symbols in Contemporary Europe

Aristotle Kallis

Introduction: How (bad) ideas spread

Ideas can often travel fast and cross boundaries effortlessly. This is as true of positive ideas (e.g. a movement for political change like the one currently being witnessed across the Arab world) as of divisive ones (e.g. stereotypes, prejudices, exclusivist and discriminatory discourses). Yet, the mechanisms for diffusion in each case are essentially the same: first, charting an alternative perspective claiming to offer distinct advantages over existing ones; then, gaining traction by receiving new adherents, mobilizing human resources and spreading further through multiple nodes and channels of communication and interaction; finally, something akin to the proverbial 'tipping point', when the new idea gathers enough momentum and support to challenge established thinking and, quite possibly, effect real change (Gladwell 2000). The above scheme applies to what could be called 'successful' ideas, that is, ideas that develop a momentum and are judged by their impact, regardless of whether they were initially considered universally 'good' or 'bad' in any sense of those words. In fact, very few ideas become truly 'infectious'; most usually follow a path that leads from inception and initial propagation to limited diffusion and (sooner or later) entropy or supersession by other ideas. However, once an idea (or 'frame' of ideas, namely interpretive filters of perception and understanding of the world: Snow & Benford 1992, Johnston & Noakes 2005) has attracted public attention and has started to mobilize human resources or effect cognitive changes to its audience, then it becomes a fascinating terrain of further enquiry into the reasons behind its apparent 'success' and the dynamic of its further diffusion.

Extreme ideas, even those considered taboo in a particular context, are no different. They begin their life cycle as politically and socially marginal and radical counterpropositions to established 'mainstream' cognition. By transgressing the widely accepted boundaries between 'acceptable' and 'unacceptable' premises or prescriptions, they are essentially attempting to remap these established cognitions and subvert the mainstream 'frames' that support them. In so doing, they invariably acquire adherents – people who are essentially 'early adopters', willing to accept and make the suggested transgression (Gladwell 2000: 30–87). The critical litmus test for their 'success' and wider propagation consists of breaking into wider political and social constituencies, well beyond the initial circle of 'early adopters'. For this to happen, demand and supply intersect in a number of unpredictable ways on each occasion. The more relevant and seemingly convincing the new counter-framing to the perceptions, fears and desires of a particular audience, the higher its capacity either to tap into suppressed demand or to appeal to, and activate, sentiments/attitudes that sustain or amplify such demand in the future. This process involves ideas and associated practices being transferred from a particular place and/or time to another – and transformed, adapted and fused with other existing context-specific elements along the way (Wodak & Fairclough 2010: 21–5). When one looks at the diffusion of the 'racial' anti-Jewish paradigm in 1930s Europe, it becomes obvious that the model pioneered by the Nazi regime with the 1935 'Nuremberg Laws' broke taboos and, in so doing, activated and/or empowered pre-existing, yet latent or partly suppressed, anti-Jewish demand in other countries. This contributed critically to its reproduction – in a 'domino effect' style – across other European countries between 1936–9. It also served as both a legitimizing (viewed as 'successful') precedent *and* a 'successful', bold model for shaping similar 'solutions' to the so-called Jewish problem outside Nazi Germany (Kallis 2008: 216–27).

At the same time, supply – in the form of social exposure, through public events and/or 'noise' from traditional and new mass media – is of crucial significance in accessing diverse social audiences and demonstrating tangibly the growing appeal of the radical counter-frame. For example, over a long period of time, Italian mainstream media sensationalized the murder of Giovanna Reggiani by a Roma immigrant in 2007, giving wide exposure to extremist views about 'revenge' against the Roma communities in Italy and the expulsion of 'illegal immigrants' propagated by figures of the far right (including many prominent local and national politicians belonging to the Lega Nord (LN)) (Sigona 2010). The cumulative result of this demand-supply dialectic (since one usually reinforces the other) is the 'mainstreaming' of either the entire counter-frame or at least aspects thereof. This is both a gradual consequence and an escalating cause for further diffusion. While initially the counter-frame enters the 'mainstream', because it activates and validates suppressed social demand (and recruits from these constituencies), it also has a powerful cyclical 'demonstration effect' on others who may, later on, be more willing to endorse it as seemingly 'mainstream' and legitimate.

'Success' is a word that has often – and more so in recent years – been used to describe the rise of the radical-populist right in contemporary Europe. The apparent 'success' of the radical-populist right in contemporary Europe can be gauged on multiple levels. The one most usually taken as a benchmark is the electoral success of extremist parties in local, regional, national and European elections alike (Eatwell 2000: 407–25, Carter 2005). While, with a few notable exceptions, far-right parties have rarely achieved a number of votes that could be classed as an electoral 'breakthrough' – and have been even less successful in sustaining high levels of voter support in the longer term – the overall trend in the last two decades has been consistently upward in this respect. In addition, new far-right parties have appeared in many European countries in recent years, making the 'new' radical-populist right a genuinely transnational political force (Mammone et al. 2009).

Beyond electoral performance, however, some far-right parties have been notably more successful in translating their poll ratings into (disproportionately stronger) political and sociocultural influence. In countries such as Austria, The Netherlands, Denmark, Italy and Switzerland, the far right emerged (in the past or more recently) as a power broker, supporting, participating in or sometimes leading government coalitions only on the basis of onerous concessions from establishment parties. This kind of political influence is very difficult to gauge, for it goes well beyond the field of party-political bargaining and parliamentary arithmetic. The initial political concessions made by so-called mainstream (typically centre-right and centre-left) parties in order to lure, appease and neutralize their far-right government or parliamentary partners may result in the gradual 'mainstreaming' of far-right parties or at least particular aspects of their programme, discourse and outlook in ways that transcend (and potentially outlive) any particular cooperative agreement.

This latter element of 'success' – namely, the indirect diffusion and 'mainstreaming' of ideas and discourses propagated by the far right – may also be witnessed even if such parties remain politically marginalized (as has been the case in France and Sweden, for example). In this case, 'mainstreaming' involves the (partial or full) endorsement by political agents of the so-called political 'mainstream', and/or by broader sectors of society, of 'extreme' (in some cases even taboo) ideas and attitudes without necessarily leading to tangible association (namely, political cooperation or voter alignment) with the extremist parties that advocate them most vociferously. This is the scenario which is most insidious and difficult to gauge, as it may involve either a gradual 'agenda-setting' or 'framing' outcome (Price & Tewksbury 1997: 173–81), or indirect ideological-political concessions by mainstream actors that are not formalized through party agreements or quantified through corresponding voter support (Eatwell 2000: 416–18, 2005: 101–20). This development has the potential to unleash previously unthinkable levels of social demand for some extreme ideas that were originally considered taboo but which have, in the process, become, allegedly, more legitimized and thus more acceptable to a wider audience.

In all three scenarios, the influence of populist ideas and outlooks is strikingly disproportionate to the actual levels of the respective parties' electoral support. Whether as a pragmatic concession by mainstream parties in order to achieve short-term government stability or as a strategy of catering to growing electoral demand and acting as a safeguard against voter alignment to extremist parties, the result is infinitely more worrying than the influence measured purely by election results (Ruzza & Fella 2009). There is, however, a further equally insidious and alarming dimension to this phenomenon of 'mainstreaming' initially extremist ideas. The diffusion dynamic of such ideas and 'frames' is not confined to the specific *national* political and social contexts in which they originate; rather, through political communication, mass media exposure and new means of interaction (e.g. the internet and new social media), they cross borders effortlessly and may have an empowering/mobilizing effect on other political and social constituencies in other parts of the world. Once again, 'successful' ideas tend to become trendsetters for new, radical political thought and action across states and societies. The positive side of this story can be witnessed in the ways in which the apparent success of the movements in Tunisia and then Egypt spread across the entire region, ushering in what has been described as 'The Arab Spring' (Beaumont 2011, CoFR 2011). But the transnational diffusion of ideas and practices can also involve negative, divisive and/or repressive ideas: this is precisely what happened in interwar Europe with the rise and spread of fascism, as well as the concurrent radicalization of anti-Semitism in many European countries at the time (Kallis 2008: chs 7–8). According to many commentators, in the past two decades we have been witnessing a comparable (in spread if not – at least yet – dynamic or devastating consequences) phenomenon of transnational social and political 'mainstreaming' of extremist ideas in many parts of the so-called Western world, particularly against immigrants and even more specifically against communities with a Muslim background. Whether identifying Jean-Marie Le Pen, Jörg Haider (Wodak & Pelinka 2002), Filip Dewinter, Geert Wilders or any other far-right leaders as their maverick *enfants terribles* (Wodak 2005: 141), these extremist discourses have developed a menacing transnational diffusion and 'mainstreaming' dynamic, in the context of which developments in one (national) context strongly influence and shape associated responses in others, usually in rapid succession.

Although the diffusion of these ideas and practices is the result of a series of very complex processes that involve strategies of appropriation and negotiation with national conditions and histories (essentially processes of *recontextualization* – Wodak & Fairclough 2010: 22–5), in this chapter I am particularly interested in how 'successful mainstreaming' in one place and moment functions as a licence to others to act in similar transgressive ways elsewhere. In other words, I focus on how particular selective taboo ideas propagated by the radical far right on one occasion, and appearing to have gained traction in a particular society, can have a similar radicalizing effect on much wider international (social and political) audiences, influencing them and being appropriated by them (Chouliaraki & Fairclough 1999). I will discuss the example of the far right's campaigns against Muslim religious spaces (mosques) and symbols (the Islamic female dress debate), focusing on how these two issues became the symbolic battlegrounds of contemporary Islamophobia and were recontextualized as 'mainstream' discourses and allegedly defensible legal measures in a number of European countries. I will illustrate how these two debates and associated landmark initiatives (namely, the 2009 Swiss referendum on minarets, and the ban on burqas in France and Belgium in 2010), while pivoting on a much broader anti-Islam/Muslim 'othering' with a long pedigree across Europe, generated a powerful 'demonstration effect' that very soon found adherents and supporters – both within each society and in many other countries.

Far-right 'contagion'?

Before embarking on an analysis of the far-right campaigns against Muslim religious spaces and symbols, it is helpful to elucidate two key concepts that have often anchored this particular discussion. The notion that, for some years now, we have been witnessing an alarming 'contagion effect' involving the gradual 'mainstreaming' and diffusion of hypernationalist, 'ethno-pluralist' (Mudde 2003, Liang 2007: 146–8) and particularly anti-Muslim ideas is not without its problems. 'Contagion' is the visible causal effect that illustrates both the strength of an 'infectious' idea and the conditional vulnerability of its receptors (Lynch 1998). Arguably, the 'contagion effect' of the new radical-populist right has been crucially propelled by previously concealed or suppressed social demand. This demand may not speak its name or it may be (socially and politically) discredited as 'extremist', but it is very often receptive to external 'confirmation' nudges that can reactivate and radicalize it. At the same time, the perceived 'success' of an idea, 'frame' or practice usually has a powerful effect on others who perceive their problems as similar and thus the 'successful' precedent as useful/applicable to their own context. Earlier 'successes' not only activate whatever similar beliefs they may hold (but were reluctant to express before) but also increase the temptation to follow the lead set by others (Conversi 1993). Yet, while the metaphor of 'contagion' eloquently captures the transnational reach and dynamic of the phenomenon, it is strikingly unidimensional. It attests to the power of particular 'extremist' ideas but says very little about how and why others are (or are not) affected by them in particular ways or at particular points in time. These ideas do not simply 'infect' people, like in the haphazard outbreak of a disease. The schema of 'contagion', 'domino' or 'snowballing' (Huntington 1991: 100–06) tends to both overdetermine the outcome (diffusion and adoption/recontextualization of the idea) and oversimplify the process (the role of particular local/national contexts and agencies in this process).

Nevertheless, broken taboos and associated practices tend to have a strong psychological empowering effect on others who have come to regard them as 'successful' and are eager to interpret this 'success' as confirmation of their already-existing similar beliefs (McAdam 1998: 48–51, Opp 2009). A 'successful' idea, frame or practice not only confirms and reinforces similar pre-existing stereotypes and beliefs in others but also 'liberates' them from the notion that such an idea is taboo, not widely shared or not respectable enough to be openly communicated and acted upon. At the same time, aspects of the overall diagnosis and framing that support the extremist idea may appear to have been validated and thus appeal to new, broader social audiences, even if they may still resist the overall framing or its wider programmatic prescriptions. For example, the current diffusion of anti-immigrant sentiment may not necessarily be nurtured by pre-existing stereotypes and prejudices against particular ethnic, religious, cultural or indeed 'racial' groups; instead, it may be indirectly 'validated' in the eyes of growing social audiences because it becomes embedded in an already internalized political narrative of existential self-defence against perceived competition and threat from 'others' (see below). Once this has happened, vulnerability to particular and more extreme ideas (e.g. targeting specific groups) or to the scaling of these ideas (e.g. from one particular group or sphere of policy to another) increases exponentially.

Thus, the apparent 'success' of the radical-populist right in contemporary Europe is the cumulative outcome of a series of discrete 'successes' on different levels. The most effective 'framing' of the discussion has been the psychological embedding of a 'zero-sum' mentality, both on the material and identity levels. The notion of fierce, almost existential, competition for material prosperity and cultural self-determination against perceived outsiders has underpinned and sustained anti-immigrant discourses across Europe for decades. This mindset rests on the principle that both prosperity and identity are more or less finite resources that the majority group should have privileged access to. Sharing them would involve a loss, but failing to safeguard them altogether could pose a serious existential threat to the majority group in the long run (Esses et al. 2001). At the same time, the 'zero-sum' mentality extends to the symbolic capital of national society – its culture, traditions, embedded values and ways of life – that fosters social reflexes deriving from a national and, in some cases, 'European' racist/ nativist mindset (Messina 2007). Again, failure or reluctance to defend those values actively against 'others' is perceived as conducive to dilution, erosion and, eventually, even extinction. To accept this kind of diagnosis/negative prognosis constitutes the first necessary and crucial step towards subscribing to aspects of the accompanying prescription – that national society should be aggressively protected, that the flow of immigrants must be arrested or even reversed and that 'integration' devices deployed by the state towards ethnic/religious minorities must become more rigid and forceful. Even if the entire 'ethno-pluralist' framing put forward by large sectors of the contemporary radical-populist right may not be endorsed in its entirety by wider 'mainstream' constituencies or its more radical prescriptions are still rejected as 'extremist', its accompanying discourses may 'succeed' in embedding the perceptions of competition and insecurity between majorities and perceived 'others'. The result is that wider social and political audiences become more receptive to ideas derived from it and more willing to subscribe to its associated negative projections for the future. In this case, a dangerous 'mainstreaming' effect may occur that is essentially open-ended and may make further and/or wider slippages into (more) extreme prescriptions in the future far more likely and acceptable.

Therefore, there is a misleading asymmetry between electoral support for the radical-populist right on the one hand, and 'success' at the level of ideas and collective perception on the other. The disproportionate emphasis on electoral performance and opinion polling of the radical right has obscured how its ideas, master-frames, diagnoses and radical (negative) prognoses have succeeded in shaping a new, broader and social 'common sense' that is accepted (and growing, in part at least) by wider political and social constituencies. The danger of this distorting viewpoint can be gauged by looking at the results of the 2007 presidential elections in France. In that case, the electoral contraction of the Front National (FN) was hailed (erroneously, in hindsight) as ushering in a period of decline for the party. Yet, a significant proportion of the voters who abandoned the FN in 2007 were attracted by the anti-immigration rhetoric of Nicolas Sarkozy, whose role in 'mainstreaming' selected ideas, diagnoses and prognoses of the FN's discourse has been correctly identified. Thus, the electoral contraction of the FN in 2007 was inversely analogous to the concessions made by Sarkozy's 'mainstream' right to the 'zero-sum' framing of the discussion by the FN – his rhetoric of 'common sense', his alleged desire to address the relevant concerns of the people and his legitimization of some ideas and policies previously considered 'extremist' (Hainsworth 2008: 121, Mondon 2011). This strategy has, in most cases, produced a win-win scenario for far-right populist parties; either their electoral contraction does not result in a stable realignment of voters with 'mainstream' parties, in which case voters soon return to the extreme parties that they perceive as being more committed to their opposition to immigration (e.g. France, Austria), or it results in a stifling of the electoral chances of far-right populist parties – in the medium term at least – but only at the onerous price of a legitimation and 'mainstreaming' of their extremist discourse (e.g. Germany, the United Kingdom).

There is a growing body of analysis that attempts to draw parallels between the diffusion of a radicalized activist variant of the anti-Semitism in 1930s Europe, on the one hand, and the growing mistrust and often belligerent animosity towards communities with a Muslim background on the continent since 9/11, on the other. The latter phenomenon – commonly described as Islamophobia – is situated at the point of intersection between three major fault lines: one that taps into long-standing anti-Muslim prejudices in Europe (Meret & Betz 2009); another relating to the similarly enduring 'nativist' prejudice vis-à-vis immigrant groups and communities; and a third one exposing socio-economic, cultural and existential insecurities that have deepened in the past decade or so (Betz 2007: 33–54). The cumulative result is the perception of a widening gap (psychological but often social and literal) between majorities and Muslim minorities on the continent, fuelled by inflammatory and divisive language from the extremes, sometimes culminating in violent encounters or at the very least resulting in tangible discrimination.

Of course history does not simply repeat itself. No matter how many similarities (in terms of the radicalization of long-standing prejudices, growing alienation, increasing militancy and escalating discrimination) may be detected, modern (post-nineteenth century) anti-Semitism and (post-late twentieth century) Islamophobia vary substantially in terms of the alleged threat that they are perceived to represent. While the former fed into historical anxieties about national identity and ethnic/'racial' homogeneity, the latter taps into a broader transnational reservoir of 'European'/'Western' civilizational angst (Bunzl 2005: 501–2). Differences also exist on the levels of numbers (Muslims represent a far larger – and growing – percentage of the population in Europe as compared to pre-1945 Jews in most countries) and perceived status (Muslims are perceived, through an 'immigrant' lens, as 'strangers in Europe', whereas Jews were viewed as the perennial 'strangers within' or 'internal outsiders' – Kallis 2008: 28–30, Kovács 2010). In addition, the wider political and societal contexts have changed dramatically. Since the end of Second World War, the achievements of European democracies in terms of institutional consolidation, cultural tolerance and the social inclusion of minorities make a repeat of the interwar tragedy appear unfathomable, not least because of the plurality and strength of the institutional and cultural checks on extremist behaviours.

The danger, however, is once again twofold. The populist right has not only sharpened its ideological framing of the contemporary discussion on immigration and Islam (not least by deploying a self-proclaimed 'post-fascist' rhetoric that attempts to distance it from the bitter memories of the interwar period and from discredited ideas associated with this period, such as race and authoritarianism), but has also embraced increasingly sophisticated techniques of communication and networking, within and across countries (Laqueur 1997: 95–110, Ruzza & Fella 2009: 42–4). For more than two decades, far-right politicians and intellectuals have unleashed an impressively wide repertoire of anti-Muslim ideas and arguments, sometimes in the context of an overarching hypernationalist anti-immigration narrative but increasingly singling out Islam as the new 'existential other' of national and 'European' identities. Their diagnoses (of alleged civilizational incompatibility (Allen 2010: 46–8) and discourse of 'zero-sum' competition for finite resources) and negative prognoses (erosion of 'European' values/Islamification (Zuquete 2008, Vossen 2010) and heightened insecurity) have found increasing reception well beyond their electoral constituencies and national audiences. But they also serve as the powerful foundation of 'cognitive liberation' for a number of symbolic, targeted battles fought by the populist right in the post-9/11 period. From the wider pressure for immigration restrictions (and indeed bans on particular categories of immigrants) to more blatantly anti-Muslim campaigns against mosques, minarets and traditional Islamic female dress, far-right politicians, activists and media (Boomgaarden & Vliegenhart 2007) have broken one taboo after another, set ever more radical precedents and often forced ostensibly 'mainstream' political forces to at least take note – and often even to concede ground to them.

Restricting Islamic religious freedoms: Three 'landmark' events

There have been some defining moments for each of these anti-Muslim campaigns. On the issue of the 'visibility' of mosques, it was the 2009 referendum that delivered the shocking (and largely unexpected) ban on minaret construction in Switzerland. For the other high-profile issue, the restriction on wearing the burqa in public places, two landmark initiatives occurred in very rapid succession – the Belgian and then the French bans in the first half of 2010. All these events deserve the appellation 'landmark' for three main reasons. First, they marked a leap from radical, divisive rhetoric against Islam to political, exclusionary praxis (Krzyżanowski & Wodak 2009: 71–122). Second, by shattering the taboo of actively restricting religious freedoms within their respective societies (Switzerland, Belgium and France), they unleashed previously concealed and/or institutionally arrested social and political demand for similar initiatives in other parts of the continent, thereby generating a wave of similar debates and proposals that are still under consideration but which have been debated far more aggressively and openly since the events outlined above – even if on numerous occasions they have been found to contravene international and national human rights stipulations. Third, the galvanizing effects that the 2009 and 2010 bans have had on radical-right parties and constituencies across Europe have been accompanied by an intensification of anti-immigration (and sometimes generally anti-multiculturalist or even openly anti-Islamic/Muslim) rhetoric derived from other parties conventionally seen as occupying (more) 'mainstream' spaces in the political spectrum. Taken together, the three shifts outlined here amount to something akin to a political and societal 'paradigm shift'. The dividing lines between acceptable and inaccessible language, as well as between desirable and inadmissible courses of action, have been redrawn in ways that are yet to be fully appreciated but which, nevertheless, constitute a dramatic transfer of previously fringe and extreme ideas onto and into increasingly mainstream political/social platforms and discourses. Meanwhile, an unfolding 'demonstration effect' from the initiatives in Switzerland, Belgium and France appears to have gained transnational traction, hijacking the debate from its initial framework of universal

human rights/respect for diversity and moving it onto the emotive terrain of (in)
security, alleged 'civilizational' clashes, fear and self-defence.

The emotional and psychological power of the precedent (i.e. the broken taboo)
can be gauged most effectively in the immediate aftermath of the three landmark
events mentioned above. The Swiss November 2009 referendum produced such a
dramatic majority (57.5%) in favour of the minaret ban (and through, ostensibly, the
most democratic of electoral devices) that it left little doubt about the level of popular
support for the initiative (Meyer 2011). The Swiss People's Party / Schweizerische
Volkspartei (SVP) itself interpreted the outcome as a further open-ended mandate
to introduce additional restrictive measures in the future, both with regard to Islam
in particular and to immigration as a whole; a year after the minaret ban vote, the
SVP forced and won yet another referendum, this time allowing the automatic
deportation of immigrants convicted of criminal activity (NYT 2010). Furthermore,
it came as little surprise that politicians from various populist right-wing parties saw
the Swiss initiative and 'successful' outcome as a legitimizing liberating precedent for
similar actions in their own countries. The result resonated across Europe, receiving
instant and enthusiastic support from radical right-wing parties from Denmark (the
Danish People's Party, the third largest in the country's Parliament and supporting
the government coalition between 2001 and 2011), France (FN), Austria (both the
Freiheitliche Partei Österreichs (FPÖ) and the Bündnis Zukunft Österreich (BZÖ)),
the Low Countries (predictably both the Dutch Partij voor de Vrijheid (PVV) and
the Vlaams Blok (VB)) and Italy (the Lega Nord, which was a primary member of
Silvio Berlusconi's governing coalition from 2008 onwards). In Italy, the then interior
minister, Roberto Maroni, and senator Roberto Calderoni (both members of the
Lega Nord) both expressed their satisfaction with the outcome and saw it as a model
for future initiatives in Italy and other European countries (IW 2009); their call was
endorsed by others in a wide circle of European countries (Garel 2009, HRW 2009a).

The ensuing debate once again caricatured Islam as an extremist religion-based
ideology of cultural aggression, expansionist aspirations and fundamental contestation
of putative 'European' values of individual and gender freedom. This kind of
discourse was by no means a novelty in the development of the European radical-
populist right. Ever since the 1990s, parties such as the VB, the FN and other populist
parties had shaped a distinct anti-Islamic narrative that was both part of their wider
anti-immigration agenda and distinct from it (growing in the intensity and power of
its negative diagnosis/prognosis) (Stuessi 2008, Todorov 2010: 8–9). In the post-9/11
period, the added layer of securitization of the strong Muslim 'immigrant' presence
in Europe strengthened the negative appeal of the message and emboldened political
entrepreneurs from the populist right, across Europe, to go further and further in the
direction of making Islamophobia a cornerstone of their negative political programmes
(Cesari 2009). Yet, the Swiss referendum result (the critical moment of transition from
rhetorical to political-plebiscitary transgression) anchored the debate about Islam and
immigration in Europe in a new semantic domain of allegedly legitimate national and
legal-constitutional defence of individual and cultural freedoms for the European
'native' majorities. The campaign poster produced by the SVP for the referendum
(showing a Swiss flag pierced by black caricatured minarets made to resemble missiles
and the silhouette of an equally caricatured Muslim woman in a niqab) transformed

Figure 4.1 SVP Minarett Poster. © GOAL AG

the image of a particular space of worship into a cultural, ideological and indeed national security existential threat and weapon of 'civilizational' warfare (Gole 2011: 8–9) (see Figure 4.1).

This was in itself a bold teasing of the boundaries of 'common sense' and societal tolerance, but the verdict from the polls turned the message into an empowering precedent for others to follow. Far more alarming, however, were two further indicators in response to the Swiss vote. On the one hand, some high-profile mainstream politicians reacted to the widespread condemnation of the measure by arguing that the underlying fears that led to this outcome must be respected and taken on board by politicians (Focus 2009, Sarkozy 2009). On the other, a series of opinion polls conducted in the wake of the Swiss referendum in many European countries revealed either majorities or very strong minorities in favour of similar restrictive measures against Muslim places of worship, including outright bans on the construction of further mosques (Allievi 2009).

The debate on the prohibition of the burqa reached its climax a few months after the Swiss referendum. In April 2010, the Belgian Parliament approved a new law banning, in all public spaces, all forms of female dress that partially or fully cover the face. Then, in July 2010, the French National Assembly voted overwhelmingly in favour of a ban on wearing the burqa or the niqab in public. In some ways, this measure was an extension of the earlier (2004) ban on 'conspicuous religious symbols' in state schools – the culmination of a much longer debate about religious traditions and secularism under the French republic. Yet, while the earlier law was restricted to specific educational environments and was predicated (controversially) on the French republic's norm of 'secularity' (*laïcité*), which in this instance prohibited all symbols regardless of creed, the 2010 vote (and the subsequent law that came into effect in April 2011) pertained specifically to full Islamic dress – and has therefore been widely criticized as discriminatory. And while the particular French discourse of *laïcité* had rendered the 2004 law less pertinent to other European countries or far-right movements (especially those with a strong commitment to 'Christian values', such as the Lega Nord in Italy and the National Orthodox Rally in Greece (Karatzaferis 2010)), the 2010 parliamentary votes in Belgium and France focused significantly on the aspects of national security and women's rights – both of which resonated far more strongly with wider social, political (for different reasons, both radical and mainstream, left and right) and indeed transnational audiences. In particular, the instrumentalization of gender issues in this debate (the ban being presented as a matter of gender equality, choice and defence against patriarchal oppression) has also attracted support from particular sectors of the left, as well as from some women's rights and feminist organizations, including ones representing Muslim women.

Unsurprisingly again, the French public debate and eventual approval of the ban ushered in a 'demonstration effect' on other countries (both at the time of the vote itself and in the wake of its implementation a year later), at least on the level of political rhetoric and legislative initiatives. In October 2010, the agreement between Dutch mainstream parties and Geert Wilders' PVV to form a new coalition government contained an explicit reference to a law banning the burqa in The Netherlands, in addition to promises to restrict immigration from outside the European Union (EU). In Italy, politicians of the Lega Nord seized the opportunity to propose a bill emulating the Belgian and French precedents. The proposal was approved by a parliamentary commission in August 2011 and was forwarded to the parliament for discussion. As for public opinion across Europe, it seems that different types of questions produced rather divergent results. When people were asked about their reactions to the French legislation in terms of either security or 'integration', strong majorities in the United Kingdom, Germany, France, Spain and Italy declared their support for the measure. When, on the other hand, the question was linked to broader issues of freedom of choice, the percentages of those in favour of the ban dropped significantly to minority (albeit sizeable) levels. It is nevertheless illustrative of the hardening of public opinion against a caricatured Islam that a strong majority of those supporting the ban on the burqa and the niqab remain reluctant to extend the prohibition to all prominent religious symbols (including Christian), as the French 2004 law had done (and this trend includes the French public itself) (Blitz 2010).

Unlike the debate on restricting minarets (and banning particular mosques – Allievi 2010), that on the Islamic female headscarf and dress has always been situated on a major fault line between the 'public' and 'private' spheres, the former viewed by state authorities as the terrain of 'integration' par excellence while the latter remaining (in spite of growing opposition from both the populist right and radical left, again for very different reasons) a matter of individual choice. Although in France and Belgium this distinction has, since 2010–11, resulted in a full separation of the two spheres in respect to the wearing of the burqa/niqab, the overall picture across the continent is far more volatile and complex. For more than a decade (particularly in the case of France), the issue of wearing headscarves in public has divided those opposing religious symbols in general and those explicitly targeting Islamic dress (Shahid & van Koningsveld 2005, Scott 2007, Kılıç et al. 2008, Joppke 2009). While the 2004 French law was predicated on the principle of secularism and was therefore religion neutral, the 2011 ban was specific to Islamic dress. Conversely, the 2004 law adopted a very specific and limited definition of the 'public sphere' by restricting the force of the prohibition to state-run schools; by contrast, the recent ban extended to the entirety of the 'public sphere' (Salvatore 2004, Asad 2005). Other countries have adopted a different approach to the controversy, generally rejecting national legislative arrangements but in some cases allowing regional and local authorities to implement their own measures in the direction of restricting either religious symbols in general or particular kinds of Islamic dress. The federal structure of Germany has enabled eight (out of a total of 16) Länder to introduce some form of restrictive legislation in this direction, starting with Baden-Württemberg in 2004 (Joppke 2007). While this initiative broke a taboo within Germany and was emulated in rapid succession in other Länder, the framework for the ban has varied from case to case. In Baden-Württemberg, the legislation specifically targeted Islamic dress in educational spaces, allowing Christian and Jewish symbols to be worn in public schools – a model also followed by Hessen, Saarland, Nordrhein Westfalen and Bayern. By contrast, in 2005, Berlin introduced a 'neutrality' law that forbade all religious symbols to be worn by a far wider selection of public employees (in education, the justice system and by the police). Two states (Niedersachsen and Bremen) have followed an intermediary approach, restricting the force of the measure to state schools but following the 'neutrality' principle in terms of banning all conspicuous religious symbols (i.e. including Christian and Jewish ones). Of the rest of the German Länder, three states (Brandenburg, Schleswig-Holstein and Rheinland-Pfalz) have considered but explicitly rejected any legislative restriction in this domain (HRW 2009b). Meanwhile, in the wake of the Belgian and French bans on the burqa, Hessen followed suit, passing a law explicitly restricting the wearing of veiled Islamic dress but adopting a limited definition of 'public space' as 'areas of public service', thus stopping short of an outright public ban like that in France (Allen 2011: 49, BBC 2011).

The poverty of the mainstream

The 'demonstration/confirmation' dynamic of all the above initiatives has already been amply felt – and its future trajectory remains unsettlingly unpredictable. After a series of bold legislative initiatives – on the local, regional and national scale – and landmark court rulings upholding the restrictions, the taboo of introducing restrictive legislation that targets (either explicitly and singularly or indirectly) Islamic religious symbols has been essentially breached. Public support for these measures has revealed a surprisingly high degree of social 'demand', either previously concealed/suppressed or fed by a master-narrative of insecurity and 'zero sum' competition – but in either case strengthened by the 'demonstration effect' of 'successful' initiatives elsewhere. The examples of Switzerland (with regard to minarets), Belgium (burqas) and France (headscarves and burqas) have legitimized the notion of 'public' restriction on Islamic spaces and symbols of faith in an otherwise liberal, humanistic and ostensibly 'multicultural' Europe.

Even more disconcertingly, however, these restrictions have now shed their original ideological and political association with the far right, being now increasingly endorsed by 'mainstream' political and social actors. The effect of this powerful 'mainstreaming' trend raises disquieting questions about the future place of universal human rights norms and freedoms in European states/societies, about the meaning of interculturalism in the post-9/11 era, as well as about the *differentia specifica* between radical-populist and 'mainstream' political spaces (Krzyżanowski & Oberhuber 2007).

The debates on Islamic symbols and places of worship in the last decade have exposed the poverty of Europe's 'mainstream' values and the waning resolve of its main political-social actors to defend the integrity of their professed 'multicultural' vision against the increasingly bold and vicious attacks from the populist right. The three landmark legislative initiatives discussed in this chapter (the 2004 and 2011 laws in France, the 2011 ban in Belgium) have emanated from, and been supported by, broad political majorities including increasingly 'mainstream' parties, even if their ideological provenance can be unambiguously traced back to the discourses of the far right. Other similar initiatives currently under consideration have followed the same trajectory of initial pressure by populist-right constituencies being translated into 'mainstreaming' social demand and party-political endorsement on the local/ regional or national level. As more and more prominent 'mainstream' political and intellectual figures across Europe have proclaimed the current model of 'state multiculturalism' to be 'dead' or 'failed', and as the discussion moves steadily away from human rights/individual freedoms towards the allegedly 'neutral' terrain of security, integration and 'European' cultural identity, so the 'demonstration effect' of initiatives for more (and more restrictive) measures against Islamic practices and symbols gathers momentum across many countries in Europe. This trend has often been presented by using the over-deterministic language of political and social 'contagion', but the term (even in its most sophisticated usage that goes beyond simplistic medical metaphors) both over-determines the outcome and oversimplifies the etiology/dynamics of diffusion. Instead, the most insidious driver of the 'demonstration effect' of Islamophobia in contemporary Europe lies (in striking similarity to the 1930s) in a lethal intersection – between the growing ability of far-right populist parties to mobilize social and political resources on a transnational basis in support of their dystopian 'zero sum' diagnoses, and the waning commitment of 'mainstream' political and social constituencies to an active and robust defence of the very principles underpinning the vision of an open, plural, multilayered, inter-cultural society that opposes extremist challenges.

References

Allen, A. (2011), *Unpopular Privacy: What Must We Hide?* Oxford: Oxford University Press.

Allen, C. (2010), *Islamophobia*, Aldershot: Ashgate.

Allievi, S. (2009), 'Conflicts over Mosques in Europe: policy issues and trends', *NEF Initiative on Religion and Democracy in Europe.* <www.nefic.org/sites/default/files/

NEF%20RelDem%20-%20RELIGION%20%26%20MOSQUES%20-%20Final.pdf>
[accessed 15 October 2011].

— (2010), 'Mosques in Europe: why a solution has become a problem', NEF Initiative
on Religion and Democracy in Europe. <www.nefic.org/sites/default/files/
mosquesinEuropefullpdf.pdf> [accessed 15 October 2011].

Asad, T. (2005), 'Reflections on Laicite and the Public Sphere', *SSRC: Items and Issues,* 5(7):
1–5.

BBC (2011): 'Germany's first burka ban imposed by state of Hesse', *BBC News,* 3
February 2011. <www.bbc.co.uk/news/world-europe-12353626> [accessed 15
October 2011].

Beaumont, P. (2011), *Summer of Unrest: Revolution Road,* London: Random House

Betz, H.-G. (2007), 'Against the "green totalitarianism": anti-Islamic nativism in
contemporary radical right-wing populism in Western Europe', in C. Schiori Liang
(ed.), *Europe for the Europeans: The Foreign and Security Policy of the Populist Radical
Right,* Aldershot: Ashgate, pp. 33–54

Blitz, J. (2010), 'Poll shows support in Europe for burka ban', *Financial Times,* 1 March
2010. <www.ft.com/cms/s/0/e0c0e732-254d-11df-9cdb-00144feab49a.html> [accessed
15 October 2011].

Boomgaarden, H. G. and Vliegenthart, R. (2007), 'Explaining the Rise of Anti-immigrant
Parties: The Role of News Media Content', *Electoral Studies,* 26(2): 407–17.

Bunzl, M. (2005), 'Between Anti-Semitism and Islamophobia: Some Thoughts on the New
Europe', *American Ethnologist,* 32(4): 499–508.

Carter, E. L. (2005), *The Extreme Right in Western Europe: Success or Failure?,* Manchester:
Manchester University Press.

Cesari, J. (2009), 'The Securitisation of Islam in Europe', *CEPS / Justice and Home Affairs,*
April 2009 (Research Paper No. 15). <http://aei.pitt.edu/10763/1/1826.pdf> [accessed
15 October 2011].

Chouliaraki, L. and Fairclough, N. (1999), *Discourse in Late Modernity,* Edinburgh:
Edinburgh University Press.

CoFR (2011), *The New Arab Revolt: What Happened, What It Means, and What Comes
Next,* Foreign Affairs ebook. <www.cfr.org/middle-east/new-arab-revolt/p24876>
[accessed 15 October 2011].

Conversi, D. (1993), 'Domino Effect or Internal Developments? The Influences of
International Events and Political Ideologies on Catalan and Basque Nationalism', *West
European Politics,* 16(3): 245–70.

Eatwell, R. (2000), "The Rebirth of the Extreme Right in Western Europe', *Parliamentary
Affairs,* 53: 407–25.

— (2005), 'Charisma and the revival of the European extreme right', in J. Rydgren (ed.),
Movements of Exclusion: Radical Right-Wing Populism in the Western World, New York:
Nova Science Publishers, pp. 101–20.

Esses, V. M., Dovidio, J. F., Jackson, L. M. and Armstrong, T. L. (2001), 'The Immigration
Dilemma: The Role of Perceived Group Competition, Ethnic Prejudice, and National
Identity', *Journal of Social Issues,* 57: 389–412.

Focus (2009), 'Westerwelle verteidigt die Schweiz', *Focus,* 4 December 2009.

Garel, D. (2009), 'The nativist response to the Swiss minaret ban', *The Centre for
Social Cohesion,* December 2009. <www.socialcohesion.co.uk/blog/2009/12/
the-nativist-response-to-the-swiss-minaret-ban.html> [accessed 15 October 2011].

Gladwell, M. (2000). *The Tipping Point: How Little Things Can Make a Big Difference,*
New York: Little, Brown & Co.

Gole, N. (2011), *Islam in Europe,* Princeton: Markus Wiener Publishers.

Hainsworth, P. (2008), *The Extreme Right in Western Europe,* London, New York: Routledge.

HRW (2009a), 'Switzerland: Minaret ban violates rights', December 2009. <www.hrw.org/ en/news/2009/12/04/switzerland-minaret-ban-violates-rights> [accessed 15 October 2011].

— (2009b), 'Discrimination in the name of neutrality', February 2009, 1–3. <www.hrw. org/reports/2009/02/25/discrimination-name-neutrality> [accessed 15 October 2011].

Huntington, S. P. (1991), *The Third Wave: Democratization in the Late Twentieth Century,* Norman OK: University of Oklahoma Press.

IW (2009), 'Lega Nord calls for Italian referendum on minaret ban', *Islamophobia Watch,* December 2009. <www.islamophobia-watch.com/islamophobia-watch/2009/12/2/lega-nord-calls-for-italian-referendum-on-minaret-ban.html> [accessed 15 October 2011].

Johnston, H. and Noakes, J. A. (eds) (2005), *Frames of Protest: Social Movements and the Framing Perspective,* Lanham: Rowman & Littlefield.

Joppke, C. (2007), 'State Neutrality and Islamic Headscarf Laws in France and Germany', *Theory and Society,* 36(4): 313–42.

— (2009), *Veil: Mirror of Identity,* Cambridge: Polity Press.

Kallis, A. (2008), *Genocide and Fascism. The Eliminationist Drive in Fascist Europe, 1919–1945,* New York, London: Routledge.

Karatzaferis, Georgios (2010), Interview with the president of LAOS, Giorgios Karatzaferis on 14 January 2010, in which he called for a referendum in Greece about the (recently granted and restricted) immigrants' right to vote. Transcript available. <www.inews. gr/29/epimenei-sto-dimopsifisma-gia-tin-ithageneia-o-g-karatzaferis.htm> (accessed on 15 October 2011; in Greek).

Kiliç, S., Saharso, S. and Sauer, B. (2008), 'Introduction: The Veil. Debating Citizenship, Gender and Religious Diversity', *Social Policy,* 15(4): 397–410.

Kovács, A. (2010), *The Stranger Within. Anti-Semitic Prejudices in Post-Communist Hungary,* Leiden: Brill.

Krzyżanowski, M. and Oberhuber, F. (2007), *Undoing Europe. Discourses and Practices of Negotiating the EU Constitution,* Bern: Peter Lang.

Krzyżanowski, M. and Wodak, R. (2009), *The Politics of Exclusion: Debating Migration in Austria,* NJ, New Brunswick: Transaction Publishers.

Laqueur, W. (1997), *Fin de Siècle and Other Essays on America and Europe,* New York: Transaction Publishers.

Liang, Schiori C. (2007), '"Nationalism Ensures Peace": The foreign and security policy of the German Populist Radical Right after (Re)unification', in C. Schiori Liang (ed.), *Europe for the Europeans: The Foreign and Security Policy of the Populist Radical Right,* Aldershot: Ashgate, pp. 146–8.

Lynch, A. (1998), *Thought Contagion: How Belief Spreads Through Society: The New Science of Memes: How Ideas Act Like Viruses,* New York: Basic Books.

Mammone, A., Godin, E. and Jenkins, B. (eds) (2009), *Mapping the Far Right in Contemporary Europe: Local, National, Comparative, Transnational,* Oxford: Berghahn Books.

McAdam, D. (1998), *Political Process and the Development of Black Insurgency, 1930–1970,* Chicago: University of Chicago Press, 2nd edn.

Meret, S. and Betz, H.-G. (2009), 'Revisiting Lepanto : the political mobilization against Islam in contemporary Western Europe', *Patterns of Prejudice,* 43(3–4): 313–34.

Messina, A. (2007), *The Logics and Politics of Post-WWII Migration to Western Europe,* Cambridge: Cambridge University Press.

Meyer, J.-F. (2011), 'A Country without Minarets: Analysis of the Background and Meaning of the Swiss Vote of 29 November 2009', *Religion,* 41(1): 11–28.

Mondon, A. (2011), 'Nicolas Sarkozy's Legitimisation of the Front National Background and Perspectives', unpublished paper presented at the conference 'Populism and Racism in Britain and Europe since 1945', University of Northampton, 21–22 September 2011.

Mudde, C. (2003), *The Ideology of the Extreme Right,* Manchester: Manchester University Press.

NYT (2010), 'Swiss right wins vote on deportation of criminals', *New York Times,* 28 November 2010. <www.nytimes.com/2010/11/29/world/europe/29iht-swiss.html> [accessed 15 October 2011].

Opp, K. D. (2009), *Theories of Political Protest and Social Movements,* New York, London: Routledge.

Price, V. and Tewksbury, D. (1997), 'News values and public opinion: A theoretical account of media priming and framing', in G. Barnett and F. Boster (eds), *Progress in communication sciences,* Norwood, N.J.: Ablex Publishing, pp. 173–212.

Ruzza, C. and Fella, S. (2009), *Reinventing the Italian Right: Territorial Politics, Populism and 'Post-fascism',* London: Routledge.

Salvatore, A. (2004), 'Making Public Space: Opportunities and Limits of Collective Action Among Muslims in Europe', *Journal of Ethnic and Migration Studies,* 30(5): 1013–31.

Sarkozy, N. (2009), 'Respecter ceux qui arrivent, respecter ceux qui accueillent', *Le Monde,* 8 December 2009.

Scott, J. W. (2007), *The Politics of the Veil,* Princeton, NJ: Princeton University Press.

Shahid, W. and van Koningsveld, P. S. (2005), 'Muslim Dress in Europe: Debates on the Headscarf', *Journal of Islamic Studies,* 16(1): 35–61.

Sigona, S. (2010). '"Gypsies out of Italy!": Social exclusion and racial discrimination of Roma and Sinti in Italy', in A. Mammone and G. A. Veltri (eds), *Italy Today. The Sick Man of Europe,* New York: Routledge, pp. 143–57.

Snow, D. A. and Benford, R. D. (1992), 'Master frames and cycles of protest', in A. D. Morris and C. M. Mueller (eds), *Frontiers in Social Movement Theory,* New Haven: Yale University Press, pp. 133–55.

Stuessi, M. (2008), 'Banning of Minarets: Addressing the Validity of a Controversial Swiss Popular Initiative', *Religion and Human Rights,* 3(2): 135–53.

Todorov, T. (2010), *The Fear of Barbarians,* Cambridge: Polity.

Vossen, K. (2010), 'Populism in the Netherlands after Fortuyn: Rita Verdonk and Geert Wilders Compared', *Perspectives on European Politics and Society,* 11(1): 22–38.

Wodak, R. (2005), 'Populist discourses: the Austrian case', in J. Rydgren (ed.), *Movements of Exclusion: Radical Right-wing Populism in the Western World,* New York: Nova Science, pp. 121–45.

Wodak, R. and Fairclough, N. (2010), 'Recontextualizing European Higher Education Policies: The Cases of Austria and Romania', *Critical Discourse Studies,* 7(1): 19–40.

Wodak, R. and Pelinka, A. (eds) (2002), *The Haider Phenomenon in Austria,* New Brunswick NJ: Transaction Press.

Zuquete, Z. P. (2008), 'The European Extreme-right and Islam: New directions?', *Journal of Political Ideologies,* 13(3): 321–44.

5

Mosques, Minarets, Burqas and Other Essential Threats: The Populist Right's Campaign against Islam in Western Europe

Hans-Georg Betz

Barcelona 2011: Three girls in miniskirts are jumping over a rope somewhere in a car park in the city. Barcelona 2025: The same three girls, same location, only the miniskirts have been replaced by burqas. This was the content of a video spot produced by Platforma per Catalunya (PxC) for the Catalan local elections in 2011.[1]

Responsible for the video was Josep Anglada, the leader of PxC. Founded in 2002 by Anglada, PxC is modelled on successful Western European right-wing populist parties, without however initially attracting much more than marginal support at the polls. This might have had something to do with the fact that, in the past, Anglada had been closely associated with Spain's post-Francoist far right (such as Blas Piñar's Fuerza Nueva and its successors) which, given the Franco regime's history of iron-fisted repression of Catalan identity, was hardly an asset in Catalonia. It took the party several years to gain some 'brand recognition', not only as a self-proclaimed advocate of ordinary people (*los catalanes primero*), but, more importantly, as a determined fighter against the alleged 'Islamization' of Catalonia. With this programme the party managed to quintuple its popular vote in the municipal elections of 2011. At the same time, the party succeeded in influencing decisions at the local level. Thus in August 2011, the administration of the town of Salt decided to delay a decision on licensing the construction of a mosque after the eruption of a PxC-inspired public protest against the project (among other things, young people from Salt buried a piglet on the proposed site for the mosque).[2] Anglada, when asked to comment on the events, claimed that Muslims and 'us' were like dogs and cats, cats and rats; in short, he explained, it was 'just a question of the compatibility of species'.[3]

---

[1] The spot can be seen on YouTube. <www.youtube.com/watch?v=BKr9yxDDqr0> [accessed 12 September 2011].

[2] See Salt prohíbe construir mezquitas tras las presiones de la xenófoba PxC, *El Pais*, 24 August 2011. <http://politica.elpais.com/politica/2011/08/24/actualidad/1314216568_327854.html> [accessed 12 September 2011].

[3] Josep Anglada (PxC) Compara A Los Musulmanes Con Los Cerdos, *la République*, 7 September 2011. <www.larepublica.es/2011/09/josep-anglada-pxc-compara-a-los-musulmanes-con-los-cerdos/> [accessed 12 September 2011]

PxC exemplifies what Jens Rydgren (2005: 415) has characterized as a 'contagion' effect on what he calls the extreme populist right. This means that marginal parties – but, as we will see below, also hitherto successful parties – adopt ideas and argumentative frames that have been proven to be political winners elsewhere in order to improve their competitive position in the electoral market. This chapter focuses on an issue which, in recent years, has become central to radical right-wing populist mobilization efforts – the integration of Muslim immigrants into Western Europe's liberal capitalist democracies.

There are several reasons why this has happened. For one, the question of whether or not Muslims – and, by extension, Islam – can and should be accorded a permanent place in Western society is a highly contentious issue, which has provoked a heated public debate in Europe. By positioning itself as the most strident and intransigent opponent of any initiative, proposal or project, in response to the legitimate demands of Western Europe's Muslim community, the populist right has gained significant exposure and publicity, particularly through the media.

At the same time, on the position of Islam in Western societies, the populist right has a significant segment of public opinion and media coverage on its side. The fact that public opinion – reflected in numerous opinion polls – has significant reservations when it comes to extending the rights of the Muslim migrant community has given the populist right an opportunity to mobilize opposition to controversial projects, such as the construction of mosques and minarets. This has helped radical right-wing populist parties to gain both attention and, to some degree at least, new political clout. Finally, the populist right has been able to frame the 'question of Islam' in terms of the larger challenges confronting Western European societies, such as the meaning and foundations of European identity and particularly how to respond to the economic, social and cultural challenges posed by globalization as issues central to radical right-wing populist ideology (Betz & Johnson 2004). The following analysis discusses three issues, which have come to assume a prominent place in the populist right's mobilization against Islam: opposition to the construction of minarets; opposition to permits for building mosques and places for prayer; and unconditional support for the state of Israel. Each of these issues serves as an example of the diffusion of arguments and rhetoric among Western Europe's populist right, which in turn has laid the foundation for the establishment and development of transnational populist networks as well as a common transnational project grounded in hostility to Islam.

The Swiss ban on minarets

In late November 2009, a thin majority of Switzerland's voters (at least those who bothered to vote) supported a proposal to ban the construction of minarets (*Minarettverbot*) throughout the country. The outcome marked a significant political victory for the Swiss populist right, even if its main representative, the Schweizer Volkspartei (SVP), had been far from unanimous in supporting the initiative (most prominently, the party's leader, Christoph Blocher, was opposed to it). The question of minarets was an ideal political issue that fitted perfectly into the Swiss populist right's identitarian strategy, which was designed to reaffirm and strengthen Swiss traditional identity while suppressing all others.

Oskar Freysinger, a rather flamboyant and outspoken SVP Member of Parliament set the tone of the campaign when he characterized minarets as a 'symbol of a political and aggressive Islam', a 'symbol of Islamic law. The minute you have minarets in Europe it means Islam will have taken over' (Foulkes 2007). A few years earlier, in 2007, Freysinger had been behind a controversial election poster which depicted Muslims praying in front of the Swiss parliamentary building (Bundeshaus) in Berne – obviously meant to evoke associations with siege, occupation and eventual takeover.[4] The anti-minaret campaign picked up this thread. Freysinger once again set the tone, justifying the campaign with the argument that the Islamic doctrine was fundamentally incompatible with Switzerland's order, based on secular law.[5] At the same time, he and other promoters of the campaign argued that minarets had nothing to do with religion, but represented 'beacons of Jihad' and landmarks of an 'intolerant culture, which put its God-given, Islamic law over the law of the country' – structures that had an 'imperialist connotation' (Freysinger 2007, Reimann 2009). A ban on the construction of minarets would constitute a first decisive step towards stopping what the promoters of the campaign considered the creeping Islamization of Switzerland: It would automatically prevent public calls to prayer and, ultimately, block the introduction of sharia law to the country. At the same time, it would represent a decisive step towards the protection and preservation of Switzerland's Christian and Western liberal values and traditions.[6]

Following the lead of right-wing populist parties in the Netherlands and Scandinavia (Akkerman & Hagelund 2007), the promoters adopted the defence of women's rights as a central issue. Claiming that they acted out of concern for gender equality, the promoters charged Muslim society with sanctioning the subordination of and discrimination against women which, they asserted, was not a result of traditional social norms and values, but an essential characteristic of Islam. All of this suggests that, for the promoters of the initiative, the main issue behind the proposed ban on minarets was not the minarets per se, but the place of Muslim immigrants and Islam itself in Swiss society.

Authoritative exit polls suggest that the populist right was highly successful in decisively shaping the discourse on the question of Islam in Switzerland. Even if a majority of almost 60 per cent of those participating in the vote agreed that the initiators were promoting pure propaganda against foreigners, an almost identical majority

---

[4] In 2004, members of the SVP had already placed an advert in several Swiss newspapers that read 'Muslims Soon in the Majority'. Next to it was a graph that suggested that by the year 2040, Muslims would constitute more than 70 per cent of the population. The figures prompted the ethics board of the Swiss office of statistics to issue a statement denouncing the numbers as purely fictitious.

[5] Interview with Oscar Freysinger, 16 December 2009. <www.swissinfo.ch/eng/Specials/Minaret_De­bate/Result_and_reactions/Minaret_vote_was_a_lesson_in_civic_spirit.html?cid=7916178> [accessed 16 September 2011]; also <www.reitschule.ch/reitschule/mediengruppe/Medienspiegel/09–04–28-MS.html> [accessed 16 September 2011].

[6] See, for example, <www.lematin.ch/actu/suisse/affiches-udc-en-valais-plainte-d%C3%A9pos%C3%A9e-46194>; <www.svp-wasserschlossregion.ch/cms/front_content.php?idart=100 for examples of campaign posters>.

agreed that minarets represented exclusively a 'religious-political demand for power and domination'. Fifty-seven per cent agreed with the statement that it was time 'to set a signal against the growing expansion of Islam in Switzerland and Western Europe'. Finally, 87 per cent supported the notion that 'in Islam, women are being oppressed' (Hirter & Vatter 2010: 33). These findings confirmed the initial observations and interpretations made immediately after the results were made public, which suggested, as the German news magazine Der Spiegel pointed out, that the main objective of the vote had been to serve as a 'symbolic referendum on the influence of Islam' (von Rohr 2009).

The Swiss populist right's anti-minaret campaign proved highly contagious. Within a short period of time, a number of Western European far-right parties, such as the British National Party and the German National Democratic Party and pro-NRW (a small anti-Islam movement originating in the city of Cologne), either adopted its text in one form or another or at least posted a more or less plagiarized copy of the Swiss anti-minaret poster on their websites.[7] The Swiss designers of the poster were not amused. At one point they went so far as to threaten to sue the Front National (FN) after the French party's youth organization had used a copy of the poster in the south-western part of the country during the FN's campaign for the regional elections of early 2010.[8] This threat, however, did not prevent the FN's rising new star, Marine Le Pen, from expressing her admiration for the Swiss system and, at least implicitly, for the SVP (Chapman 2011).

In defence of Western civilization against Islamization

In fact, the success of the Swiss populist right has served as an inspiration for a larger transnational project designed to unite the European populist right under one common banner – the defence of Europe's Christian heritage and its Western liberal and democratic values against, as one of the project's sponsors recently put it, 'the third Islam invasion of Europe' (Dewinter 2010a). Once again, the initiators of this project focused on a concrete issue – the construction of mosques in Western European towns and cities.

In early 2009, leading right-wing populist politicians gathered in Cologne to devise strategies to impede, and eventually reverse, the advance of Islam in Europe. This was in line with the transnational radical right-wing populist project 'Cities against Islamization', a 'European initiative' launched in early 2008 by Filip Dewinter (the leader of Vlaams Belang), Heinz-Christian Strache (head of the Freiheitliche Partei Österreichs (FPÖ)) and other right-wing populist representatives. One of the main objectives of the initiative was to develop a coherent theoretical doctrine that would

---

[7]   See http://tempsreel.nouvelobs.com/actualite/politique/20110301.OBS8873/
       affiche- non-a-l-islamisme-le-pen-a-nouveau-en-proces-a-nanterre.html
[8]   Rechtsextremist Le Pen kopiert SVP-Plakat, *Der Tagesanzeiger*, 25 February 2010. <www.tagesan-
       zeiger.ch/schweiz/standard/Rechtsextremist-Le-Pen-kopiert-SVPPlakat/story/15840499> [accessed
       18 September 2011].

serve as an ideological foundation and justification for the radical-populist right's campaign against mosques, minarets and other symbols and aspects of Islam's alleged encroachment on Western Europe's liberal democratic societies. For this purpose the initiative's 'charter' advanced the charge that Western society and Islam constituted two fundamentally different, diametrically opposed and mutually exclusive cultural spheres. There was always the risk that Muslim immigrant communities, as long as their members preferred Islam's divine laws to Western civil laws, would become radicalized, as reflected in the growing hostility towards Western civilization and its liberal values. According to the charter, mosques play a particularly pernicious role in this process, given their emphasis on the 'strict observance of Islam'. In fact, as far as the organizers of the initiative were concerned, mosques served as 'catalysts' for the Islamization 'of entire neighbourhoods', thus effectively preventing the integration of Muslim immigrant minorities.[9]

By the end of 2010, the radical-populist right's anti-Islam campaign had developed a core set of arguments, advanced and repeated on numerous occasions. The most important charge against Islam was that it was not actually a religion but, as Filip Dewinter put it in a speech against the planned construction of a grand mosque in the small town of Lier, Flanders, a 'political religion, an ideology, which seeks to subject our free Western society to Islam'. The building of mosques represented above all an attempt to increase Islam's influence on the community, a first step towards the conquest of an area and, therefore, a 'symbol of its Islamization'. Thus Western Europe was confronted with the fact that in its midst there was a steadily growing community which 'subscribed to a fundamentally different social ideology', which instead of integrating into the larger society turned its back 'on our society and culture'. The result was what Dewinter called a process of 'reversed colonization'. The '50 million Muslims already living in Europe' were supposed 'to make Europe Muslim within the next few decades'. This was part of a 'master plan' designed first to subject 'our cities' to Islam, and then all of Europe. From this it logically followed that mobilization against the construction of new mosques – via transnational initiatives such as Cities against Islamization – was an act of resistance, a first step towards both stopping and reversing Islamization and defending Europe's fundamental values, such as 'democracy, freedom of opinion, equality between man and woman' (Dewinter 2010b).

'Cities against Islamization' served as an important platform, not only helping to diffuse core right-wing populist arguments against Islam but also serving to establish contacts with various leading anti-Islamic politicians, such as Oskar Freysinger and Geert Wilders, and members of the Lega Nord, the Sverigedemokraterna, the FN and PxC. Some of these politicians, in turn, established contacts with smaller parties and movements and thus helped to extend the network. Oskar Freysinger, for instance, agreed to take part in an anti-Islam conference organized by the French far-right groups Riposte laïque and Bloc identitaire in late 2010. The two groups had gained notoriety with highly mediatized events designed to provoke France's Muslim community (such

---

[9] Cities against Islamization, Charter. <www.citiesagainstislamisation.com/En/2/> [accessed 30 September 2011]. See www.filipdewinter.be/9-december-spoedmanifestatie-geen-supermoskee-in-lier for the respective poster.

as organizing an '*apéro saucisson et pinard*', a street festival with sausages and red wine, in the Paris neighbourhood of Goutte d'or, an area heavily frequented by Muslim immigrants from North Africa and elsewhere). Freysinger defended his participation at this conference, charging that groups such as Bloc identitaire were merely defending France against the advance of 'the halal society' (a reference to the decision by the Franco-Belgian fast food chain Quick to introduce halal hamburgers in some of its French affiliates), which threatened to undermine the country's secular principles (Blumer 2010).

The growing influence of radical right-wing populist Islamophobic ideology can even be seen in the case of established parties, such as the FN, which hitherto had themselves served as a model. Until recently, the FN had been rather ambiguous on the question of Islam. This was in part due to the fact that a significant number of Algerian Muslims (the so-called *harki*) had fought on the side of the French during the war of independence, in part also because Jean-Marie Le Pen did not want the question of Islam to distract from what he considered the main issue – immigration (Lecœur 2007: 185–6). The election of his daughter, Marine Le Pen, in January 2011 marked a decisive turning point with regard to the question of Islam. Under Marine Le Pen, the FN adopted the Islamophobic rhetoric of the Western European populist right, undoubtedly because Marine Le Pen recognized its potential as a winning issue. Not only did she equate radical Islam with totalitarianism, she also went so far as to characterize the presence of Muslims praying on the streets of Paris and other cities as a sort of territorial conquest comparable to Nazi occupation during the Second World War. At the same time, Marine Le Pen promoted herself as the only true defender of secularism (*laicité*) and the republic, calling for the 'reconquest' of its values (Chabrout 2010). One prominent example of this strategy was her campaign against what she claimed was the advance of halal meat into canteens, school cafeterias and elsewhere, characterized as the intrusion of the religious into secular society (Le Bars 2012).[10] The campaign culminated in her charge made during a speech given in February 2012 in Lille that, unknown to French consumers, virtually all meat sold in the Paris region was halal. The remark provoked a major controversy, particularly after it was revealed in the media that Marine Le Pen had been at least partially correct (Jaillette 2012a). All of these references were thinly veiled attacks on Islam and France's Muslim community, designed to appeal to lower-class voters who, as surveys suggested, formed an increasingly significant constituency for the FN.

Islamophobia, anti-Semitism and the populist Right's commitment to the state of Israel

Shortly after Marine Le Pen was elected president of the FN at the party's congress in January 2011 in Tours, there occurred a telling incident in the corridors of the meeting

---

[10] Marine Le Pen started her campaign against the 'Islamization of France' before her election as new president of the Front National in January 2011. See, for example, her interview with Thierry Guerrier, the host of the TV programme 'C'à dire', France 5, 10 September 2010. <www.youtube.com/watch?v=nH8EiIFlOx8> [accessed 12 March 2012].

hall. Farid Smahi, until recently a member of the party's politburo, emerged from the congress, hardly able to contain his anger after having lost his politburo seat. Furious, he charged that he had lost his seat because of his pro-Palestinian position, which obviously no longer jibed with the new party line. Smahi went so far as to accuse Marine Le Pen of being in the pocket of the 'Zionists' (Zaiane 2011). Smahi's attack was not entirely unfounded. In late March 2010, Adar Primor, in an article for Israel's centre-left daily newspaper *Haaretz* (Primor, 2010), posed the provocative question, 'Where have all the anti-Semites gone?' In the article, Primor noted that, in recent years, a growing number of prominent European radical right-wing politicians, such as Heinz-Christian Strache of the FPÖ, had sought 'Israeli recognition' by adopting positions – both on the question of the Holocaust and on the state of Israel – which radically diverged from traditional far-right anti-Semitism.

The case of Marine Le Pen has been emblematic of this development, which has spread in similar fashion throughout Western Europe's populist right in recent years. If Jean-Marie Le Pen hardly ever missed an occasion to flirt with Holocaust denial and anti-Semitism, his daughter has made it her policy to eradicate both these from the new FN. Even her detractors concede that her commitment to ridding the party of the *nostalgiques* of historical French anti-Semitism (in the tradition of Charles Maurras and the Vichy regime) is genuine (Daniel 2011: 7).

Marine Le Pen established her position in a lengthy interview accorded *Le Point*, one of France's leading weekly news magazines. Although the interview covered a number of issues, the headlines were dominated by Le Pen's responses to questions about the Holocaust. Not only did she declare herself 'irritated' by anyone who showed any 'ambiguity' with regard to the Holocaust, she also made it completely clear that there was no doubt as to what had happened in the camps and 'under what conditions' and that, in her view, the Holocaust constituted 'the height of barbarism' (*le summum de la barbarie*).[11] A few months later, the international edition of *Israel Magazine* gave Marine Le Pen the opportunity (after the French Jewish radio station, Radio J, had cancelled an invitation for an interview with the new leader of the FN) to clarify her position on France's Jewish community and on the state of Israel. Once again, Marine Le Pen reiterated that she and her party were neither racist nor antisemitic. With regard to Israel – for which in the past she had expressed great admiration – she pointed out her party's official position supporting the right of the state of Israel (as well as a sovereign Palestinian state) to 'sure and secure borders'.[12] At the same time, she aggressively courted France's Jewish community and tried to persuade Israel's government to invite her for an official visit (see Mahrane 2011). When this failed, she sent her partner (and vice-president of the FN), Louis Aliot, on a secret mission to Israel (in early December) to 'warm up the atmosphere' and meet with a group of French Jews resident in Israel and interested in Marine Le Pen's platform (Ettinger 2011). When asked in an interview with the Israeli news portal *Guysen News* what might explain Marine Le Pen's recent

---

[11] 'Les camps ont été le summum de la barbarie', *Le Point*, 3 February 2011. <www.lepoint.fr/politique/les-camps-ont-ete-le-summum-de-la-barbarie-03-02-2011-135109_20.php> [accessed 18 September 2011].

[12] Entretien avec Marine Le Pen, *Israel Magazine*, May 2011, pp. 10–12.

'change of direction' with respect to the Holocaust and the state of Israel, Aliot gave the new party line: thus, he argued, both the FN and Jews (including Israelis) defended common Greek-Roman and Judeo-Christian values, which were under heavy attack on the international scene today. Under the circumstances, it would be important to stand together in the defence of common ideas and a common civilization (Bahloul 2011). Aliot's Israeli interview partner was not convinced, pointing out that at no point during the interview had Aliot clearly distanced himself from Jean-Marie Le Pen's infamous antisemitic and negationist statements, qualifying them instead as 'ambiguities'. Under the circumstances, it was hardly surprising if official French Jewish circles remained highly suspicious of Marine Le Pen's FN.

There certainly are good reasons to remain cautious. For one, Jean-Marie Le Pen still plays a major and highly visible role behind Marine Le Pen, presumably to reassure the party's hard-core clientele that the FN has not fundamentally deviated from its traditional course (Jaillette 2012b). At the same time, Marine Le Pen has made a significant effort to dispel doubts about her own sincerity. The question is what has motivated her to adopt this course. Strategic considerations are an obvious answer. There can be no doubt that anti-Semitism has proved to be a major reason for the FN's marginalization during the past several decades – a position which Jean-Marie Le Pen appears to have relished, since it allowed him to project himself as both victim and uncompromising detractor of 'the system', a people's tribune. Against that, Marine Le Pen has made it her strategic priority to 'mainstream' the party via a process of 'de-demonization' and 'de-diabolization' which is supposed to bring the FN closer to power (Le Pen 2012). De-demonization, in turn, necessarily presupposes a strong and unequivocal disavowal of anything that might be construed as antisemitic (such as questioning the Holocaust and/or questioning Israel's policies in the name of anti-Zionism). This was also behind Marine Le Pen's highly controversial meeting with Israel's ambassador to the United Nations during her visit to New York in early November 2011. Although Israel's government tried to dismiss the meeting as a misunderstanding, casual statements made by the ambassador after the meeting suggest the opposite (see Perrault 2011).[13] Strategic considerations were also behind Louis Aliot's meeting with ex-pat French Jews in Israel. As the far-right paper *Minute* maintained, the objective was to appeal to a community which has the right – since July 2008 – to vote in one of the 11 constituencies (in this case number 8, which includes French residents of Israel – some 70,000 potential voters, according to *Minute*) for the French National Assembly reserved for French citizens residing abroad (Humbert 2011).

---

[13] On 18 December 2011 the French pay TV channel Canal+ aired a documentary on 'the hidden face of the Front National' which gave ample space to Marine Le Pen's visit to the United States in early November 2011, including her meeting with the Israeli ambassador and influential Jewish community leaders in Florida, among them William Diamond, head of the Palms Beach synagogue and a member of American Israel Public Affairs Committee (AIPAC). La face cache du nouveau front, Canal+, 18 December 2011, 12.45h. <www.canalplus.fr/c-infos-documentaires/pid3354-c-dimanche.html?vid=561600> [accessed 19 December 2011]. For a brief account of these meetings see also Folch 2011.

The ideological U-turn on the 'Jewish question' is hardly a new development on the French far right. As early as 2007, Guillaume Faye, once a leading intellectual figure of Alain de Benoist's *nouvelle droite*, published a book on the 'New Jewish Question', in which he chastised and ridiculed the 'inanity' of the 'revisionist theories' of Holocaust deniers such as Robert Faurisson, a former professor at the University of Lyon, who gained notoriety beyond France's borders for his claim that the Nazis had never used gas chambers or systematically exterminated Jews (Faurisson 2000). Faurisson and other prominent 'negationists' such as Switzerland's Jürgen Graf were not amused. In fact Graf, writing from 'exile' in Moscow, declared that, with this book, Faye's reputation on the far right was ruined forever (Graf 2007). Marine Le Pen obviously disagreed, adopting instead the notion that Holocaust denial and anti-Semitism in general represented a political dead end and should therefore be abandoned. This is a lesson that appears to have spread throughout the Western European populist right.

Equally important, the disavowal of anti-Semitism is intricately linked to the Western European populist right's broader anti-Islamic ideological turn, which targets Western Europe's Muslim migrant community as the main enemy, eclipsing any other (including the Jews). In short, if Western European radical right-wing populist parties have increasingly sought to embrace Israel, it has been in order 'to unite against what they perceive to be a common threat' (Theil 2011). Geert Wilders, the leader of the Dutch anti-Islamic right, laid out the rationale behind this strategy during a speech he delivered in Tel Aviv in December 2010:

> Let us never forget that Islam threatens not just Israel; Islam threatens the entire world. Without Judea and Samaria, Israel cannot protect Jerusalem. The future of the world depends on Jerusalem. If Jerusalem falls, Athens and Rome – and Paris, London and Washington – will be next. Thus, Jerusalem is the main front protecting our common civilization. When the flag of Israel no longer flies over the walls of Jerusalem, the West will no longer be free . . . Because it is here that our civilization is under attack as we speak. It is here that we, men and women of the West, must show our resolve to defend ourselves. It is here that Israel has lit the light of freedom and that Europeans and Americans must help the Israelis to keep that light shining in the darkness. For Israel's sake and for the sake of all of us.[14]

In a similar vein, Filip Dewinter, during the visit of a delegation of right-wing populist politicians to Israel in December 2010 (unrelated to Wilders' appearance), characterized Israel as being on the front line in the clash between two civilizations: one living in freedom, the other one bent on subjecting the rest of the world to 'Islamic theocracy'. The bombs and rockets that threatened Israel on a daily basis, all in the name of Islam, were the 'true face' of an ideology seeking to conquer Europe. The main difference, he argued, was that in Europe, Islam conducted an 'undercover, cultural jihad', which used mosques, minarets, burqas, halal food and sharia to undermine freedom, democracy and 'our way of life'. In this struggle, Israel represented 'the outpost of our European

---

[14] Speech delivered in Tel Aviv, 5 December 2010. <http://gatesofvienna.blogspot.com/2010/12/geert-wilders-speech-in-tel-aviv.html> [accessed 16 October 2011].

civilization', an island of freedom and democracy, which had agreed to engage in the fight against 'an extremist, fundamentalist Islam', something Europe was 'too cowardly' to do (Dewinter 2010c).

Dewinter's engagement with the state of Israel was motivated in part by the same strategic considerations that explain Marine Le Pen's break with the FN's history of anti-Semitism. Like Marine Le Pen, Dewinter has sought to gain political respectability in order to break the *cordon sanitaire* which the traditional parties in Flanders erected around his party (Coffé 2005). At the same time, Dewinter, who has had ambitions of becoming the mayor of Antwerp, has a history of appealing to Antwerp's sizeable Jewish community for support by both evoking images of an Islamic threat and promoting himself as an ardent supporter of the state of Israel (Betz 2007: 33–4).

This led Dewinter, as early as 2005 (in an interview with *Haaretz*), to declare that he distanced himself from 'all of those individuals and groups with antisemitic tendencies and from Holocaust deniers' and wanted nothing to do with them. It was in this context that Dewinter expressed his desire to visit Israel, not only to express his affinity with a state that he regarded as 'a sort of outpost for our Western society' but also to prove that he was sincere in his disavowal of anti-Semitism and Holocaust negationism (Schwartz 2005). It should not be forgotten, however, that Dewinter's visit to Israel in 2010 was on the invitation of extreme right-wing Israeli political circles and settler groups. The latter characterized Dewinter and the other members of the delegation as representatives of parties 'that support Israel, renounce anti-Semitism and see the Islamic takeover of Europe as a clear danger', and thus promoted the visit as an expression of political support for 'the struggle against a common foe – Islamic jihadism and expansionism' (Ronen & Kempinski 2010). Israeli critics of the visit were not convinced. For one opposition politician, the delegation's visit was nothing surprising given the general deterioration of the political culture in Israel, as reflected in the growing acceptability of 'racist opinions spreading throughout large sections of the public' and receiving only a feeble, if any, response from the government. At the same time, the visit was symptomatic of Israel's growing international isolation, which had reached the point that the country was forced to 'take comfort in the arms of radicals, just because they prefer at this stage to pursue Muslims rather than Jews' (Whbee 2010).

These doubts are well-founded. Even if right-wing populist leaders no longer hesitate to keep their distance from anti-Semitism, their sincerity is very much in doubt, given the composition of their political constituency, which consists of a significant number of extreme nationalists. It was hardly a coincidence that delegation member Heinz-Christian Strache, during a visit to Yad Vashem, chose not to wear a kippah to show respect to the victims of the Holocaust. Instead he donned a cap worn by life-long members of Vandalia, an Austrian right-wing student fraternity which has a long history of Pan-German nationalism and anti-Semitism. Although Strache rejected the charge that this had been a deliberate provocation, other members of the delegation had their own interpretations. Thus a German member maintained that Strache was playing to his Austrian audience, delivering a coded message to his constituency that not everything is as it seems (Theil 2011). This suggests that the populist right's embrace of the state of Israel represents above all a tactical move, in the process of which both Western European populists and Israeli right-wing circles have found a perfect opportunity to instrumentalize each other in their common campaign against Muslims and Islam.

For the European populist right, the support accorded to the State of Israel and its government's policies (especially with regard to new settlements) is, like the campaigns against minarets and the construction of new mosques, part of the new common platform on the basis of which some of the major representatives of the Western European populist right have sought to coordinate their activities against the alleged 'Islamization' of Europe. And like the anti-minaret and anti-mosque rhetoric, the discourse on Israel has started to be adopted even among some right-wing extremist groups. A case in point is the English Defence League (EDL), which promotes itself as a staunch defender of liberal democracy against the advance, in Britain, of Islam, which is characterized as a political and social ideology bent on dominating all non-believers and imposing a system hostile to democratic accountability and to human rights. At the same time, its leader has maintained that one of the 'fundamental beliefs' of his movement is 'its support for Israel's right to defend itself'. The reason for the EDL's 'support of Israel and the Jewish people' was that Israel 'is a shining star of democracy', a 'beacon of democracy amid repressive Arab states . . . If Israel falls, we all fall'. At the same time, the leader of the EDL strongly affirmed that the EDL 'reject(ed) all anti-Semitism' and stood 'where it always has stood, which is side-by-side with Israel'.[15]

Anti-Islamic mobilization and the populist Right

The analysis presented so far demonstrates that fanning the flames of anti-Islamic sentiments has become central to right-wing populist mobilization in Western Europe, and that too for good reasons: Right-wing populist parties have generally promoted themselves as 'identititarian' movements, committed to the defence of national traditions, customs and values. At the same time, in recent years, right-wing populist discourse on immigration has increasingly focused on the challenges posed by the integration of Western Europe's migrant communities, which have been used as a justification for exclusion in the name of the preservation of identity (Betz & Johnson 2004: 317). According to this discourse, whether or not a migrant can be integrated depends crucially on whether or not his or her cultural background is compatible with the values of the local majority population. For the populist right, Islam is fundamentally incompatible with Western values and the Western way of life, and so Western Europe's Muslim migrant community is therefore deemed to be 'unassimilable' (Betz & Meret 2009).[16]

The overwhelming emphasis on culture in the populist right's campaign against Muslim migrants and Islam in general is, to a large extent, also motivated by political

---

[15] Statement by Tommy Robinson to Stop the Islamization of America (SIOA), 30 June 2011. <http://atlasshrugs2000.typepad.com/atlas_shrugs/2011/06/tommy-robinson-any-rogue-elements-within-the-edl-that-go-against-our-mission-statement-will-be-remov.html> [accessed 13 October 2011].

[16] See also www.filipdewinter.be/vlaams-belang-start-met-%E2%80%9Cvrouwen-tegen-islamisering%E2%80%9D for an example of this belief system.

calculation. In a recent article on anti-immigrant attitudes in present-day Western Europe, Silke Schneider (2008: 63) has demonstrated that cultural distance, rather than the economic status of immigrants (either as competitors for jobs or welfare benefits), 'adds to the average level of perceived ethnic threat in European countries. The higher the percentage of non-Western immigrants, the higher the country's average level of perceived ethnic threat.' These results jibe well with the findings of studies that have shown that radical right-wing populist support at the polls is significantly influenced by a voter's cultural disposition. This is particularly true for lower-class voters (such as skilled blue-collar workers, routine operatives and low-skilled service employees), who have increasingly become the core constituency of radical right-wing populist support (Bornschier 2010). Under the circumstances, Marine Le Pen's anti-Islamic turn is hardly surprising, given her strategy to appeal in particular to those lower-class voters disenchanted with the mainstream right.

Recent surveys conducted in various West European countries to gauge public attitudes towards Muslim migrants and various issues related to Islam suggest that, at least on this subject, the populist right's position resonates with a significant segment of public opinion. With respect to Islam in general, a German survey from 2006 found over 90 per cent of respondents agreeing with the notion that Islam was hostile to women; 71 per cent thought Islam was intolerant; and over half of the respondents agreed with Samuel P. Huntington that the relationship between the West and the Muslim world was best described in terms of a clash of civilizations (between the West and the Muslim world).[17] In the same year, a British YouGov poll found more than 50 per cent of British respondents agreeing with the statement that 'Islam' posed a threat to Western liberal democracy (Johnston 2006). French polls suggest that the populist right's campaign against the construction of mosques and minarets has considerable public support beyond Switzerland's borders. In 2009, more than 40 per cent of French respondents said they opposed the construction of mosques and 46 per cent came out in favour of a law prohibiting the construction of minarets. Support for a ban on the construction of mosques and minarets was (at more than 60 per cent) particularly pronounced among workers (ifop 2009).

Some of the latest surveys indicate that Islamophobia remains strong among a considerable proportion of public opinion. In a representative Austrian survey from 2010, for instance, 71 per cent of respondents agreed with the statement that Islam was fundamentally incompatible with Western ideas of democracy, freedom and tolerance. Fifty-four per cent thought that Islam represented a threat to the West and its way of life; and more than 70 per cent of respondents thought Muslim migrants living in Austria did too little to adapt to Austria's way of life (IMAS 2010). A comparative French/German survey from December 2010 found similar results. Thus, in both countries, four out of ten respondents thought that the Muslim community in their country represented a threat, twice as many as thought it represented a 'factor of enrichment' for the country. Between 68 (France) and 75 (Germany) per cent thought

---

[17] Eine fremde, bedrohliche Welt, *Frankfurter Allgemeine Zeitung*, 17 May 2006. <www.faz.net/ aktuell/ politik/inland/allensbach-analyse-eine-fremde-bedrohliche-welt-1328270.html> [accessed 17 October 2011].

Muslims were not integrated into society. Among those who held this view, more than 60 per cent charged Muslim migrants with refusing to integrate into society. Finally, when asked which three characteristics best reflected their idea of Islam, two-thirds of respondents chose characteristics with negative connotations (rejection of Western values, fanaticism and submission). In both cases, negative views of Islam and the country's Muslim community were particularly pronounced among lower-class respondents (ifop 2010). Islamophobia, however, is hardly a lower-class phenomenon. Wilhelm Heitmeyer has shown, on the basis of time-series data, that over recent years attitudes hostile towards Islam and the Muslim community in Germany have been growing dramatically among the affluent, reaching far into the educated middle class (2010: 24–5).

The media have done their part to reinforce existing impressions that not only is Islam – and Western Europe's resident Muslim community – to a large extent incommensurable with Western values and the European way of life but also that it represents a serious threat. A telling example is *Der Spiegel*, Germany's left-leaning news magazine, which has generally been at the forefront of the fight against xenophobia, prejudice and the populist right. Yet in early 2007, the magazine devoted both its cover and lead article to the 'silent Islamization' of Germany (under the headline 'Mecca Germany'). Islamophobic tendencies have been even more pronounced in Western Europe's yellow press, which generally seeks to appeal to lower-class voters and those media close to the populist right. Take, for instance, the Swiss weekly newsmagazine *Die Weltwoche*, which does not hide its sympathies for Blocher's SVP. In May 2010, the cover of the magazine raised the provocative question of whether 'Islam should be outlawed' (*Muss der Islam verboten werden*).[18] Given Switzerland's recent decision to ban the construction of minarets, this was hardly a moot question.

A few years ago, the American historian Philip Jenkins (2003) referred to anti-Catholicism as the 'last acceptable prejudice' in the United States, for good reason: Ever since the 1830s, Catholicism – and particularly Catholic immigrants from Ireland and Germany entering the United States in record numbers – represented the favourite target of American nativists bent on safeguarding the Protestant nature of the United States against a creed they considered fundamentally at odds (i.e. incompatible) with the very foundations of liberty, democracy and the American way of life. In the eyes of leading nativists, Catholics represented an 'ignorant mob ready to sacrifice rational individualism to Church hierarchy', and thus a fundamental threat to American democracy (Fenton 2011: 53).

Nativism gave rise to the 'Know-nothing' movement of the mid-1850s (later renamed the American Party), which the American historian Ronald Formisano (2008: 198) has characterized as 'one of the largest populist mobilizations of U.S. history'. As it was, Know-nothingism (in the form of the American Party, one of the most important third parties in American history) proved to be short-lived, torn apart over the question of slavery (much of the party was soon absorbed by the newly formed Republican Party). Yet nativism was to continue to have a lasting impact on American political culture.

[18] *Weltwoche*, No. 19, 2010. <www.weltwoche.ch/ausgaben/2010–19/artikel-2010–19-seite-3.html> [accessed 15 October 2011].

Elizabeth Fenton (2011: 21) has even argued that anti-Catholic nativist mobilization was instrumental in shaping American conceptions of pluralism and liberalism, conceptions fundamental to American identity.

Anti-Catholicism did not disappear with the beginning of the Civil War. In fact, it re-emerged in the latter part of the nineteenth century, giving rise to a second wave of nativist mobilization (ironically during a period which is generally referred to as the 'Progressive Era'), which lasted well into the early decades of the twentieth century (Nordstrom 2006). Tom Watson for instance – a once eminent figure in the agrarian populist movement of the 1870s and 1880s from Georgia and candidate for the vice-presidency on the 'fusion' (i.e. Populist/Democratic) ticket for the 1896 presidential election (together with Democrat William Jennings Bryan) – warned in 1912 of the 'Roman Catholic Designs on the American Nation' (ibid.: 30–1). Even Franklin D. Roosevelt's embracing of Roman Catholics two decades later did not prevent large numbers of native-born Protestants from continuing to harbour profound suspicions toward the 'popists' (Gerstle 2001: 46). Later on, a few years after the end of the Second World War, Paul Blanshard (an associate editor for *The Nation*) gained notoriety through his anti-Catholic writings. In them he characterized Catholicism as 'an authoritarian cultural system, directed by foreign (and foreign-appointed) figures', which raised the question of how to confront a 'hierarchy that operates in twentieth-century America under medieval European controls' and asked what would happen if Catholics became a majority in the country. This he considered a real possibility, given the fact, as he warned, that Catholics were 'outbreeding the non-Catholic elements in our population' (Wolfe 2000: 17, Massa 2001: 554).

For enlightened Western Europeans today, this might sound arcane and a bit ridiculous – were it not for the fact that the tropes and arguments advanced in today's right-wing populist campaign (such as the conjuring up of images of invasion, subversion and the eventual displacement of the local population as a result of demographic trends) against the Muslim migrant community and Islam in general represent an almost exact replica – some might say a pastiche – of American anti-Catholic nativist mobilization. Today, in the United States, Catholics are fully accepted as a vital part of the fabric of American society. However, it took more than a century for Catholics to be fully accepted as loyal citizens of the United States who could be entrusted with the country's highest political office without fear of betrayal. If the American experience has any relevance for the situation of Muslims in contemporary Western Europe, Western Europe's Muslim community – and with it Islam – has a long way to go.

References

Akkerman, T. and Hagelund, A. (2007), '"Women and children first!" Antiimmigration parties and gender in Norway and the Netherlands', *Patterns of Prejudice*, 41: 197–214.

Bahloul, J., 'Interview du numéro 2 du FN en visite en Israël', Guysen News, 12 December 2011. <www.guysen.com/article_Interview-du-numero-2-du-FN-en-visite-en-Israel_16922.html> [accessed 21 December 2011].

Betz, H.-G. (2007), 'Against the "green totalitarianism": Anti-Islamic nativism in contemporary radical right-wing populism in Western Europe', in C. Schori Liang (ed.), *Europe for the Europeans: The Foreign and Security Policy of the Populist Radical Right*, Aldershot: Ashgate, pp. 33–54.

Betz, H.-G. and Johnson, C. (2004), 'Against the Current – Stemming the Tide: The Nostalgic Ideology of the Contemporary Radical Populist Right', *Journal of Political Ideologies*, 9: 311–27.

Betz, H.-G. and Meret, S. (2009), 'Revisiting Lepanto: The Political Mobilization Against Islam in Contemporary Western Europe', *Patterns of Prejudice*, 43: 313–34.

Blumer, C. 'Wer etwas gegen Multikulti sagt, ist ein Faschist', interview with Oskar Freysinger, *TagesAnzeiger*, 23 December 2010. <www.tagesanzeiger.ch/schweiz/standard/Wer-etwas-gegen-Multikulti-sagt-ist-ein-Faschist/story/24359861> [accessed 25 September 2011].

Bornschier, S. (2010), *Cleavage Politics and the Populist Right*, Philadelphia: Temple University Press.

Chabrout, J., 'Marine Le Pen persiste', *L'Express*, 13 December 2010. <www.lexpress.fr/actualite/politique/marine-le-pen-persiste_944871.html> [accessed 25 September 2011].

Chapman, M., 'Marine Le Pen sucht die Nähe zur SVP', *Der Bund*, 7 January 2011. <www.derbund.ch/schweiz/standard/Marine-Le-Pen-sucht-die-Naehe-zur-SVP/story/17424807> [accessed 20 September 2011].

Coffé, H. (2005), 'The Adaptation of the Extreme Right's Discourse: The Case of the Vlaams Blok', *Ethical Perspectives*, 12: 205–30.

Daniel, J., 'Les ides de mai', *Le Nouvel Observateur*, 1 December 2011, p. 7.

Dewinter, F., 'Islam is een roofdier', speech given at the party conference of pro-NRW, Duisburg, 29 March 2010a. <www.filipdewinter.be/tag/islamisering/> [accessed 25 September 2011).

— 'Geen supermoskee in Lier!' Speech given 9 December 2010b. <www.filipdewinter.be/geen-supermoskee-in-lier-toespraak-fdw> [accessed 2 October 2011].

— Speech given in Ashkelon, 9 December 2010c. <www.filipdewinter.be/toespraak-filip-dewinter-colloquium-%C2%AB-de-strijd-tegen-radicale-islam-en-moslimterrorisme-een-kwestie-van-zelfverdediging-%C2%BB> [accessed 5 October 2011].

Ettinger. Y., 'French National Front Heads to Israel to Stump for Support Ahead of Election', *Haaretz*, 13 December 2011. <www.haaretz.com/print-edition/news/french-national-front-heads-to-israel-to-stump-for-support-ahead-of-election-1.401091> [accessed 21 December 2011].

Faurisson, R. (2000), 'Impact and Future of Holocaust Revisionism', *The Journal of Historical Review*, 19: 2–31. <www.ihr.org/jhr/v19/v19n1p-2_Faurisson.html> [accessed 12 March 2012].

Fenton, E. (2011), *Religious Liberties: Anti-Catholicism and Liberal Democracy in Nineteenth-Century U.S. Literature and Culture*, New York: Oxford University Press.

Folch, A., 'Les secrets du voyage de Marine Le Pen aux États-Unis', *Valeurs actuelles*, 17 November 2011. <www.valeursactuelles.com/dossier-d039actualit%C3%A9/dossier-d039actualit%C3%A9/secrets-voyage-de-marine-pen20111117.html> [accessed 19 December 20011].

Formisano, R. P. (2008), *For the People: American Populist Movements from the Revolution to the 1850s*. Chapel Hill: University of North Carolina Press.

Foulkes, I., 'Swiss Move to Ban Minarets', BBC News, 28 May 2007. <http://news.bbc.co.uk/2/hi/6676271.stm> [accessed 15 September 2011].

Freysinger, O., 'Les phares du Jihad,' 3 May 2007. <www.minarets.ch/20.html> [accessed 15 September 2011].

Gerstle, G. (2001), *American Crucible: Race and Nation in the Twentieth Century*, Princeton: Princeton University Press.

Graf, J., 'La nouvelle question juive ou la fin de Guillaume Faye', Altermedia.info, 11 November 2007. <http://ca.altermedia.info/histoire/jurgen-graf-repond-a-guillaume-f aye_3520.html> [accessed 18 December 2011].

Heitmeyer, W. (2010), 'Disparate Entwicklungen in Krisenzeiten, Entsolidarisierung und gruppenbezogene Menschenfeindlichkeit, in W. Heitmeyer (ed.), *Deutsche Zustände*, Folge 9, Berlin: Suhrkamp Verlag.

Hirter, H. and Vatter, A. (2010), *Analyse der eidgenössischen Abstimmung vom 20. November 2009, Vox Analysen eidgenössischer Urnengänge*, Bern: gfs and Institut für Politikwissenschaft.

Humbert, L., 'Louis Aliot sur la ligne de front israélienne', *Minute*, 21 December 2011, p. 9.

Ifop, 'Les Français et la construction des mosquées et des minarets en France', December 2009. <www.lefigaro.fr/assets/pdf/Sondage-minaret.pdf > [accessed 12 August 2011].

— 'Regard croisé France/Allemagne sur l'Islam', 13 December 2010. <www.ifop.com/ media/poll/1365-1-study_file.pdf> [accessed 15 December 2011].

IMAS, 'Der Islam in den Augen der Bevölkerung', IMAS International Report, No. 6, April 2010. <www.imas.at/images/imas-report/2010/06-2010.pdf> [accessed 17 October 2011].

Jaillette, J.-C., 'Viande halal et kasher : Le cadeau fait à Marine Le Pen', *Marianne*, 25 February 2012a, pp. 42–3.

— 'Front national : Jean-Marie Le Pen reprend la campagne', *Marianne*, 10 March 2012b, p. 26.

Jenkins, P. (2003), *The New Anti-Catholicism: The Last Acceptable Prejudice*, New York: Oxford University Press.

Johnston, P., 'Islam poses a threat to the West, say 53pc in poll', The Telegraph, 25 August 2006. <www.telegraph.co.uk/news/1527192/Islam-poses-a-threat-to-the-West-say-53pc-in-poll.html> [accessed 17 October 2011].

Le Bars, S., 'Le halal à la cantine, un fantasme loin de la réalité', *Le Monde*, 10 March 2012. <www.lemonde.fr/societe/article/2012/03/10/le-halal-a-la-cantine-un-fantasme-loin-de-la-realite_1655942_3224.html> [accessed 12 March 2012].

Lecœur, E. (ed.) (2007), *Dictionnaire de l'extrême droite*, Paris: Larousse.

Le Pen, M. (2012), *Pour que vive la France*, Paris: Editions Grancher.

Mahrane, S., 'Marine Le Pen fait la cour aux juifs', *Le Point*, 24 November 2011, pp. 46–8.

Massa, M. (2001), 'The New and Old Anti-Catholicism and the Analogical Imagination', *Theological Studies*, 62: 549–70. <http://findarticles.com/p/articles/mI_hb6404/ is_3_62/aI_n28861217/pg_2/> [accessed 16 December 2011].

Nordstrom, J. (2006), *Danger on the Doorstep: Anti-Catholicism and American Print Culture in the Progressive Era*, Notre Dame: University of Notre Dame Press.

Perrault, G., 'Le « malentendu» de la rencontre Le Pen/Prosor', *Le Figaro*, 3 November 2011. <www.lefigaro.fr/politique/2011/11/03/01002-20111103ARTFIG00718-marine-le-pen -rencontre-l-ambassadeur-d-israel-a-l-onu.php> [accessed 18 December 2011].

Primor, A., 'Where Have All the Anti-Semites Gone?', *Haaretz*, 26 March 2010. <www. haaretz.com/print-edition/opinion/where-have-all-the-anti-semites-gone-1.266764> [accessed 3 October 2011].

Reimann, L., ' SVP-Fraktion: Einstimmiges Ja zum Minarettverbot', 22 February 2009. <http://reimann-blog.ch/?p=64> [accessed 19 September 2011].

Ronen, G. and Kempinski, Y., 'European "New Right" MPs in Samaria: "This is Jewish Land!"', Arutz Sheva 7, 6 December 2010. <www.israelnationalnews.com/News/News. aspx/141016#.TvCz81bnNkG> [accessed 18 December 2011].

Rydgren, J. (2005), 'Is Extreme Right-Wing Populism Contagious? Explaining the Emergence of a New Party Family?', *European Journal of Political Research*, 44: 413–37.

Schneider, S. (2008), 'Anti-Immigrant Attitudes in Europe: Outgroup Size and Perceived Ethnic Threat', *European Sociological Review*, 24: 53–67.

Schwartz, A., 'Between Haider and a Hard Place', *Haaretz*, 28 August 2005. <www.haaretz. com/print-edition/features/between-haider-and-a-hard-place-1.168287> [accessed 18 December 2011].

Theil, S., 'Europe's Extreme Righteous: Far-right European politicians find love – and common cause – in Israel', The Daily Beast, 27 February 2011. <www.thedailybeast. com/newsweek/2011/02/27/europe-s-extreme-righteous.html> [accessed 10 October 2011].

von Rohr, M., 'Swiss Minaret Ban Reflects Fear of Islam, not Real Problems', Spiegel Online, 30 November 2009. <www.spiegel.de/international/europe/0,1518,664176,00.html> [accessed 19 September 2011].

Whbee, M., 'Has Racism Become Acceptable?', *The Jerusalem Post*, 20 December 2011. <www.jpost.com/Opinion/Op-EdContributors/Article.aspx?id=200328> [accessed 18 December 2011].

Wolfe, A. (2000), 'Liberalism and Catholicism', *The American Prospect*, 11: 16–21.

Zaiane, A., 'Clash : « Farid Smahi s'en prend à la pro-sioniste » Marine Le Pen et claque la porte', Bondy Blog, 16 January 12011. <http://yahoo.bondyblog.fr/201101161515/ clash-farid-smahi-s%E2%80%99en-prend-a-la-%C2%AB-pro-sioniste-% C2%BB-marine-le-pen-et-claque-la-porte/> [accessed 5 October 2011].

6

Hate Across the Waters: The Role of American Extremists in Fostering an International White Consciousness

Heidi Beirich

In the summer of 2011, Norwegian Anders Behring Breivik decided that he had had enough. A 32-year-old right-wing extremist who had consumed a steady diet of rabid anti-Islamic propaganda about Muslim hordes reoccupying European Christendom, Breivik concluded that, according to his 1,500-page manifesto, '2083: A European Declaration of Independence' (Breivk 2011), what was needed was the formation of a revived Christian army. He called for a new Knights Templar to wage 'guerrilla warfare against the Multiculturalist Alliance through a constant campaign of shock attacks'. His manifesto predicted a coming war that would kill or injure more than a million people as he and his small group of warriors seized 'political and military control of Western European countries' and forcibly put into place 'a cultural conservative political agenda'. Deciding to take matters into his own hands and start that war, on the morning of 22 July, Breivik bombed a government building in central Oslo and then shot to death dozens of children of Labour Party officials, whom he blamed for Muslim immigration and whose children he feared would further that policy. A million were not killed that day, but 77 people died in the horrific bloodbath.

While Breivik acted on his own, the ideology that fuelled his shooting spree derived from a number of racist and anti-Islamic sources. Norway has long had an extremist scene, with neo-Nazis and other white supremacists promoting their racist and antisemitic beliefs. Breivik had made his way through Norway's extremist scene, joining the anti-immigrant Progress Party and participating in the racist Web forum Nordisk where a favourite topic was the race-war novel *The Turner Diaries* (Ridgeway 2011). Breivik was also influenced by European anti-Muslim ideologues and greatly admired Stop Islamization of Europe (SIOE), which he suggested people join. SIOE, which has a Norwegian chapter, has been calling for an end to Muslim immigration into the continent. In addition, Breivik expressed support for the English Defence League (EDL), which has held violent protests involving soccer hooligans and racists against mosques in England (Warner 2010). Breivik claimed he had contact with senior members of the EDL and that a Norwegian version of the group was 'in the process of gaining strength' (Breivik 2011: 1435).

But the primary sources for the anti-Muslim propaganda that had helped give voice to Breivik's manifesto were American. The anti-Muslim author Robert Spencer, who runs the Jihad Watch website, was cited by Breivik 64 times in his manifesto and excerpted extensively. 'About Islam I recommend essentially everything written by Robert Spencer', Breivik wrote, adding that Spencer should be awarded the Nobel Peace Prize (Lenz 2011). Along with Spencer, Breivik also drew inspiration from anti-Muslim American blogger and close Spencer ally Pam Geller. She, along with Spencer, established Stop Islamization of America (SIOA), which is closely allied with SIOE. Geller calls the head of SIOE, Anders Gravers, her 'colleague' (Geller 2011). On 11 September 2011, Geller brought Gravers to New York to speak at a rally where she gathered anti-Muslim extremists from Europe, the United States and Canada to mark the ten-year anniversary of the terrorist attacks (ibid.). Geller has spoken glowingly about the EDL and invited members of the group to New York, to one of her protests.

The relationships between Breivik, Spencer, Geller, the EDL, SIOA, etc. reveal a thickening web of connections between individuals and groups on the extreme right in the United States and Europe. In the decades after the Second World War, these links were at first tenuous, involving a handful of German ex-Nazis and their fascist American allies. For the most part, such connections between American extremists have been among small groups or isolated individuals reaching out to Europeans, not organized party politics. The American two-party political system has made the organizing of extremist political entities almost impossible and attempts at far-right parties, such as the Populist Party or the relatively recent American Third Position party, have garnered very few votes. Few American political figures with extremist racial views have made it into high political offices since the end of segregation.

But in the last two decades, the connections between American extremists and Europeans have grown precipitously, as racists and extremists of all persuasions find solace and compatriots, not in their backyards necessarily, but in places where extremists may share the belief that whites are facing a diminution of demographic power. This is as true among anti-Muslim thinkers as in other racist movements, as indicated by the frequent meetings between American white nationalists and members of extremist European political parties such as the British National Party (BNP) and the German National Democratic Party (NPD). The concept of forming alliances across borders with other whites is dubbed 'pan-Aryanism' in neo-Nazi circles and indicates a unifying ideology and common world view that emphasizes the need to create a worldwide white political space (Southern Poverty Law Center 2001d). These various forms of extremism are now a transnational phenomenon, an unsurprising development in the era of the internet and cheap air travel, as extremists find more common cause with others abroad who share their views.

The West's anti-Muslim network

In the summer of 2010, a furore erupted in the New York City area over the planned establishment of an Islamic Community Center in lower Manhattan called the 'Park

51 Project'. Anti-Muslim activists Pam Geller and Robert Spencer led a crusade against the planned building, calling it a 'Victory Mosque' that did not deserve to be placed within a few blocks of Ground Zero, the site of the 9/11 attacks. The attack by Geller began in May 2010 when Geller's group, SIOA, launched its 'Campaign Offensive: Stop the 911 Mosque!' (Spencer serves as SIOA's associate director). Geller posted the names and contact information for the mayor and members of a community board involved in sanctioning the project. Within days, the board chair reported getting 'hundreds and hundreds' of calls and e-mails from around the world (Elliott 2010).

Geller's protests, which were self-financed by the wealthy Long Islander, went viral when they were picked up by prominent public figures. By June 2010, former New York City Mayor Rudy Giuliani had called the mosque a 'desecration'. And former vice-presidential candidate Sarah Palin had tweeted 'peaceful Muslims, pls refudiate [sic]' the project. Former Republican House Speaker Newt Gingrich may have been the most extreme of all, comparing the backers of the project to 'Nazis' (DeLong 2010). The furore brought a new strain of anti-Muslim hatred to the public's consciousness, raising the profile of anti-Muslim Americans whose work, even though it started in the months after 9/11, had hitherto been obscure.

The movement that seemed to spring up around the New York protests was not a case of spontaneous public-opinion combustion. In the decade since 9/11, a coterie of core activists – most importantly, hard liners Spencer, Geller and other Americans, most notably Brigitte Gabriel, Frank Gaffney, David Horowitz and David Yerushalmi, along with the more moderate Daniel Pipes and Steve Emerson – had been warning that an Islamic sky was falling (Steinback 2011a). These activists have been backed by a handful of right-wing foundations, most importantly the Richard Mellon Scaife foundations, the Lynde and Harry Bradley Foundation, the Newton D. & Rochelle F. Becker Foundation and the Russell Berrie Foundation. According to the Center for American Progress, 'Just seven charitable groups provided $42.6m. to Islamophobia think tanks between 2001 and 2009 – funding that supports the scholars and experts . . . as well as some of the grassroots groups' (Ali et al. 2011). In December 2010, Max Blumenthal, a journalist with *The Nation* and an expert in American extremism, called it 'the Great Islamophobic Crusade'. 'It's the fruit of an organized, long-term campaign by a tight confederation of right-wing activists and operatives who first focused on Islamophobia soon after the September 11th attacks, but only attained critical mass during the Obama era', Blumenthal opined. 'This network is obsessively fixated on the supposed spread of Muslim influence in America' (Blumenthal 2010).

What is interesting about this attack on the Muslim community is that in the United States, Muslims are quite well-integrated into American life and not very likely to be interested in radical politics. They are also a small community that is extremely diverse, including persons from several different countries and faiths (Gallup 2009). About a quarter of the Muslim population consists of converts, many are African Americans. Polling has also shown that Muslim Americans are more likely than other faith groups to reject attacks on civilians, a quite different picture of that community than that presented by Geller and her allies (Naurath 2011).

Paying the reality of the Muslim American community no heed, the anti-Muslim movement in the 2000s was intent upon demonizing this population. The movement relies heavily on two key tactics. The first is arguing that the most radical

Muslims – men like Osama bin Laden – are properly interpreting the Koran, while peaceful moderate Muslims either do not understand their own holy book or are strategically faking their moderation. The second key tactic is relentlessly to attack individuals and organizations that purport to represent moderate Islam in America, painting them as secret operatives in the grand Muslim scheme (typically attributed to a conspiracy led by the Egypt-based Muslim Brotherhood) to destroy the West. The attack on the Park 51 Project was of this kind. The mosque's leader, Imam Feisal Abdul Rauf, had long been seen as a moderate voice arguing against radical Islam (Ghosh 2010). At their most extreme, far-right activists, particularly in Europe, go so far as to argue, as did Breivik, that immigrants and asylum seekers are 'pioneers in a Muslim army of conquest' (Merkl & Weinberg 2003: 294).

The primary architect of these anti-Islamic tactics is SIOA co-founder Robert Spencer. An entirely self-taught 'expert' in the study of modern Islam and the Koran, he often takes the Koran literally, as an innately extremist and violent text – something typical of anti-Muslim writers (Marranci 2004: 107).'As I have pointed out many times', Spencer wrote in 2006, 'traditional Islam itself is not moderate or peaceful. It is the only major world religion with a developed doctrine and tradition of warfare against unbelievers' (Steinback 2011b). Critics charge that Spencer ignores other passages and centuries of interpretive scholarship that mitigate the Koran's occasional violent verses (Armstrong 2007). Former Pakistani Prime Minister Benazir Bhutto accused Spencer of 'falsely constructing a divide between Islam and the West' and providing what was a 'skewed, one-sided, and inflammatory story that only helps to sow the seed of civilizational conflict' (Bhutto 2008: 245–6). Some also point out that the many violent admonitions of other holy books, including the Bible, are not usually taken literally by believers (Soharwardy 2010). Scholars believe this anti-Muslim bias 'is of increasing sociological and political importance' (Miles & Brown 2003: 163).

Geller's views of Islam, published on her website Atlas Shrugs, are simply defamatory. She has posted (and later removed) a video implying that Muslims practised bestiality with goats and a cartoon depicting the Muslim prophet Mohammad with a pig's face (observant Muslims do not eat pork). Geller has denied the genocide of Bosnian Muslims by Serbian forces in Srebrenica – calling it the 'Srebrenica Genocide Myth', even though the Serbian government itself issued a state apology for the massacre. This is akin to Holocaust denial in that Geller, due to her anti-Muslim bias, refuses to accept that Muslims can be victims of genocide in the same manner that neo-Nazis and others refused to accept the slaughter of Jews in Germany by their heroes as possible (Beirich 2009). Geller wrote, 'Westerners are admitting to their role in something that didn't happen, and digging their own graves' (Southern Poverty Law Center 2012b).

The anti-Muslim network built in the 2000s is not confined to the United States; Geller has significant overseas connections, proving that fears of a possible coming 'Eurabia' do not only exist in Europe (Bat 2005). In 2009, Geller was invited to address the German far-right organization Pro Köln, described as a successor group to the neo-fascist German League for People and Homeland. As of early 2011, Pro Köln was officially deemed a right-wing extremist group by the German authorities (Schlatter 2011a). Geller and the EDL have worked hand-in-glove on this issue, and members of the EDL joined her 11 September 2010 protest in Manhattan, sporting flags (and ski masks) bearing a St. George's Cross. White with red crossbars, the mediaeval flag is most famous for its use by British Crusaders (Zaitchik 2010). In February 2010, Geller wrote admiringly of the EDL on her blog. 'I share the E.D.L.'s goals' she said. 'We need to encourage rational, reasonable groups that oppose the Islamisation of the West' (Southern Poverty Law Center 2012b).

A big fan of anti-Muslim Dutch politician Geert Wilders, Geller, in March 2010, glowingly advertised an upcoming EDL protest that was to feature him (Geller 2010). She invited Wilders to speak at a June 2010 'Ground Zero Mosque' rally. On the tenth anniversary of the 9/11 attacks, Geller and Spencer held a rally in Manhattan that featured a 'Who's Who' of anti-Muslim activists from the United States, Canada and Europe. Among those attending were René Stadtkewitz, a right-wing German Parliament member from the anti-Islamic Freedom Party and Ezra Levant, a Canadian lawyer and founder of the libertarian-conservative news source *The Western Standard* (Schlatter 2011b).

These close working relationships show that this anti-Muslim network is now transnational in nature. Besides Breivik, these anti-Muslim activists have drawn the admiration of white nationalist and even neo-Nazi proponents on the extreme right – a rather remarkable feat, considering Geller is proudly Jewish and very pro-Israel, something that is anathema to anti-Semites. Geller has also been the subject of positive postings on racist American websites such as Stormfront, VDARE, American Renaissance and the neo-Confederate League of the South (Southern Poverty Law Center 2012b). But anti-Muslim extremists have been quite willing to set aside parts of their ideology for the greater cause. This has been true of Nick Griffin, the head of the BNP and a man convicted of Holocaust denial, who began in the mid-2000s to reach out to the British Jewish community on the basis of his anti-Muslim platform. At a 2006 meeting of the white nationalist group American Renaissance, that included prominent anti-Semites in the audience including former Klansman David Duke, Griffin denounced those who see behind every evil some kind of 'world-Jewish conspiracy' and claimed that Jews are a natural ally in the battle against Islam (Beirich 2006).

Hardcore racists

Another world that Breivik frequented was that of neo-Nazis and other hardcore extremists. In the wake of his attacks, Breivik reportedly sent his manifesto to more than 1,000 contacts, including anti-immigrant political activists from the EDL and the Vlaams Belang, a Belgian party that was banned for 'xenophobia and racism' in its former incarnation, but also Combat 18, a neo-Nazi skinhead group with affiliates in the United Kingdom and the United States (Taylor 2011). This was not his only contact with hardcore extremists. Breivik frequently posted to a Web forum whose major topic of conversation was, reportedly, *The Turner Diaries*, a race-war novel penned by American neo-Nazi William Pierce (the book served as a blueprint for Oklahoma City bomber Timothy McVeigh) (Kay 2011).

That a Norwegian racist would spend time on forums devoted to an American race-war novel is not all that surprising. Since the Second World War, a significant and growing number of American right-wing extremists have worked for or advocated a transnational approach to revolutionary politics. While these budding internationalists have included Klansmen and many other types of radical rightists, the most important have been neo-Nazis – men who believe in the rehabilitation of some form of German National Socialism, but with a far more global scope than that espoused by Adolf Hitler. The shared movement grew slowly, as neo-Nazism and Holocaust denial became more common in the United States as memories of the war faded.

By the 1990s, shared contacts were quite common among neo-Nazis and other hardcore racists, such as racist skinheads, street toughs known for engaging in hate crimes. This is partly because of the rise of 'pan-Aryanism', a white supremacist philosophy that emphasizes the idea that white revolutionaries must adopt a global strategy to succeed. In the words of American neo-Nazi William Pierce, leader of the National Alliance (NA), 'We must understand that we are in a planet-wide race war, and survival of our race depends on our winning this war' (Southern Poverty Law Center 2001a).

Interchanges between leaders of neo-Nazi and similar groups have been common in the last few decades. During the 1990s, Pierce, who died in 2002, travelled regularly to Europe, speaking to neo-fascist groups like the BNP (he was banned from the United Kingdom after a 1997 speech to the BNP), Greece's neo-Nazi Golden Dawn and Germany's racist and antisemitic NPD (Southern Poverty Law Center 2001a). In 1999, Pierce summed up his views to an NPD audience, saying, 'It is essential – not just helpful, but necessary – for genuine nationalist groups everywhere to increase their degree of collaboration across national borders . . . The National Alliance is really unique in that it . . . define[s] nationality in terms of race, not geography.' Pierce concluded: 'our destinies are linked' (Southern Poverty Law Center 2001b).

Over the years, many other extremist leaders have made the trek to Europe to find like-minded extremists. In September 1991, Dennis Mahon, the then Oklahoma leader of the White Knights of the Ku Klux Klan, took a nine-day tour of reunified Germany. The trip peaked with a Klan-style cross burning, organized by the neo-Nazi Nationalist Front (Nationalistische Front) and led by Mahon in a German forest near Berlin. In August 1998, an American delegation from the white supremacist Council of Conservative Citizens, including top leaders Gordon Lee Baum and Tom Dover, participated in a National Front festival in France (Southern Poverty Law Center 2001a). David Duke, perhaps America's best-known racist political figure and a former state senator from Louisiana, has long had a major international presence. He has travelled widely in Europe, selling his antisemitic autobiography, *My Awakening: A Path to Racial Understanding*. Duke began visiting Russia at the turn of the millennium and made his second trip to Russia in the summer of 2000 at the invitation of Alexander Prokhanov, editor of the ultranationalist newspaper *Zavtra*, and Konstantin Kasimovsky, head of an antisemitic outfit called Russian Action. In the early 2000s, Duke resided in Moscow, Russia, while he was being sought by authorities in the United States for fraud (Lee 2003, Southern Poverty Law Center 2012a). He spent time promoting his last book, *The Ultimate Supremacism: My Awakening on the Jewish Question*, which was for years openly offered in the lobby of the Russian Congress. Boris Mironov, who was once press secretary to former president Boris Yeltsin, wrote the preface to Duke's book (Duke 2003).

The other area of long-standing, tight racial collaboration between Americans and Europeans is in the realm of white power music, which began in Britain but soon spread to the rest of Europe and then America. As Anton Shekhovtsov has pointed out:

> Extreme-right political parties and groups have produced their own music scene which is known as White Power music, or White Noise . . . It [was] originated in Britain in 1978 by two Leeds-based bands, the Ventz and the Dentists . . . From 1979 onward, [these] ideas were taken up by the main publication of the Young Nation Front, *Bulldog*, edited by Joe Pearce. It was not, however, until the early 1980s, that the far right musical scene began to flourish . . . During the 1980s, White Power music rapidly spread all over Europe. The French far-right music label Rebelles Européens was set up in 1987 by Bodilis Gael, who was active in the youth wing of the French National Front, Third Way, and, afterwards, the French and European Nationalist Party. Socialist Europe was not left behind either. At the end of the 1980s, sympathisers of the National Rebirth of Poland party formed the far-right band Legion that helped the organisation recruit skinheads for the political cause. By the mid-1990s, the far-right scene appeared in Russia, where the band Russkoe Getto, later renamed Kolovrat, was formed and rapidly reached cult status amongst Russian neo-Nazis. (Shekhovtsov forthcoming)

White power music, which is often illegal in Europe and thus mainly produced and distributed in and from the United States, has acted as a unifying element among racist skinheads. It has allowed for connections to develop between American distributors, in terms of websites and various hate groups, and European and American bands. Hate music bands travel frequently to the United States and vice versa to spread their message. As Shekhovtsov notes, 'The 1990s were undoubtedly the heyday of the White Power music scene in Europe. [These networks] played a crucial role in the rise of the scene that also became increasingly profitable' (forthcoming).

The growing white power music industry, valued at millions of dollars in annual sales and in the early 2000s estimated by Interpol to be worth more than the Hashish trade, is not just the largest source of money and recruits for the Western world's most dynamic racist revolutionaries (Southern Poverty Law Center 2001d). It is also astonishingly international. Through websites and cheaper travel, racist music has spread over the last quarter of a century from Britain to the rest of Europe and on to the United States. In many ways, this remarkably violent music is accomplishing for the radical right what decades of racist theorizing did not: It has given skinheads and many other extremists around the world a common language and a unifying ideology – an ideology that replaces old-fashioned state-based nativism with the concept of 'pan-Aryanism'. To this day, skinheads remain remarkably integrated across borders with European racist bands from across the continent playing gigs in the United States and vice versa.

The West's white nationalist network

Breivik's manifesto pointed to a particular ideology, called 'cultural Marxism', as being responsible for Europe allowing in foreign populations and turning its back on the greatness of Western civilization. His manifesto explicitly equates liberalism and multiculturalism with cultural Marxism, something Breivik says is destroying European Christian civilization. The manifesto is literally a call to arms against this evil trend. But Breivik did not learn about cultural Marxism by reading European thinkers; it is an idea created by American thinkers, most of them white nationalists, to explain the rise of political correctness and anti-racist beliefs as well as the advent of multiculturalism. Over time, the idea spread to Europe as racist ideologues on both sides of the Atlantic came to believe that their countries would no longer be healthy functioning societies or democracies once whites were supplanted by other populations (Beirich & Hicks 2009: 109). Many white nationalists see the changes in American society, particularly since the hated decade of the 1960s, as the result of an orchestrated plan by leftist intellectuals, or cultural Marxists, to destroy the American way of life as established by whites.

In a nutshell, the cultural Marxism argument posits that the ideas and actions of a tiny group of philosophers – mainly Jews who taught at the Institute for Social Research in Frankfurt, Germany, and who fled Germany in the 1930s – dramatically changed American society (Owens 2000: 34, Berkowitz 2003). These men set up shop at Columbia University in New York City and founded the 'Frankfurt School' of philosophy. White nationalists allege they devised an unorthodox form of Marxism that took aim at American culture, rather than its economic system, and worked to undermine the culture by introducing leftist ideas, particularly by extending civil rights to marginalized groups, such as minorities, the lesbian and gay community and women. As social psychology professor Richard Lichtman of the Berkeley-based Wright Institute has pointed out, cultural Marxism is

> a convenient target that very few people really know anything about. By grounding their critique in Marxism and using the Frankfurt School, [extremists] make it seem like it's quite foreign to anything American. It takes on a mysterious cast and translates as an incomprehensible, anti-American, foreign movement that is only interested in undermining the U.S. . . . The idea being transmitted is that we are being infected from the outside. (Berkowitz 2003)

Cultural Marxism, a term popularized by William Lind of the Free Congress Foundation and spread through white nationalist circles, largely by a video put out by the white supremacist Council of Conservative Citizens that features Lind, has allegedly had another extremely deleterious effect: these assaults on American culture have made whites unable to form a coherent identity for themselves. White nationalists argue that this has been encouraged to happen among minority groups, who have created their own identities, such as African Americans and Latinos, and their own lobbying groups (Lind 2000, Council of Conservative Citizens 2007). White nationalists allege that a double standard has been put into place, whereby minorities in groups such as the National Council of La Raza or the National Association for the Advancement of Colored People (NAACP) can celebrate their culture and create institutions to further their interests, but whites cannot (racist activists ignore the fact that these groups are multiracial and open to membership to anyone who agrees with their beliefs). 'Racial pride is fine for blacks and everyone else, but verboten . . . for whites. Not just American whites, mind you, but all whites everywhere' is how Jared Taylor has explained this result of cultural Marxism (Taylor 2004). Because of this, one of the primary political goals of white nationalism is to forge a white identity, which it believes will be the first step to re-establishing white political power. In Taylor's words, 'No group can survive without group identity. This is a law of nature. Deny to whites their identity as a group and you condemn them to obliteration and oblivion. And that, of course, is precisely what we refuse! We are not going quietly' (ibid.).

And what does Taylor fear losing? At its core, the white nationalist movement is defined by its fundamental belief in a biological conception of race. Here is how Taylor put it in a speech to his American Renaissance group's 2004 biannual gathering:

[W]e just want to be left alone. We are the heirs to the magnificent traditions of Europe. We are a biologically distinct group known as white people. We want to be left alone to carry forward our traditions and to pursue our own destiny. It is as simple as that. We wish other groups well, but we cannot welcome them in our midst because they are not us. We have a deep, healthy loyalty to our own kind, and we know populations are not replaceable or interchangeable. We have the right to be us, and only we can be us. (ibid.)

For white nationalists, humankind is made up of a number of naturally occurring racial divisions; each race possesses traits that are the product of genetic inheritance and that serve to characterize it as a distinct human type. Culture is the partner of this inheritance and what binds together members of the same race in a community of common interests, habits and characteristics (Beirich & Hicks 2009: 114). When members of the same race create political organizations, like the nation state, these institutions are necessarily an expression of both the race and culture of their creators. In the case of America, white nationalists see it as an intrinsically white nation, the result of a superior Western European racial and cultural inheritance. As a result, white nationalists believe that whites created the highest level of human civilization: Western civilization.

White nationalists are very concerned about the genetic deterioration of their 'race' and the diminution of its power. White nationalists view the 'interbreeding', to use their word, of the increasingly multicultural societies in the West, particularly the United States, as a disaster that only political alliance among whites can avoid (ibid.: 116). 'Some are more desirable than others' is how Thomas Jackson put it in the October 2011 issue of *American Renaissance*. 'When people with desirable characteristics have more children than those with undesirable characteristics we evolve. When they do not we degenerate' (Jackson 2011: 1). They look for hope to Europe, where the ravages of cultural Marxism are not seen as having been quite so deleterious, at least not yet.

The fact that Europe has several political parties that are organized around either racist or xenophobic anti-immigrant views provides hope to American white nationalists (Mudde 2003, Givens 2005, Norris 2005). This is how Taylor has assessed the situation: 'In just about every white country there is a nationalist political party that stands explicitly for national preservation – sometimes even for nothing less than ethnic or racial preservation – and gets voters because of this' (Taylor 2006: 11). Anti-immigrant right-wing populist parties in Europe, such as the BNP and the anti-immigrant Sweden Democrats, whose 2010 electoral success is celebrated by Taylor's organization, *American Renaissance,* have serious fans and allies in the United States (Widmark 2010). In addition, American white nationalists look to the Swiss People's Party, one of the most successful anti-immigrant parties in Europe. In October 2007, it took 29 per cent of the votes for that nation's lower house, the best result for any Swiss party since 1919, which translated into 62 seats in the nation's 200-seat National Council. The party's campaign was simple and appealing to America's white nationalists: the expulsion of foreign criminals and other immigrants, a continued refusal to join the European Union and tax cuts, which appeal to extremists as they shrink governments that are seen as multicultural and anathema to their goals.

There is a relatively integrated circuit of white nationalists who speak on both sides of the Atlantic, fundraise, share beliefs and repeatedly link to each other's websites (Southern Poverty Law Center 2001b). In the early 2000s, the BNP had an American fundraising arm called the American Friends of the British National Party (AFBNP). The AFBNP brought together dozens of prominent American racists at events held specifically to raise funds for the BNP. Nick Griffin, the BNP's leader, spoke of the need for supporting movements such as his at AFBNP events where a basket was passed around for donations (Southern Poverty Law Center 2001c). Ultimately, the leader of the group, Mark Cotterill, was deported from the United States after it was revealed by the Southern Poverty Law Center that he had never registered as a foreign agent with the US Government (ibid.). In June 2000, Taylor travelled to London to address a meeting of supporters of *Right Now!,* an English pseudo-academic 'racialist' publication similar to his own. Taylor, the British anti-fascist magazine *Searchlight* reported, described multiculturalism as 'a conspiracy to destroy white society' (Southern Poverty Law Center 2001a). Leaders of the French National Front have come to the United States to fundraise and speak at extremist events, and in 2007, leaders of the Belgian Vlaams Belang came to the United States to speak to the Robert Taft Club, whose leader attends American Renaissance events, and the Federation for American Immigration Reform (Beirich 2007a, b). Just this past February, the party's leader, Filip Dewinter, spoke at the 2011 American Renaissance conference. The most recent attempt at white nationalist American political action is the establishment of the American Third Position, a political party begun in 2009 by skinheads but now run predominantly by academics and other professionals that calls for the removal of non-whites from the United States. The party relies on European expertise (Beirich 2011). One of its directors, appointed in 2010, is Tomislav Sunic, a graduate of the University of Zagreb who has become an outspoken white nationalist and speaks frequently in Europe (American Third Position 2011).

Conclusion

Breivik was no lone wolf and he did not reach his terrifying conclusions in a vacuum. Breivik was deeply involved online and in Norway in anti-immigrant and racist movements. He learned his hatred of Muslims at the feet of American ideologues and he spread his hatred to extremists in Europe and the United States. The spider's web of hate he functioned in is part and parcel of a growing transnational web of hatred that is available to anyone with an internet connection.

These racist networks are the real world outcome of massive change in terms of globalization and demography, and they are only likely to intensify over the coming years. Growing anxieties on both sides of the Atlantic over factors such as changing demographics, immigration from the developing world and economic disparities brought about by globalization are seen, by certain sectors of the population, as resulting in a precipitous decline in white power. These changes have given rise to a transnational movement that is bringing together various types of extremists, regardless of whether their priorities are anti-Muslim proselytizing, advocating white nationalism or pushing more extreme and often more openly violent racist ideologies such as neo-Nazism.

References

Ali, W., Clifton, E., Duss, M., Fang, L., Keyes, S. and Shakir, F. (2011), *Fear, Inc. The Roots of the Islamophobia Network in America*, Washington, DC: Center for American Progress.

American Third Position (2011), 'Leadership'. <http://american3rdposition.com/leadership/> [accessed 4 February 2012].

Armstrong, K. (2007), 'Balancing the Prophet', *Financial Times*, 27 April.

Bat, Y. (2005), *Eurabia: The Euro-Arab Axis*, Madison, NJ: Fairleigh Dickinson University Press.

Beirich, H. (2006), 'Irreconcilable Differences', *Intelligence Report* 122. <www.splcenter.org/get-informed/intelligence-report/browse-all-issues/2006/summer/irreconcilable-differences> [accessed 4 February 2012].

— (2007a), 'Extremist Group Announces Speech by Congressman', *Hatewatch*. 8 October. <www.splcenter.org/blog/2007/10/08/extremist-group-announces-speech-by-congressman/> [accessed 4 February 2012].

— (2007b), 'The Teflon Nativists', *Intelligence Report*, 128. <www.splcenter.org/get-informed/intelligence-report/browse-all-issues/2007/winter/the-teflon-nativists> [accessed 4 February 2012].

— (2009), 'The Holocaust Denial Movement', *Southern Poverty Law Center*. <www.splcenter.org/get-informed/intelligence-files/ideology/holocaust-denial/essay-the-holocaust-denial-movement> [accessed 4 February 2012].

— (2011), 'Racist Prof Latest to Join Group that Seeks White Rule in America', *Hatewatch*. 27 June. <www.splcenter.org/blog/2011/06/27/racist-emeritus-prof-latest-to-join-group-that-seeks-white-rule-in-america/> [accessed 4 February 2012].

Beirich, H. and Hicks, K. (2009), 'White Nationalism in America', in Barbara Perry (ed.), *Hate Crimes*, 1, New York: Praeger, pp. 109–31.

Berkowitz, W. (2003), 'Reframing the Enemy', *Intelligence Report* 110. <www.
splcenter.org/get-informed/intelligence-report/browse-all-issues/2003/summer/
reframing-the-enemy?page=0,1> [accessed 4 February 2012].

Bhutto, B. (2008), *Reconciliation: Islam, Democracy, and the West*, New York: Harper.

Blumenthal, Max (2010), 'The Great Islamophobic Crusade', *The Nation*, 19 December.
<www.nationinstitute.org/featuredwork/fellows/1271/ the_great_islamophobic_
crusade/?page=entire> [accessed 4 February 2012].

Breivik, A. (2011), '2083: A European Declaration of Independence', *Kevin I Slaughter: An
Unwanted Advocate*. 23 August. <www.kevinislaughter.com/2011/anders-behring-
breivik-2083-a-european-declaration-of-independence-manifesto/> [accessed 4
February 2012].

Council of Conservative Citizens (2007), 'The Frankfurt School'. <www.youtube.com/
watch?v=hh2DdJLycPM> [accessed 4 February 2012].

DeLong, M. (2010), 'Newt Gingrich Compares 'Ground Zero Mosque' Backers to Nazis',
Washington Post, 16 August. <http://voices.washingtonpost.com/44/2010/08/
newt-gingrich-compares-ground.html> [accessed 4 February 2012].

Duke, D. (2003), *The Ultimate Supremacism: My Awakening on the Jewish Question*,
Mandeville, LA: Free Speech Press.

Elliott, J. (2010), 'How the "ground zero mosque" fear mongering began', *Salon*, 16 August.
<www.salon.com/news/politics/war_room/2010/08/16/ground_zero_mosque_
origins> [accessed 4 February 2012].

Gallup Center for Muslim Studies (2009), *Muslim Americans: A National Portrait*,
Washington, DC: Gallup.

Geller, P. (2010), 'English Defence League London Rally In Defence of Geert Wilders',
Atlas Shrugs, 3 March. <http://atlasshrugs2000.typepad.com/atlas_shrugs/2010/03/
english-defense-league-edl-london-rally-in-defense-of-geert-wilders-friday-2pm-go.
html> [accessed 4 February 2012].

— (2011), '9/11 Remember', *Atlas Shrugs*, 9 September. <http://atlasshrugs2000.typepad.
com/atlas_shrugs/2011/09/911-remember.html> [accessed 4 February 2012].

Ghosh, R. (2010), 'The Moderate Imam Behind the "Ground Zero Mosque"', *Time
Magazine*, 3 August. <www.time.com/time/nation/article/0,8599,2008432,00.html>
[accessed 4 February 2012].

Givens, T. E. (2005), *Voting Radical Right in Western Europe*, Cambridge: Cambridge
University Press.

Jackson, T. (2011), 'The Decline of the West', *American Renaissance*, 21: 1.

Kay, J. (2011), 'We've Heard This Story Before', *National Post*, 26 July. <www.canada.com/
story_print.html?id=5157815&sponsor> [accessed 4 February 2012].

Lee, M. A. (2003), 'Duke Travels in European Anti-Semitic Circles', *Intelligence Report*, 109.
<www.splcenter.org/get-informed/intelligence-report/browse-all-issues/2003/spring/
insatiable/the-wandering-jew-hater> [accessed 4 February 2012].

Lenz, R. (2011), 'Christian Crusader', *Intelligence Report* 143. <www.splcenter.org/
get-informed/intelligence-report/browse-all-issues/2011/fall/christian-crusader>
[accessed 4 February 2012].

Lind, W. (2000), 'The Origins of Political Correctness', 5 February. <www.academia.org/
the-origins-of-political-correctness/> [accessed 4 February 2012].

Marranci, G. (2004), 'Multiculturalism, Islam and the Clash of Civilizations Theory:
Rethinking Islamophobia', *Culture and Religion*, 5: 105–17.

Merkl, P. H. and Weinberg, L. (2003), *Right-Wing Extremism in the Twenty-First Century*,
Portland, OR: Frank Cass Publishers.

Miles, R. and Brown, M. (2003), *Racism*. New York: Routledge.

Mudde, C. (2003), *The Ideology of the Extreme Right*, Manchester: Manchester University Press.

Naurath, N. (2011), 'Most Muslim Americans See No Justification for Violence', *Gallup*, 2 August. <www.gallup.com/poll/148763/muslim-americans-no-justification-violence.aspx> [accessed 4 February 2012].

Norris, P. (2005), *Radical Right, Voters and Parties in the Electoral Market*, Cambridge: Cambridge University Press.

Owens, J. (2000), 'Ending the Race Crisis in the 21st Century'. <www.cofcc.org/foundation/racecrisis> [accessed 4 February 2012].

Ridgeway, J. (2011), 'Anders Breivik, Stieg Larsson, and the Men with the Nazi Tattoos', *Mother Jones*, 26 July. <http://motherjones.com/mojo/2011/07/anders-breivik-stieg-larsson> [accessed 4 February 2012].

Schlatter, E. (2011a), 'Far-Right Student Group Building Ties to Right-Wing European Extremists', *Hatewatch*, 20 April. <www.splcenter.org/blog/2011/04/20/ far-right-student-group-building-ties-to-right-wing-european-extremists/> [accessed 4 February 2012].

— (2011b), '9/11 Rally to Include Hard Rightists from Around the World', *Hatewatch*, 7 September. <www.splcenter.org/blog/2011/09/07/911-rally-to-include-hard-rightists-from-around-world/> [accessed 4 February 2012].

Shekhovtsov, A. (2012), 'European Far-Right Music and Its Enemies', in Ruth Wodak and John E. Richardson (eds), *Analyzing Fascist Discourse: European Fascism in Talk and Text*, London: Routledge (in press).

Soharwardy, S. (2010), 'Qu'ran Misinterpreted, just like Bible', *The Calgary Herald*, 19 September.

Southern Poverty Law Center (2001a), 'The Ties That Bind', *Intelligence Report*, 103. <www.splcenter.org/get-informed/intelligence-report/browse-all-issues/2001/fall/the-ties-that-bind?page=0,1> [accessed 4 February 2012].

— (2001b), 'The Internationalists', *Intelligence Report*, 103. <www.splcenter.org/get-informed/intelligence-report/browse-all-issues/2001/fall/hands-across-the-water/the-internationa> [accessed 4 February 2012].

— (2001c), 'Hands Across the Water', *Intelligence Report*, 103. <www.splcenter.org/get-informed/intelligence-report/browse-all-issues/2001/fall/hands-across-the-water> [accessed 4 February 2012].

— (2001d), 'White Pride Worldwide', *Intelligence Report*, 103. <www.splcenter.org/get-informed/intelligence-report/browse-all-issues/2001/fall/white-pride-worldwide> [accessed 4 February 2012].

— (2012a), 'David Duke'. <www.splcenter.org/get-informed/intelligence-files/profiles/david-duke> [accessed 4 February 2012].

— (2012b), 'Pamela Geller', <www.splcenter.org/get-informed/intelligence-files/profiles/pamela-geller> [accessed 4 February 2012].

Steinback, R. (2011a), 'Jihad Against Islam', *Intelligence Report*, 142. <www.splcenter.org/get-informed/intelligence-report/browse-all-issues/2011/summer/jihad-against-islam> [accessed 4 February 2012].

— (2011b), 'The Anti-Muslim Inner Circle', *Intelligence Report*, 142. <www.splcenter.org/get-informed/intelligence-report/browse-all-issues/2011/summer/the-anti-muslim-inner-circle> [accessed 4 February 2012].

Taylor, J. (2004), 'Prospects for Our Movement', 21 February. <www.amren.com/news/news04/02/27/jtconf2004talk.html> [accessed 4 February 2012].

— (2006), 'Jews and *American Renaissance*', *American Renaissance*, 17: 11.

Taylor, M. (2011), 'Anders Breivik Had Links to Far Right EDL, Says Antiracism Group', *The Guardian*, 26 July. <www.guardian.co.uk/world/2011/jul/26/anders-behring-breivik-edl-searchlight> [accessed 4 February 2012].

Warner, W. (2010), 'New York City Blogger Pamela Geller Support Of The Neo-Nazi EDL Group, So Who Are The Nazis? Meet Atlas's Thugs', *Zimbio*, 5 March. <www.zimbio.com/Orly Taitz/articles/LxnfF1cWiY6/New York City Blogger Pamela Geller Support> [accessed 4 February 2012].

Widmark, M. (2010), 'Nationalists Win At Great Odds', *American Renaissance*, 21. <www.amren.com/ar/2010/11/index.html> [accessed 4 February 2012].

Zaitchik, A. (2010), 'The British (Extremists) Are Coming – or the English Defence League Hearts Pam Geller', *Hatewatch*, 16 September. <www.splcenter.org/blog/2010/09/16/ the-british-extremists-are-coming-or-the-english-defence-league-hearts-pam-geller/> [accessed 4 February 2012].

Section II

Case Studies – Western Europe

7

Ploughing the Same Furrow? Continuity and Change on Britain's Extreme-Right Fringe

John E. Richardson

In this chapter, I discuss two British political organizations and their relationships to British fascism. The first of these is the British National Party (BNP) – which is, at the time of writing, the largest extreme right-wing party in Britain. In contrast to certain published academic work (e.g. Mudde 2007, Fella 2008, Mastropaolo 2008), this chapter will argue that the BNP should not be categorized as a 'populist radical right-wing' party. Operating at the highest levels of the BNP, a coterie of hardcore (ex-)National Socialists can be identified who, across the decades, have acted like a 'container group', ensuring the continuation of their political ideology. The origins of this coterie date from the re-establishment of the British tradition of National Socialism in the late 1950s, since which time it has acted to protect and maintain the flame of British fascist ideology. Accordingly, categorizing the party as ideologically 'populist' 'may serve as an unintended form of democratic legitimization of modern xenophobia and neo-fascism' (Mammone 2009: 174). The second organization discussed in this chapter is the street-fighting movement the English Defence League (EDL), whose nascent ideology contains populist and radical elements. However, the EDL is not a political party and, as such, it lacks a mandated leadership, a stable ideological position and a widely agreed upon programme of political action. These facts create difficulties for both the classification and policing of the EDL, as I discuss below.

Working from the arguments of previous analysts of British fascist ideology – primarily those of Billig (1978) and Copsey (2007, 2008) – I argue that an understanding of extremist parties requires comparative analysis of texts produced at different times and for different audiences (insider and outsider; potential voter and party initiates) (see, for example, Richardson & Wodak 2009a, 2009b, Richardson 2011). This analysis needs to be contextualized through examining the histories and activities of the party, 'their history, cultures and heritage, on forms of party socialization and membership, and ideology and internal discourse' (Mammone 2009: 176). The remainder of this chapter briefly discusses the surface and depths of BNP ideology, the political records of certain party members, the associations between the BNP and other European fascist parties and organizations and the party's continued anti-Semitism. Following this, I will briefly discuss the EDL and the ways that the ideology of this fractious movement could develop in the future.

BNP ideology: Surface and depth

As the BNP Leader Nick Griffin has himself noted, the BNP has its ideological roots 'in the sub-Mosleyite whackiness of Arnold Leese's Imperial Fascist League' (Griffin 2003, cited in Copsey 2007: 70). Arnold Leese has been described as the 'high priest' of British Nazism (Thayer 1965) and, until very recently, there were core members of the BNP who had been his contemporaries in the 1950s – John Bean, for example, the last editor of the BNP's magazine *Identity*. In essence, the BNP's political ideology still draws strength from Leese's antisemitic racial fascism and remains committed to the racial purification of the national space by anti-democratic paramilitary means.

This is not to claim that the BNP core ideology is a simple mimetic reproduction of the concerns that dominated the fascist parties of the inter-war period. Nor do I regard the ideological commitments of the Imperial Fascist League (IFL), the British Union of Fascists (BUF) or any other fascist party of that period as a touchstone against which contemporary movements can be measured. As Paxton (2005: 14–15) has argued, such an emphasis on historic definitions provides 'a static picture of something that is better perceived in movement . . . It is like observing . . . birds mounted in a glass case instead of alive in their habitat'. Other political ideologies have mutated and transformed relative to changing social and political circumstances, so it would be odd to believe that fascism has not also.[1] Fascism is, as Weber (1964) put it, a dynamic but vague ideology, with few specific predetermined objectives, and is inherently prone to opportunist shifts. However, this much I believe we can argue – this much *does* remain a constant: when analysing the discourses of fascist parties and movements, 'more than in most others, it is essential to separate the propaganda from the real attitude in order to gain an understanding of its essential character' (Mannheim 1960: 120). The history and core ideology of the BNP are concealed from the wider public through the adoption of a 'dual style' of political communication: 'esoteric appeals' are used to communicate to 'intellectual' insiders and grossly simplified 'exoteric appeals' to address both the mass membership and the electorate (see Taylor 1979: 127). The current leader of the BNP, Nick Griffin, is on record as arguing explicitly for this Janus-faced communications policy. In an article published in the magazine *Patriot* shortly after his first trial for incitement to racial hatred, Griffin outlined to BNP activists his plans for 'modernization' of the party:

---

[1] Following Billig (1978) I argue that fascism is characterized by a shifting constellation of: (1) strong-to-extreme nationalism; (2) support for a capitalist political economy (given the nationalism, this is usually of an autarkic nature); (3) and opposition to communism (and any mobilization of the working class as a class for itself); (4) these are 'advocated in such a way that fascism will pose a direct threat to democracy and personal freedom' (p. 7). More specifically, fascism is a reactionary, nationalist and largely petty-bourgeois mass movement, which advocates, employs and/or tolerates violence against political opponents to further its goals. Fascism can rise to power as the 'party of counter-revolutionary despair' (Trotsky) during periods of hegemonic crisis and working class defeat.

As long as our own cadres understand the full implications of our struggle, then there is no need for us to do anything to give the public cause for concern . . . we must at all times present them with an image of moderate reasonableness . . . Of course, we must teach the truth to the hardcore, for, like you, I do not intend this movement to lose its way. But when it comes to influencing the public, forget about racial differences, genetics, Zionism, historical revisionism and so on – all ordinary people want to know is what we can do for them that the other parties can't or won't. (*Patriot*, No. 4, 1999)

The importance of this extract – acknowledging that the BNP adopts a 'moderate' public face to hide an ideological core – cannot be over-emphasized. Here, Griffin explicitly makes a distinction between exoteric and esoteric appeal, arguing that it is both possible and desirable to appeal to 'ordinary people' while teaching 'the truth to the hardcore' by more covert means. Further, the article indexes this strategy of exoteric/esoteric appeal in a more fundamental way. Even here, writing for party members on the subject of strategically moderating the BNP's 'careless extremism', Griffin partially conceals 'the truth' to which he and his party remain wedded: in British fascist discourse, 'racial differences' is a code for racial hierarchies; 'genetics' is a code for scientific racism, and theories of genetic racial superiority/inferiority more specifically; 'Zionism' is a code word for Jews, the 'Jewish Question' and the myth of a Jewish world conspiracy in particular (Billig 1978); and 'historical revisionism' refers to Holocaust denial. In their place, Griffin argues that the party needs to concentrate its propaganda on 'idealistic, unobjectionable, motherhood and apple pie concepts' (ibid.): freedom, democracy, security and identity (see Copsey 2007, 2008).

British National Party members

The actions of party leaders, members and supporters reveal an enduring commitment to fascist politics. To take an anecdotal example first, I personally took the photographs below (Figures 7.1a and 7.1b), at the BNP's *Red, White and Blue* Festival, in August 2009. The man, saluting the crowd I was part of, was later arrested by the attending police.

The man pictured below is by no means an aberrant case among BNP members. And, in case readers may feel I am selecting only the most extreme outlying members of the party, fascist tendencies can also be identified in the party's senior members. On the eve of the 2010 UK General Election, *Searchlight* published brief biographies of 19 BNP election candidates showing their commitment to racism and political extremism. Two of the more straightforwardly fascist of these included:

Barry Bennett (Parliamentary candidate for Gosport) who wrote the following on the Stormfront website: 'I believe in National Socialism, WW2 style, it was best, no other power had anything like it. The ideology was fantastic. The culture, nothing like it. If it was here now, I'd defect to Germany.'

Jeffrey Marshall (Eastbury ward, Barking and Dagenham Council), the Central London BNP organizer, who in response to the death of David Cameron's six-year-old

Figure 7.1a Fascist salutes at the BNP 'Red, White and Blue' festival, August 2009. © John E. Richardson.

son, wrote in an internet politics group: 'We live in a country today which is unhealthily dominated by an excess of sentimentality towards the weak and unproductive. No good will come of it . . . There is actually not a great deal of point in keeping these sort of people alive, after all' (see Williams and Cressy 2010: 12–13, Richardson 2011).

Given that the people above were selected to stand as parliamentary candidates, it should come as no surprise that the leadership of the party also has similar political inclinations. Nick Griffin has been a leading member of fascist parties since the 1970s – initially the National Front (NF), and later the International Third Position (ITP). He has also edited, written and published various fascist publications, including the pamphlet *Who are the MIND-BENDERS?* (Anon 1997), which drew on the antisemitic fraud the *Protocols* and adopted the structure of *Who Rules America?* written by an American neo-Nazi, William Pierce. In more detail, *Who are the MIND-BENDERS?* (ibid.) detailed the 'Jewish conspiracy' to brainwash the British (white) people in their own country. In this pamphlet, Griffin claimed: 'The mass media in Britain today have managed to implant into many people's minds the idea that it is "anti-Semitic" even to acknowledge that members of the Jewish community play a large part in controlling our news'. Jews are also accused of 'providing us with an endless diet of pro-multiracial, pro-homosexual, anti-British trash'.

Griffin has been prosecuted for incitement to racial hatred on two occasions – successfully in 1998 for Holocaust denial material published in his magazine *The Rune*, for which he received a nine-month suspended sentence. When interviewed by the police during this investigation, Griffin argued:

Figure 7.1b Fascist salutes at the BNP 'Red, White and Blue' festival, August 2009. © John E. Richardson.

[Griffin] I cannot see how any Jew should be upset, erm, if they find out that such large numbers of their people weren't horribly killed. It's good news! I can't see it's insulting to anybody....

[Police questioner] By promoting the fact that they believe, as history bears out, that the Holocaust occurred-

[Griffin] History does not bear that out.

[Police questioner] Well, the recognized history, for the majority of people then, the-

[Griffin] The orthodox history accepts it in the same way that people once thought that, erm, that the sun goes round the earth, yes.

He has never distanced himself from these statements. Indeed footage filmed by journalist Dominic Carman (Griffin's unofficial biographer), in 2004 using a concealed camera, shows he still believes 'The Jews' have 'simply bought the West, in terms of press and so on, for their own political ends', and 'If Hitler hadn't been so daft, they'd have exterminated the German Jews'.[2] I see little evidence in this of the claimed 'modernization' and rejection of fascist ideology in the BNP.

Griffin currently represents North England in the European Parliament, but until 2012 the BNP also had a second MEP, Andrew Brons, who represented Yorkshire and the Humber. Bron's links to British and European fascist movements go back

---

[2] <www.youtube.com/watch?v=9LR8-uXEHAM> [accessed 12 May 2010].

almost 50 years. A briefing document, produced by the campaigning website *Nothing British* on his election as an MEP, describes him as follows: 'Brons is a true ideologue from the National Socialist wing of the British politics. He is a strong believer in the pseudo-science of racial hygiene'.[3] In 1964, aged 17, he joined the National Socialist Movement, an organization deliberately founded on 20 April 1962 (Adolf Hitler's birthday) and led by Colin Jordan, the leading figure of post-war British Nazism. Throughout the 1960s, NSM members were responsible for an arson campaign against Jewish property and synagogues. In a letter to Jordan's wife, Françoise Dior – who was herself charged with arson attacks against London synagogues in 1965 – Brons said: 'I feel that our public image may suffer considerable damage as a result of these activities. I am however open to correction on this point.' Towards the end of the 1960s, with Jordan serving another jail term under the Public Order Act for a highly racist pamphlet *The Coloured Invasion*, Brons joined John Tyndall's Greater Britain Movement (GBM). This party was founded on what Tyndall termed 'British National Socialism', though its constitution looked as Nazi influenced as the NSM, arguing 'Only those of British or kindred Aryan blood should be members of the nation' and that 'The removal of the Jews from Britain must be a cardinal aim of the new order'. Brons then joined the NF, was voted onto its National Directorate in 1974, and became party Chairman in 1980, when Tyndall left to form his *New* National Front. His leadership of the NF did not lessen his contribution to street politics however, and in June 1984 Brons was convicted by Leeds magistrates of using insulting words and behaviour likely to cause a breach of the peace. The court heard how Brons and another NF member were heard shouting slogans such as 'Death to Jews', 'White Power' and 'National Front'.[4]

In a speech at the 2009 *Red, White and Blue* festival, Griffin acknowledged the ideological debt that the party owed to Brons, identifying him as the person who introduced distributism to party policy. Distributism (also known as distributionism, distributivism) is a political-economic theory developed chiefly by G. K. Chesterton and Hilaire Belloc in which the means of production (but *not* wealth) are spread as widely as possible, rather than concentrated in either the hands of the state or with a small number of monopolistic (*international*) corporations. It accepts the capitalist mode of production but seeks to restrict capitalist ownership within national boundaries and share the alleged benefits of the accumulation of surplus value among as many as possible. It is these commitments that made it attractive to fascists – an economic system that posits a spurious equality between the propertied classes and workers and which aims to insulate the Nation from the influence of 'International Finance'. As the organization Church in History Information Centre has argued, in a pamphlet written in *support* of Belloc:

> Belloc detested both international finance, which exploited and manipulated the ordinary working people, and Marxist socialism which, by making the state the owner of all productive wealth, would be destructive of freedom of the spirit. It was widely believed at the time that the leaders of both these forces were small

---

[3] <www.nothingbritish.com/research/> [accessed 30 January 2012].
[4] <www.nothingbritish.com/research/> [accessed 30 January 2012].

groups of Jews. Because of this, a negative feeling developed towards them . . . In this way, Belloc's campaigning against corruption in high places became entwined with opposition to certain rich and potentially influential Jews.

Distributism is not, in and of itself, antisemitic. However, it does provide another opportunity for British fascists to position finance capitalism and communism as tools of a single enemy: the 'International Jew'. Such a 'reconciliation of contradictions' (Billig 1978: 162) also brings a rhetorical benefit for fascist political campaigning:

> If both communism and capitalism are seen as common enemies in the same evil conspiracy then working-class support can be solicited with an anti-capitalist rhetoric and middle-class support can be solicited with an anti-communist rhetoric. The language of revolution can be used simultaneously with the language of tradition. (ibid.)

Distributism was also the basis of NF economic policy in the 1980s – as indicated by numerous articles that Brons wrote on the subject when he was a member – as well as other smaller British parties including International Third Position, The Voice of St George and Third Way. Griffin's spontaneous advocacy of Brons in this speech therefore indexes yet another ideological continuity with fascist parties of the recent past and signals, to those who understand the code, the continued commitment of the BNP leadership to antisemitic conspiracy theories.

BNP: Political associates

The BNP has links with parties and organizations, across Europe, which belong directly and clearly within the fascist political tradition. For example, Nick Griffin has long-standing personal associations with Roberto Fiore, the leader of Forza Nuova (FN). As Mammone (2009: 173) points out, 'the label neo-fascist is not usually disputed' by members of FN, 'indeed it would be difficult to deny this because they regularly organize pilgrimages to the tomb of Benito Mussolini in order to commemorate certain fascist anniversaries'. The friendship between Fiore and Griffin stretches back to the start of the 1980s, when Griffin was the leader of Young National Front. Wanted by Italian police in connection with his role in the Bolgona station bombing on 1 August 1980 – which killed 86 people and injured 260 others – Fiore was provided with a safe house in London, and eventually made a small fortune from employment and housing agencies for Italian and Spanish migrants he ran with the help of Griffin. Fiore also had a significant political influence on Griffin, leading him to introduce Evola-inspired 'Third Positionist' politics into the NF, and to develop the political soldier philosophy that would lead the NF down a pseudo-revolutionary cul-de-sac for the remainder of the decade. Fiore and Griffin remain close, with Fiore giving the keynote address at the BNP's 2009 *Red, White and Blue* festival. As part of his introduction to Fiore's speech, Griffin described him in glowing terms and acknowledged his influence on the British extreme right:

... this group of young Italians, basically the same age as us, but coming from a place where they had been engaged in a physical and also an intellectual struggle with the far left and with liberalism, which is far more honed than the nationalist movement in Britain had yet come to. But although they were the same age, they brought a huge amount in fact of experience and a new way of looking at things [. . . One of these Italians] who is now here with us, Roberto Fiore, who to my mind was really always the leader of that operation, and a tremendous influence for good on this party and our nationalist cause in Britain . . . a man who has had a great influence on nationalism all over Europe, Roberto Fiore.[5]

Members of the BNP are regularly welcomed at fascist meetings on mainland Europe. Among many activities recorded by Searchlight Magazine, four BNP activists attended the Nazi music and politics festival, Fest der Völker, in East Germany on 12 September 2009. Nina Brown, a BNP councillor in Brinsley (Nottingham) and her husband Dave Brown, also a Brinsley councillor and the BNP candidate for Broxtowe District Council, were photographed in front of 'a banner depicting two steel-helmeted soldiers of the German army and bearing the clapped-out fascist slogan Europe Awake!'.[6] Nina Brown spoke to the festival crowd, sharing the stage with leading European fascists in attendance, including Sweden's Dan Erikkson, a representative of the violent antisemitic Info14 network. Similarly, on 5 April 2009, the BNP Deputy Leader, Simon Darby, spoke at an international fascist conference in Milan, entitled 'Our Europe: Peoples and Traditions Against Banks and Big Powers'. Originally, the title of the conference was to be 'Our Europe: Peoples and Traditions Against Banks and Usury', but perhaps this reference to usury was thought to index the fascist pedigree of the conference to an unacceptable degree, given its historic importance in fascist discourse as ambivalent coded reference to Jews and to the mythic 'International Conspiracy' in particular.[7]

BNP: Ambivalent and open anti-Semitism

BNP literature is replete with references to vague or unidentified people who are working against the interests of Britons (i.e. white Britons). These people are a crucial link in the BNP's ideological chain – an explanation for why, in the words of the 'racial scientist' Philippe Rushton, whites have adopted ideologies that 'discourage nationalist and religious beliefs' (cited in Mehler 1989: 20). The explanation is 'the Jews'. For British fascists, 'it has long been axiomatic that multiculturalism is a Jewish conspiracy' (Copsey 2007: 74). It is the Jew ('*Der Jude*' in Nazi argumentation), the arch-internationalist architect of both communism and capitalism, who is the real enemy of the nationalist; it is the Jew that is responsible for mass immigration, in a bid to weaken the white race; it is the Jew that has pulled the wool over the eyes of

---

[5] <http://bnptv.org.uk/2009/08/italian-roberto-fiore-of-the-forza-nuova-party/> [accessed 30 January 2012].

[6] hopenothate.org.uk/news/article/1356/midlands-bnp-officers-speak-at-german-neo-naz

[7] <www.indymedia.org.uk/en/2009/04/426708.html> or <www.hopenothate.org.uk/news/article/1145/bnp-deputy-leader-addresses-international-fas> [both accessed 30 January 2012].

white people, through their control of the mass media (see Billig 1978 for an extensive discussion, Nugent & King 1979). Significant portions of the BNP remain wedded to such antisemitic conspiracy theories and to Holocaust denial. For example, just before the 2010 General Election, Alby Walker, the Stoke BNP council group leader and local branch organizer, left the party and announced on a regional BBC programme that 'there's a vein of Holocaust denying within the BNP that I cannot identify myself with. They've still got senior members of the BNP who will be candidates in the general election that have Nazi, Nazi-esque sympathies.'[8]

At points in the history of British fascism, this *Judenhass* has been open and unambiguous. However, given the overwhelming distaste for political anti-Semitism, and its association with Nazism and the Holocaust, references in modern fascist literature to this conspiracy are almost always coded, even in esoteric arguments. There are, instead, frequent ambivalent references to the men in 'International Finance', unnamed-but-financially-powerful-string-pullers, 'big business', money power, the backers of international political or economic institutions (e.g. the EU, the IMF, the UN) and, increasingly, globalists.

A casual intertextual reference is also another principal way in which an adept writer can index the antisemitic conspiracy theory. As Copsey points out:

> The January 2005 issue of *Identity* featured an article entitled 'The Hidden Hand' that argued that, as the work of the likes of the British conspiracy theorist A. K. Chesterton had shown, the Bilderberg Group was taking all the major decisions affecting the world and that its final goal was one of world dictatorship. (2007: 77)

Fascist initiates would not have missed the significance of an article on global conspiracy, with such a headline, that also referred to the work of A. K. Chesterton. Chesterton was a key figure in the development of British fascism, being a leading member of the British Union of Fascists in the 1930s, the leader of the League of Empire Loyalists in the 1950–60s and the first Chairman of the NF from 1967. As late as 1996, the catalogue for the BNP Book Service still sold Chesterton's conspiracy text *The New Unhappy Lords*. This book asks the question 'Are these master manipulators and master-conspirators Jewish?', and takes over 200 pages to answer:

> . . . almost certainly 'yes'. Whether or not One World is the secret final objective of Zionism, World Jewry is the most powerful single force on earth and it follows that all major policies which have been ruthlessly pursued through the last several decades must have had the stamp of Jewish approval. (Chesterton 1965: 204)

The Hidden Hand was an alternative title for the viciously antisemitic magazine *Jewry über alles*, published in the 1920s by The Britons and still advertised for sale in British publications, such as *Spearhead*, throughout the 1970s and 1980s. Referring to Chesterton's work and invoking *The Hidden Hand* – in this 2005 article in the BNP's

---

[8] David Walker (2010) Dissident derails Stoke BNP election campaign, *Searchlight Online*.<www.searchlightmagazine.com/index.php?link=template&story=320> [accessed 3 November 2011].

leading magazine – demonstrates an unbroken link back through the 'populist' fascism of the 1970s, British National Socialism in the 1960s as far as the British Union of Fascists and National Socialists in the 1930s. The intertextual reference is a favourite method of the modern-day fascist, in which they hide their devotion to antisemitic conspiracy theories in clear view.

The English Defence League

At the time of writing, the EDL is not, and does not consider itself to be, a political party, 'but a grass-roots single-issue movement. The EDL is best understood as a right-wing social movement, that deploys mass mobilization, or the threat of mass mobilization, as its prime source of influence' (Copsey 2010: 11, see also Jackson 2011b). The lack of centralized management makes the politics and discourse of the EDL less controlled, and hence more heterogeneous, than with most political parties. The EDL were formed on, or immediately before, 27 June 2009 at an anti-Muslim demonstration at a mosque in the East End of London. The formation of the EDL occurred, at least initially, outside the influence of traditional fascist, far- and extreme-right parties, such as the NF and the BNP. A variety of small 'ultra-patriotic' groups developed to fight the (perceived) greater influence of Islam in the British public sphere, and specifically in response to the hostile reception several small Islamist groups gave to some British soldiers returning from service in Afghanistan (Copsey 2010, Bartlett & Littler 2011). These groups banded together, initially under the name of the English and Welsh Defence League. They were later joined by the members of Casuals United – a football 'hooligan' organization, aimed at putting aside the differences between fans of rival football teams in order to fight 'the enemies of our nation, those who wish to enslave and or murder us'.[9]

The size of the EDL is difficult to measure accurately, due to the nature of the movement itself: there is no official membership nor any formal joining procedure; most of the recorded discourse of the EDL takes place on social forums, such as Facebook, between individuals who voluntarily 'like' the movement. However, using such groups as a means of recruiting a sample of respondents, one recent study has estimated the 'membership' of the EDL to be between 25,000–35,000 people (Bartlett & Littler 2011). Of these, 'around half have been involved in demonstrations and/or marches' (ibid.: 4) while the remainder could perhaps be better categorized as sympathizers. The number of activists is therefore roughly comparable to the BNP membership at the height of the party's popularity.

The success of the EDL – which within six months was able to organize demonstrations of 1,500 people (Copsey 2010) – took many people by surprise. Indeed the achievements of EDL led rivals from Britain's fascist fringe to cast doubts on the origins and motivations of the movement's organizers. Predictably, the leadership of the BNP alleged that the movement was evidence of a 'Zionist' conspiracy, based upon

---

[9] See Casual United blog. <http://casualsunited.wordpress.com/photos/> [accessed 3 November 2011].

the support that the tabloid newspaper the *Daily Star* gave to them. In a recorded conversation broadcast on a BNP multimedia website, Nick Griffin and Simon Darby discussed the EDL in some depth. Darby opens the subject, introducing the conspiracy:

> Darby: It's been set up by a powerful organisation. People with the power to manipulate, who are used to manipulating and have the organisational structure, the facility and the financial clout to promote it.
>
> Griffin: Let's spell it out shall we? . . . Spelling it out in simple terms, you look at the owners of the *Daily Express*, the *Daily Star* and their interests. This is a neo-con operation. This is a Zionist false flag operation, designed to create a real clash of civilisations right here on our streets between Islam and the rest of us.[10]

In interviews, the leadership of the EDL has always strenuously denied that it is a far-right or even a racist movement, pointing to their Sikh and Jewish Divisions and their few Black members as evidence.[11] However, it is clear that the movement has attracted far-right activists since its very earliest days, and now counts neo-Nazi factions within its ranks. Copsey (2010) details the role that BNP activists such as Chris Renton, Peter Fehr, Laurence Jones and Chris Mitchell have played in the development of the movement, and points out that members of the BNP and the NF, including the leader Tom Holmes, have been present at their demonstrations. The influence of such people, in the run-up to the breakthrough demonstration in Birmingham (8 August 2009), led EDL organizer Paul Ray to claim that neo-Nazis had 'hijacked the movement' (quoted in Copsey 2010: 13). 'Anyone with the slightest bit of knowledge about neo-Nazis', he argued, 'knows the meaning of 8/8 [the date the demonstration was planned] which is why I pulled out of any active participation' (ibid.) – 88 standing for the eighth letter of the alphabet, giving HH or Heil Hitler.

However, for the most part, EDL supporters and EDL ideology accord with the 'new wave of populist, nativist far-right politics sweeping Europe' (Jackson 2011a: 7). The key themes of their still developing ideology – communicated via Facebook, Youtube and blogs of members and affiliated groups – appear to draw most strongly on 'ethno-nationalism based on "cultural racism" . . . [and] anti-political establishment rhetoric' (Rydgren 2005: 416). Their arguments are populist, aimed at demonstrating that the needs and sensitivities of the common (working-class) Englishman are being ignored, and that their grievances are caused by a Muslim folk devil who political élites pander to in order to serve their own interests. The ideology is therefore specific enough that it provides 'followers [with] a clear sense of how to frame and interpret their grievances with the wider world' and yet flexible enough that it allows for 'a wide range of seemingly unrelated social issues to be refracted through the unifying lens

---

[10] <www.hopenothate.org.uk/blog/article/520/bnp-blame-zionists-for-edl> [accessed 30 January 2012].

[11] For example, Tommy Robinson (real name Stephen Yaxley-Lennon) was interviewed on the flagship BBC news programme Newsnight on 1 February 2011 and again on 25 July 2011. For footage of this second interview, see <www.youtube.com/watch?v=4RdJ4dpRQeE>. He was interviewed on the ITV morning show Daybreak two days later <www.youtube.com/watch?v=_ZpdhdUOoJ4> [both links accessed 30 January 2012].

of perceived injustices' (Jackson 2011a: 9). It is recognizably far right due to the way it links steep national decline to a (racialized) scapegoat figure, and populist in the ways this decline is blamed on 'the neglect of the political elite . . . It is a tenor that can connect individual instances of alleged corruption and decay to an overarching narrative of future crisis and decline' (ibid.).

Jackson (2011a) details the ways in which the ideology of the EDL has developed since the formation of the movement, and its relations with fellow travellers of the extreme right. What is key here, at least in my view, is the potential for their populist ethno-nationalism to develop into a more fully fledged conspiracy theory. It is only a small inductive leap from claiming that a political élite panders to immigrant communities, to their own advantage and against the interests of the (white) majority, to asking who these political élites are, and perhaps pointing an accusing finger. Indeed, recently, the leader of the radical splinter group within the EDL, The Infidels – a group mainly based in the north of England – has discovered the infamous antisemitic tract *The Protocols of the Elders of Zion*. Writing on his Facebook page, John 'Snowy' Shaw declared that the book has already begun to make things 'click' in his head, and suggests that 'all true British patriots take the time to read this'.[12]

In keeping with such ideological developments, the actions of EDL activists have recently taken on a more threatening air. For instance, elsewhere on the Facebook walls of members of the EDL, 'we can find references to neo-Nazi rallying cries such as David Lane's 14 Words slogan' (Jackson 2011a: 18). Anders Behring Breivik, the far-right terrorist convicted of murdering 77 people on 22 July 2011, was in contact with the EDL through Facebook groups and may have met leaders of the EDL during a visit to London in March 2010.[13] The willingness of the EDL to use violence against political enemies is reflected in the data collected by Bartlett and Littler (2011: 23): they show that 37 per cent of their respondents (n = 1,295) 'agree entirely' or 'agree a little' with the statement that in certain circumstances it can be acceptable to use violence to achieve political goals. And when asked what they rated as their most important personal value, bottom of their respondents' lists were tolerance (9%) and respect for other cultures (3%) (ibid.: 24). Indeed, EDL rallies and demonstrations have always been marked by violence, harassment and arrests (Copsey 2010, Jackson 2011b).[14] The violent activities of the EDL and their various splinter groups are likely to continue in the near future, just as their ideological arguments and explanations are likely to continue to develop.

Conclusion

There remains a constituency of the British population which remains attracted to anti-egalitarian politics *in extremis*, whose views fascist political parties accommodate in

---

[12] <www.hopenothate.org.uk/blog/article/1287/infidel-leader-praises-the-protocols> [accessed 30 January 2012].
[13] <www.telegraph.co.uk/news/worldnews/europe/norway/8661139/Norway-killer-Anders-Behring-Breivik-had-extensive-links-to-English-Defence-League.html> and <www.guardian.co.uk/world/2011/jul/23/norway-attacks-utoya-gunman> [both accessed 30 January 2012].
[14] www.indymedia.org.uk/en/2011/10/487677.html?c=on#c274923> and <http://blog.fredrikwalloe.com/2011/10/edl-supporters-attack-occupy-newcastle.html> [both accessed 30 January 2012].

order to attract and retain them as activists. However, while they need to communicate to such people, they cannot alienate the more sizable rump of the country who 'simply' oppose immigration, or think that there are too many jobs/homes/opportunities going to 'non-British' people. This, and the obvious legal restrictions on open hate speech, has meant that extreme-right wing parties have developed ambiguous and coded ways of constructing arguments, of referring to social problems and proposing (final) solutions. Ironically, it seems that many people attracted to parties like the BNP do not understand this rich tradition of double-talk. Periodically, factions break off to form more openly extreme organizations that speak more directly about conspiracies etc., before eventually attenuating their position to gain support, and so setting up another cycle of splits. Currently, we are witnessing such a period within the BNP – which may not exist by the time this chapter is published, or at least will be a party greatly changed by internal feuding and legal investigations for breaches of electoral law. But whatever the future for the BNP, the mixed constituency to which it speaks – from the unrepentant National Socialist to the conservative rural shopkeeper concerned to 'keep out' asylum seekers – will still exist, and so will continue to act as a driver for political agitation.

In some ways the EDL appears to be something new in Britain. Their fusion of ultra-patriotism, 'traditional English values', cyber-activism and street violence has acted like a lightning rod for a wide assortment of activists, from far- and extreme-right racists to anti-Muslim defenders of 'liberal values'. The EDL, like other 'new far-right' groups across Europe, 'lay claim to the mantle of the enlightenment, espousing support for fundamental liberal values of free speech, democracy and equality' (Bartlett & Littler 2011: 7) while simultaneously aiming to deny these same rights to those whose 'culture' – acting as a homologue for race – they deem to be threateningly different. A binary is constructed in EDL ideological discourse wherein Western culture is deemed tolerant and progressive and Islam is deemed intolerant and backward (Jackson 2011b). Accordingly, the EDL must protect Western tolerance by not tolerating intolerant Muslims; their stated objectives, to protect liberality and the Rule of Law, act as little more than a pretext for xenophobia, bigotry and violent criminality; and this mismatch between words and deed allows a space wherein supporters are able to associate themselves with either (both?) their tolerant/law-abiding aims and/or their intolerant/ law-breaking activities. Though clearly riven with contradictions, this strategy appears to have gained ground, as evidenced by the large numbers of demonstrators and supporters the EDL has attracted in a short period of time. Despite, or perhaps because of, this success, the future of the movement currently looks uncertain, due to a variety of intense rivalries – both political and between opposing football hooligan 'firms' – that continue to surface in their ranks.

References

Bartlett, J. and Littler, M. (2011), *Inside the EDL: Populist Politics in a Digital Age*, London: Demos.

Billig, M. (1978), *Fascists: A Social Psychological View of the National Front*, London: Harcourt Brace Jovanovitch.

Copsey, N. (2007), 'Changing course or changing clothes? Reflections on the ideological evolution of the British National Party 1999–2006', *Patterns of Prejudice*, 41(1): 61–82.
— (2008), *Contemporary British Fascism: The British National Party and the Quest for Legitimacy*, 2nd edn, Basingstoke: Palgrave-Macmillan.
— (2010), *The English Defence League: Challenging our Country and our Values of Social Inclusion, Fairness and Equality*, Research Report for Faith Matters.
Fella, S. (2008), Britain: Imperial Legacies, Institutional Constraints and New Political Opportunities, in D. Albertazzi and D. McDonnell (eds), *Twenty-First Century Populism: The Spectre of Western European Democracy*, Houndmills: Palgrave, pp.181–97.
Jackson, P. (2011a), 'English Defence League: Anti-Muslim politics online', in P. Jackson, and G. Gable (eds), *Far-Right.Com: Nationalist Extremism on the Internet*, Northampton: RNM Publications, pp. 7–20.
— (2011b), *The EDL: Britain's Far Right Social Movement*, Northampton: RNM Publications.
Mammone, A. (2009), '*The Eternal Return?* Faux Populism and Contemporarization of Neo-Fascism across Britain, France and Italy', *Journal of Contemporary European Studies*, 17(2): 171–92.
Mannheim, K. (1960), *Ideology and Utopia*, London: Routledge & Kegan Paul.
Mastropaolo, A. (2008), 'Politics against democracy: Party withdrawal and populist breakthrough', in D. Albertazzi and D. McDonnell (eds), *Twenty-First Century Populism: The Spectre of Western European Democracy*, Houndmills: Palgrave, pp. 30–48.
Mehler, B. (1989), 'Foundation for Fascism: the New Eugenics Movement in the United States', *Patterns of Prejudice*, 23(4): 17–25.
Mudde, C. (2007), *Populist Radical Right Parties in Europe*, Cambridge: Cambridge University Press.
Nugent, N. and King, R. (1979), 'Ethnic minorities, scapegoating and the extreme right', in R. Miles and A. Phizacklea (eds), *Racism and Political Action*, London: Routledge & Kegan Paul. pp. 28–49.
Paxton, R. O. (2005), *The Anatomy of Fascism*, New York: Vintage.
Richardson, J. E. (2011), 'Race and Racial Difference: The Surface and Depth of BNP Ideology', in N. Copsey and G. Macklin (eds), *British National Party: Contemporary Perspectives*, London: Routledge, pp. 38–61.
Richardson, J. E. and Wodak, R. (2009a), 'The Impact of Visual Racism: Visual Arguments in Political Leaflets of Austrian and British Far-right Parties', *Controversia*, 6(2): 45–77.
— (2009b), 'Recontextualising Fascist Ideologies of the Past: Right-wing Discourses on Employment and Nativism in Austria and the United Kingdom', *Critical Discourse Studies*, 6(4): 251–67.
Rydgren, J. (2005), 'Is Extreme-right Wing Populism Contagious? Explaining the Emergence of a New Political Family', *European Journal of Political Research*, 44: 413–37.
Taylor, S. (1979), 'The National Front: Anatomy of a political movement', in R. Miles and A. Phizacklea (eds), *Racism and Political Action*, London: Routledge & Kegan Paul, pp. 125–46.
Thayer, G. (1965), *The British Political Fringe*, London: Anthony Blond.
Weber, E. (1964), *Varieties of Fascism*, Princeton, NJ: D. Van Nostrand.
Williams, D. and Cressy, S. (2010) 'New BNP? Same Old Nazis and Thugs', *Searchlight*, May 2010, 120–17.

Primary sources

Anon. [attributed to Nick Griffin] (1997), *Who are the MIND-BENDERS?* [pamphlet].

Chesterton, A. K. (1965), *The New Unhappy Lords,* London: Candour Publishing Co.

Church in History Information Centre (n.d.), *In Defence of Hilaire Belloc* [pamphlet].

Griffin, N. (1999) 'BNP – Freedom Party!', Patriot no. 4 Spring 1999, reproduced at www.
whatnextjournal.co.uk/Pages/Politics/Griffin.html [consulted 12 October 2012].

— (2003) 'At the crossroads', *Identity*, no. 34, July 2003.

8

Contemporary Forms of Racist Movements and Mobilization in Britain

John Solomos

During the first two decades of the twenty-first century we have seen important transformations in both the ideologies and organizational forms of racist, extreme right and populist movements and political parties. These transformations have been particularly important within both the political cultures and civil society in contemporary European societies. In the British context, the efforts by the British National Party (BNP) to rebrand itself as an ethno-nationalist movement have been a key feature of this period, even if their efforts have met with only limited success. The foundation of the English Defence League (EDL), in 2009, as a street-level direct-action movement aimed at countering forms of radical Muslim mobilization and a perceived threat to national identity as a result of immigration, represents another important innovation in far-right mobilizations over recent years. In Britain, as well as various other European societies, such movements and parties have sought to mobilize support by focusing on such issues as immigration and asylum, the role of radical political Islam and terrorism, economic crisis and social dislocation, and fears about the impact of greater religious and cultural diversity (Eatwell & Goodwin 2010). More specifically, they have been able to develop their political language in such a way as to articulate what they perceive as new discourses about race, culture and national identity that have formed the basis of their evolving political strategies and agendas (Eatwell & Mudde 2004, Eatwell & Goodwin 2010, Bleich 2011, Goodwin 2011a). They have also been able to seek to give voice to popular concerns within sections of white working-class communities about their seeming marginalization in the face of the growing role of racial and ethnic diversity (John & Margetts 2009, Cutts et al. 2010).

These broad developments have helped to reshape the role of the racist right as both a social and political force and have created the potential for these movements and parties to play an important role in influencing both public debates and policy interventions on issues such as immigration, multicultural policies and integration strategies. Over the same period, there has been intense debate within political institutions as well as in civil society about how best to develop strategies for responding to the growth of extreme right and racist movements and parties (Lentin 2004, Ford & Goodwin 2010).

Much of this debate has been framed by a concern to develop anti-racist initiatives that will provide an alternative to the political language of the extreme right, as well as potentially reducing, in the medium term, the basis of support for racist movements and parties.

In this environment it is important for researchers to try to understand the conditions that have led to the current situation and to make sense of the likely impact of these trends on political mobilizations by the extreme right in specific countries. The various chapters in this collection are tied together by a common concern to frame and analyse the changing role of right-wing racist populism across a range of national and regional contexts. The concerns of this chapter are linked to this common concern as well, but it will focus on two key issues in order to give more depth to our analysis. First are the changing forms of extreme right mobilizations in contemporary British society, including the evolving role of the BNP and the EDL. In looking at this issue we shall, in particular, seek to place the contemporary forms of mobilization and activism within a broader historical context. Second, we shall explore the challenges posed by new forms of racist and populist mobilizations for the development of anti-racist strategies. It will be argued that it is important to situate the contemporary role of the BNP and EDL in a wider historical context, reflecting the evolving and changing politics of immigration and race within British society over the past few decades (for a somewhat different account of this history see Richardson 2011, 2012). Issues such as immigration, race relations and cultural and religious diversity are at the heart of the political impact of organizations such as the BNP. At the same time, during the past decade, we have seen some significant changes in the ways in which racist movements have mobilized. In the British context, the mix of 9/11, urban unrest and 7/7 helped to push the extreme right to mobilize around issues of religion and cultural identity as well as immigration and race relations. This chapter will look at the role of these mobilizations in shaping the political and ideological formations of the extreme right. It will also explore the shifting forms of political mobilization among the extreme right as well as the responses of policy-makers and civil-society actors to their growing popularity.

Situating racist and extreme right-wing movements

Political and social movements espousing racist and populist extreme-right ideologies may have grown substantially in the past two decades, but we should not lose sight of the reality that they have a longer-term history. In the case of Britain, for example, they have been a feature of political debates about race and immigration from the 1960s and 1970s onwards (Billig 1978, Walker 1978, Fielding 1981, Husbands 1983). Indeed, since the 1970s, a number of extreme right-wing movements have sought to develop a broader political base, often using a mixture of neo-fascist ideas, anti-immigrant feelings and ethno-nationalist sentiment in their rhetoric and political language (Billig 1978, Thurlow 1998). Such movements have gone through cycles of growing support both nationally and in specific localities, and they have managed to gain a voice in public debates about race and immigration. They have on the whole remained at the margins of political institutions and have not succeeded in gaining a strong foothold either in national political institutions or in local government. At various points since the 1970s, however, racist populist mobilizations have succeeded in giving a high profile to the extreme right as a social and political force. During the 1970s and early 1980s, this was the case with the National Front (NF), which gained a degree of support in some areas and became a focus for public concern about the influence of racial populism. Subsequently, much of the attention shifted to the BNP, which has been the most prominent movement with a national as well as a local presence. For both of these movements, questions about immigration and race, the rights of the white majority in Britain and the threats posed by increasing cultural diversity have constituted a core element of their political language.

During the past two decades in particular, an important element in the rhetoric and the practice of such mobilizations has shifted to questions such as religious diversity, the impact of immigration on white working-class communities and on the threats posed by radical political Islam. In the late 1990s and 2000s, much of the rhetoric of the BNP shifted towards mobilizations focused on popular fears and concerns within the white majority communities, both nationally and locally. This approach became most clear in the political strategies developed by the BNP under the leadership of Nick Griffin since 1999 (Copsey 2008, Copsey & Macklin 2011, Goodwin 2011b). The BNP can, in some ways, be seen as a movement that espouses ideas with a familial similarity to the earlier racist movements, such as the NF, but it is also the case that they have been adept at representing themselves as racial populists whose concern is to protect the rights of the white British majority in this evolving and changing social and political environment (Rhodes 2006, Wemyss 2006). Perhaps the highpoint of this strategy was the election, in the June 2009 European Elections, of two BNP members to the European Parliament, namely Nick Griffin and Andrew Brons, with 943,000 votes cast for the party nationally. In the aftermath of this relative success there was intense public debate as well as media-led discussion about both the reasons for the support that the BNP attracted and how best to develop both national and local strategies to counter their ideas and influence (Hartley-Brewer 2009, Rhodes 2009, Ford 2010).

From the NF to the BNP

The rise of the NF during the 1970s as a more or less credible political force was intimately linked to the politicization of immigration and race relations. Indeed there was serious concern during the late 1970s and early 1980s that the NF might become an established entity on the formal political scene. The history and political impact of the NF have been paid considerable attention by academics. There have been a number of studies of its rise and decline, and of the social context of the support received by it and other neo-fascist and racist political groups (Fielding 1981, Thurlow 1998). In addition, a number of studies have explored the role of racialized ideologies and the prospect of the future mobilization of racist beliefs and ideologies by political parties and movements. These studies, written mostly between the 1970s and the early 1990s, focused on the impact of the NF on both local and national political life.

The NF was founded in 1967 as a united organization of groups with neo-fascist and anti-immigration views. One of the primary motivations for its formation was the perception among extreme-right activists that immigration and race-related issues were being relatively neglected by the mainstream political parties. This was seen as providing an opportunity for a party openly committed to the defence of racial purity and to a clear anti-immigration stance to capture support from both of the main political parties. As a union of the right-wing BNP and the League of Empire Loyalists, the NF inherited the ideological baggage of anti-Semitism and resistance to Britain's post-war decolonization, two prominent themes among far right-wing political groups in the 1960s and 1970s. In its political rhetoric, it made clear its links to the politics of anti-Semitism and its commitment to a nationalist ideology based on racial purity (Thurlow 1975, 1976).

Research, on the social basis of support for the NF and other racist political groups, revealed two important features. First, some research argued that it was important to look at social and economic factors in order to understand the attraction of sections of the white working class to the politics of the NF. Scholars such as Phizacklea and Miles, for example, explored the changing dynamics of working class support for the NF in specific parts of the country (Miles & Phizacklea 1979, Phizacklea & Miles 1980). Drawing on research conducted in London, they argued that one of the most important factors in the growth of support for racist political groups was the economic and social restructuring of many inner-city working-class areas (Phizacklea & Miles 1980). Based on a study of NF support in localities such as the East End area of London, Husbands argued that it was particularly important to look at the influence of such issues as the presence of black communities, changes in the national and local politics of race and the restructuring of local political economies in order to understand the level and solidity of NF support in some areas and its relative weakness in others (Husbands 1983). Hence these studies emphasized the need to locate the support for racism in a wider social, economic and geographical context. A similar theme was taken up by Cashmore in his detailed analysis of the social basis of racism in Birmingham and its environs during the 1980s (Cashmore 1987).

But it is important not to lose sight of the part played by broader transformations in politics and ideology in the mobilization of this support. It is interesting to remember, for example, that during the 1970s and early 1980s both the Conservative Party and the Labour Party lost voters to the NF. Throughout the 1970s, the NF's membership and level of electoral support ebbed and flowed with the tide of political debate on, and public controversy over, racial questions. Its membership rose from 14,000 to 20,000 between 1972 and 1974, at the height of the arrival of the Ugandan Asians. In 1973 it achieved a vote of 16.2 per cent in the West Bromwich by-election, and it also achieved respectable results in local elections in 1976 and the London local elections in 1977. This level of support was not maintained, however, and fell dramatically during the 1980s, particularly as the Conservative Party adopted a hard-line stance on immigration and the 'swamping' of British culture as a result of immigration (Thurlow 1998, Copsey 2008).

From its foundation, the issue of black immigration occupied a central place in the NF's political rhetoric and propaganda. Despite periodic attempts by its leadership to broaden the movement's appeal and political platform, immigration and race remained the two most salient issues among its members and sympathizers during the 1970s. It was the ability of the party to play on this issue at both local and national level that enabled it to mobilize electoral support and attract members. The political discourses of the NF, as well as those of subsequent neo-fascist political groupings, resonated with references to racial purity, cultural superiority or difference and defence of 'the nation'. Indeed, according to the NF, the main threats to Britain were immigration and racial mixing. The alien, the stranger and the 'subhuman' were common themes, and the anti-Semitism embedded in the pages of the main neo-fascist journals tied them closely to Nazi ideology. What was also at play in the ever-changing politics of the extreme right was an attempt to create a mass nationalist movement that would attract popular support on a scale never before witnessed in Britain.

After the election of the first Thatcher government in 1979, there was a decline in the electoral success of the NF, and during the 1980s it splintered into various factions. This has been interpreted from a number of perspectives as indicating the marginalization of the racist message the NF was propounding, as the outcome of the absorption of some of the NF's ideas by mainstream political parties and as the result of factional strife and conflict within the racist groups themselves. It is also important to note that this was a period of important anti-racist mobilization in the political and culture spheres. During the late 1970s and early 1980s, the activities of the NF also became the focus of anti-racist political actions orchestrated by the Anti-Nazi League and Rock against Racism, which helped to counter the NF's claim to be a defender of the national interest and to spread awareness of the political dangers that its growth as a major political force presented (Gilroy 1987).

Evolving forms of racial populism

During most of the 1980s and 1990s, the BNP noticeably failed to have any significant impact on electoral politics. Although it became the most successful organization to emerge from the collapse of the NF, the BNP struggled for some time to escape the links it shared with earlier racist movements and ideologies. It founder, John Tyndall, was linked to the neo-Nazi political groupings of the 1960s and 1970s. In his personal monthly journal, *Spearhead*, he espoused a mixture of anti-immigration politics, anti-Semitism and ethno-national politics. Initially, the BNP did not have the degree of national attention garnered by the NF in the 1970s, but it did have some success in particular localities. In 1993, for example, BNP member Derek Beackon briefly held the Millwall ward in the London borough of Tower Hamlets. After his surprise victory in the by-election, Beackon commented 'I put my own people first – by that I mean white people' (*Independent on Sunday*, 19 September 1993). Beackon's success was short-lived and the BNP did not gain the foothold in local politics it had hoped for. It continued to be active in some localities throughout the 1990s, but it too suffered from factionalism and splits. Part of its political agenda during the 1990s was its adoption of a nationalist rhetoric. In its newspaper, the *British Nationalist*, there was constant emphasis on the need for the party to fight for the interests of the white majority in British society, and a call for the adoption of the Union Jack by its members as a symbol of their political stance. By the late 1990s the BNP was also showing an interest in developing an electoral strategy to gain influence in both national and local politics.

This was perhaps reflective of a broader shift by sections of the extreme right towards a more overt nationalist political stance, and particularly by one of the rising young leaders of the organization, Nick Griffin, who had been active in the NF and was a member of one of the 'third position' factions that had emerged from the split in the early 1980s. In the mid-1990s, he became active in the BNP and was involved in the editing of *Spearhead* and another journal called *Rune*. He gained a sufficient power base to challenge Tyndall for leadership of the BNP and became its leader in 1999. Although Griffin retained some of the NF's political rhetoric on race and immigration, he sought to reinvent the party in order to give it a broader electoral appeal. In one sense his vision of the BNP involved its evolution along the path of racial populism similar to Le Pen's Front National.

As part of its new electoral strategy, the BNP sought to gain a higher profile for its candidates in both national and local elections. This became evident in the 1997 general election and was taken further during the 2001, 2005 and, most recently, 2010 general elections. The urban unrest in Oldham, Burnley and Bradford featured prominently in the BNP's electoral strategy for the 2001 general election and it stood for 33 seats, gaining an average of 3.9 per cent of the votes. Its most successful result was Nick Griffin's 16.4 per cent in Oldham West and Royton. The BNP also did relatively well in Burnley, Bradford and in parts of the West Midlands and East London. Encouraged by this performance, the BNP adopted a similarly aggressive electoral strategy in the 2005 and 2010 general elections. It met with mixed results on the ground though this strategy highlighted the potential of the BNP's approach in particular localities.

This relative success encouraged the BNP to move further towards presenting itself as essentially a white nationalist party. Through the late 1990s and 2000s, it refashioned itself as a party focused on issues such as radical Islam, asylum-seekers and gaining rights for whites on a range of social and economic issues, including housing, crime and the environment. The 9/11 terrorist attacks in New York and the 7/7 terrorist attacks in London encouraged the BNP to give a higher profile to its attacks on Islam, framed around its idea that the West needed to be defended against the enemies within as well as without. More importantly, it refashioned itself through this period around ideas of national identity and white nationalism.

The past and the present

Perhaps the most important lesson to be learnt from the experiences of the past two decades or so is that racist mobilizations are constantly evolving and changing, as demonstrated by the emergence of new forms of racist politics, violent attacks on ethnic minority people and a rapid expansion in the use of cultural symbols by racist and neo-fascist movements. This has been the subject of considerable journalistic attention and research over the past few years, with wide-ranging discussions in the press and among researchers and policy-makers on the origins of these new racist activities and their impact on specific environments. A good case in point is the strategy that the BNP has adopted over the past decade of developing local and community-based forms of political mobilization. The mobilization of support for the BNP on a local basis has taken a number of forms, including attempts to play on fears about the impact of immigration, the role of Islam in British society as well as more localized concerns about housing and access to public services (Rhodes 2011, Bloch et al. forthcoming). In areas such as Burnley, Dagenham and Luton, the exploitation of anti-Muslim attitudes has been an important theme in its local propaganda.

Perhaps the most important theme in contemporary political discourses on race in Britain, even after successive attempts to institutionalize anti-discrimination policies, is the portrayal of the whole of black and ethnic minority communities, or particular groups of them, as a threat to the unity and order of British society. One way in which this tendency is expressed is in attempts to attribute the persistence of racial inequality not to racism but to the presence of black minorities and the problems that result from their presence. This is by no means unique to the post-1945 period or to Britain. Edelman (1971), writing about the United States, shows how, in situations of conflict and protest, one of the ways in which dominant groups or political institutions defend themselves is to rationalize the events as the product of outsiders whose social and moral values are removed from those of society as a whole. For example, referring to the race riots of the 1960s, he argues that the dominant élite attempted to reduce the political impact of the events by portraying them as the work of enemies of American society and its values.

In Britain, in the 1990s and 2000s, the new right portrayed black and ethnic minority communities not as an enemy from without but as an enemy within: as endangering the cultural and political values of the nation. Meanwhile, the media depicted them as a threat to the way of life of the white population and as being difficult to integrate into mainstream British society. More recently, Muslims have been portrayed as a kind of fifth column, particularly at times of global tension, and other racialized groups, such as refugees and asylum-seekers, have been said to pose a threat to cultural and religious unity.

An integral part of the BNP's political strategy since the 1990s can be seen in its adoption of a political rhetoric that draws on a self-image of the party as one of the silent white minority communities, particularly those in areas that have been transformed by immigration and religious and cultural diversity. It has sought, in particular, to play on fears about the loss of voice and rights for the white majority communities. It is interesting that the BNP has sought to play on white working fears about immigration and race by using slogans such as 'People Like You' on billboards in the period leading to the 2009 European elections.

The growing importance of Islam in the political language of the BNP is another central feature of the way it has sought to place itself in the position of defending the cultural and religious values of British society. The issue of Islam has been highlighted even further by the EDL in street-level mobilizations in various localities up and down the country from 2009 onwards. The EDL has focused on two key issues since its foundation in 2009. First, the role of 'Muslim extremism' nationally and in specific cities and towns has been perhaps their key concern (Allen 2011). They have also mobilized on issues such as immigration, multiculturalism, lack of jobs, crime and the financial crisis. Underlying these mobilizations has been a concern over the question of national identity and the threats posed by increasing cultural and religious diversity. Interestingly enough, research carried out by Demos among supporters and sympathizers of the EDL during 2011 highlighted immigration and fear of Islamic extremism as strong concerns, followed by issues such as crime, unemployment and multiculturalism (Bartlett et al. 2011, Bartlett & Littler 2011). The combination of these concerns is perhaps not surprising in itself, since historical research on right-wing ideologies has highlighted the way that they adapt to changing social and economic environments (Mosse 1981, 1985). But the growing importance of fears about Islamic extremism also highlights the contingent nature of issues as a tool for mobilization.

Countering or accommodating racism?

We can now turn to the question of how best to respond to the actions of movements such as the BNP and the EDL. This has been a recurrent theme in political debates and controversies in Britain for some time (Kyriakides 2008; Lentin 2008). During the New Labour administrations from 1997 to 2010, there were recurrent attempts to respond to the mobilizations of the extreme right by combining initiatives aimed at enhancing community cohesion in specific localities with a tough stance on immigration and asylum. Successive Labour politicians argued that there was a need to balance opposition to the BNP with recognition of 'real fears' about immigration and race relations in the wider society. Norman Tebbit, a right-wing Tory politician, commented acerbically that 'Mr Blunkett is more outspoken on race than I ever was and we should be grateful to him' (*Mail on Sunday*, 10 February 2002).

Certainly, a core element of New Labour policies at the beginning of the twenty-first century involved attempts to assuage popular concerns about issues such as housing, employment and terrorism. This was often justified in terms of the claim that the 'real fears' of sections of the white working class about immigration and increasing religious and cultural diversity needed to be addressed. This kind of approach was based on the assumption that the best way to manage fears about such issues as immigration and political Islam was to develop a strategy of engaging in dialogue with those sections of white working-class communities that were attracted to racial populist ideologies. This also involved attempts to distance governmental policies from a strong commitment to multiculturalism in favour of policies that aimed to emphasize the need for minorities to integrate with majority norms and values. The bombings in London on 7 July 2005 emphasized the tenuous nature of policy agendas in this area, and led to a wide-ranging public debate about the limits of multicultural policies in producing community cohesion. Indeed, some commentators argued that there was a need to question the very idea of multiculturalism and to emphasize the need for greater social cohesion alongside diversity. It was in this context that the Commission on Integration and Cohesion was set up, with the remit of looking at how best to develop policies that would strengthen integration and cohesion (Keith 2008, Bloch et al. forthcoming). In their final report, *Our Shared Future*, they made a total of 57 recommendations across a range of areas for refining and extending the cohesion and integration agenda. The report argued that it was more important to focus on people's perceptions of and feelings for their localities and stressed that it should be interdependency, mutuality and social separation rather than residential separation that should be the focus of attention.

The potential threat of terrorism from violent groups within political Islam accentuated the growing emphasis in policy terms on integration and social cohesion. This has become a recurring theme in the period since 2001, and has influenced both political and media discourses. In the aftermath of the 7/7 terrorist attacks on London, Tony Blair reflected this theme when he argued that 'radical Muslims must integrate' or endanger the possibilities for social cohesion (Blair 2006). In the context of the 2010 General Election in the United Kingdom, the *Daily Telegraph* reflected an even stronger version of this strand of analysis when it argued that 'Immigration is not an insoluble problem, assimilation, not multiculturalism, is the best way' (*Daily Telegraph*, 10 June 2009). Such arguments reflected the growing fears that there was increasingly a potential for communities to live what some commentators called 'parallel lives' rather than to interact and develop new ways of living together.

A clear example of the influence of this shift can be found in the policies and agendas developed by the coalition government of David Cameron since 2010. In his most forthright intervention on this question, Cameron defines multiculturalism largely in a positive manner:

> Multiculturalism, the notion that this country would be enriched by allowing each community to maintain and develop its own culture, lifestyle and value system, was founded on tolerance and fair play. (*The Times*, 7 February 2011)

While defining himself as being in favour of this notion of multiculturalism he does not see it as succeeding in practice:

> It has sadly, failed. Instead of new stream enriching the lifeblood of this country, all too often separate cultures have remained separate. Communities have become ghettos, mental and physical. (*The Times*, 7 February 2011)

In opposition to this failing multiculturalism, Cameron argues that 'we need less of the passive tolerance and much more active, muscular liberalism'. By implication, the way forward lies in strategies that emphasize common values and interests, what holds people together rather than keeps them apart.

Another facet of contemporary political discourses is represented by the conflation between the actions of groups like the BNP and EDL and radical Muslim groups in fostering a climate of fear in multicultural communities. This is a strong theme in the interventions made by David Cameron since he became the leader of the coalition government of Conservatives and Liberal Democrats in the aftermath of the 2010 general election. He has sought to highlight his opposition to what he sees as the 'extremism' of radical right-wing groups as well as radical Muslim groupings by arguing for a stronger sense of what it means to be British in these changing times.

Arguing against what he sees as the excesses of multiculturalism he has positioned himself in favour of a 'muscular liberalism' that would help to prioritize a sense of national identity (Cameron 2011).

This approach is not only articulated by the Conservatives. Although perhaps in a more nuanced manner, the Labour Party has also argued for the need to enhance community cohesion by directing attention to common British values. In the aftermath of the 7/7 attacks Tony Blair warned that:

> When it comes to our essential values – belief in democracy, the rule of law, tolerance, equal treatment for all, respect for this country and its shared heritage – then that is where we come together, it is what we hold in common. It is what gives us the right to call ourselves British. At that point no distinctive culture or religion supersedes our duty to be part of an integrated United Kingdom. (Blair 2006)

In the context of the relative success of the BNP in local politics, David Miliband has also articulated a similar line of analysis. Referring to the situation in places such as Bradford, Luton, Barking and Dagenham, Miliband has highlighted the potential for the mobilizations of the extreme right and radical Islam to fuel a politics of hatred:

> Groups like the BNP, the English Defence League and Islam4UK are only ever likely to appeal to a small minority: their violent rhetoric, aggression and warped politics provide the source of their downfall. But we should not understate their impact locally in creating a climate of division, fear and hatred. (Miliband 2011)

Although Miliband is also clear that the BNP and the EDL are a substantive threat to community cohesion, his inclusion of a radical Islamic group is also symptomatic of efforts to balance attacks on the politics of the extreme right with efforts to address fears and concerns within white working-class communities. From this standpoint, the role of policies should be to oppose all extremist ideologies and not just those of the populist right.

In pursuing strategies such as these, both New Labour and the coalition government have touched on a concern that is likely to remain an important issue in debates about how best to develop policies that can undermine the appeal of racist and populist movements. But they also highlight the potential dangers of accommodating rather than countering the political language used by such movements. The attempts by the EDL to mobilize locally on issues such as Muslim radicalism, immigration and unemployment are also reflective of the range of issues that have become the focus of extreme right mobilization in recent years (Bartlett & Littler 2011).

Conclusion

We have argued in this chapter that the core reasons why racist and ethno-nationalist populist movements and parties are an important part of the contemporary political scene, as well as of civil society in many countries in contemporary Europe, and can be linked to the current waves of fear and public debate about immigration, cultural diversity and national identity, Muslim minorities and political Islam. We have also suggested that a rounded analysis of contemporary forms of racist politics and racial populism needs to (i) take account of contemporary trends within a broader historical context, and (ii) explore the ways in which racial populism has evolved in response to changing patterns of migration and racialized politics. Given current trends, it is likely that extreme right and racial populist movements will remain an important political issue in British society for some time to come. This is not to say that specific movements and organizations will remain unchallenged. A good case in point is the failure of the BNP to sustain the gains it made during 2009 and in the May 2010 general election. It suffered losses in a number of local contexts, including in Barking and Dagenham in East London, the parliamentary constituency in which Nick Griffin stood. In the aftermath of his weak performance and the defeat of the BNP's six local councillors in Barking and Dagenham, some commentators argued that this highlighted the importance of developing locally based strategies to tackle the influence of the BNP and the EDL (Taylor & Muir 2010).

An important challenge that we face in the contemporary environment is the question of how we can develop a better understanding of the ways in which racist and populist movements are developing and taking on new issues and concerns in order to underpin their ideologies. Contemporary racist and populist movements are in many ways ideologically linked to earlier movements and mobilizations, particularly when we look at issues such as immigration and opposition to racial and ethnic diversity. But it is also important to analyse the emergence of discourses that have allowed them to take on new issues and reinvent themselves through political discourses about radical Islam and multiculturalism. It is through this process of reinvention that such movements are likely to gain more influence in the future and it is important therefore that we are able to analyse the discourses of racist and populist movements in all their complexity. It is therefore of some importance that the complexities of contemporary racist ideologies and forms of mobilization are understood.

References

Allen, C. (2011), 'Opposing Islamification or Promoting Islamophobia? Understanding the English Defence League', *Patterns of Prejudice*, 45(4): 279–94.

Bartlett, J., Birdwell, J. and Littler, M. (2011), *The New Face of Digital Populism*, London: Demos.

Bartlett, J. and Littler, M. (2011), *Inside the EDL: Populist Politics in a Digital Age*, London: Demos.

Billig, M. (1978), *Fascists: A Social Psychological View of the National Front*, London: Harcourt, Brace Jovanovich.

Blair, T. (2006), 'Radical Muslims Must Integrate', *The Guardian*, 9 December.

Bleich, E. (2011), *The Freedom to be Racist?: How the United States and Europe Struggle to Preserve Freedom and Combat Racism*, New York: Oxford University Press.

Bloch, A., Neal, S. and Solomos, J. (forthcoming), *Race, Multiculture and Social Policy*, Basingstoke: Palgrave Macmillan.

Cameron, D. (2011), 'No Place for the Intolerant', *The Times*, 7 February.

Cashmore, E. (1987), *The Logic of Racism*, London: Allen & Unwin.

Copsey, N. (2008), *Contemporary British Fascism: The British National Party and the Quest for Legitimacy*, 2nd edn, Basingstoke: Palgrave Macmillan.

Copsey, N. and Macklin, G. (2011), *The British National Party: Contemporary Perspectives*, London: Routledge.

Cutts, D., Ford, R. and Goodwin, M. J. (2010), 'Anti-immigrant, Politically Disaffected or Still Racist after All? Examining the Attitudinal Drivers of Extreme Right Support in Britain in the 2009 European Elections', *European Journal of Political Research*, 50(3): 418–40.

Eatwell, R. and Goodwin, M. J. (eds) (2010), *The New Extremism in 21st Century Britain*, London: Routledge.

Eatwell, R. and Mudde, C. (eds) (2004), *Western Democracies and the New Extreme Right Challenge*, London: Routledge.

Edelman, M. J. (1971), *Politics as Symbolic Action: Mass Arousal and Quiescence*, Chicago: Markham.

Fielding, N. (1981), *The National Front*, London: Routledge & Kegan Paul.

Ford, R. (2010), 'Who might vote for the BNP?: Survey evidence on the electoral potential of the extreme right in Britain', in R. Eatwell and M. J. Goodwin (eds), *The New Extremism in 21st Century Britain*, London: Routledge.

Ford, R. and Goodwin, M. J. (2010), 'Angry White Men: Individual and Contextual Predictors of Support for the British National Party', *Political Studies*, 58(1): 1–25.

Gilroy, P. (1987), *There Ain't No Black in the Union Jack: The Cultural Politics of Race and Nation*, London: Hutchinson.

Goodwin, M. J. (2011a), *Right Response: Understanding and Countering Populist Extremism in Europe*, London: Chatham House.

— (2011b), *New British Fascism: The Rise of the British National Party*, London: Routledge.

Hartley-Brewer, J. (2009), 'Government Arrogance Let in the BNP Fascists', *Sunday Express*, 14 June.

Husbands, C. T. (1983), *Racial Exclusionism and the City*, London: Allen and Unwin.

John, P. and Margetts, H. (2009), 'The Latent Support for the Extreme Right in British Politics', *West European Politics*, 32(3): 496–513.

Keith, M. (2008), 'Public Sociology? Between Herioc Immersion and Critical Distance: Personal Reflections on Academic Engagement with Political Life', *Critical Social Policy*, 28(3): 320–34.

Kyriakides, C. (2008), 'Third Way Anti-racism: A Contextual Constructionist Approach', *Ethnic and Racial Studies*, 31(3): 592–610.

Lentin, A. (2004), 'Racial States, Anti-Racist Responses: Picking Holes in "Culture" and "Human Rights"', *European Journal of Social Theory*, 7(4): 427–43.

— (2008), 'After Anti-Racism?', *European Journal of Cultural Studies*, 11, 3: 311–31.

Miles, R. and Phizacklea, A. (eds) (1979), *Racism and Political Action in Britain*, London: Routledge and Kegan Paul.

Miliband, D. (2011), 'Insecurity is Fuel to Hate', *The Guardian*, 28 February 2011.

Mosse, G. L. (1985), *Toward the Final Solution: A History of European Racism*, Madison: University of Wisconsin Press.

Mosse, G. L. (ed.) (1981), *Nazi Culture: Intellectual, Cultural and Social Life in the Third Reich*, New York: Schocken Books.

Phizacklea, A. and Miles, R. (1980), *Labour and Racism*, London: Routledge & Kegan Paul.

Rhodes, J. (2006), 'The "Local" Politics of the British National Party', *Sage Race Relations Abstracts*, 31(4): 5–20.

— (2009), 'The Political Breakthrough of the BNP: The Case of Burnley', *British Politics*, 4(1): 22–46.

— (2011), 'Multiculturalism and the subcultural politics of the British National Party', in N. Copsey and G. Macklin (eds), *The British National Party: Contemporary Perspectives*, London: Routledge, pp. 62–78.

Richardson, J. E. (2011), 'Race and racial difference: The surface and depth of BNP ideology', in N. Copsey and G. Macklin (eds), *The British National Party: Contemporary Perspectives*, London: Routledge, pp. 38–61.

— (2012), 'Ploughing the same furrow? Continuity and change on Britain's extreme-right fringe', in Wodak, R., KhosraviNik, M. and Mral, B. (eds), *Right Wing Populism in Europe: Politics and Discourse*, London: Bloomsbury Academic (in press).

Taylor, M. and Muir, H. (2010), 'Is this the End of the BNP?', *The Guardian*, 14 May.

Thurlow, R. C. (1975), 'National Front Ideology: The Witches Brew', *Patterns of Prejudice*, 9(1): 1–9.

— (1976), 'The Powers of Darkness: Conspiracy Belief and Political Strategy', *Patterns of Prejudice*, 12(6): 1–23.

— (1998), *Fascism in Britain: From Oswald Mosley's Blackshirts to the National Front*, London: I. B. Tauris.

Walker, M. (1978), *The National Front*, London: Fontana/Collins.

Wemyss, G. (2006), '"Outside Extremists", "White East Enders", "Passive Bengalis": Tracking Constructions, Mobilizations and Contestions of Racial Categories in Media Discourses', *Sage Race Relations Abstracts*, 31(4): 21–47.

9

From Anti-Immigration and Nationalist Revisionism to Islamophobia: Continuities and Shifts in Recent Discourses and Patterns of Political Communication of the Freedom Party of Austria (FPÖ)

Michał Krzyżanowski

Introduction

This chapter analyses the dynamics of discourses of the right wing populist Freedom Party of Austria (FPÖ). In order to portray significant changes as well as key continuities in the FPÖ discourse over time, the chapter focuses on two distinct periods: on the one hand, late 1990s and early 2000s and, on the other hand, mid/late 2000s. Whereas in the former period the FPÖ was still a government member under the (either official or symbolic) leadership of its charismatic head Jörg Haider, the arrival of mid/late 2000s saw the secession of the party (into Haider-led BZÖ and the FPÖ as of 2005) and the FPÖ's return to the opposition as well as the arrival of the party's new chairman H. C. Strache.

The main aim of this paper is to show that, whereas several continuities can be observed in FPÖ discourses over time, there are also significant shifts[1] in the party's populist rhetoric adjusted to the changing national and, to some extent also international, political conditions. The key shift is the FPÖ's departure from its many Austrian-specific arguments of the first analysed period (e.g. Austrian-specific forms of anti-Semitism, revisionism of Austria's NS past, etc.; in Haider times), towards a

---

[1] The notion of (discursive) shifts is used here in line with a theoretical model which portrays them as more or less localized (micro-level) responses to (macro-level) social-political and discursive change. Discursive shifts are seen as local appropriations of global changes and as produced by selected individual or collective actors (e.g. political parties) in their discursive and communicative practices (for further details, see Krzyżanowski *forthcoming*).

different rhetoric of the second period when more 'international' arguments (which have also been used by other right-wing populist movements across Europe[2] such as Islamophobia and strong Euroscepticism under Strache) have become salient.

Theoretical background

This paper subscribes to the ideas proposed by Beck (1992 and 1994) within his theories of *risk society* and of *reflexive modernisation*. As argued by Beck, contemporary societies – especially their Western forms – do not undergo any abrupt changes or transformative periods of crisis (such as previous revolutions, uprisings, etc.) but instead *are in the state of context flux and of quasi ongoing transformation*. That transformation is particularly visible in the political field in which we witness a vivid development of re-invented civil society which is 'naturally' closer to the social. On the other hand, what occurs simultaneously is the growing 'political vacuity of the institutions' (Beck 1994: 17) which stems from the general weakening of traditional politics which is not capable anymore of responding to both local and global tendencies and changes in the social environment (see also Beck & Grande 2007).

Such a situation provides a fertile ground for right-wing populist movements, which, paradoxically (i.e. as members of the political class themselves), subscribe to the criticism of the mainstream political parties which have apparently lost touch with the larger portions of the society. By providing 'simple answers to complex questions' (Reisigl & Wodak 2001) as well as subsequent (and indeed constant) critique of the entire political establishment, right wing populist movements opportunistically respond to, on the one hand, public fears of the late-modern developments, including the alleged loss of security, and, on the other, to the growing public disenchantment with politics (Wodak 2011).

In a similar vein, discourses of Right-Wing Populist parties (RWPs) also display the feature of 'ongoing transformation' postulated by Beck (see above). Whereas earlier, the RWPs were much more eager to respond in their actions to grand moments of social and political transformation (as was the case with the FPÖ's 1992/93 'Austria First' referendum, initiated in the aftermath of the fall of the Iron Curtain),[3] they currently mostly rely on constant self-re-invention and auto-construction of 'crises' to which they can then find populist quasi-solutions. As we see in the recent actions of the FPÖ, the latter is found in the *constant process of campaigning* which, unlike before, is not tied only to elections but is in fact also an ongoing practice which provides the party with the ability to be constantly present in the media.

In this context, special attention should be paid to recent transformations in political landscapes in Europe. These changes, which result in the ongoing blurring (if not the actual disappearance) of divisions between political 'left' and 'right' (Azmanova 2004),

---

[2] See Boréus (this volume) for the comparative analysis of discourses in Austria, Denmark and Sweden.

[3] See Reisigl and Wodak (2000 and 2001), Wodak (2001), Krzyżanowski and Wodak (2009).

are mainly ascribed to the awakening and spread of the global neoliberal tendencies of the 1990s and 2000s (see Jessop 2002a, b). Such tendencies contribute to the visible transformation of the forms as well as the contents of political competition. The latter is now no longer based on the rivalry between different and/or alternative proposals of varied models of the state, but, instead, between different types of responses proposed by political actors with regard to largely similar sets of issues. According to Azmanova (2009) those issues include both globalization (in both economic and sociopolitical terms) and political internationalization (e.g. at the level of the EU). The former is most aptly associated in the European context with accelerating politics of the European integration which meets with the ever-larger waves of Euroscepticism (see Taggart & Szczerbiak 2008) fuelled by national-populist movements. On the other hand, implications of the latter – that is, transnationalization – are manifold and include cross-national migration and otherwise conceived human and labour mobility as well as the transnationalization of economy (again, all widely contested in national public spheres; see Azmanova 2009).

Importantly, many of the topics outlined above – especially migration – are the ones which were not traditionally 'discursively' embraced by Europe's political mainstreams. While having had an obviously profound impact in shaping migration policies in the post-war period, many mainstream parties have for a long time avoided making the topic into the central element of their official discourses and media appearances. This has changed since the mid-to-late 1990s, with migration now at the centre of debates about national 'security' and gradually becoming the most important topic in political debates in which it is not only perceived in international but also, and primarily, in home affairs. (Such was the case in, for example, the first televised pre-election political debate in the United Kingdom in 2010 which, focussing on home affairs, started from debating 'immigration'). At the same time, right-wing populist parties, which traditionally embrace migration – or more specifically anti-immigration – as the central point of their political agendas are now rising in importance as 'champions of public debates' and as 'agenda setters' who 'knew all along' that migration was a 'problem' (Krzyżanowski & Wodak 2009). Accordingly, RWPs appear as those who have a better recognition of social problems than the mainstream parties and as those who ask the often uneasy questions (e.g. about 'costs' and 'limits' of migration).

Such is also the case with Austria where the FPÖ's activities led to migration becoming a mainstream political topic already in the early 1990s (with the 'Austria First Petition', etc., see above) and consequently focused public opinion as well as pre-election debates on that topic (see Wodak & Krzyżanowski 2008a). Since the mid-2000s – as a response to social and political changes (and, for example, an inability to further oppose migration from former-communist and now European Union member states) – that discourse has also shifted to 'third-country' refugees and asylum seekers (already to some extent targeted by Haider in the 1990s) rather than focussing on migrants as such. This shift has recently been continued further and now encompasses different Islamophobic slogans (see below) which allow the placing of local aspects of migration in the global context of, for example, struggle between different cultures and religions.

Methodology and categories of analysis

My study draws on previous research on the dynamics of FPÖ discourses in early and late 1990s[4] as well as in early 2000s.[5] It also builds on earlier explorations of forms of racism and discrimination in public discourses (see van Dijk 1988, Wodak & van Dijk 2000), on cross-national receptions of right-wing populist politics (Krzyżanowski 2002) as well as on recent studies on Islamophobia in European public spheres.[6]

The study is rooted in the methodological tradition of Critical Discourse Analysis (CDA) and especially the Discourse-Historical Approach.[7] The analysis focuses mainly on *strategies of self- and other-presentation* which investigate dynamics of discursive formation and legitimation of in- and out-groups (see Reisigl & Wodak 2001 for further details). Of the said categories, the central ones remain those related to strategies of argumentation which show how arguments for/against certain issues (e.g. Islam) are constructed in discourse. Here, *topoi* which are understood as headings of arguments constructed in discourse by means of different constellations of contents of texts at hand (see Krzyżanowski 2010 for further details) are treated as the central categories. For example, the *topos of danger and threat*, encountered frequently in the analysed material (see below), is realized by means of different parts of analysed texts which describe Islam from the point of view of its mainly negative features (e.g. radical education, terrorism, etc.) all of which help in constructing an argument about a set of more or less obvious 'threats' posed by Islam to European, and especially Austrian, social reality.

While the aforementioned categories will be crucial in analysing the textual material, multimodal genres (e.g. billboards) will be examined by means of a combination of strategies of self- and other presentation and of *strategies of representation of social actors in discourse* (van Leeuwen 2008). The latter allow for the recognition of dynamics of discursive representation, including processes of foregrounding or backgrounding of social actors. Analysis of the inter-semiotic genres will also be supplemented by means of related forms of 'multimodal' or 'visual-semiotic analysis' (Kress & van Leeuwen 1996, O'Halloran 2008; see also Scollon & Levine 2004, Pollak 2008).

Exploring the context

Due to limitations of space, this chapter is unable to describe in detail the history of the FPÖ from its beginnings in the late 1940s (for further details and earlier studies, see, inter alia, Pelinka 1990, 1993, 2005, Manoschek 2002, Krzyżanowski & Wodak 2009). Therefore, the present contextualizing section only sketches out key developments of the FPÖ since 2000.

---

[4]   See Matouschek et al. (1995), Reisigl and Wodak (2001).
[5]   See Pelinka and Wodak (2002), Wodak and Pelinka (2002), Wodak and Krzyżanowski (2008a), Krzyżanowski and Wodak (2009), Wodak (2009); see also Geden (2005 and 2006).
[6]   See Richardson (2004), Richardson and Wodak (2009a and 2009b), Wodak and Köhler (2010).
[7]   See Reisigl and Wodak (2001 and 2009), Wodak (2001, 2011), Wodak and Krzyżanowski (2008b), Krzyżanowski (2010).

The new millennium started successfully for the FPÖ which, following a significant gain in public support, scored 27.4 per cent of the votes (second best) in elections to the National Council (*Nationalratswahl*) of the late 1999. In early 2000 the FPÖ then entered the Austrian federal government as the coalition partner of the conservative Austrian People's Party (ÖVP). This led, however, to repercussions of both a national and international nature. The latter mainly took the form of sanctions imposed by the then remaining EU-14 countries against the Austrian government, as a response to allowing into government a party such as FPÖ which was widely known for its uncritical stance towards National Socialism and its frequent use of antisemitic slogans (the sanctions were lifted on 12 September 2000). These international repercussions eventually led to the national occurrences during which, in view of the growing discontent in the party, FPÖ leader Jörg Haider resigned as the party chairman. However, despite his official resignation, Haider maintained considerable influence on the succeeding party leaders such as Susanne Riess-Passer, Matthias Reichhold, Herbert Haupt and Ursula Haubner (Haider's sister).

Due to the turmoil within the FPÖ and, especially, in view of the party's inability to effectively act as a coalition partner, the *Nationalratswahl* of 24 November 2002 brought a disappointing result of only ca. 10 per cent of the national votes. Despite this, the FPÖ yet again entered a coalition government with the ÖVP in 2003 and remained part of the government until 2005. However, despite remaining within national government politics, the weakening of the FPÖ's position across the country was soon proved by electoral defeats between 2003 and 2005 when the party lost in all of the Austrian regional elections except for Carinthia (where Haider – as provincial governor since 1999 – led the local FPÖ to significant victory). This, however, proved rather destructive for the party as it fuelled the ensuing conflict between Haider and his national and regional party colleagues such as the then Party-Chairman Hilmar Kabas or the Viennese faction leader Heinz-Christian (HC) Strache.

This, as well as several other conflicts in the party, resulted in the eventual split of the FPÖ in 2005 when Haider and his close followers left the party and founded the *Alliance for the Future of Austria* (BZÖ). The split proved very influential not only for the party-internal politics but also for the FPÖ's partaking in the national government. As several members of the latter included close allies of Haider and joined him in the new formation – including the then federal Vice-Chancellor Hubert Gorbach – the BZÖ automatically entered the federal government while the FPÖ was, in fact, forced to move into opposition. This, expectedly, caused an open conflict between the now two Austrian RWPs, with the FPÖ soon electing (on 23 April 2005) a new leader HC Strache to lead the party into the post-Haider era.

The first years of Strache's FPÖ leadership proved to be rather unsuccessful with the party suffering clear loses. Such was the case especially in the new leader's hometown of Vienna where, despite a fierce campaign led by Strache in 2006, the FPÖ lost significantly against the Austrian Social-Democratic Party (SPÖ) who thus regained majority in the Viennese regional parliament (*Wiener Landtag*). Similarly, the FPÖ's gains in the ensuing national-parliamentary elections of 2006 were rather modest with the party gaining only 1 per cent of votes (thus scoring 11% compared to 10% in 2002. such an electoral gain was still low when compared to the support the party used to win in the heyday of the Haider era).

The unsuccessful first years of Strache's FPÖ leadership were, however, soon followed by a thorough rethinking of the party's marketing and communication strategies (increased mediatization, focus on a new, 'young' leader, etc.) as well as a shift in focus from the traditionally FPÖ-like topics (e.g. anti-Semitism, revisionism, etc.) to new slogans (especially Islamophobia which had already proved fruitful for RWPs in other Western-European countries; see below). In view of this significant change in the image and rhetoric of the party and also in light of the growing public insecurity fuelled by the evolving Global Financial Crisis, the FPÖ soon started to clearly gain ground as far as both regional and national elections were concerned. In the *Nationalratswahl* of 2008, the FPÖ managed to score 17.5 per cent of the votes (BZÖ and FPÖ together scored almost 25%) which showed that the party was gradually on the rise. Its increase of votes was soon followed by a further boost in popularity which coincided with a significant weakening of the BZÖ's popularity after Jörg Haider's death in October 2008.[8]

Despite some unsuccessful electoral attempts by the FPÖ (when, for example, the party's 2010 Presidential candidate Barbara Rosenkranz scored only 15% of the votes compared to 80% gained by her social-democratic opponent Heinz Fischer), the party has recently been experiencing a relatively steady increase in support. The latter has been fuelled by, on the one hand, the prolonged economic turmoil in Europe, the Euro-zone and worldwide (although it has not affected Austria as much as many other EU countries) and, on the other, the ever-more frequent crises in the SPÖ-ÖVP Austrian coalition government. The FPÖ gained almost 6 per cent in the European Parliamentary elections of 2009 (scoring altogether 12.7%) as well as almost topped its record level of support in the Viennese regional elections of 2010 (scoring 25.8%). Its recent nationwide support is estimated at ca. 30 per cent, often exceeding support for Austria's two mainstream social-democratic and conservative parties which presently form the federal coalition government. The party also seems to be increasingly boosted by the ongoing crisis in the BZÖ.

FPÖ politics and rhetoric in late 1990s and early 2000s: The Haider era

Allowing for the abundance of studies which have dealt with FPÖ during party's leadership by Jörg Haider (see above), the current section will only briefly describe the party's politics and rhetoric of late 1990s and early 2000s. In doing so, it will construct a comparative basis for the later exploration of the FPÖ rhetoric as of 2005 (see below).

As a typical *Führerpartei*, the Haider-led FPÖ of late 1990s and early 2000s was strongly focussed on its charismatic leader who was always present in the media whenever FPÖ's opinion was sought or whenever significant televised and other debates were taking place. Although this changed slightly following Haider's retreat from the party leadership in 2000, it was still obvious up to 2005 (secession of the FPÖ)

---

[8]   Jörg Haider died in a car accident in south Carinthia on 11 October 2008.

that, although not officially in post, Haider remained the party's actual leader who controlled FPÖ's discourse and guarded the central aspects of its programme.

The central frame of the Haider-led FPÖ discourse was the strong anti-immigration stance which was the party's concern since the early 1990s ('Austria First'; see above) and which occupied the party even more after it entered the federal government in 2000. There, the anti-immigration slogans were soon put into practice by means of different official anti-immigration acts, of which the 2002 Integration Agreement (*Integrationsvereinbarung*) remains central. The FPÖ's anti-immigration discourse was often characterized by the use of catchy yet clearly ambivalent slogans such as 'the Right to Fatherland' (*Recht aufs Heimat*) which not only denoted Austrian's right to live in their own *Heimat* but also voiced the call for the 'right' of migrants to return to their own fatherlands.

A further key element of the rhetoric of FPÖ under Haider was its stringent nationalistic stance. The latter often resulted in many antisemitic slogans and expressions (several of which, Haider was tried and sentenced for; see Pelinka & Wodak 2002) as well as in the related quasi-denial and de-facto glorification of Austria's National-Socialist past. Using such rhetoric had obvious strategic motivations as it allowed the FPÖ to retain the backing of one of its core support groups, that is, elderly sections of the electorate including those who were once involved in Austrian NS politics (see Engel & Wodak 2009). As a typical populist party, the FPÖ's discourse under Haider was also characterized by strong anti-establishment rhetoric (directed mainly at the Austrian mainstream parties SPÖ and ÖVP) which, however, gradually faded especially once the FPÖ itself became part of the 'establishment' by entering the Austrian government as of the early 2000s (see also chapter by Boréus in this volume).

The FPÖ since 2005: The Strache years

Contrary to the Haider era when FPÖ discourse was dominated by anti-immigrant, nationalistic, revisionist and anti-establishment rhetoric, the recent years have been dominated by the party's overt turn to Islamophobia as its central discursive and policy frame. Looking at how Islamophobic discourse is actually constructed in FPÖ's recent campaign posters – for example, in the 2009 Viennese Local Election Posters 'Away with Mosques and Minarets' (*Aus für Moscheen und Minarete*) or the 2008 National Election Poster 'At Home instead of Islam' (*Daham statt Islam*)[9] – one notices a vast array of strategies which draw on 'us' versus 'them' oppositions. Whereas the first of the posters constructs those oppositions within the visual aspects of the design ('us' is symbolized by the smiling and colourful image of HC Strache and 'them' by the faint and 'worried' image of Vienna's long-term social-democrat Mayor Michael Häupl), the second poster refers to the textual opposition constructed in the main slogan ('at home' – *da Heim* – spoken in Viennese dialect as '*Daham*' is rhymed and thus semantically juxtaposed with 'Islam').

[9] See www.hcstrache.at/home/?id=48 for further details.

While both of the posters focus on the said binary oppositions, the remaining textual material supports the thus constructed general anti-Islam message. In the first case, the visual opposition Strache-Häupl is supported by statements which claim that the Viennese Mayor and other politicians (including from the conservative government party ÖVP) have for years shied away from halting radical Islamist groups from spreading in Austria. Those statements are then, again, juxtaposed with FPÖ's anti-Islam proposals which start with the general statement that 'FPÖ's HC-Strache says' (*FPÖ-HC Strache sagt . . .*) that 'keeping freedom and security means fighting the radical Islamism' (*Freiheit und Sicherheit erhalten heist, den radikalen Islamismus bekämpfen*). In what follows, we encounter an enumeration of concrete actions that the FPÖ is proposing within the said 'fight'. Those actions include, inter alia, a 'construction ban on mosques and minarets' (*Bauverbot für Moscheen und Minarette*), 'prayers in German only' (*Predigten nur in deutscher Sprache*) or 'no EU accession for Turkey and Israel' (*kein EU-Beitritt für Türkei und Israel*). The use of anti-Turkish arguments in that context is especially significant as the FPÖ's Islamophobic slogans are often 'exemplified' by references to members of Austria's Turkish community stereotyped as consisting as if only of Muslims.

On the other hand the second poster (*Daham statt Islam*) actually resorts to the presentation of quasi-facts and statistics which are supposed to support the party's stance. In the presented case, those facts say that '45% of Muslims do not want to integrate' which is followed by statements directed at the FPÖ's political opponents who, apparently, do not understand the gravity of such a situation. The following statements also include some – quite paradoxical – ideas about the 'division between the Church and the state' (e.g. implying that any other solution might in fact foster Islamism) and claiming that the party is pleading for 'women's rights' (FPÖ's strategic statement referring to its opposition towards headscarves worn by Muslim women and allegedly, to other aspects of violation of women's rights by Islam).

Further to billboards and other usual genres of 'open' political communication, Islamophobia plays a prominent role in FPÖ's discourses expressing the party's official goals and viewpoints. The key document which proves this is the Handbook of Freedomite Politics (*Handbuch Freiheitlicher Politik*, hereinafter HFP) which, contrary to the usually politically correct official documents from the Haider era, includes a range of Islamophobic and related statements and arguments including overt and blatant stereotypes. In the 283-page document, which is defined as 'guidelines for leading functionaries and mandate holders for the FPÖ', Islam is thematized within a variety of topics which include self-presentation of the FPÖ as Austrian *Heimatpartei*, FPÖ's stance on Austrian internal affairs or, last but not least, FPÖ's viewpoint on international and European matters.

The most explicit anti-Islamic statements are placed in section 2.1.3 of the HFP (29–32) which concerns 'the Christian and enlightened Occident' (*Das christliche und aufgeklärte Abendland*). Presented in Figure 9.1, the semantic field of key themes discussed in that section shows that it is not as much about Christianity or Enlightenment as it is about different aspects of Islam. The latter is thematized in topics which range from Minarets as symbols of Muslim violence, through to the growing number of Muslims in Austria up until the aforementioned peculiar understanding of

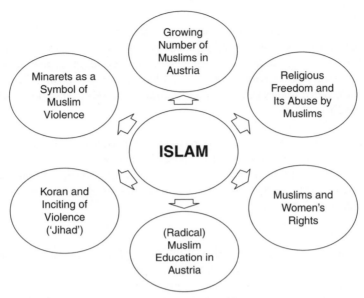

Figure 9.1 Semantic Field of 'Islam' in Section 2.1.3. of the HFP

Muslims and women's rights. What is worth noting is that, as such, all of the discussed aspects of Islam are clearly negative with almost every topic implying that, for example, Muslim education is 'radical' or that religious freedoms are 'abused' by Muslims.

Moreover, it is worth mentioning that practically all of the arguments constructed therein serve to present Islam as an omnipresent threat not only to the headlined Christianity but also to Austria and Europe as a whole. Accordingly, the arguments are constructed along the key *topoi of danger and threat* which help to portray Islam and its dangers in a wide range of contexts from terrorism to social cohesion. There, one for example encounters a set of general fallacious statements about Islam such as below (see Example 1).

Example 1:
Islam is a religion which sees the world as a war-theatre, and indeed as long as the entire world would not become Islamic. [*Der Islam ist eine Religion, die die Welt als Kriegsschauplatz ansieht – und zwar solange, bis die gesamte Menschheit islamisch ist*]. (HFP, Section 2.1.3., 31)

However, the expressions of such blatant stereotypes are also followed by some more detailed and apparently 'analytically founded' arguments. For example, one encounters a prolonged argument about the dangers of Islamic education which, as the HFP suggests, is already widely practiced in Austria with the help of textbooks that allegedly call for Jihad against other religions. As presented in Example 2 (see below), which describes a textbook allegedly used in some of the Austrian secondary schools, Islam is teaching its followers to not only disobey but in fact act against Western-like law and order due to claims of becoming the world-ruling religion.

Example 2:
The claim to rule the world by Islam is already being sketched out in the introduction to the textbook. Accordingly, the Islamic law of Sharia is set to stand above the legal order of Western democracies. [*Bereits in der Einleitung des buches wird der Weltherrschaftsanspruch des Islam untermauert. Die Scharia, die islamische Gesetzgebung, stehe über dem Rechtstaat westlicher Demokratien*]. (HFP, Section 2.1.3., 30)

Arguments such as those portrayed above are also used in the HFP to explain the FPÖ's stance against minarets (see also above). Namely, as it is blatantly claimed in the analysed section of the document (see Example 3), minarets do not actually serve as towers used to call Muslims to prayer, but as symbols of Islamic aggression against other religions and cultures.

Example 3:
A mosque with minaret is a symbol of this [MK: Muslim] teaching and law. A minaret is a construction which symbolises religious and symbolic issues. Just like triumphal monuments the minarets spring out of the ground to represent the victory of Islam over other religions or over the unfaithful. [*Das Symbol dieser Lehre und dieses Rechtssystems ist die Moschee mit dem Minarett. Ein Minarett stellt einen Bau mit religiösem Charakter und Symbolwirkung dar. Wie Siegesstatuen spriessen Minarette als Sinnbild und Zeichen des Sieges des Islam gegenüber Anders-beziehungsweise Ungläubigen aus dem Boden*]. (HFP, Section 2.1.3., 32)

Further, the document also refers to the rather undefined experts or analyses (*topos of authority*) allegedly supporting the claims put forth by the FPÖ with regard to the dangers of Islam. As shown in Example 4 (see below), those dangers are, inter alia, of demographic nature with Austria soon not only becoming 'overpopulated' by Muslims but also with Austrian (native?) children soon turning to Islam. Interestingly the example calls upon an unspecified study of a certain 'Academy of Sciences' which also remains undefined.

Example 4:
According to a study by the Academy of Sciences, over 50 percent of Austrian children will, by 2050, belong to the Muslim religious community. [*Bereits im Jahr 2050 sollen laut einer Studie der Akademie der Wissenschaften mehr als 50 Prozent der österreichischen Kinder der islamischen Glaubengemeinschaft angehören*]. (HFP, 30)

Further, the HFP's section 2.1.3 also resorts to many attempts at redefining the meanings of, inter alia, lessons of Koran or women's rights within Islam (*topos of definition*; see Reisigl & Wodak, 2001). In the first case, several arguments are put forward with the aim of explaining or highlighting some of the teachings of the Koran which, as it appears from the document, do not stipulate anything else but Jihad against the West and Christianity. As argued in the following example (see Example 5), the Koran is indeed in its majority supposed to be devoted to Jihad. What is interesting, is that the

Jihad is no longer defined here – as if anyway known to the recipients of the document – contrary to other aspects such as the *Sunna*[10] (this aims to show that the FPÖ and/or the authors of the text in fact possess some degree of knowledge of Islam and Koran).

Example 5:
Large parts of the work (MK: Koran) which describe Sunna – Mohammad's norm regulating behaviour – are devoted to Jihad against followers of other religions. [*Umfangreiche Kapitel der Werke, die die Sunna – das Norm setzende Handeln Mohammeds – enthalten, sind dem Jihad gegen Andersgläubige gewidmet*]. (HFP, 31)

However, a standard element of the FPÖ's redefinitions of Islam and its teachings concerns the issue of women's rights and their alleged violation in different aspects of Muslims' both religious and everyday life. In this context, the redefinition of women's rights is quite broad and spans from the bare presentations of what is allowed or forbidden for Muslim women to the more elaborate discussions of how – and why – the FPÖ must be against Islam in order to protect women's rights.

Example 6:
In order to avoid bodily contact with men in a bus, cinema or elsewhere, the (MK: Muslim) woman should at best not leave her house at all. However, she should not be locked out: whenever she asks her husband if she can go to a mosque to pray, he cannot forbid her to do that. [*Das Haus soll die Frau am besten gar nicht verlassen, um eventuellen Körperkontakt mit Männern im Autobus oder im Kino o.ä. zu vermeiden. Das heisse aber nicht, dass sie eingesperrt sei: Wenn sie ihren Mann bittet, die Moschee besuchen zu dürfen, darf er ihr das nicht verweigern.*]. (HFP, 30)

As shown in Example 6 (see above), the HFP examples of what Muslim women are allowed or not are built on untrue and unsubstantiated presentations of women as totally subjected to men (who are elsewhere portrayed as 'Lords' of their families, page 30). As suggested in the example, Muslim women are totally subjected to the will of their husbands who only cannot forbid them to go and pray in a mosque if they so wish (note the sarcasm implied in this statement).

Conclusions

As evidenced above, the Freedom Party of Austria has recently undergone a change which not only results in the personal shift from the party's once charismatic leader Jörg Haider to its new chairman HC Strache but also pertains to the intensified dynamics of the FPÖ's message (discourse). Particularly, the FPÖ's discursive shift

---

[10] Though the term carries different meanings, *Sunna* – or *Sunnah* – denotes in some Islamic traditions a set of religious and related laws and habits practiced by the followers of Prophet Muhammad.

towards Islamophobia is worth highlighting. On the one hand, that change helps 'modernizing' the party's image by showing that the FPÖ accommodates arguments expressed by many other contemporary European RWPs which resort to Islamophobia as a standard element of their discourses and policies. On the other hand, however, the move towards Islamophobia also allows the FPÖ to find a new overarching frame for its discourses which, while targeting Muslims, still retain such 'old' features of the FPÖ rhetoric as, inter alia, anti-immigration stance (in fact introduced and developed during the Haider years).

Indeed, as the analysis above illustrates, recent discursive shifts in the FPÖ are (quite paradoxically) based on patterns of both continuity and discontinuity. While HC Strache and his party officials often emphasize how different their politics now is from the Haider era and how the FPÖ has now become 'truly freedomite' (*echt freiheitlich*) compared to the earlier years, it is more than obvious that many of the current FPÖ postulates date back to the early 1990s with many supporting slogans – most notably Haider's famous 'Austria First' (*Österreich zuerst*) – often recontextualized.

What the analysis illustrates is that, at a more general level, party-political communicative and discursive practices of RWPs such as the FPÖ remain very ambiguous in nature and become an example of a peculiar 'jack of all trades' that emphasizes the paradoxes of contemporary (right-wing) populism (for other example, see Krzyżanowski 2012). The latter is, as shown, based on both discursive discontinuity and continuity (even if the latter is veiled as an actual 'new beginning') which, in general, aims to gain new voters while not losing the old ones and to propose new issues and slogans (see Islamophobia) while in fact reusing those from the past (e.g. anti-immigration). It is argued here that the said partial and often ambiguous discursive shifts of the FPÖ constitute a vital example of the ongoing transformation and constant invention of crises in the realm of the political (as theorized in line with Beck, see above). As shown, in such a context, especially the right-wing populist movements – in particular those in opposition roles and struggling for power – aim to remain quasi all-embracing in their opinions and thus able to please different sections of the electorate which might be prone to follow different (old and/or new) slogans.

In a similar vein, the discursive dynamics depicted above show that, while revamping their discourses and slogans, RWPs such as the FPÖ accommodate discourses about (in)security into their rhetoric. This is an example of the change in politics which, following Azmanova (see above), nowadays ceases to form alternative visions of 'local' social reality and instead responds to – or accommodates – different aspects of global and transnational ideas (in our case Islamophobia, insecurity, etc.). As shown in the example of the recent discourses of the FPÖ, RWPs now often use such transnational frames to justify their arguments related to, inter alia, exclusion of large portions of societies (in the present case the Muslims). The latter are, accordingly, viewed by the FPÖ as profoundly not 'integrated' and by and large threatening the overall social cohesion and the collective well-being of the – always more or less 'native' – majority (see also Buonfino 2004, Ibrahim 2005). While, to be sure, such discriminating arguments have long been at the core of FPÖ discourses, they have recently seen a 'nominational' turn towards 'Muslims' as the key targeted social groups.

References

Azmanova, A. (2004), 'The Mobilisation of the European Left in the Early 21st Century', *Arch. Europ. Sociol.*, XLV(2): 273–306.

— (2009), '1989 and the European Social Model. Transition without Emancipation?', *Philosophy and Social Criticism*, 35(9): 1019–37.

Beck, U. (1992), *Risk Society: Towards a New Modernity*, London: Sage.

— (1994), 'The reinvention of politics: Towards a theory of reflexive modernisation', in U. Beck, A. Giddens and S. Lash, *Reflexive Modernization: Politics, Tradition and Aesthetics in the Modern Social Order*, Cambridge: Polity Press, pp. 1–56.

Beck, U. and Grande, E. (2007), *Cosmopolitan Europe*, Cambridge: Polity Press.

Buonfino, A. (2004), 'Between Unity and Plurality: The Politicization and Securitization of the Discourse of Immigration in Europe', *New Political Science*, 26(1): 23–49.

Engel, J. and Wodak, R. (2009), 'Kalkulierte Ambivalenz, "Störungen" und das "Gedankenjahr": Die Causen Siegfried Kampl und John Gudenus' in R. de Cillia and R. Wodak (eds), *Gedenken im Gedankenjahr*, Innsbruck: Studienverlag, pp. 79–100.

Geden, O. (2005), 'The Discursive Representation of Masculinity in the Freedom Party of Austria (FPÖ)', *Journal of Language and Politics*, 4(3): 397–421.

— (2006), *Diskursstrategien im Rechtspopulismus. Freiheitliche Partei Österreichs und Schweizerische Volkspartei zwischen Opposition und Regierungsbeteiligung*, Wiesbaden: VS Verlag für Sozialwissenschaften.

Hanf, T. (2008), 'Foreword', in T. Hanf (ed.), *Power Sharing: Concepts and Cases*, Byblos: UNESCO International Centre for Human Sciences, pp. 5–9.

Ibrahim, M. (2005), 'The Securitization of Migration: A Racial Discourse', *International Migration*, 43(5): 163–87.

Jessop, R. D. (2002a), *The Future of the Capitalist State*, Cambridge: Polity Press.

— (2002b), 'Liberalism, Neoliberalism and Urban Governance: A State-Theoretical Perspective', *Antipode*, 34: 452–72.

Kress, G. and van Leeuwen, T. (1996), *Reading Images*, London: Routledge.

Krzyżanowski, M. (2002) 'Haider: the new symbolic element in the ongoing discourse of the past', in R. Wodak and A. Pelinka, (eds), *The Haider Phenomenon in Austria,* New Brunswick, NJ: Transaction Publishers, pp. 121–57.

— (2010), *The Discursive Construction of European Identities*, Frankfurt am Main: Peter Lang.

— (2012), 'Right-Wing Populism, Opportunism and Political Catholicism: On Recent Rhetorics and Political Communication of Polish PiS (Law and Justice) Party', in A. Pelinka and Sir Peter Ustinov Institute (eds), *Populismus - Herausforderung oder Gefahr für die Demokratie?* Vienna: Braumüller Verlag (in press).

Krzyżanowski, M. and Wodak, R. (2009), *The Politics of Exclusion: Debating Migration in Austria*, New Brunswick, NJ: Transaction Publishers.

Manoschek, W. (2002), 'FPÖ, ÖVP and Austria's Nazi past', in R. Wodak and A. Pelinka (eds), *The Haider Phenomenon in Austria,* New Brunswick, NJ: Transaction Publishers, pp. 3–17.

O'Halloran, K. L. (2008), 'Systemic Functional-Multimodal Discourse Analysis (SF-MDA): Constructing Ideational Meaning Using Language and Visual Imagery', *Visual Communication*, 7(4): 443–75.

Pelinka, A. (1990), *Zur österreichischen Identität. Zwischen deutscher Vereinigung und Mitteleuropa*, Vienna: Ueberreuter.

— (1993), *Die Kleine Koalition. SPÖ – FPÖ 1983–1986,* Vienna: Böhlau.

— (2005), *Vom Glanz und Elend der Parteien. Struktur- und Funktionswandel des österreichischen Parteiensystems,* Innsbruck: Studien Verlag.

Pelinka, A. and Wodak, R. (eds) (2002), '*Dreck am Stecken*'. *Politik der Ausgrenzung,* Vienna: Czernin Verlag.

Pollak, A. (2008), 'Analysing documentaries', in R. Wodak and M. Krzyżanowski (eds), *Qualitative Discourse Analysis in the Social Sciences,* Basingstoke: Palgrave Macmillan, pp. 77–96.

Richardson, J. E. (2004), *(Mis)Representing Islam. The Racism and Rhetoric of British Broadcast Newspapers,* Amsterdam: John Benjamins.

Richardson, J. E. and Wodak, R. (2009a). 'Recontextualising Fascist Ideologies of the Past: Right-wing Discourses on Employment and Nativism in Austria and the United Kingdom', *Critical Discourse Studies,* 6(4): 251–67.

— (2009b). 'The Impact of Visual Racism: Visual Arguments in Political Leaflets of Austrian and British Far-right Parties', *Controversia,* 6(2): 45–77.

Reisigl, M. and Wodak, R. (2000), *The Semiotics of Racism: Approaches in CDA,* Vienna: Passagen Verlag.

— (2001), *Discourse and Discrimination. Rhetorics of Racism and Anti-Semitism,* London: Routledge.

— (2009), 'The discourse-historical approach (DHA)', in R. Wodak and M. Meyer (eds), *Methods of Critical Discourse Analysis* (2nd edn), London: Sage, pp. 87–121.

Scollon, R. and Levine, P. (2004), 'Multimodal Discourse Analysis as the Confluence of Discourse and Technology', in P. Levine and R. Scollon (eds), *Discourse and Technology: Multimodal Discourse Analysis,* Washington, DC: Georgetown University Press, pp. 1–7.

Taggart, P. and Szczerbiak A. (eds) (2008), *Opposing Europe? The Comparative Party Politics of Euroscepticism* (Vols 1 and 2), Oxford: Oxford University Press.

van Dijk, T. A. (1988), *News as Discourse,* Hillsdale, NJ: Lawrence Erlbaum Associates.

van Leeuwen, T. (2008), *Discourse as Practice: New Tools for Critical Discourse Analysis,* Cambridge: Cambridge University Press.

Wodak, R. (2001), 'The discourse-historical approach' in R. Wodak and M. Meyer (eds), *Methods of Critical Discourse Analysis,* London: Sage, pp. 63–95.

— (2009) 'In Österreich nichts Neues – oder doch?', *Zukunft,* 7(8): 18–22.

— (2011). 'Suppression of the nazi past, coded languages, and discourse of silence: Applying the discourse-historical approach to post-war anti-Semitism in Austria' in W. Steinmetz (ed.) *Political Languages in the Age of Extremes,* Oxford: Oxford University Press, pp. 351–79.

Wodak, R. and Köhler, K. (2010), 'Wer oder was ist »fremd«? Diskurshistorische Analyse fremdenfeindlicher Rhetorik in Österreich', *SWS Rundschau,* 1: 33–55.

Wodak, R. and Krzyżanowski, M. (2008a), 'Migration und Rassismus in Österreich', in B. Gomes, A. Hofbauer, W. Schicho and A. Sonderegger (eds), *Rassismus. Beiträge zu einem vielgesichtigen Phänomen,* Wien: Mandelbaum, pp. 257–79.

— (2008b), *Qualitative Discourse Analysis in the Social Sciences.* Basingstoke: Palgrave Macmillan.

Wodak, R. and Pelinka, A. (eds) (2002), *The Haider Phenomenon in Austria,* New Brunswick, NJ: Transaction Publishers.

Wodak, R. and van Dijk, T. A. (eds) (2000), *Racism at the Top,* Klagenfurt: Drava.

10

Developments within the Radical Right in Germany: Discourses, Attitudes and Actors

Britta Schellenberg[1]

Public discourse and attitudes

The Sarrazin debate

Even though there is wider acceptance of heterogeneity, recently we have also witnessed a new Social-Darwinistic discourse in Germany, defaming certain groups, especially Muslims. The best example of such a discourse is the so-called Sarrazin debate. The starting point was an interview with Thilo Sarrazin (Sozialdemokratische Partei Deutschlands/Social Democratic Party (SPD)), a former Senator of Finance for Berlin and board member of the German Federal Bank, in the cultural magazine *Lettre Internationale* in autumn 2009 (Sarrazin 2009: 197–201). In the interview, Sarrazin complained of a steady increase in Arab and Turkish migrants in Berlin and called this a 'negative selection'. Muslims were '*integrationsunwillig*' (unwilling to integrate) and '*integrationsunfähig*' (unable to integrate), Sarrazin said. Shortly afterwards, in 2010, he published a book, with a provocative title, describing the outcome of such 'negative selection': '*Deutschland schafft sich ab*' (Germany Abolishes Itself) (Sarrazin 2010). Within two months the title became Germany's best-selling book on politics in a decade. This reflects the willingness of many to consume his claims, the attraction of his assertions and the public controversy about them.

In his book, Sarrazin categorizes people according to their intellectual ability and their assumed (economic) value to society. Sarrazin claims that an individual's ability is largely determined by his or her genes. And he connects the quality of genes to certain groups established along ethnic/religious and class lines. For instance, he believes that the children of uneducated and poor families deserve a minor place in German society because their intelligence quotient is – in his view – low. He elaborates at length on the 'problem' of a growing number of schoolchildren having a Muslim, Arab or Turkish background. The combined impact of a growing lower class, Muslim immigration

---

[1] The author wishes to thank Toby Axelrod for her proofreading.

and a decline in the birth rate among ethnic Germans would lead to the abolition of Germany. Typical of the German situation is that Sarrazin, at one point in the debate, also employs stereotypes that are understood as antisemitic: He states that every '*Volk*' (people) has its own genetic identity and he points at Jews who, he alleges, all share a certain gene (*Berliner Morgenpost*, 29 August 2010).

Sarrazin's statements were and remain a source of controversy, criticism and encouragement. They also provoked a dispute with his employer, the German Federal Bank, which led to his resignation. However, despite severe criticism within the SPD, attempts to exclude him from the party failed. The first ousting procedures against Sarrazin took place after the publication of his interview in *Lettre Internationale*. Even though a branch of the SPD Berlin had commissioned a report by the University of Potsdam that claimed Sarrazin's statements were racist, the SPD State Arbitration Commission in Berlin ultimately rejected the ousting procedures. An attempt to exclude Sarrazin from the party also was initiated by the SPD party executive after the publication of his book. However, Sarrazin had prominent advocates within the party, so when he promised to uphold Social Democratic norms a compromise was found. In SPD hearings, Sarrazin stated he did not intend to endanger equal opportunity norms in education by introducing a selective system and testified to his belief that all children are equally worthy as human beings. In a defensive statement he also said that he did not mean to argue on an ethnic basis but was rather looking at the cultural differences between people (*Zeit-online*, 21 April 2011).

Both Sarrazin's book and the debate surrounding it reflect the hostility towards Muslims and the lower classes, as well as a social-Darwinist orientation. However, in the media and even in politics, the Sarrazin debate has focused primarily on migration and Islam. It became clear (surprising some German Muslims) that many participants in the discussion made a distinction between 'Germans' and 'Muslims'.

Before looking at how the radical right reacts to the Sarrazin debate and tries to prosper from it, I will present results of attitudinal surveys. Here we can see how widespread 'group focused enmity' (Heitmeyer 2002–11)[2] is within the German population.

Radical-right attitudes in the general population

Attitude surveys indicate that about 8.2 per cent of the German population hold hard-core right-wing extremist views (Decker et al. 2010: 96). Extreme right-wing views had been declining continuously since 2002, but opinion polls show an increase in 2010. According to a study by the University of Leipzig, *Die Mitte in der Krise*, commissioned by the *Friedrich-Ebert-Stiftung*, almost 35 per cent of the population believe that 'the presence of so many foreigners is a threat to Germany'. There is a rise in the categories of: 'approval of dictatorship' (5.1%), 'chauvinism' (19.3%), 'xenophobia' (24.7%) and 'social Darwinism' (3.9%). In the former East Germany,

---

[2] 'Group focused enmity' is a syndrome that W. Heitmeyer of the Bielefeld Institute analyses in his long-term study, 'Deutsche Zustände' (State of affairs in Germany). It focuses on dimensions like Islamophobia, anti-Semitism and hostility against the homeless.

some of the categories found much more approval than in the former West ('approval of dictatorship' 6.8%, 'xenophobia' 35%, 'social Darwinism' 6.2%) (Decker et al., 2010). The study on 'group focused enmity' (GMF) by the Bielefeld Institute records similarly high acceptance of xenophobic statements. The study, which collects data on an annual basis, illustrates a sharp rise in Islamophobia among the German population. Despite the relatively low proportion of Muslims in the German population (around 5%), the study shows that 46 per cent agree with the statement 'There are too many Muslims in Germany' and 52.2 per cent of respondents held the view that Islam is an intolerant religion. The opinions of Germans towards Muslims and Islam therefore largely correspond to opinions held in the rest of the European countries covered by the study (average country samples: 44.2%; 54.4%). However, German respondents agreed least frequently with the statement: 'Muslim culture fits in well in Germany' (16.6%); in other words, of all the Europeans sampled, Germans are the most critical of Muslim culture (country sample average: 31.3%) (Zick & Küpper 2009).[3]

Recent studies also show a fairly high agreement with classic antisemitic statements: Almost 15 per cent of respondents agreed with the statements, 'Jews are more prone than other people to use nasty tricks to get what they want' and 'Jews simply have something special and unique about them, and don't fit in so well with us' (Decker et al. 2010: 73f., 79). Concerning antisemitic attitudes, a new phenomenon can be detected: anti-Semitism in the guise of criticism against Israel or finding expression through criticism of Holocaust remembrance. Far more people agree with antisemitic statements in those contexts, as the following examples show: 44.4 per cent agree with the statement: 'Looking at Israel's politics I can understand that people dislike Jews', and 51.2 per cent agree with the direct comparison between Israel and the National Socialist regime (Heyder et al. 2005: 151); 54 per cent agree with the statement 'the Jews use the commemoration of the Holocaust for their own purposes' (Rensmann 2004: 492). While this 'new' anti-Semitism is widespread, the levels of agreement with openly antisemitic statements are still fairly high.

A further interesting finding is that various hostile attitudes show a positive correlation, proving the existence of a phenomenon Heitmeyer calls 'group-focused enmity'. The annual surveys show another trend in Germany: increasing enmity against the homeless and jobless (Heitmeyer 2002: 10–11). At this point it is possible to conclude that the themes Sarrazin put on the agenda correspond with attitudes in the general population: widespread anti-Muslim sentiment, indirectly voiced antisemitic attitudes and derogation of socially 'weak' groups.

The radical right

The ethnicization of problematic social relations or individual dispositions creates favourable conditions for a radical right-wing perception of reality. Indeed, radical right-wing parties took their chances and campaigned with Thilo Sarrazin: The right-wing extremists (NPD) stated that 'Sarrazin is right' and the recent election

---

[3]   Countries studied: France, Germany, Great Britain, Hungary, Italy, Netherlands, Poland, Portugal.

campaign of the right-wing populist party Pro-Deutschland (Pro-Germany)[4] (Berlin, September 2011) read: 'Cast a vote for Thilo's theses' (*Wählen gehen für Thilos Thesen*).[5] René Stadtkewitz, a former Christian Democratic Union (CDU) member of the Berlin State Parliament, emphasized – when announcing the formation of a new Islamophobic party, Die Freiheit, in October 2010 – the need to stop blaming Sarrazin, who in his view had singled out the most important theme of the day ('Muslim immigrants'). Actors on the radical right agree with the overall picture drawn in the debate: Certain conflicts are interpreted as 'survival battles of specific groups of people or races', and individuals are attributed a certain value by virtue of their membership of a specific ethnic or cultural group. However, those on the radical right applaud only Sarrazin's anti-Muslim statements and his criticism of migration. The fact that Sarrazin defames the lower classes[6] as being (economically) useless is largely ignored. Being incongruent with a primarily National Socialist radical right (parties, subculture), the 'economic usefulness discourse' is rather characteristic of a racist élitism held by less visible right-wing radical players: Members of the duelling and non-duelling fraternities and segments of the (old) German élite.

The radical right in Germany shares not only a belief in a homogeneous and superior German nation or '*Volk*' that is threatened by 'the others' or certain destructive powers, it also opposes the great triggers of cultural shifts since the reign of National Socialism: the Allied 'occupation' of Germany, especially liberal and allegedly 'decadent' American impulses, the political movement of 1968 and Germany's immigration policy. However, as the radical right is a heterogeneous phenomenon, it is necessary to acknowledge (at least roughly) its different ideological groups. It is also important to stress that these different groups often have close contacts with each other and even intermingle.

National socialist-oriented groups

Right-wing extremism in Germany has been marked by a lively subculture and diverse movement-type organizations. The Freie Kameradschaften (Free Associations), loose networks of 10–30 neo-Nazis, were developed in reaction to perceived State repression. The Freie Kameradschaften regard themselves as part of a 'national resistance', a 'radical-right united front'. There are about 150 regional and supra-regional groups in Germany. Since around 2002, a new group has become an established part of the far right in Germany – and an export: the Autonome Nationalisten (Autonomous Nationalists). Their supporters are mostly very young and adopt the clothing styles and some of the habits of left-wing groups,[7] particularly the autonomous Schwarze Blocks (Black Blocks). The group is attractive to some young people in precarious situations, offering temporary accommodation (e.g. beds for homeless youths) and

---

[4] The party was founded 2005 in Cologne as the national branch of *Pro Cologne*, which had just been elected to the Civil Council of Cologne. For a description of the party, see below.
[5] Sarrazin sued those parties.
[6] He includes Turkish and Arab migrants in this category.
[7] For instance, they live in a commune, gather and listen to 'protest' music, join protest marches and even shout slogans only slightly (but decisively) different from those of the left: *Hoch die nationale Solidarität!* (Long live national solidarity!) instead of *Hoch die internationale Solidarität!* (Long live international solidarity!).

jobs (Borstel 2010). This extreme right scene is characterized by high levels of violence (Schellenberg 2011a: 70–2).

With the NPD, which was set up in 1964, Germany also has a hard-core right-wing extremist party. Many of its members and functionaries are former Nazis. Today, while the party is recruiting its personnel partly from violence-prone neo-Nazi groups like the Freie Kameradschaften, it also is trying to appear gentrified and to attract members from the common middle class. For some years now the NPD has increasingly won local and regional mandates, especially in rural areas of eastern Germany. Moreover, it recently had electoral success[8] in the federal states of Saxony (2004 election: 9.2%; 2009: 5.6%) and Mecklenburg-West Pomerania (2006 election: 7.3%; 2011: 6.0%). In Thuringia (2009: 4.3%) and Saxony-Anhalt (2011: 4.6%) the NPD just missed entering the Federal State Assembly (2009: 4.3%). Today the former 'old men's party' is particularly active in reaching out to young people, including through leisure activities or the distribution of free CDs. The NPD's 'School Playground' CD, which has appeared in various versions since 2006, promotes right-wing ideology and boastfully describes the party as 'the movement'.[9] These groups are particularly successful in rural areas of the former East Germany.

Elitist racists and xenophobic anti-Muslim groups

In addition to the National Socialist scene there is an élitist radical right with a long tradition. Its supporters are likely to be both quite wealthy (or descended from rich families) and well-educated. In this group, ideas à la Sarrazin are a matter of course. They have nationalistic and social-Darwinist beliefs. Typical exponents are: student fraternities and duelling fraternities as well as media, such as the weekly paper *Junge Freiheit* (Young Freedom/Liberty) and the internet-newspaper/blog 'Politically Incorrect'. They seek to build a bridge between hard-core neo-Nazi ideologies and more complex nationalistic and conservative attitudes.

On the political level, the ideology is represented by parties like the Republikaner (REP), which – after having had some regional successes (mainly in the 1980s and 1990s) – has become quite meaningless, or the Schill Party, which was only briefly successful in Hamburg at the beginning of the millennium. So far, those parties have found no permanent space in politics.

However, there is a fairly new party group that takes up anti-Muslim propaganda as its central theme: Member groups describe themselves as 'populist' or 'citizens' movements and put the topic of Islam – with its widespread connotations of fear – at the heart of their political agenda. Today the civic action group Pro Köln (Pro Cologne) is the most successful of these. Its branches Pro NRW in the state of North Rhine-Westphalia (regional) and Pro Deutschland (national) are less important. A typical slogan of the party is: 'We oppose the Islamisation of Cologne'. Pro Cologne was set up as an association in 1996 and survived into the new millennium through the efforts of activists from the extreme right-wing scene. The initiators and members of

---

[8]   A party must receive 5 per cent of the vote in order to gain seats in a regional or federal legislature.
[9]   The contents and aims of the CDs are presented and analysed in detail in Schellenberg 2011b.

these anti-Muslim parties are often linked to the right-wing extremist scene (Häusler 2008). In 2004, Pro Cologne succeeded in winning 4.7 per cent of the vote, thus gaining four seats on the Cologne City Council. The party particularly attracts attention through initiatives against the building of mosques. Another party is Bürgerinitative Ausländerstopp (civic action group to stop foreigners). It was founded in Nuremberg in 2001 and was able to send two representatives to the Nuremberg City Council and one to the Munich City Council.[10]

A rather new party that seems (so far) not to be influenced by the right-wing extremist scene is Die Freiheit (freedom/liberty), formed in October 2010 by René Stadtkewitz, then a member of Berlin's State Parliament for the CDU. He was excluded from the CDU after having initiated a round table called 'Islam as obstacle to integration' and inviting the Dutch populist Geert Wilders as speaker. The agenda of this new party is mainly anti-Muslim. Die Freiheit seems to be inspired by Wilders and his right-wing populist Partij voor de Vrijheid (Party for Freedom, PVV). Wilders participated in the election campaign for Stadtkewitz's new party in Berlin. However, so far, Die Freiheit has failed to succeed in elections. Despite its intensive election campaign in Berlin – using Sarrazin allusions – it received less than 1 per cent of the vote for the Berlin Parliament in September 2011.

Characteristically, these players have intensive European liaisons. For instance, Pro Cologne is a member of the European network 'Cities Against Islamisation' and receives support from the Freiheitliche Partei Österreichs (Freedom Party Austria, FPÖ) and the Belgian Vlaams Belang (Flemish Interest). Anti-Muslim political parties in Germany are not only linked with those in other European countries but inspired by them. These currently active groups are highly xenophobic and today identify 'the Muslim' as the prototypical 'other'. The main goal of those groups is to declare cultural war on Islam and Muslims and to fight the 'multicultural society'. But they have other hate targets, including Roma and migrants in general, whom they describe as 'criminal elements'.

However, it may be important to note that, in Germany, these parties have no modern spin to them – they usually appear authoritarian and their protagonists are almost exclusively male. For an understanding of the phenomenon in Germany, it is also helpful to note that all the described groups cling to Germany's political traditions: In contrast to other European countries, Germany has at best few liberal and democratic historical reference points; it also has a short history as 'a' or 'one' nation. The radical right relates to authoritarian and neurotic nationalist traditions and movements.

Failure and success

Given their electoral results on the national level, all these parties are quite unimportant. The NPD scored relatively well in 2009, gaining 1.5 per cent of the vote in the national election (its best result was 4.3% in 1969). So far, parties of the radical right have gained only regional and local success. An exception was the European success of the

---

[10] Since their politicians come from the right-wing extremist subcultural scene and foster contacts with this scene and the NPD, the Bürgerinitative Ausländerstopp is often called a 'Tarnorganisation' (cover organization) in the media.

Republikaner (Republican, REP) in 1989. It won 7.1 per cent of the vote and entered the European Parliament.

However, there are some tendencies that need to be noted: As early as 2005, German journalist and publicist Toralf Staud spoke of right-wing extremism dominating everyday culture in some rural areas of eastern Germany and described this phenomenon as the 'process of the east German provinces becoming fascist' (Staud 2005). Recent scientific research has examined the expansion of right-wing radicalism at the local level and confirmed Staud's point. There are clear indications of a growing presence of far-right structures at the local level and people are increasingly accepting its manifestations (e.g. organizations, political parties) Buchstein & Heinrich 2010, Schellenberg 2012).[11] In some areas today, right-wing radicals are seen as acceptable political players (Staud 2005, Buchstein & Heinrich 2010, Schellenberg 2012).

Special situation in Germany?

Despite the evident potential for extreme right-wing attitudes among the German population and its vibrant subcultural scene,[12] current radical right-wing parties have considerable difficulties in gaining credibility and acceptance among the wider population. Basically, radical-right parties do not enjoy a good reputation. A set of legal and historical conditions as well as developments in political culture make it difficult for the radical right to become widely acceptable political players in Germany.

Legal and political consequences from the history of national socialism

German law orients itself strictly against all actors and movements that exhibit a relationship to National Socialism. The political system of the Federal Republic of Germany, built on a free democratic order, understands itself to be a '*Wehrhafte Demokratie*' (defensive democracy). That means that the democratic State is supposed to prevent attacks against it and thus a repetition of history, namely the hegemony of National Socialism. Against this background, comprehensive legislation is to be understood as being against offences defined as right-wing extremism in Germany. Everything that opposes the German Constitution or refers to an affinity with National Socialism, whether in writing, speech, symbols or structure, is forbidden. The basic principle of the legislation is a variety of State measures against right-wing extremism, particularly those with limitations on associations and demonstrations.

Parties of the radical right are discredited in many people's eyes simply by their relationship to Nazism. Most people reject Nazism and believe their life within a pluralist democracy is preferable to the conditions of the Third Reich. Denying the Holocaust, using National Socialist symbols or wording, is prohibited by German law

---

[11] This trend is embedded in a set of occurrences and sensitivities that lead to a dissociation from federal politics and its general norms (like pluralism and liberalism).

[12] In Germany not only is there more violence committed by right-wing radicals than in other Western European countries, there also is an innovative far-right subculture (as mentioned, *Freie Kameradschaften* and *Autonome Nationalisten*).

and politicians from right-wing radical parties are regularly accused or convicted of such offences. In broad sections of society those parties are still suspected of wishing to resurrect National Socialism. This accusation is made not only against the clearly National Socialist-oriented groups but also against today's anti-immigrant and anti-Islam parties.[13]

Recent political choices and agendas

Moreover, there are quite a few developments in German society that make it difficult for political parties of the radical right to gain more support: In contrast to other European countries, Germany has – after a long phase of scepticism and denial that Germany is a land of immigration – seen a recent opening up towards migration and a trend to accept migrants as part of society.[14] A milestone was set only in 2000 when regulations on German nationality were reformed: Nationality is no longer based on '*Blutsrecht*' (*jus sanguinis*), a purely ethnic definition of nationality, but now includes aspects of '*Bodenrecht*' (*jus soli*). Also, the German immigration law of 2002/2004 reflects the country's new perception of itself as a land of immigration. Today, all mainstream political parties welcome qualified immigrants and foster their integration. This change was prompted first and foremost by economic conditions: Germany's population is decreasing and it is increasingly difficult to find enough qualified workers to keep the economy running smoothly.

It is also only quite recently that wider parts of society have become increasingly vigilant about radical right aspirations.[15] A key year was 2000, when – after some serious cases of violence – Chancellor Gerhard Schröder called for an 'uprising of all decent people'. This is due to the tireless commitment of some individuals with an influence on public opinion and decision-making, such as journalists, politicians and lawyers, as well as civil-rights activists. One big step forward was the initiation of State funding programmes for activities against right-wing extremism, xenophobia and anti-Semitism. Even though the programmes have been changed slightly by the present liberal-conservative government coalition (CDU/CSU and FDP), their core direction has been maintained: engagement for diversity, countering right-wing extremism.[16]

Another main losing formula for the radical right seems to be the growing support for plurality and individualism. Attitude surveys show that the oldest generation (people born before or during the Nazi era) tend towards right-wing extremism more strongly than people born and socialized in the Federal Republic of Germany. Younger

[13] One indicator is that the Federal Office for the Protection of the Constitution, or a Länderbranch (State branch), watches these parties and reports on them – which is only permitted if a party or group is officially assessed as (potentially) anti-constitutional.

[14] Since the 1950s, Germany has had agreements with foreign countries on labour recruitment and a growing percentage of migrants in the population, but it had never accepted the definition of being a country of immigrants who make a permanent home in Germany.

[15] For instance: politicians (especially federal), journalists, clergy (especially Protestant ministers), stars (musicians, football players) and active citizens.

[16] However, the government has initiated programmes against 'left-wing extremism' and 'Islamist extremism', and thus is partly relativizing the threat posed by the radical/extremist right (which – as mentioned above – is very violent in Germany, being responsible for at least 182 murders since 1990).

generations tend to be more liberal and cosmopolitan, even if not free of extreme right-wing attitudes (Bergmann 2001). The latest Shell Youth Study showed that most young people have a generally positive attitude towards social change; 84 per cent of them actually associate globalization with the freedom to travel, work and study all over the world. They appreciate a society that has become more open to pluralism and embraces internationality, for instance in cultural realms (e.g. music) (Albert et al. 2010).[17]

Is the radical right changing?

The radical right interprets the increased public engagement against right-wing extremism and for diversity as an attack against itself. It tries to discredit this attack (by claiming it is foreign led or politically triggered by the far left). The radical right sees 'natural' German culture and its nationalistic norms as being at stake, and is looking for new forms and spaces to articulate its concerns.[18]

The radical right is reacting to the losing formula of national socialism

Attempting to shake off its bad reputation, the radical right reacts to certain 'losing formulas'. Parties of the radical right are responding to the widespread dislike of National Socialism with their own ambivalent relationship to it. On the one hand, they allude to its ideology and even to its crimes: For instance, the NPD campaigned in the 2011 Berlin elections with the slogan '*Gas geben*' (the wording is ambiguous in German: it could mean 'accelerate' or 'give/treat with gas' which is seen by many as a reference to and glorification of the National Socialist concentration camps). On the other hand, the NPD is distancing itself from Nazism and accuses political opponents of trying to discredit the party by making absurd comparisons. Recently, the party has even started to accuse political adversaries of being Nazi-like or being related to Nazism.[19] Even though National Socialist allusions are still common, radical right-wing parties of today fight associations with National Socialism.

Populist and revolutionary?

Political parties of the radical right take advantage of popular fears of relegation and loss to act as so-called advocates for the common people, or the losers in globalized economic processes. They propagate a 'national and social' policy, welcoming a welfare state that takes care of (only) its ethnic-national citizens. This is reflected in slogans

---

[17] However, some segments of the younger population are sceptical about social change in general, and 10 per cent of young people experience a depressing lack of opportunity within society.

[18] One sad example is the 'Nationalsozialistische Untergrund' (NSU), whose members murdered at least ten people (Turkish and Greek migrants and a policewoman) in the last decade.

[19] For instance, a NPD member of the Parliament of Saxony accused a CDU MP of having a father who was a high-level National Socialist functionary. In this context, the NPD representative demanded that this fact be discussed in public. Speech of Jürgen Gansel (NPD) in the Parliament of Saxony (Sächsischer Landtag 2007: 7,840).

such as 'jobs for Germans first' (e.g. NPD, REP), '*sozial geht nur national*' (the only way to be social is to be nationalist) (NPD) or 'social security for our people' (REP).

National Socialist-oriented groups in particular, but also the protagonists of the anti-Muslim parties, call mainstream political parties and their politicians élitist, corrupt and profoundly antisocial. They attack them as 'the ruling class' and 'fat cats' and call their politics 'dirty tricks' and '*Asozialpolitik*' (anti-social politics). A big issue for radical right-wing parties like the NPD was the recent 'Hartz IV' reform of basic social services. In this context they argued that 'the rich' would let their people down. Of course, this socialist bias of the radical right has its tradition in Germany – but it gains new importance in a rapidly changing world that leaves many behind and creates a growing gap between the advantaged and the disadvantaged. The agitation of the radical right on those issues reflects a populist undercurrent as well as a revolutionary bias. As research on the radical right shows, young people on the street and less advantaged people are most vulnerable to these arguments (Schellenberg 2011a: 67).

Euphemistic language

Changes in the use of language are also characteristic of the fight of the radical right for greater public acceptance:[20] First the language becomes softer and the vocabulary of the old extreme right is expelled. One example is the word '*Rassentrennung*' (racial segregation). Today, such National Socialist vocabulary loses its appeal within the radical right, which instead uses terms such as '*Ethnopluralismus*' (ethnopluralism), which sounds harmless and positive and relates to popular concepts like diversity. However, it is the same old concept with the same old goals. Another term frequently used by the radical right is '*Freiheit*' (freedom/liberty) – even taken up as party name by the most recently founded right-wing radical party in Germany. '*Freiheit*' is used especially to refer to freedom of opinion and (discriminatory) speech and demands for the disregard or elimination of anti-discrimination legislation. This change in language and approach can be seen tentatively within the NPD (the old right-wing extremists) (Schellenberg 2011a), but is practised even more cleverly by the younger players in this ideological family. Especially *Die Freiheit* strives for soft language and distances itself from neo-Nazi thugs.

Ideological change or contradictions?

The goal of right-wing radicalism is an ethnically and culturally homogenous society: a right-wing utopia that promises to solve social and individual problems by excluding 'the guilty' or 'the other'. According to this logic, all that is alien must be identified and ruled out in order to ensure the nation's/people's survival. The definition of 'the other' is rather mutable and subject to the zeitgeist. Discourse analyses and attitude surveys make it clear: Today it is 'the Moslem' culture and religion in particular that are considered 'others'. Anti-Semitism, however, continues to be a core element of the radical right in Germany, with different guises for different right-wing players: from open hatred calling for violence among the extreme right, to codes and secondary allusions (such as

---

[20] This is not the case within the National Socialist-oriented subcultural scene.

in the reference to the 'American East Coast') among moderate right-wing radicals and public players. The very young political party, Die Freiheit, is among those European populist parties (like the Danish People's Party and Wilders' Party for Freedom) that exclude anti-Semitism and even seek proximity to the State of Israel (Jäger 2010). In Germany there are two explanations for this course of action: First it is a strategic turning away from Nazism. Especially, anti-Semitism is still (though decreasingly) taboo in the political arena and has – if expressed – always resulted in resignation from political office.[21] Secondly, by pointing out that Muslims are threatening Israel, these parties aim at further discrediting the Muslim population at home as naturally aggressive and destructive. However, Die Freiheit has never gained much support, which might be characteristic of the present situation in Germany: Since the party is categorized publicly as right-wing radical, it has to cope with being related to National Socialism and the extreme right. In addition, it is hard to imagine that abstinence from anti-Semitism and support for Israel help the party gain popularity.

In Germany, not only does anti-Semitism have a long tradition; there also is a tradition of good relations between the radical right and the Arab/Persian world and its (Muslim) leaders, especially when they are against Israel and Jews. One example is the relationship between the Nazis and the Mufti of Jerusalem, Hajj Amin al-Husaini. He found refuge in National Socialist Germany in 1941, where he settled (Nordbruch 2008: 261). More recent examples are the close contacts between right-wing extremist groups like the neo-Nazi Wehrsportgruppe Hoffmann (Paramilitary Sport Group Hoffmann[22]) and Arab countries: The group had an extraterritorial group in Lebanon. And one of their members fled Germany for Lebanon after having committed, in 1980, a double murder with antisemitic motivations (Virchow 2011). Another recent example of such relations is the visit of NPD functionaries[23] to the Holocaust denial conference in Teheran in 2006, which was hosted by Iranian President Mahmoud Ahmadinejad. An ideological closeness to extremist Islamist groups was visible when the right-wing extremist scene celebrated the terror attacks of 9/11 as pay-off to the United States, Jews and Western decadence.[24] However, it is not only the extreme right that is deeply antisemitic but also the right and left fringe of mainstream parties.[25] Even though there are some signs that actors of the radical right strategically approach Israel, it cannot be taken for granted that parties like Die Freiheit will ever find a space in Germany's

---

[21] The latest example is that of Martin Hohmann, who was a member of the German Bundestag (CDU). He gave a speech that used antisemitic reasoning and sources and characterized the Jews as 'a nation of perpetrators' in the time of Stalinism. As a consequence he was excluded from the CDU/ CSU faction of the Bundestag (2005) and later also from the CDU. See Benz 2011: 168–73.

[22] Hoffmann is the surname of the founder of this paramilitary group.

[23] Two prominent right-wing radicals, Horst Mahler and Günter Deckert, were prevented by the State from leaving Germany to attend the conference. The conference was attended by NPD functionaries Carsten Bormann, Benedikt Frings, Markus Haverkamp, Arnold Höfs and Herbert Hoff, as well Christian Lindtner, a member of the NPD, and Peter Töpfer, another right-wing activist from Germany.

[24] See for instance the text and video to the songs 'ZOG I' and 'ZOG II' by the band Stahlgewitter. The latter is printed in: Schellenberg 2011b: 50.

[25] This is not only shown by attitude surveys but also by statements from people of the right fringe of mainstream parties like Hohmann (CDU) and Möllemann (FDP). Both attracted attention by making antisemitic statements (see fn. 18).

political arena or that other right-wing radical parties will distance themselves from anti-Semitism.

Conclusion

Unlike radical-right parties in most European countries, those in Germany have so far failed to break through at the national level. This is due in large part to a comprehensive repression of neo-Nazi activities in Germany and to the fact that political parties are related to Nazism and therewith discredited. However, as parts of society dissociate from political developments, norms and the changing zeitgeist, a certain degree of right-wing radical stabilization is becoming apparent in specific groups (modernity losers, parts of the old élite) and areas (rural remote areas).

Moreover, the radical right has taken up the struggle against 'losing formulae' and against its own slow demise: It has developed an ambivalent relationship to Nazism in public, offensively distancing itself from it.[26] Some far-right leaders soften their language, striving to be democratic and to give positively connoted words (like freedom/liberty and pluralism) a new ideological meaning. In addition, they participate in the public debate about political culture and societal norms. Here they try to fight developments towards a liberal pluralist society in which people are seen as individuals and worthy members with equal rights. Finally, they take the opportunity to engage with public debate, which is increasingly directed against Muslims. However, this causes friction for at least some sections of the radical right – as German right-wing radicals are, traditionally, committed anti-Semites and tend to have rather good relations with Arab/Persian countries and (Muslim) leaders. On the ideological level, the belief in an existential threat to German identity from conspiratorial powers still plays a dominant role.

However, right-wing radical ideas are widespread among the German population. A trend in public discourse is hostility towards Muslims and other population groups such as migrants, the unemployed and the homeless. These attitudes are found well beyond the far-right spectrum. A discourse of economic 'usefulness' is currently superimposed over the xenophobic discourse in Germany. But for right-wing radical parties that target the disadvantaged, these two discourses are difficult to reconcile. It remains unclear whether or how the radical right can gain from them: On the one hand the 'economic usefulness discourse' might promote discrimination against Muslims – as this group comprises mainly former labour migrants and their descendants and is highly impacted by unemployment due to the increased need for skilled labour. On the other hand, the intermingling of those two discourses might make it difficult to attract the traditional target group of the radical right because this attack is also directed against them: people who feel dissociated from society and its norms and are living in fragile economic situations or feel that they are losing status within society. This group might feel excluded and discriminated against by aims à la Sarrazin: 'Positive selection'

---

[26] While, however, protesting about any debate over Germany's National Socialist past.

means – for the racist élitist group – diminishing or excluding certain ethnic groups as well as members of those families with little education and low status. The racist élitists believe the genes of members of those groups to be less promising and less worthy than those of the 'white élite'. That is the essential message of Sarrazin's 'Germany Abolishes Itself' – and the pattern of most populist discourse in Germany today.

References

Albert, M., Hurrelmann, K. and Quenzel, G. (eds) (2010), *Jugend 2010. 16. Shell Jugendstudie*, Frankfurt am Main: Fischer.

Bergmann, W. (2001), 'Wie viele Deutsche sind rechtsextrem, fremdenfeindlich und antisemitisch? Ergebnisse der empirischen Forschung von 1990–2000', in W. Benz (ed.), *Auf dem Weg zum Bürgerkrieg? Rechtsextremismus und Gewalt gegen Fremde in Deutschland*, Frankfurt am Main: Fischer, pp. 41–62.

Borstel, D. (2010), 'Der immergleiche braune Sumpf? Neuere Entwicklungen der rechtsextremen Szene', in J. P. Albrecht (ed.), *Strategien gegen Rechtsextremismus*, Berlin: The Greens/European Free Alliance in the European Parliament, pp. 9–20.

Buchstein, H. and Heinrich, G. (eds) (2010), *Rechtsextremismus in Ostdeutschland. Demokratie und Rechtsextremismus im ländischen Raum*, Schwalbach/TS: Wochenschau Verlag.

Decker, O., Weissmann, M., Kiess, J. and Brähler, E. (2010), *Die Mitte in der Krise: Rechtsextreme Einstellungen in Deutschland 2010*, Berlin: Friedrich-Ebert-Stiftung.

Häusler, A. (ed.) (2008), *Rechtspopulismus als 'Bürgerbewegung'. Kampagnen gegen Islam und Moscheebau und kommunale Gegenstratgeien*, Wiesbaden: Verlag für Sozialwissenschaften.

Heitmeyer, W. (ed.) (2002–11), *Deutsche Zustände*, Series 1–9, Frankfurt am Main: Suhrkamp.

Heyder, A., Iser, J. and Schmidt, P. (2005), 'Israelkritik oder Antisemitismus? Meinungsbildung zwischen Öffentichkeit, Medien und Tabus', in W. Heitmeyer (ed.), *Deutsche Zustände*, Series 3, Frankfurt am Main: Suhrkamp, pp. 144–65.

Jäger, L., 'Neue Freunde für Israel. Reise nach Jerusalem', *FAZ-net*, 13 December 2010. <www.faz.net/aktuell/feuilleton/debatten/neue-freunde-fuer-israel-reise-nach-jerusalem-15591.html> [accessed 17 October 2011].

Nordbruch, G. (2008), 'Palästina', in W. Benz (ed.), *Handbuch des Antisemitisus. Judenfeindschaft in Geschichte und Gegenwart*, Vol. 1, Länder und Regionen, München: Saur, pp. 259–64.

Rensmann, L. (2004), *Demokratie und Judenbild. Antisemtismus in der politischen Kultur der Bundesrepublik Deutschalnd*, Wiesbaden: Verlag für Sozialwissenschaften.

Sächsischer Landtag, 4. Wahlperiode, 94. Sitzung vom 12 December 2007, Tagesordnungspunkt 9, 'Schlägerei beim Mügelner Altstadtfest am 18/19 August 2007', Drucksache 4/9692.

Sarrazin, T. (2010), *Deutschland schafft sich ab*, München: DVA.

— (2009), 'Berlin auf der Couch (Interview)', *Lettre Internationale*, 86: 197–201.

— 'Ich bin kein Rassist (Interview)', *Berliner Morgenpost*, 29 August 2010. <www.morgenpost.de/berlin-aktuell/article1385382/Thilo-Sarrazin-Ich-bin-kein-Rassist.html> [accessed 17 October 2011].

Schellenberg, B. (2011a), 'The radical right in Germany: Its prohibition and reinvention', in N. Langenbacher and B. Schellenberg (eds), *Is Europe on the 'right' path? Right-wing*

Extremism and Right-wing Populism in Europe, Berlin: Friedrich-Ebert Foundation, pp. 57–81. <http://library.fes.de/pdf-files/do/08338.pdf> [accessed 31 March 2012].

— (2011b), *Unterrichtspaket Rechtsextremismus und Demokratie. Auseinandersetzung mit Rechtsextremismus anhand von Musik.* Schwalbach/Ts.: Wochenschau Verlag.

Schellenberg, B. (2012), 'Rechtsextremismus' und 'Fremdenfeindlichkeit' im öffentlichen Diskurs der Bundesrepublik Deutschland. Die Debatte über den Fall Mügeln. Diss. TU Berlin Juli 2012.

Staud, T. (2005), *Moderne Nazis. Die neuen Rechten und der Aufstieg der NPD*, Cologne: Kiepenheuer & Witsch.

Staud, T. (2005), *Moderne Nazis. Die neuen Rechten und der Aufstieg der NPD*, Cologne: Kiepenheuer & Witsch.

Virchow, F. (2011), 'Levin-Poeschke-Mord (1980)', in W. Benz (ed.), *Handbuch des Antisemitismus. Judenfeindschaft in Geschichte und Gegenwart.* Vol. 4, Ereignisse, Dekrete, Kontroversen, Berlin: De Gruyter/Saur, pp. 232–3.

Zeit-online, 'Parteiausschussverfahren. Sarrazin darf SPD-Mitglied bleiben', *Zeit-online*, 21 April 2011. <www.zeit.de/politik/deutschland/2011–04/sarrazin-spd-ausschluss> [accessed 17 October 2011].

Zick, A. and Küpper, B. (2009), 'Meinungen zum Islam und Muslimen in Deutschland und Europa. Ausgewählte Ergebnisse der Umfrage Gruppenbezogene Menschenfeindlichkeit in Europa', *Bielefeld University*. <www.uni-bielefeld.de/ikg/zick/ Islam_GFE_zick.pdf> [accessed 17 October 2011].

11

Italian Populism and the Trajectories of Two Leaders: Silvio Berlusconi and Umberto Bossi

Carlo Ruzza and Laura Balbo

In November 2011, Silvio Berlusconi resigned as Prime Minister of Italy. A few months earlier he had resigned as head of the Popolo della Libertà party (People of Freedom) – the leading partner in the right-wing coalition that had ruled Italy for most of the previous 15 years. These resignations marked a pause in the political career of one of the most visible and controversial leaders of Italian politics in recent years, whom several observers have characterized as a 'populist' (Meny & Surel 2002, Edwards 2005, Albertazzi & McDonnell 2008, Pasquino 2008, Ruzza & Fella 2011). Berlusconi's two resignations took place as Italy was sliding towards economic disaster, with a collapsing stock market and a crisis of confidence in the ability of the Italian state to service its large and mounting public debt. Following this resignation a new government of university professors and bankers briefly replaced Berlusconi and implemented a programme of financial austerity.

While most political parties supported this programme, including, although reluctantly, Berlusconi's party, the other notable 'populist' charismatic figure and Berlusconi's long-standing ally – Umberto Bossi, leader of the separatist party 'The Northern League' – reacted with a new wave of oratorical radicalism and theatrical actions in Parliament, reversing his previously more sedate pro-government stance. Thus the two former allies manifested different and incompatible views.

The deepening of the financial crisis unsettled the populist political axis which had characterized Italian politics in recent decades The centre-right coalition that ruled Italy in recent years had now lost its unity and a great deal of public support. However, through its leader and his vast financial empire, it retains control of much of the Italian media and enjoys continuing approval from large sections of the Italian social and political élites. Accordingly, now is a good time to reflect on the long-term legacy of this axis – and on the sociological consequences and impact on Italian society. We will argue that these consequences are even more important than the political ones, which many observers agree have been momentous, providing Italy with a new electoral law, a distinctive and different political culture and a set of new political parties. The social consequences are equally important, however. In the view of observers such as Albertazzi, Mazzoleni and Zaslove, these two leaders and their parties 'colonized' society with their values, their styles of communication, their strongly polarized views of enemies and friends, the personal qualities that they value and those that they condemn (Mazzoleni 2008, Zaslove 2008, Albertazzi & Rothenberg 2009) – a 'syndrome' often referred to as the 'Berlusconization' of Italy (Ginsborg 2004, Albertazzi & Rothenberg 2009: 8, Ginsborg & Asquer 2011). By reviewing the political trajectories of these two leaders, we shall seek to assess the impact of their ideas on Italian society. We also believe that reflecting on these two leaders, their strategies and the political opportunities that they exploited will also allow more general lessons to be drawn for Europe, where manifestations of populism are widespread. Although their impact is by no means historically concluded, enough evidence has now accumulated for more general reflection to be possible. We shall not provide an historical account of recent Italian political history, this is available from other sources (Ginsborg 2001, Bull & Newell 2005, Donovan & Onofri 2008). We shall instead concentrate on the sociological relevance of the visions and political communication of these two leaders.

It should be emphasized that Berlusconi's resignation has certainly not put an end to his long political career, but it nonetheless marks a momentous change in Italian politics. It signals the conclusion of a period which has been described as being characterized by the emergence and affirmation of populist politics to an extent possibly unique in contemporary European politics, albeit not unique to Italy (Ginsborg 2001, Tarchi 2008). The Italian case has been seen as epitomizing a more general European context in which complex dynamics have interacted to produce distinctive political alignments whose sociological counterpart is an equally distinctive configuration. We refer to dynamics such as the personalization of politics, the normalization of forms of 'hard' and 'soft' populism in civil society, the concentration of media ownership under the control of tycoons who have used it to advance their right-wing political views, the emergence of racism and xenophobia in the context of various types of 'enemy politics' and the growing legitimation of a right-wing political agenda across the public policy landscape (Mudde 2007). Equally important are mounting forms of anti-political reliance on charismatic leaders to remedy the perceived shortcomings of democratic institutions (Betz 1994). More generally, this has been a long period of triumph for the ideology of unfettered markets and retrenchment of the State – a period of affirmation for the ideologies of New Public Management in the public sector and glorification of deregulation in the private sector, an emerging ethos which has also notably characterized Italy (Kicker 2007). However, it has also been a period in which a clash has often been noted between the public affirmation of these pro-market ideologies and a concomitant, much slower implementation of liberalizing economic change. This has sometimes been labelled a triumph of style over substance, and in this regard populism has been seen as a political style, rather than as a coherent ideology or set of policies (Mair 2002, Taggart 2002).

In the Italian context, this process has sometimes been referred to as the 'Berlusconization' of Italy, with reference to both the glorification of markets and the 'politics of announcements' – a politics of style over substance, of declarations of principles over the implementation of policies. Similar phenomena have, however, been noted in other countries. The connections between them have not escaped analysts, and they are typically reflected in publications with titles such as *Le Sarkoberlusconisme* (Musso 2008).

Thus the financial crisis of 2008 and its long aftermath come at the conclusion of a long cycle of both neo-liberal and populist politics which has seen the affirmation and sometimes decline of populist European leaders. Although some have declined or died and some are still exerting political impact, over the years, a long list of influential populist political leaders has emerged. They have included well-known politicians such as Jörg Haider, Jean Marie Le Pen, Pim Fortuyn and the Kaczyński brothers. The rise of recent Italian populism in Italy began with Berlusconi's outstanding electoral success in 1994, amid promises of economic liberalization, meritocracy, efficiency and, above all, empowerment of 'the people', whom Berlusconi purported to represent directly, in contrast to the previous corrupt political élites that had ruled Italy during the post-war period (Poli 2001). Large sections of the Italian population accepted this recipe and shaped their identities accordingly. The victory of Berlusconi coincided with the birth of 'the Second Italian Republic' and the demise of an entire party system dominated by the Italian Christian Democratic Party, which disappeared after its involvement in a series of corruption trials. The early 1990s were therefore not only a period of political renewal, of which Berlusconi was seen as the main initiator, but also a period of social renewal, and carried hopes for a better society.

To gain a full understanding of the importance of this fact, one should follow Pierre Bourdieu's advice 'to try and think politics sociologically' (Bourdieu 2001). Hence, we shall seek to reconceptualize populism 'sociologically' by directing attention to the interrelated aspects of political and social change that it activates.

However, we argue that merely reporting a 'Berlusconization' of Italian society is not sufficient. This process must be framed in a broader context of mounting populist sentiments and of multiple, and even possibly incompatible, populisms (Tarchi 2002, 2008). A necessary first step is to conduct a parallel analysis of two populist figures, Berlusconi and Bossi. Both are 'winners' in the Italian political competition; both are charismatic leaders, both are deeply connected to their *popolo* (we shall use Italian *popolo* as it is a word reminiscent of the fascist rhetoric of an internally undifferentiated and externally exclusionary entity). And both of them are evidently important actors within a right-wing populist framework. But their 'stories' are very different.

We shall compare their public images and their political programmes and argue that their definition of *il popolo* is key to both. They embrace a vision of *il popolo* which requires and legitimizes an anti-immigration political discourse, xenophobic attitudes and language. Both Berlusconi and Bossi, with some differences, have contributed to disseminating exclusionary forms of public discourse which are now widely accepted, taken for granted by the public and recurrent in everyday language and practices.

Populism in Italy

The theme of Italian populism has been examined by historians, philosophers and political scientists, and it is central to ongoing debates (McDonnell 2006, Mastropaolo 2008, Tarchi 2008, Ruzza & Fella 2011). It would be difficult to summarize the relevant contributions adequately. Suffice it to say that, in the Italian context, the complex and historically late process of 'becoming a nation' has produced a recurring 'populist temptation'. Fascism was, of course, a long dramatic experience in Italian 'populism'. A nation divided by large geographical, cultural and even linguistic barriers attempted to reconstruct its identity with reference to ideologies concerning an invented and glorified historical heritage, enforced internal homogeneity and belligerent attitudes to invented threats (Berezin 1999). However, different visions of the nation, its enemies and its aspirations repeatedly clashed, and redefinitions were imposed by the outcomes of those clashes. An endeavour to redefine *il popolo* ensued from the defeat of fascism.

Over time, new attempts to redefine *il popolo* were prompted by the unsuitability of other ideologies that developed and then at least partially waned, such as visions of a re-Christianization of Italy, or of a socialist society. The late 1980s and early 1990s – the period of inception of the current populist right – were in this sense a crucial period of ideological collapse and renewed collective identity foundation (Cartocci 1996). The collapse of the Eastern Bloc and processes of secularization called for new visions of *il popolo*. Two such visions were embodied by Berlusconi and Bossi (ibid.).

Berlusconi and the 'people of freedom' (popolo della liberta')

Silvio Berlusconi has for years represented the ideal of the successful businessman, the very wealthy, very active and very 'modern' embodiment of the American model of success based on a 'work hard, play hard' lifestyle. This cultural icon has been embodied by his lifestyle, and it has been popularized by his media empire. With Berlusconi, post-war Italian national television, controlled by the Christian Democrats and intended as an instrument of mass literacy, popular education and indoctrination into the Christian values of charity and frugality, has been replaced by television centred on entertainment and portraying a world of scantily dressed women and affluent lifestyles. Once Berlusconi was in government, a combination of influence, through political control of public television channels and nearly total control of private television channels, cemented his impact on Italian culture and society (Andrews 2005, Edwards 2005, Pasquino 2007).

Through personal direct forms of communication, Berlusconi introduced a new model of political leadership onto the public stage – a model very different from the traditional one. The old model was based on long convoluted speeches by bland politicians using a set of complex metaphors only fully understandable to political insiders (Amadori 2002, Mazzoleni 2008). Berlusconi's political communication relies instead on the frequent use of jokes – often 'politically incorrect' ones – in which his adversaries are derided. He offers musical performances to the audience; he sings, makes joking references to aspects of his private life, including ones to his wealth and his body, his illnesses, hair transplants, cosmetic surgery and height (Mazzoleni 2008). Thus this is a 'personalization' of politics, which also alludes to a redefinition of the individual as a modern consumer – a powerful consumer of beauty treatments and quality clothes, with an affluent lifestyle. By means of his irreverence and flaunted wealth, Berlusconi takes the personalization of politics a step further than other politicians. He embodies the aspirations and qualities of *il popolo* that he claims to represent – the Westernized affluent consumer, the entrepreneur who despises politics and politicians. He claims that he engages in the discredited profession of politics purely for the sake of 'his people', not because he needs to, and not for career purposes. He claims that he is only 'lending' his entrepreneurial skills temporarily to an otherwise discredited occupation: that of the professional politician. And his is a people who idealize him precisely because of his unusual style, unprofessional behaviour and humorous remarks.

An emotional identification with their leader creates a symbolic bridge for voters – a connection between his charisma and their needs and hopes – bypassing the corrupt intermediating élites, the professional profiteers of the political world that Berlusconi despises. Thus in Berlusconi's case, the 'personalization of politics' is achieved through public performance which symbolizes anti-élitism but also hedonism and success, and which then justifies public political power through private social and economic power. In the words of his voters, 'he is so rich he does not need to steal' and 'he has been so successful as an entrepreneur, he can only be good for Italy' and also 'he will protect our economic interests in the financial world and in the business world because they are his own economic interests as well'. Messages of this kind are collected in a book of letters from his supporters that Berlusconi published in 2010 (Berlusconi 2010).

Anchoring his political spectacle to his body enables Berlusconi to claim a 'real' existence – a personal and emotional relevance that goes beyond what he often calls 'the theatre of politics'. In December 2009, he was attacked in Milan by a mentally unstable bystander who hit him in the face with a pointed object. Revealingly, he chose to be pictured and televised immediately afterwards, showing his wounds. His bloodied face thus attested to his 'real existence'. It cemented his connection with real people and negated his membership of unreachable social élites. It was also part of another spectacle. His wounded body echoed the stories of martyrdom and altruistic sacrifice so close to Catholic culture. It was suggested that he appeared to be undergoing a collective process of beatification (Ceri 2011).

This claimed self-sacrifice is naturally derided by Berlusconi's detractors, but among his supporters it has been accompanied by a rhetoric which vilifies all political enemies, typically described as morally unsound, unappreciative and prejudiced. This has resulted in a strong polarization of political views. Observers have noted that this climate has been conducive to Berlusconi's communication strategies, which are based on moralized anti-communist stances. Connections between the horrors of Soviet communist persecutions and his enemies are used as standard rhetorical devices in his speeches. Conversely, he portrays himself and his *popolo* as loving and caring – as affluent and happy, and therefore not full of the envy and hatred typical of losers in the capitalist economic competition. The title of the book previously mentioned, which collected the views of Berlusconi's supporters, conveys this view: 'Love always wins over envy and hatred' (Berlusconi 2010).

However, in 2008, Berlusconi's power and influence started to unravel. A series of sexual scandals erupted at precisely the time when the Italian economic situation was deteriorating. Initially, he tried to deny or minimize accusations of sexual misconduct, and once again he reinterpreted these scandals through the filter of his public persona: that is, he utilized them to prove his own anti-political nature, his exceptionality and therefore his membership of *il popolo* of affluent Western consumers whose hedonism allows occasional minor transgressions. Berlusconi's sexual misconduct was reinterpreted through a public performance consisting of jokes, denials and reinterpretations of events by his media, himself and his political allies. He reiterated his optimism, denying the seriousness of the financial crisis emerging throughout Europe and in Italy in particular.[1]

However, as the crisis began to affect the lifestyles of his constituents, Berlusconi gradually appeared to be the highly privileged member of an élite. His private vices started to be framed in public opinion as a logical extension of his conflict of interests, whereby he could do things precluded to others with the means at his disposal. It was only at this stage that the self-serving policies promoted by a Parliament that he effectively controlled became gradually less accepted, and in 2011 his electoral support started to wane (Ginsborg & Asquer 2011, Salvati 2012).

Umberto Bossi and the Northern League

The success of Berlusconi over such a long period would not have been possible without the protracted support of an ethno-nationalist party with roots in the affluent north. Umberto Bossi and his party, the Northern League, attracted national attention as a new phenomenon in the late 1980s, at a time when the 'new social movements' of the left-liberal family were beginning to decline. The 'Lega Nord' (The League – initially a smaller movement called the Lombard League) was, at the outset, generally seen as an eccentric and politically irrelevant formation. The League exhibited a distinctive repertoire of ethno-nationalist rituals (Albertazzi & McDonnell 2005, Huysseune 2006), which included the adoption of medieval costumes claimed to be typical of the northern Italian regions in medieval times, and advocated the use of local dialects. These traits were meant to reclaim the legitimacy of local traditions, and they were generally regarded as inappropriate by an Italian cultural establishment still grappling with both state-building and nation-building strategies. The cultural unification of Italy was a goal still widely accepted by all the social classes and political ideologies dominant at the time of the League's ascendency.

The League also manifested an openly anti-intellectual ethos, which included the adoption of simple and immediate language in political speeches, a refusal to legitimate and empower intellectuals among cadres and the rejection of the cosmopolitan ethos that marked the culture of educated Italian élites. The League's political discourse was thus strongly anti-political and anti-élitist from the outset (Ruzza & Schmidtke 1993, Cento Bull & Gilbert 2001, Gomez-Reino Cachafeiro 2001).

Umberto Bossi – the charismatic leader of this formation – epitomized cultural values and a political style which, at the time, appeared novel in their anti-modern ethos and unashamedly localist character. In contrast to Berlusconi, Bossi came from a small village, and from a culturally and economically modest background (Tambini 1993).

---

[1] For instance Christine Lagarde, noted: 'To have had him say at a press conference that there was no crisis in Italy because the restaurants were full, the planes were booked ... where was he?' (cited in *Newsweek*, 30 January 2012, 35).

He remained proudly attached to his origins and village. His political vision was one of a society radically different from Berlusconi's – a society of small producers rooted in strong morals and families, and grounded in strong communities. This vision, however, also attracted popular support and over the years became increasingly characterized in exclusionary ethno-nationalist terms, with open and recurrent xenophobic overtones and an increasing social conservativism.

Bossi therefore embodied a different vision of *il popolo* – not modern consumers but village dwellers. His vision appealed to a different audience, and it represented a powerful ideological alternative to the dominant ideologies of the post-war period – an ideology, at the time, as new and persuasive as Berlusconi's recipe for self-affirmation and personal freedom through consumerism. For instance, Berlusconi has referred to his hair transplants as a means to construct a better image and therefore enjoy a better life. For Bossi however, self-affirmation was a collective communal pursuit within which strong solidarities had to be cemented, with the exclusion of those who did not belong to the community – initially Italian southern workers, and then migrants.

In 2004 Bossi fell seriously ill and was forced off the public scene for a lengthy period. He returned as a deeply transformed person, an elderly man in bad physical shape but still determined to lead his party, and with a different kind of charisma – that of the great sage, the elder statesman.

Bossi had once abandoned his ally Berlusconi, leading to the collapse of the first Berlusconi government in 1994. However, after his illness, he remained a faithful ally until after Berlusconi's 2011 resignation, when Bossi once again withdrew his support for the coalition.

However, in the intervening period, he and his party remained strong allies of Berlusconi, and for over a decade they were a central component of his coalition. This was thus a coalition of two populisms – or, more precisely, a coalition of three populisms, because the third component of the centre-right coalition adopted a populist stance for a long period, although not as vehemently as the Berlusconi and Bossi formations. The third component was a party that represented the heirs of fascism – a mix of ageing, nostalgic members of pre-war fascism and younger modernizers, including the party leader, Gianfranco Fini. For them, the concept of *il popolo* was based on classic nation-building nationalism. For instance, the 1995 Statute of National Alliance – the then party of Fini – declared:

> National Alliance is a political movement which has as its objective the guarantee of the spiritual dignity and the social and economic aspirations of the Italian people, in respect of their civil traditions and national unity. (Alleanza-Nazionale 1995: 1)

These heirs of fascism thus embodied an opposite vision, of a united Italy, and consequently they often conflicted with the nation-dissolving efforts of the League. Their vision of *il popolo* was grounded in a reassertion of the fascist myths of past, but they were also aware of the limited historical viability of their goals, and therefore were less able to proclaim them (Ruzza & Fella 2009). Fini's political formation changed its name over the years. In the post-war period he led the Movimento Sociale Italiano

(Italian Social Movement); then, with the incorporation of conservative Catholics and a neoliberal component, he headed Alleanza Nazionale (National Alliance), which gradually merged with Berlusconi's party, Forza Italia, to form the Popolo delle Libertà. After breaking with Berlusconi, Fini left the coalition. In all these transformations the dominant ideological emphasis was always on Italian nationalism. However, after founding the new party, Futuro e Libertà, in 2011, Fini joined a centrist coalition with a large Christian component, which tempered much of his remaining populist rhetoric.

In recent years, Bossi's support became increasingly important for Berlusconi. As his personal relations with Fini gradually deteriorated, Berlusconi's political reliance on the League grew. The relation between two charismatic leaders and their two parties thus increasingly characterized Italian politics, and it can be described as the union of two populisms, and as the related and intertwined story of two contrasting, but in some areas compatible, political visions.

Berlusconi and Bossi were like-minded in their reliance on a politics of the enemy, in their anti-communism, in their sometimes implicit and sometimes explicit xenophobia – much more central for Bossi – and in their constant use of theatrical politics and a reliance on staged public events. Their anti-political stance forced them to appear as if they were not in government but in opposition, while – as their critics often argued – they nevertheless used the power and resources of office to reward and retain their electorate, and in the case of Berlusconi to steer parliamentary approval for self-serving policies (Ginsborg & Asquer 2011, Salvati 2012). Indeed, the problematic relation between public discourse and public policy has often been pointed out by analysts of Italian politics (Mastropaolo 2008).

In the meantime, however, despite its political rhetoric, the League sought to become institutionalized at local level. It learned how to administer municipalities and developed stable connections with important social and political actors, such as the Church. A new generation of local administrators emerged and learned the language and skills of public administration. They then acquired the distinctive ability to speak and operate with multiple political registers – appearing bombastic in their activist media while acting responsibly in their roles as mayors and city councillors. The League learned to rely on younger and competent administrators closely tied to their *popolo*, whose primary values were the defence and celebration of local identities and traditional culture, but who were also good at local government and efficiency. These administrators often ritualistically opposed the nation-building efforts and cosmopolitan ethos of Italian élite culture. Conversely, Berlusconi's party remained a 'plastic party', as his critics have often argued, with little or no grounding in local communities. This difference in party structure reflects the different communities of reference of the unattached cosmopolitan consumer and the small-city dweller (Mammone et al. 2008, Bar-on 2009).

However, despite examples of good governance at local level, integrating incompatible policy blueprints with other coalition partners at national level proved difficult. Even the political communication efforts of the different coalition partners remained very different and often incompatible. A comparative analysis of their electoral party manifestos shows, for instance, that they were unable to agree on fundamental values and stressed different priorities. Berlusconi's party typically emphasized economic competitiveness, and focused on an inefficient state bureaucracy seen as hindering business efficiency, and also on personal security and family values. Fini's party typically emphasized a strong executive and law and order policies – issues stemming from its fascist roots. The Northern League focused on the regional devolution of power and rallied against state assistance to southern regions. This has been evidenced by Ruzza and Fella's content analysis of over ten years of the League's written policy texts and party manifestos (Ruzza & Fella 2009).

The only rhetorical device that enabled the coalition partners to appear united was a shared insistence on the importance of *il popolo* – a value that appeared among the ten highest priorities of all three parties (ibid.). Populism was thus a conceptual 'glue', providing the appearance of cohesion and enabling incompatible parties with incompatible visions to appear united, if not to govern effectively together.

A country of competing populism

The lifestyles, values and political trajectories of Bossi and Berlusconi can now be reconceptualized sociologically. Not only their alliance but also their recent differences and tensions indicate that populism is a complex and multifarious process – a language and a set of policy approaches that interpret the cleavages that characterize Italian social and political life. For instance, analyses of the political language of Berlusconi and Bossi have shown that Berlusconi typically uses the aspirational language of the *petite bourgeoisie*, which aims to achieve social distinction through coded references to wealth, higher education and the adoption of the language of business and finance (Amadori 2002). Conversely, Bossi uses a language of the Northern working classes – a language that one would expect to see used in pubs and which is based on hyperbole and intentional defiance of the opinions perceived to reflect the rules of 'political correctness' of the Left (Ruzza 2008).

Dreams of cosmopolitan consumer happiness coexist in the same political coalition with visions of glorified localism and exclusionary xenophobic politics, thanks to an unspecific glorification of the people where, however, different constituencies understand the people differently and are sometimes uncertain of their own definitions of friends and enemies. The electoral flows of votes between the parties of Berlusconi and Bossi suggest that the same voters often oscillated between competing visions of their *popolo* of reference (Diamanti 2003, Ruzza & Fella 2009).

We may therefore posit that Italian populism is a weak political ideology which allows for constant restatements of alliances and values (Freeden 1996). It is a language adopted by political actors to justify their fears, and to legitimate their egoistic drive. But it may also be an expression of social uncertainty – the expression of a need for a community of reference which is lacking in contemporary Italian society. It indicates the importance of a political project to rebuild communities, one that effectively bridges the gap between modernity and tradition, between individual liberty and communal reassurance, between cosmopolitanism and belonging.

Constant electoral changes in the fortunes of these populist parties indicate that although voters may sometimes support right-wing positions, they do so only peripherally. Exclusionary stances may remain dormant and be activated by interpretations of events in the world of public communication that make an exclusionary discourse appear sensible. But the same voters may turn their backs on the populist vision, as the recent collapse of support for the right-wing coalition seems to suggest. Yet the coalition partners retain the capacity to seek, accept and legitimate populist solutions in a sort of everyday populism which relies on, by now, strongly entrenched anti-political stances and exclusionary attitudes ready to be reawakened by socially disruptive events.

We would also posit the existence of an 'everyday populism' as a syndrome that parallels 'everyday racism' (Essed 1991), which in the Italian context is characterized by a narrow and exclusionary community-defending character, but is also one in which the conceptual boundaries of the community of reference are differently defined by different political groups and their leaders. This everyday populism is predicated upon the implicit assumption of a culturally homogeneous 'people' engaged in unwanted cultural relations with an 'other people', which is seen as incompatible and different, and therefore rejected. It is then an implicit popular theory of cultural encounters of a particular type – encounters leading to polarization and a shared unwillingness to engage in meaningful forms of interaction (Delanty 2011: 644–5).

Each of the two parties' idealized communities can be cemented through enhancing inclusion or by asserting exclusionary essentialist boundaries. Each of the three parties has chosen to adopt a culturally essentialist conception of their community – their *popolo*. Berlusconi's idealized community of affluent consumers, Bossi's ethno-nationalist community, with its dialects, folklore and cultural values, and Fini's nationalist community based on historical myths of the homeland are all culturally essentialist communities. Although they are not biological, they are difficult to modify because they acquired their features through long processes which lend themselves to processes of exclusion. Each of these communities is also cemented by an emphasis on external threats, and the three leaders define their identities in opposition to these threats. Berlusconi's stereotype of the 'Communists' gripped by envy and anger points to a vision that legitimates social inequalities and excludes. The League's propaganda is Islamophobic, and it stresses religious affiliation and ethnic background as conditions for incorporation into the community. Possibly to a lesser extent, Fini's rhetoric emphasizes the threats to national cohesion raised by migrants. In this climate of cultural essentialism, a state-of-siege atmosphere has characterized Italy's political culture and permeated its society for many years. In other words, non-Italians are conceptualized as carriers of a culture that is fundamentally unchanging and incompatible with the values of Western societies.

Social intolerance and perceptions of threat have resulted in the recurrent racist attacks against minorities that have characterized Italian society in recent decades (Balbo & Manconi 1990). Examples include the destruction of Roma camps and the organized beatings of minorities. This has produced a polarization of Italian political culture between, on the one hand, racism and, on the other, an anti-racist movement occasionally able to rally strong support, notably when unjustified and violent attacks against migrants are reported in the media. However, the anti-racist movement has been more frequently concerned with educational initiatives and with providing support to minorities in key sectors such as housing, health and the labour market (Ruzza 2008). On the other hand, 'everyday populism' remains the dominant cultural context for sizeable sections of the population.

References

Albertazzi, D. and McDonnell, D. (2005), 'The Lega Nord in the Second Berlusconi Government: In a League of its own', *Western European Politics*, 28(5): 952–72.
— (2008), *Twenty-first Century Populism: The Spectre of Western European Democracy*, Basingstoke: Palgrave Macmillan.
Albertazzi, D. and Rothenberg, N. (2009), *The Tide is not for Turning. Resisting the Tide: Cultures of Opposition under Berlusconi (2001–2006)*, London: Continuum.
Alleanza-Nazionale (1995), *Statuto di Alleanza Nazionale*.
Amadori, A. (2002), *Mi consenta. Metafore, messaggi e simboli. Come Silvio Berlusconi ha conquistato il consenso degli italiani*, Milano: Libri Scheiwiller.
Andrews, G. (2005), *Not a Normal Country – Italy After Berlusconi*, London: Pluto Press.
Balbo, L. and Manconi, L. (1990), *I razzismi possibili*, Milano: Feltrinelli.
Bar-On, T. (2009), 'Understanding Political Conversion and Mimetic Rivalry', *Totalitarian Movements and Political Religions*, 10(3–4): 241–64.
Berezin, M. (1999), 'Political belonging: Emotion, nation and identity in fascist Italy', in G. Steinmetz (ed.), *State/Culture: State Formation after the Cultural Turn*, Ithaca: Cornell University Press, pp. 355–77.
Berlusconi, S. (2010), *L'amore vince sempre sull' invidia e l'odio*, Milan: Mondadori.
Betz, H.-G. (1994), *Radical Right-wing Populism in Western Europe*, New York: St. Martins Press.
Bourdieu, P. (2001), *Science de la Science et Reflexivité*, Paris: Raisons d'Agir.
Bull, M. and Newell, J. (2005), *Italian Politics: Adjustment under Duress*, Cambridge: Polity.
Cartocci, R. (1996), 'L' Italia unita del populismo', *Rassegna Italiana di Sociologia*, 287–95.
Cento Bull, A. and Gilbert, M. (2001), *The Lega Nord and the Northern Question in Italian Politics*, Basingstoke: Palgrave.
Ceri, P. (2011), *Gli italiani spiegati da Berlusconi*, Bari: Laterza.
Delanty, G. (2011), 'Cultural Diversity, Democracy and the Prospects of Cosmopolitanism: A Theory of Cultural Encounters', *The British Journal of Sociology*, 62(4): 633–56.
Diamanti, I. (2003), *Bianco, rosso, verde . . . e azzurro. Mappe e colori dell'Italia politica*, Bologna: Il Mulino.
Donovan, M. and Onofri, P. (2008), *Italian Politics: Frustrated Aspirations for Change*, New York: Berghahn Books.
Edwards, P. (2005), 'The Berlusconi Anomaly: Populism and Patrimony in Italy's Long Transition', *South European Society and Politics*, 10(2): 232–3.
Essed, P. (1991), *Understanding Everyday Racism: An Interdisciplinary Theory*, London: Sage.
Freeden, M. (1996), *Ideologies and Political Theory: A Conceptual Approach*, Oxford: Clarendon Press.
Ginsborg, P. (2001), *Italy and its Discontents: Family, Civil Society, State 1980–2001*, London: Allen Lane.
— (2004), *Silvio Berlusconi: Television, Power and Patrimony*, London: Verso.
Ginsborg, P. and Asquer, E. (2011), *Berlusconismo. Analisi di un sistema di potere*, Bari: Laterza.

Gomez-Reino Cachafeiro, M. (2001), *Ethnicity and Nationalism in Italian Politics: Inventing the Padania: Lega Nord and the Northern Question*, Aldershot: Ashgate.

Huysseune, M. (2006), *Modernity and Secession. The Social Sciences and the Political Discourse of the Lega Nord in Italy*, Oxford: Berghahn.

Kicker, W. (2007), 'Public management refoms in countries with a Napoleonic state model: France, Italy and Spain', in C. Pollitt, S.V. Thiel and V. Homburg (eds), *New Public Management in Europe*, London: Palgrave Macmillan, pp. 26–51.

Mair, P. (2002), 'Populist democracy vs. party democracy', in Y. Mény and Y. Surel (eds), *Democracies and the Populist Challenge*, Basingstoke: Palgrave, pp. 81–98.

Mammone, A., Godin E., Jenkins, B. (2008), 'The Extreme Right in Contemporary Europe: Cultural and Spatial Perspectives', *Journal of Contemporary European Studies*, 16(3): 323–6.

Mastropaolo, A. (2008), 'Populism and democracy', in D. Albertazzi and D. McDonnell (eds), *Twenty-first Century Populism: The Spectre of Western European Democracy*, Basingstoke: Palgrave Macmillan, pp. 30–45.

Mazzoleni, G. (2008), 'Populism and the media', in D. Albertazzi and D. McDonnell (eds), *Twenty-first Century Populism: The Spectre of Western European Democracy*, Basingstoke: Palgrave Macmillan, pp. 49–64.

McDonnell, D. (2006), 'A Weekend in Padania: Regionalist Populism and the Lega Nord', *Politics and Society*, 26(2): 126–32.

Meny, Y. and Surel, Y. (2002), *Democracies and the Populist Challenge*, Basingstoke: Palgrave.

Mudde, C. (2007), *Populist Radical Right Parties in Europe*, Cambridge: Cambridge University Press.

Musso, P. (2008), *Le Sarkoberlusconisme*, Paris: Editions de l'Aube.

Pasquino, G. (2007), 'The Five Faces of Silvio Berlusconi: The Knight of Anti-Politics', *Modern Italy*, 12(1): 39–54.

Pasquino, G. (2008), 'Populism and democracy', in D. Albertazzi and D. McDonnell (eds), *Twenty-first Century Populism: The Spectre of Western European Democracy*, Basingstoke: Palgrave Macmillan, pp. 15–29.

Poli, E. (2001), *Forza Italia: Strutture, Leadership e Radicamento Territoriale*, Milano: Il Mulino.

Ruzza, C. (2008a), 'The Italian Antiracist Movement Between Advocacy, Service Delivery, and Political Protest', *International Journal of Sociology*, 38(2): 55–64.

— (2008b), 'Language and Territorial Identity in Minority Nationalism: The Case of the Northern League', in R. Baccolini and P. Leech (eds), *Constructing Identity*, Bologna: University Press Bologna, pp. 101–21.

Ruzza, C. and Fella, S. (2009), *Re-inventing the Italian Right: Territorial Politics, Popularism and 'Post-facism'*, London: Routledge.

— (2011), 'Populism and the Italian Right', *Acta Politica*, 46(2): 158–79.

Ruzza, C. and Schmidtke, O. (1993), 'Roots of Success of the Lega Lombarda: Mobilization Dynamics and the Media', *West European Politics*, 16(2): 1–23.

Salvati, M. (2012), *Tre pezzi facili sull'Italia: democrazia, crisi economica, Berlusconi*, Bologna: il Mulino.

Taggart, P. (2002), 'Populism and the Pathology of Representative Politics', in Y. Meny and Y. Surel (eds), *Democracies and the Populist Challenge*, Basingstoke: Palgrave, xii, p. 258.

Tambini, D. (1993), 'Strategy or identity? The Northern League at a Crossroad – Two Interviews with Bossi and Rocchetta', *Telos*, 98–9(Winter 1993–4): 229–48.

Tarchi, M. (2002), 'Populism Italian Style', in Y. Mény Y. Surel (eds), *Democracies and the Populist Challenge*, Basingstoke: Palgrave, pp. 120–38.

— (2008), 'Italy: A Country of Many Populisms', in D. Albertazzi and D. McDonnell (eds), *Twenty-first Century Populism: The Spectre of Western European Democracy*, Basingstoke: Palgrave Macmillan, pp. 84–99.

Zaslove, A. (2008), 'Here to Stay? Populism as a New Party Type', *European Review*, 16: 319–36.

12

Explaining the Rise of the Front National to Electoral Prominence: Multi-Faceted or Contradictory Models?

Brigitte Beauzamy

Introduction: Contradictory accounts of the Front National's electoral potential

Studies of the Front National (FN) form an enormous body of literature, spreading across varied disciplines, languages (since it is by no means limited to francophone contributions) and methods. It is hardly a unified field since conclusions vary a great deal. Despite this unchallenged interest in the radical right, no agreement is found among scholars on how serious the threat of electoral FN victory is for other parties. For Auberger and Dubois (2005), the FN is a mere 'electoral nuisance' (381), while Bonnetain (2004) claims that 'the *Front National* has emerged as a strong challenger in the presidential race' (420). This lack of a common view may be explained by the shortcomings of empirical research itself. In their review of the literature on right-wing extremism, De Lange and Mudde (2005) point to the shortcomings of country case analyses. There is a danger of constantly reanalyzing the better known case studies, among which is the FN, while leaving more obscure cases unexplored. This bias entails a strong risk of tautology when authors try to generalize their findings to other European radical-right parties (RRPs). Whether the FN is considered to be the result of idiosyncratic French dynamics or part of a radical-right European tidal wave, its electoral future remains very much in dispute, not only in academic circles but also in the media, as the coverage of Marine Le Pen's campaign for the 2012 presidential elections so clearly illustrates.

Multi-explanation models

The absence of a shared evaluation of the electoral potential of the FN may derive from diverging theoretical models mobilized by various studies. Many analyses fail to display a fully fledged causal model to support their accounts of radical-right parties' electoral success, including that of the FN. This lack does not derive from an absence of background theory, but instead points to a wealth of different and sometimes competing theories mobilized in a single study. For instance, Falter (1999), looking for explanations of the RRP vote in the Federal Republic of Germany, includes such factors as the impact of the openness of political systems and the importance of a charismatic leader. He also lists the sociological characteristics of voters, such as gender, women being less likely to vote for RRPs, as well as age, since these parties appeal mostly to youth and older people. These accounts fall into the trap described by De Lange and Mudde (2005): authors usually provide long lists of factors (socio-economic, political, media, etc.) without ranking them. Veugelers (2005) summarizes the factors often cited for their impact on FN electoral success:

> Explanations for the resurgence of far-right parties in Europe since the 1970s tend to focus on: variation in the nature of electoral systems; the leadership, resources, and organizational unity of far-right parties; social insecurity caused by rising unemployment, economic liberalization, and shrinking welfare-state protections; the wish, within a segment of the electorate, to punish politicians and parties tainted by scandal and corruption. (409)

All these elements, he argues, are too often mobilized without taking their historical roots into account.

Besides the lack of a clear explanatory model, which greatly diminishes their predictive capacity, the multi-explanation theories fall short of agreeing on a common list of causes. Such is the case when it come to accounting for the FN's breakthrough in the 1984 European elections. Elements of the national Political Opportunity Structure (POS), such as proportional representation, are often cited, to which authors like Bréchon and Mitra (1992) add the specificity of European elections and their 'second-order elections' status. However, they also include other aspects in their model such as the rhetoric excellence of Jean-Marie Le Pen or the media attention he received. Conversely, Birenbaum (1987), in his account of the take-off of the FN between 1984 and 1986, focuses on a variety of domestic factors: the conjunction between a long-term economic crisis and immigration, the victory of François Mitterrand and the government participation of Communist ministers (4). These last two examples are studies which make an otherwise very convincing case in favour of a single factor explaining the FN success – rising xenophobia for Bréchon and Mitra and the clever strategy of the party, between ideology and pragmatism, for Birenbaum – but they seem to feel obliged to list a large number of other factors whose impact remains unexplained.

Demand-side models

The defining social characteristics of the FN electorate have been the topic of many studies, and Evans (2005) identified the convergence of the sociological profiles of RRP voters, as the parties' constituencies gradually became more proletarian. Grunberg and Schweisguth (2003: 332) point to the impact of secularism, since the FN attracts a higher proportion of members of the working class, who in France are statistically less religious than other electorates. The impact of other religious factors has been confirmed in comparative research on RRPs; Minkenberg (2003: 165) argues that they scored higher in Catholic countries than in Protestant ones, where radical-right social movements might be stronger. Some elements remain disputed: most studies point to the lower educational level of RRP voters, yet Evans surprisingly argues that 'in the 1980s, the French FN electorate was one of the most educated among French parties' (81). Polls carried out during the 2012 presidential campaign confirmed that working-class and active voters were more likely to express sympathy with the FN than would retired voters (Vivavoice poll, quoted in La Dépêche, 9 January 2012).

Models explaining the far-right vote with socio-economic models reached their peak with the success of the so-called modernization's losers thesis. A term fruitfully coined by Hans-Georg Betz (see, among others, 1993 and 1994), it tied the impact of unemployment and progressive marginalization of the working class in post-industrial states to its increasing rejection of older political parties (Betz 1993). In his application of this model to radical-right voting in Germany during the late 1960s, Falter notes the impact of a climate characterized by economic and social crisis which might render right-wing populism more appealing to a poorer population experiencing precarious circumstances (1999). Yet, some authors consider such models to be outdated (Van Der Brug et al. 2005) and no longer sustained by empirical evidence. Bonnetain (2004) examines how voters potentially concerned by issues mentioned in the FN platform – among them the appeal of socio-economic measures such as tax cuts to voters particularly afflicted by tax burdens, or of law-and-order measures to those most likely to be victims of crime – might be prone to vote for a radical-right party. He concludes that socio-economic factors, such as unemployment, have a significant impact on the FN vote.

Indeed, attempts to measure the impact of 'real-life' indicators pertaining to the environment for voting behaviour have shown mixed results. Among them, environmental factors related to two topics rated high on the FN's agenda – crime and immigration – do not appear to impact directly on voting behaviour. For Bonnetain (2004), indicators such as the actual presence of many immigrants or local crime rates do not seem to influence the decision to vote for the radical right in any significant way. Bréchon and Mitra (1992: 68) note that although statistical correlation between the FN vote and the percentage of immigrants is valid at the *département* (French territorial administrative division) level, it is not the case in local elections. Yet this does not prevent a general rise in anti-immigrant sentiment, as shown by poll data: 'The electors of the *Front National* appear much more xenophobic than the average voters' (70). These results lead them to conclude that two kinds of FN voters should be distinguished: the ideological hardcore supporting conservative or reactionary authoritarianism, and protest voters reacting to immigration issues.

This remark leads many authors to focus on voter's representations rather than on their material situations, and to attempt to reconstruct the path from subjective perceptions to ideology. For Minkenberg and Perrineau (2007: 32–42), radical-right voters see themselves as 'modernization's losers' in subjective rather than objective terms, and share a strong level of anti-immigrant feeling – a result confirming Veugelers' emphasis on the importance of racial prejudice in predicting far-right voting (2005: 424). Two original contributions are particularly useful in order to conceptualize this articulation between self-perception and ideological orientation. In her study of the psycho-sociological factors impacting on FN adhesion, Birgitta Orfali (1990) focuses on the psychological rewards associated with joining the FN. The party's tightly connected community will be especially appealing to people suffering from social marginalization that, regardless, form a minority of sympathizers. Beyond these incentives tied to radical-right subcultures, she states that the party's arguments may appeal to specific psychological profiles: law-and-order arguments appeal to a certain category of male members ('order men') as opposed to the antisemitic arguments preferred by Catholic, female and rather subdued members ('*assujettis*'). This direction leads to a renewed interest in the psychological appeal of authoritarian politics initially theorized by Adorno et al. (1993), which for Kitschelt (1995) forms a key part of the policy preferences of radical-right voters when teamed with right-wing economic liberalism. For Veugelers (1997), this appeal is inherent to a fraction of the electorate and opportunities may arise for the radical right if other parties are unable to satisfy the wishes of authoritarian voters – and one may add, following Spektorowski (2000), of anti-egalitarian voters as well.

Beyond psychological factors, the appeal of authoritarian politics and a dislike of foreigners therefore appear to be ideologically connected for FN voters: noting that the main emphasis of the FN is ideological, with 'xenophobia and punitiveness [being] the core of FN voter's ideology' (ibid.: 337), Grunberg and Schweisguth (2003) conclude that 'the FN electorate is highly structured from an ideological standpoint and therefore cannot be considered merely as a protest electorate, or simply as being to the right of the right' (339). This type of explanation departs from models considering the FN vote as a manifestation of problems – psychological or socio-economic – afflicting voters, as one is led to investigate how the party's specific ideology translates into fully fledged partisanship: Gschwend and Leuffen (2005) go as far as to assert that 'ideology, candidate evaluation and partisan preferences are the main determinants of the [FN] vote in France' (704), a claim which certainly clashes with their popular representation as social outcasts. If typical FN voters are often referred to as '*petits blancs*' (white trash), for instance, by Bréchon and Mitra (1992: 70), this depiction leaves aside the question of the roles played by repressive and xenophobic ideologies in their representations and their sociability, which impact directly on their voting preferences.

Supply-side models

Supply side explanatory models of the electoral rise of the FN emphasize the strategic means used by its party leaders to shape and tap into this specific electorate. Founded in the 1970s, as a synthesis of diverse trends and small splinter groups, the party reached electoral significance in the 1980s and early 1990s, before undergoing a split in 1999 which, for many commentators at the time, was expected to be fatal. Contrary to these predictions, the FN obtained its most remarkable achievements to date in the early 2000s: first, during the 2002 presidential elections, where Jean-Marie Le Pen bypassed the Socialist candidate and reached the second round; and secondly in 2005, with the victory of the 'No' vote to the referendum on the Constitutional Treaty of the European Union (EU) which the RRP claimed as its own. Throughout its history, the FN has increasingly been able to attract voters who had previously favoured the conservative right, especially during its take-off in the 1980s (Veugelers 1997: 40). The party's growing electorate now incorporates new voters recruited from among previous non-voters (Mayer & Perrineau 1990: 42) and beyond its appeal as a one-time 'protest vote', the FN was also able to establish loyalty from recurrent voters (ibid.: 45). Yet, some authors underline the capacity of the party to advance its own candidates, in a context where the heterogeneity of the electorates of the moderate and radical right renders alliances is problematic anyway (Gschwend & Leuffen 2005). The relative strength of the FN in the 2002 legislative elections made it possible for the party to maintain its candidates in a number of constituencies at the second ballot, thereby weakening the moderate right and creating incentives for the latter to form alliances with the left (Blais & Indridason 2007). The strength of the party may also be confirmed by the amounts spent on the election (Epstein & Franck 2007) – before its financial resources were endangered by the party putting itself heavily in debt. As a whole, the increased capacity to function as a party whose aim is to conquer through electoral victories, instead of being an anti-system protest, has been cited as a key element to the longevity of the FN (Crépon 2006, Dézé 2012).

The party has managed to retain the support from core like-minded communities: cultural approaches emphasize the key role of extreme-right subcultures which intermediate between the party and its constituency. In the French case, such links have been repeatedly noted, despite the heterogeneity of the radical-right social movement sector, stretching from skinheads and 'identity rock' fans to small élitist and occultist groups (François 2006). Civil society organizations may propagate world views close to the FN's ideology without actually being organizationally tied to the party. Support for FN politics ranks high among ex-colonials and repatriates, especially if they belong to associations valuing a colonial past (Veugelers 2005). Far-right associations are neither completely disconnected from the party nor a mere communication channel for it. Minkenberg (2003) argues that radical-right social movements do not represent a radicalized and more dangerous form of extreme-right politics than parties, but they do prepare the ground for them when they rely less on violent modes of action.

One of the major points of contention in the literature regarding FN strategies to attract supporters relates to which form of ideological positioning, between moderation and radicalization, has been more successful. Many authors such as Veugelers (1997), following Ignazi (1992), have emphasized the agenda-setting role of RRPs, for instance concerning immigration or national identity, or opposition to a corrupt system – a position coined as 'populist antistatism' by Kitschelt (1995). In contemporary FN discourses, this part is played by anti-Islam positions, for example, vilifying street prayer or the spread of halal butchers in poor neighbourhoods, both elements which have been widely commented upon in the media, and sometimes integrated into the topics of mainstream parties' candidates. This impact on the mainstream political agenda reveals the growing acceptability of FN theses: the normalization ('*banalization*') of the party's standpoints (especially with regard to immigration) may therefore be understood as a crucial element in obtaining more electoral success (Berezin 2006: 271): 'it may no longer be accurate to categorize [the FN] as simply representing the politics of the *refus* – those left behind by society' (ibid.: 272). The acceptability of FN ideology is on the increase, not as a consequence of its toning down in order to appeal to moderate voters, but because the whole space of political discourses has shifted to include FN themes and vocabulary. This confirms Birenbaum's results (1987: 6) that the party conducted a strategy of simultaneous openness and radicalization. These trends were represented by different party leaders, except for Jean-Marie Le Pen who managed to combine both dimensions in his rhetoric, and did not hesitate to rely on provocation by intentionally adopting Vichyist images and metaphors. Supply side models ought therefore to consider the multiple constituencies and publics to which the FN is trying to appeal.

Assessing the impact of leadership change on the FN's modernization

Inspired by research into fascism, many authors have scrutinized the FN leadership in order to explain the longevity of the party, even though the history of its electoral fate is by no means linear. Studies have focused on the style of its historical leader, Jean-Marie Le Pen, and the characteristics of his rhetoric have been described in much detail (see for instance Souchard et al. 1998). For others, the main competence displayed by the FN leadership does not lie in its electoral strategy but in its communication and media outreach. Bernard (2007) underlines the impact of a strategy based on scandal and provocation and suggests that the negative media coverage following Le Pen's infamous remarks may indeed have been beneficial to the party (40). They allowed the leader to defend his right to use, in good faith, shocking metaphors to convey his ideas, while arguing that they could be widely understood. This strategy renders alliances with the conservative right more problematic – and therefore reinforces loyalty among FN candidates who might otherwise be tempted to appear moderate so as to reach electoral agreements with the conservative right. It also favours the FN with continuous media coverage, even between elections, while allowing party leaders to portray themselves as the victims of a media conspiracy aimed at silencing them (Beauzamy & Naves 2010).

The recent change in the party's leadership following Jean-Marie Le Pen's retirement – though he still remains its honorary president – and the nomination of his youngest daughter, Marine, as the presidential candidate for 2012 have led to a renewal of leadership-centred examinations of the party's strategy. A controversial thesis argues that the rise of Marine Le Pen to FN leadership is a sign of the party's modernization and renunciation of its roots – be they fundamentalist Catholic and counter-revolutionary or fascist. A lawyer, like her father, Marine Le Pen is presented as a 'modern' candidate because of her non-traditional lifestyle – she is a twice-divorced single mother of two. Her ideology has also been described as being markedly more culturally liberal than the party's official position – she claims to be pro-choice, although with some reservations, and has made several attempts to seduce gay and Jewish electorates. Yet continuity prevails with regard to her favourite themes, with a strong denunciation of Islam and of European integration, and a reaffirmed nationalist stance. She has also borrowed her father's populist tribune style and has increased the attacks on journalists, claiming that they present her ideas in a simplified or erroneous fashion. She has also maintained her father's strategy of considering the mainstream right and Nicolas Sarkozy to be her main adversaries.

Political Opportunity Structure models

Van Der Brug, Fennema and Tillie's article (2005) is a model case of the POS approach, in which they integrate such elements as the level of electoral competition and institutional arrangements by which votes are transformed into seats (544) – that is, proportional representation rather than majority elections. In opposition to the 'protest vote' hypothesis, they claim that RRP voters want their vote to matter when it comes to curbing immigration. The authors tested hypotheses related to the party system – the level of support for the political system, voting loyalty to one particular party – but also added variables relating to the economic and/or immigration situation. They found that RRPs are likely to fare poorly in elections when faced with strong competition from mainstream-right candidates close to their own ideology (ibid.: 566). This result sheds some light on why such mainstream parties as the Union for a Popular Movement (UMP) may choose to incorporate FN themes as a counter strategy – as in the case of the appropriation of the theme of 'national identity' by Nicolas Sarkozy in his 2007 presidential campaign. However, one finds that the trivialization of its ideas does not necessarily benefit the FN.

If the use of POS is a promising direction, the previous example illustrates that it is not exempt from the problem of integrating multiple and heterogeneous factors into a single model – factors which have already been examined separately, in many cases with inconclusive results. Such is the case for the impact of the electoral system on voters' preferences for the FN, which appears limited. According to Minkenberg (2003), the low level of proportional representation has not prevented the party from winning a faithful electorate. Examining the impact of voters' regime preference – unified if the presidency and the majority at the National Assembly are from the same party, divided in the case of *cohabitation* – Gschwend and Leuffen (2005) distinguish patterns of strategic voting and preferred voting according to the institutional consequences of electoral results. Yet the FN's greatest electoral breakthroughs have not been obtained at national level, and Birenbaum's (1987) emphasis on the importance of local politics for the electoral fate of the FN is still salient, a result confirmed by Bréchon and Mitra's indepth analysis of the rise of the party in its stronghold of Dreux (1992). Local political and socio-economic dynamics played a key role in the electoral victory of the Stirbois, the élite local FN couple, but Bréchon and Mitra stress the importance of the FN vote as a form of protest against government immigration policies (Bréchon and Mitra 1992: 77). In this case, it is a complex interplay between local variables and national policies which created a favourable situation for the FN. Similarly, the tendency of the FN to fare better in European elections has been explained concurrently by either a disinterest towards the stakes of the elections – the second-order elections phenomenon (Minkenberg & Perrineau 2007) – or by voters' actual hostility to the European construction which may render them more receptive to RRPs ultra-nationalist discourses (34). Yet the authors state that: 'In the EU of 25, the radical right has not gained significant strength' (50). Such models are useful because they disaggregate the 'FN vote' as a single phenomenon, pointing to the very real impact of the electoral system and thereby making sense of otherwise puzzling variations in electoral results.

A key element of POS explanations for the RRP vote is the nature of the political environment created by competing candidates. Some re-examine the protest vote hypothesis, that is, a decision motivated by dissent with the system or with the ruling élite(s) (van Der Brug et al. 2005: 541), or simply by the wish to punish the ruling majority for poor economic performance (Auberger & Dubois 2005). The dealignment of voters from mainstream parties also impacts on FN electoral performances (Veugelers 1997), which are likely to be higher when support for the two main parties' candidates (socialist and conservative right) is eroded, thereby supporting the description of the FN as being anti-systemic (Bonnetain 2004). For Grunberg and Schweisguth (2003), the French political space is no longer adequately mapped as bipolarized by a Right-Left cleavage, since the far right constitutes a third pole distinct from the mainstream right. Minkenberg complicates this concept by pointing to the complex relationship between both political ensembles: 'the French established right's response to the FN since 1988 reflects a reversal of strategies. A combination of ideological demarcation and organizational co-optation was followed by one of ideological co-optation and organizational demarcation' (2003: 163). Both rights therefore entertain close and complex relations, with part of the mainstream right still very much attached to a strategy of Republican distinction from the FN, while other UMP politicians adopt much of the FN's doctrine and vocabulary. The electoral outcome of President Nicolas Sarkozy's appropriation of the theme of 'national identity' in his mandate – for instance by adding it to the title of the 'Ministry for Immigration, Integration and National Identity' from 2007 until 2010 – among other FN-inspired policy themes, may prove to be a key direction for research into the 2012 presidential elections. The 2012 presidential campaigns illustrate this dynamic, with close followers of Nicolas Sarkozy borrowing radical-right ideological features – such as theories of racial inequality for his Ministry of the Interior Claude Guéant – while Marine Le Pen herself concentrates her attacks on the president's poor policy record with regard to immigration.

Lastly, some argue that the structural elements impacting on the FN vote include the overall significance of political cleavages relating to immigration and national identity in France. Since, as we have seen, no straightforward correlation can be observed between the percentage of immigrants – or even of people perceived as such – and FN electoral results, the general climate of hostility towards foreigners should be integrated into explanatory models in a more subtle way. Some authors focus on how events focusing on the media's agenda contribute to the materialization of more diffusive opinion trends favourable to the radical right. These events might be public debates, such as the headscarf affair (Bréchon & Mitra 1992: 66), but also electoral events per se. Berezin (2006) explains, for instance, how the 'shock' of 21 April 2002 – when Jean-Marie Le Pen reached the second round of the presidential elections instead of the socialist candidate – created favourable conditions for other victories. For example, she identifies, perhaps too categorically, the influence of the FN in the other 'shock', the victory of the 'No' vote in the 29 May 2005 referendum on the European Constitutional Treaty. There is, however, a risk of circularity in this argument: FN victories create the conditions for more triumphs to come. Yet a key conclusion is that the party is a serious electoral contender and not only a troublemaker in a political space dominated by mainstream parties. The hypothesis that a more profound alignment between FN ideology and some elements shared by media discourses and public debates might be responsible for the party's growing strength has been examined by van der Valk (2003), using a Critical Discourse Analysis-informed approach. In both France and the Netherlands, anti-immigrant discourse is commonplace in both right and radical-right discourses, where similar discursive strategies may be found, such as negative presentation of the Other (200). Yet anti-immigrant stances are more pronounced in France, which suggests that the content of public debates on themes related to immigration and/or national identity is shaped in a way which welcomes radical-right contributions as quasi-normal and legitimate ones.

Ethnicization models

This last remark points us towards including dimensions pertaining to how ethnic identities – including white ones – are transformed into legitimate political topics and thus lead to the ethnicization of French politics. In a French context marked by the well-researched distrust of public acknowledgement of ethnic minorities (Amiraux & Simon 2006), accounts of ethnicization have mostly been the stuff of pessimistic and sometimes apocalyptic depictions of growing ethnic tensions in multiracial France (see for instance Costa-Lascoux 2001, or Lagrange 2010) – a discourse which in many ways parallels FN analyses. Prophets of the ethnicization of France generally fail to provide convincing backgrounds for their arguments because of a shared tendency to overgeneralize while reifying cultural elements (such as forms of sociability or family structure) which they associate with ethnicity. This dimension is usually scrutinized only in Others, traditionally Arabs, but recently increasingly defined as Africans or Muslims: Black families are for instance increasingly blamed for the poor educational results, and participation in youth gangs, of their children (Beauzamy & Montes 2011). Yet this should not lead us to discard ethnicization from the array of legitimate topics for inquiry, especially when examining the fate of radical-right ethno-racial politics and its electoral impact.

Following Brubaker and Laitin's results pertaining to the study of mobilizing the power of ethnicity as an ideology in violent conflicts (1998), a first direction is to attempt to make sense of the relative growth of debates on ethnicity and national identities in the French context. In their study, Brubaker and Laitin find that 'even without direct positive incentives to frame conflicts in ethnic terms, this has led to a marked ethnicization of violent challenger-incumbent contests as the major non-ethnic framing for such contests has become less plausible and profitable' (op. cit., 425) – which in our case suggests looking into the possible exhaustion of other ideological macro-discourses to make sense of certain events or grievances. For instance, media discourses aimed at explaining the major riots of 2005 show a marked shift away from the traditional socio-economic accounts of urban conflicts to include élite-based (and especially governmental) explanations focusing on subcultures and ethnicity (Beauzamy & Naves 2006). Public debates on national history also display an increasingly ethnicized view of 'Frenchhood', thereby revealing the rise of an ethnic definition of the nation (Terrio 1999). This ethnicization does not completely coincide with xenophobia, nor does it derive directly from anti-immigrant sentiment: 'The saliency of ethnic, religious and regional identities cannot be definitively linked to a "backlash" against immigrants [or] minorities' (Tossuti 2002: 66). It may therefore be fruitful to examine the regional pattern of ethnicization in Europe, following Tossuti's results (op. cit.) concerning the role of transnational factors and of globalization in explaining attachments to national or sub-national identities, which may materialize in support of nationalist, ethnic or religious parties. Similarly Köves, in her attempt to make sense of what she interprets as a revival of fascism (2004), examines the link between globalization and 'ethnic polarization' and sees ethnicity as a by-product of the remains of a class struggle under decomposition in post-industrial France: 'Ethnicity is a form of protest against the demands of neoliberalism and globalization' (46) – an argument which takes us back to the vicinity of the 'modernization's losers' thesis. This regional trend would resonate particularly in France, where the dominant Republican view of nationhood promotes the integration of migrants through their socio-cultural assimilation – a model which Spektorowski calls 'ethnocentric' (2000: 286).

Returning to the FN and the strategies of its leaders, one finds that it may be described as an ethnocentric party, and in fact the only party that defines the nation in ethno-nationalist terms, thereby fulfilling Köves' definition of contemporary fascism as 'the articulation and translation of racism and ethnicity into politics' (2004: 36). It may rely on an elaborate ethno-differentialist theorization of race relations framed by *Nouvelle Droite* (New Right) ideologues (Taguieff 1994, Spektorowski 2000) – even though such ethno-differentialism translates into FN party programmes only obliquely, and some ideological divergences between the two may be identified. However, the FN can still boast that it is the first party to address issues related to ethnicization openly – the topos of the 'absence of taboo' has been appropriated by other political actors, particularly from the mainstream right.

Conclusion

Many approaches have been used to examine the FN's appeal to its voters, from indepth accounts of its organizational structure and leadership issues – recently focusing on the replacement of historical leader Jean-Marie Le Pen by his daughter Marine, supposedly in favour of the 'modernization' of the party's discourse and ideology – to wide and far-ranging examinations of the social, economic and political conditions in which the party may thrive. As we have seen, simply adding or superposing these approaches does not give us a clearer picture of the situation. While providing a comprehensive alternative framework is too ambitious a goal for this chapter, some different directions do however appear to be promising.

On the supply side of FN party politics – which, De Lange and Mudde argue (2005: 483), is a relatively underdeveloped field of RRP studies – a key question is the nature of the interaction between the FN and the mainstream right – chiefly the Union pour un Mouvement Populaire, the main conservative party – especially under UMP governance and a Sarkozy presidency. While certain authors have examined ruptures or proximities between members of both parties, the overall impact of the appropriation of FN themes and their inscription on the government agenda remains by and large unknown so far.

Demand-side models ought to go beyond the quest for straightforward socio-economic and socio-cultural explanations of the decision to vote for FN candidates. Poor socio-economic conditions and belonging to an increasingly unemployed working class do not mechanically lead to voting for the FN, since these factors are mediated by social representations of one's situation. Increasingly, stereotyped and polarized perceptions of Self and Other are likely to encourage xenophobic attitudes and ideologies. We ought to be particularly attentive to not covertly return to the '*petit blancs*' thesis, leading to a description of the FN electorate as white trash. Insights pertaining to the ethnicization of current definitions of Self and Other in France show that factors other than a sense of loss and resentment may be at play. Pride and belonging should also be examined in this construction of an ethnicized – primarily white – Self potentially attracted to FN candidates, as studies pertaining to radical-right sociability suggest. Rather than treating the FN vote as a problem disfiguring French politics, such a way of envisioning the French radical right could open a gateway to explore more general issues pertaining to multiethnic French society, such as the marked rise of anti-immigrant and Islamophobic attitudes.

References

Adorno, T. W., Frenkel-Brunswick, E. and Levinson, D. J. (1993/1950), The Authoritarian Personality (1st edn), New York: Norton & Cie.

Amiraux, V. and Simon, P. (2006), 'There are no Minorities Here. Cultures of Scholarship and Public Debate on Immigrants and Integration in France', *International Journal of Comparative Sociology,* 47(3/4): 191–215.

Auberger, A. and Dubois, E. (2005), 'The Influence of Local and National Economic Conditions on French Legislative Elections', *Public Choice,* 125(3/4): 363–83.

Beauzamy, B. and Montes, A. (2011), 'The politicization of black identities and "agonistic democracy": a comparative analysis of France and Colombia', paper presented at the CES International Conference 'Challenging Citizenship', Coimbra, Portugal.

Beauzamy, B. and Naves, M.-C. (2006), 'Förortsupploppen i Frankrike hösten 2005: Mediebevakning och tolkningsskillnader', in Masoud Kamali (ed.), *Den segregerande integrationen,* Stockholm: Fritzes, pp. 220–50.

Berezin, M. (2006), 'Appropriating the "No": The French National Front, the Vote on the Constitution, and the "New" April 21', *PS: Political Science and Politics,* 39(2): 269–72.

Bernard, M. (2007), 'Le Pen, un provocateur en politique (1984–2002)', *Vingtième Siècle,* 93: 37–45.

Betz, H.-G. (1993), 'The New Politics of Resentment: Radical Right-Wing Populist Parties in Western Europe', *Comparative Politics*, 25: 413–27.
— (1994), *Radical Right-Wing Populism in Western Europe*, London: Macmillan.
Birenbaum, G. (1987), 'Les stratégies du front national: Mars 1986-Mai 1987', Vingtième Siècle, 16: 3–20.
Blais, A. and Indridason, I. H. (2007), 'Making Candidates Count: The Logic of Electoral Alliances in Two-Round Legislative Elections', *The Journal of Politics*, 69(1): 193–205.
Bonnetain, P. (2004), 'Behind the Polling-Booth Curtain and beyond Simple Speculations: Toward a Causal Model of Far-right Voting Behaviour – Some Evidence from the French Presidential Elections of 2002', *Canadian Journal of Political Science*, 37(2): 419–29.
Bréchon, P. and Mitra, S. K. (1992), 'The National Front in France: The Emergence of an Extreme Right Protest Movement', *Comparative Politics*, 25(1): 63–82.
Brubaker, R. and Laitin, D. (1998), 'Ethnic and Nationalist Violence', *Annual Review of Sociology*, 24: 423–52.
Costa-Lascoux, J. (2001), 'L'ethnicisation du lien social dans les banlieues françaises', *Revue Européenne des Migrations Internationales*, 17(2): 123–38.
Crépon, S. (2006), *La Nouvelle extrême droite. Enquête sur les jeunes militants du Front national*, Paris: l'Harmattan.
De Lange, S. and Mudde, C. (2005), 'Political Extremism in Europe', *European Political Science*, 4: 476–88.
Dézé, A. (2012), *Le Front national : à la conquête du pouvoir?*, Paris, Armand Colin.
Epstein, G. S. and Franck, R. (2007), 'Campaign Resources and Electoral Success: Evidence from the 2002 French Parliamentary Elections', *Public Choice*, 131(3/4): 469–89.
Evans, J. (2005), 'The Dynamics of Social Change in Radical Right-Wing Populist Party Support', *Comparative Politics*, 3: 76–101.
Falter, J. W. (1999), 'Le vote des partis d'extrême-droite', *Vingtième Siècle*, 55/56: 33–9.
François, S. (2006), *La Musique europaïenne. Ethnographie politique d'une subculture de droite*, Paris: l'Harmattan.
Grunberg, G. and Schweisguth, E. (2003), 'French Political Space: Two, Three or Four Blocs?', *French Politics*, 1: 331–47.
Gschwend, T. and Leuffen, D. (2005), 'Divided We Stand: Unified We Govern? Cohabitation and Regime Voting in the 2002 French Elections', *British Journal of Political Science*, 35(4): 691–712.
Ignazi, P. (1992), 'The Silent Counter-Revolution: Hypotheses on the Emergence of Extreme Right-Wing Parties in Europe', *European Journal of Political Research*, 9: 75–99.
Kitschelt, H. (1995), *The Radical Right in Western Europe: A Comparative Analysis*, Ann Arbor, University of Michigan Press.
Köves, M. (2004), 'Fascism in the Age of Global Capitalism', *Social Scientist*, 32(9/10): 36–71.
Lagrange, H. (2010), *Le déni des cultures*, Paris, Seuil.
Mayer, N. and Perrineau, P. (1990), 'Pourquoi votent-ils pour le Front National?' *Pouvoirs*, 55: 163–84.
Minkenberg, M. (2003), 'The West European Radical Right as a Collective Actor: Modeling the Impact of Cultural and Structural Variables on Party Formation and Movement Mobilization', *Comparative European Politics*, 1: 149–70.
Minkenberg, M. and Perrineau, P. (2007), 'The Radical Right in the European Elections 2004', *International Political Science Review*, 28(1): 29–55.

Orfali, B. (1990), *L'Adhésion au Front National. De la minorité active au mouvement social,* Paris: Kimé.

Souchard, M., Wahnich, S., Cuminal, I. and Wathier, V. (1998), *Le Pen, les mots. Analyse d'un discours d'extrême droite,* Paris: La Découverte.

Spektorowski, A. (2000), 'The French New Right: Differentialism and the Idea of Ethnophilian Exclusionism', *Polity,* 33(2): 283–303.

Taguieff, P.-A. (1994), *Sur la Nouvelle Droite,* Paris: Descartes & Cie.

Terrio, S. (1999), 'Crucible of the Millenium? The Clovis Affair in Contemporary France', *Comparative Studies in Society and History,* 41(3): 438–57.

Tossuti, L. (2002), 'How Transnational Factors Influence The Success of Ethnic, Religious and Regional Parties in 21 States', *Party Politics,* 8(1): 51–74.

van Der Brug, W., Fennema, M. and Tillie, J. (2005), 'Why Some Anti-Immigrant Parties Fail and Others Succeed: A Two-Step Model of Aggregate Electoral Support', *Comparative Political Studies,* 38(5): 537–73.

van der Valk, I. (2003), 'Political Discourse on Ethnic Minority Issues: A Comparison of the Right and Extreme-right in the Netherlands and France (1990–97)', *Ethnicities,* 3(2): 183–213.

Veugelers, J. (1997), 'Social Cleavage and the Revival of Far Right Parties: The Case of France's National Front', *Acta Sociologica,* (40)1: 31–49.

— (2005), 'Ex-Colonials, Voluntary Associations, and Electoral Support for the Contemporary Far Right', *Comparative European Politics,* 3: 408–31.

13

Explaining the Swing to the Right: The Dutch Debate on the Rise of Right-Wing Populism

Merijn Oudenampsen

Introduction

In these last ten years the Netherlands has experienced a dramatic swing to the Right. Long considered the epitome of tolerance and liberalism, the country now finds itself at the forefront of the political revival of nationalist and anti-immigrant sentiments in Europe. The motor behind this remarkable turnaround is the spectacular rise of right-wing populism since the 1990s, an ascendancy that reached yet a new climax with the 2010 elections, which resulted in a resounding victory for the right-wing populist and anti-Islamist Freedom Party (PVV) of Geert Wilders.[1] The election was followed by the formation of a minority government of right-wing Liberals (VVD) and Christian Democrats (CDA), dependent on the strategic support of the PVV to obtain a parliamentary majority. It is generally seen as the most right-wing government in Dutch post-war history.

The newfound status of the Freedom Party as a strategic partner of the government marks a transition towards the incorporation of right-wing populism as a more permanent and accepted feature of the Dutch political landscape. Thus, the Netherlands seems to have joined the club of European countries with large and entrenched right-wing populist parties (Belgium, Denmark, Austria, Italy, France, Hungary). At the same time, right-wing populist discourse has proven itself capable of achieving a

---

[1] The Freedom Party (PVV) of Geert Wilders won 24 seats at the 2010 elections, 16 per cent of the vote. The party was founded in 2006 when its leader, Geert Wilders, left the right-wing Liberal Party (VVD). The PVV won nine seats in the 2006 elections.

[2] One of the more interesting examples is the hugely popular television show *Ik Hou van Holland* (I love Holland), where Dutch celebrities are asked questions about Dutch society. The show is explicitly inspired by the integration test for foreign immigrants devised by the right-wing populist politician Rita Verdonk when she was still Minister of Immigration and Integration.

much wider resonance, as it is taken up by the mainstream media[2] and by established political parties. A case in point is the controversial pronouncement of Prime Minister Mark Rutte at the installation of the new government in 2010, stating that his cabinet aimed to 'give the country back to the hardworking Dutchman.'[3] Taken together with the recent assertion of the Christian Democrat leader, Maxime Verhagen, that popular fears about immigrants and contaminated foreign vegetables are 'comprehensible' and 'legitimate',[4] it becomes clear that a certain normalization of populist, nationalist and anti-immigrant rhetoric has occurred.

Several lines of enquiry have emerged to explain these developments. One way of dealing with the issue of populism is to adopt a nominalist approach, look at the electoral fortunes and practices of political parties that are commonly defined as populist, and classify these according to a certain taxonomy (Ionescu & Gellner 1969, Canovan 1981). Such an approach quickly runs into a series of problems. First of all, the term populism remains contested and unclear (Taggart 2000, Panizza 2005, Arditi 2007). Existing studies of populism typically start out with the observation that the label populism is often used in a pejorative sense and lacks clarity: 'A scientific consensus is thoroughly lacking on any definition of populism' (Canovan 1981: 175). Secondly, populism is not a neatly contained phenomenon. The Dutch political landscape, for example, has been affected in a much broader sense, with almost all political parties moving to the Right and some of them openly adopting right-wing populist discourse. Lacking any exhaustive definition of populism, it becomes difficult and rather arbitrary to draw a line, defining certain parties or figures as populist and others as 'normal' instances of political practice. A third and perhaps even more important problem is that describing the success of populist parties is not the same as explaining it.

Another common strategy is to portray the emergence of right-wing populism in Europe as a reflection of the growing popularity of certain values and attitudes among the general population. These are defined either in terms of adherence to classic right-wing issues (such as immigration, Europe and law and order) or more general sentiments (such as political cynicism, resentment and the desire for a strong leader). This is the dominant approach in the Dutch academic debate, where leading scholars reduce populism to voter behaviour, and thus follow in the footsteps of either the mass culture paradigm or the pluralist behavioural science tradition. The consequence is that the most prominent studies (Houtman et al. 2008, Bovens & Wille 2009) offer a rather one-sided reading of recent political developments in the Netherlands. The emergence of populism is generally accounted for by the impact of all sorts of long-term trends on voter behaviour, whereas politics itself is reduced to a derivative factor. Often, the most important figures and events are not even mentioned. The practical consequence of this omission is that research into voter behaviour in the Netherlands has a hard time explaining political change (Aarts 2005). While in the Dutch case, rapid change

---

[3] Source: NOS Dutch national news, 30 September 2010. <http://nos.nl/artikel/188117-land-weer-vo or-hardwerkende-nederlander.html> [accessed 15 February 2012].

[4] The statement was part of a controversial speech at a CDA party symposium on populism, 28 June 2011. <www.nrc.nl/nieuws/2011/06/28/toespraak-maxim-verhagen/> [accessed 15 February 2012].

is exactly what needs to be explained: the breakthrough of populism occurred amid a sweeping reversal of political sentiment among the wider population.

This chapter, taking the Dutch case as an example, will outline the shortcomings of the reflective approach described above. A more fruitful strategy, I will argue, is to see populism not as the reflection or expression of the opinions of the electorate, but rather as a technique, style or mode of representation that aims to constitute the very political opinions that it claims to represent (Laclau 2005a, Arditi 2007). Besides helping to explain the inner logic of populism itself, the use of a constructivist approach (Bourdieu 1984) can explain rapid change in terms of the influence of events and political action on public opinion and institutional structures.

The structure of this chapter is as follows. In the first part of this text I will discuss the origins and problems of the reflective approach used by leading Dutch scholars to explain the emergence of populism in the Netherlands. The second part first develops a constructivist reading of populism. It goes on to introduce the reader to the Dutch political context and the wider elements of Dutch political culture that could explain the profoundness of the changes we have seen in the past decade. Subsequently, an outline of a constructivist reading of the emergence of Dutch populism will be presented, after which I will conclude.

The shortcomings of the reflective approach

The approaches that attempt to explain the emergence of populism through voter behaviour stem from a particular theoretical background. In an essay entitled *The rediscovery of ideology; return of the repressed in media studies*, Stuart Hall (2006) traced a development in social science, which he subdivided into three periods: 1) In most of the nineteenth and the beginning of the twentieth century, mass culture theory is dominant, 2) In the 1940s, what Hall terms the 'behavioural' and 'scientifistic tradition' emerges in the United States and swiftly becomes the new global norm and 3) From the 1960s onwards, the behavioural tradition finds itself increasingly challenged by a range of critical social-constructivist perspectives. Much of the epistemological critique of the mass culture debate and the behavioural science tradition, as advanced by Hall and others within this later current (Lukes 1974, Bourdieu 1984), is still of relevance today. The defining Dutch studies on populism continue apace in these old repertoires, where political change is reduced to changes in the opinions of the electorate.

The mass culture debate

The rise of populism in the Netherlands led to a remarkable revival of mass culture theory. Its negative vision of modernization resulting in anomy and uprootedness, and the idea of a high culture, threatened by the growing self-assertion of mass culture and mass man, functioned as an important framework to explain the political developments in the Netherlands from an élite perspective. A good example of the classic mass-culture logic is that of famous Dutch author Menno ter Braak, who in the 1930s used the following argumentation, inspired by Nietzsche, to explain the rise of fascism: 'It is the ideal of equality that, given the biological and sociological impossibility of equality between people, promotes rancour in society to a power of the first degree; who is not equal to the other, but wishes to be equal nonetheless, is not being told off with reverence to rank or caste, but is awarded a premium!' (Ter Braak 1992/1937: 173, author's translation).

A similar image of the disgruntled masses started to surface with the electoral breakthrough of the right-wing populist party of Pim Fortuyn (LPF) in 2002. Sometimes this took place in a very literal sense: the influential commentator H. J. A. Hofland explained the electoral victory of the LPF with the above quote from Ter Braak.[5] Another example is the bestselling polemic *The Eternal Return of Fascism* (2010) by the philosopher Rob Riemen, a study portraying right-wing populism as a form of fascism stemming from the cultural degeneration of the masses, on the basis of Ortega y Gasset and other mass culture theorists. But a subtler and more pervasive version of the mass culture thesis is present as well. It is the idea of the electorate as 'spoiled consumers', who vote out of resentment or rancour. Just as democratization for Ter Braak leads to resentment, here it is the rise in prosperity of the masses that leads to a popular revolt by 'spoiled voters'. Resentment returns in the form of a 'jealousy model' (Oosterbaan 2002) or an 'envy system' attributed to the petit bourgeois and nouveau riche that have done well, but feel they deserve even better (van Stokkum 2002). Prominent opinion-makers and social scientists started using this rationale to explain the voters' revolt, such as the well-known economist Heertje and the political scientist De Beus, who stated after the 2002 elections that a combination of Alexis de Tocqueville and disposable income could explain 90 per cent of the populist vote (Banning 2002). The two researchers quoted Emile Durkheim to explain how a rise in prosperity could lead to resentment: 'With increased prosperity desires increase. At the very moment when traditional rules have lost their authority, the richer prize offered [to] these appetites stimulates them and makes them more exigent and impatient of control' (Durkheim 2002/1897: 214).

General critiques of the mass culture framework have been around for some time (Strinati 1995). But in particular, the shortcomings of these attempts to explain the emergence of Dutch right-wing populism according to the mass culture repertoire are threefold. First, the claims are so broadly postulated that they have little explanatory power. Second, there is little empirical basis for these claims: Dutch election research indicates that voters for the party of Pim Fortuyn did not deviate much from the rest of the electorate, either in terms of demographics or in terms of their (supposedly resentful) voting motivations (van Praag 2001, van der Brug 2003, 2004, Bélanger & Aarts 2006). A third problem is of a more general nature: when using social characteristics (e.g. income or education) of the electorate to explain voting behaviour, or processes such as modernization and the mass-commodification of culture, the limitation is that these factors change very gradually over time. As a consequence, rapid changes in voting behaviour cannot be explained (Aarts 2005).

---

[5]   Oosterbaan, W. 'Het Onbehagen kan weer Ondergronds', *NRC Handelsblad*, 2 November 2002.

The behaviouralist tradition

Arguably, the dominant reading of the emergence of Dutch populism is provided by a series of studies inspired by the American behaviouralist and pluralist tradition. In these studies, populism is addressed through a quantitative analysis of changing voting behaviour (Achterberg & Houtman 2006, van der Waal et al. 2007, 2010, Houtman et al. 2008) and unequal political participation (Bovens & Wille 2009). The rise of populism is attributed to the emergence of a new political cleavage between highly educated 'culturally progressive' and lower educated 'culturally conservative' voters. Two studies in particular have received large amounts of attention in the Dutch debate. There is the study for the Dutch national research council (NWO) by Mark Bovens and Anchrit Wille, entitled *Diplomademocracy* (2009) and the work of the Rotterdam sociologists Dick Houtman and Peter Achterberg, of which the book *Farewell to the Leftist Working Class* (2008) is the most well-known.

Though it presented itself as empirically grounded, according to critics like Hall, the behaviouralist and pluralist tradition 'was predicated on a very specific set of political and ideological presuppositions' (Hall 2006: 127). The two most important of these presuppositions were 1) the assumption of the end of ideology and 2) a mimetic or reflective idea of representation: politics functions – and should function – as a neutral reflection of the policy preferences of the population, seen as rational autonomous individuals. This framework, as became clear in the political turmoil of the 1960s, severely impinged on the ability of behavioural science to explain change and dissent. As I will show, similar problems occur using this approach in the present Dutch context, with very particular political implications.

In *Diplomademocracy* (Bovens & Wille 2009), the influential report of the Dutch research council (NWO), we find the assumptions mentioned above almost literally reproduced.[6] The report presents a narrative on the emergence of populism that has grown to become the most authoritative explanation in Dutch public opinion. The rise of populism is presented as a rebellion of the lower educated against the political over-representation of the higher educated, who dominate both civil society and political parties. This over-representation is seen as exceedingly problematic, since higher-educated and lower-educated constituencies have different interests and concerns, and therefore different policy preferences. Higher-educated people are cosmopolitans, we are told, whereas the lower educated are nationalists (ibid.: 85). This is not due to their ideas but follows from their purported rational interests: higher-educated people reap the benefits from globalization, and the lower educated bear its costs. The lower educated, according to data cited by the DPES (Dutch Parliamentary Election Studies), are more concerned about crime and immigration, whereas other survey data show they tend to be more negative about the European

---

[6] The study uses a reference to an article by Converse from 1964 to declare that in the present Dutch situation 'the role of ideology or belief systems as a common yardstick for masses and elites has lost much of its importance' (Bovens & Wille 2009: 71). And the study is an explicit defence of a weak version of mimetic representation (ibid.: 9).

Union (EU).[7] Because the political process does not sufficiently represent the interests of the lower educated, widespread disenchantment with politics has occurred, which has led to a populist revolt in the last decade, 'the "revolt" of Fortuyn and the subsequent rise of populist parties in the first decade of the 21st century is a manifestation of a sudden eruption of resentment against the rise of diploma democracy' (ibid.: 88).

The emergence of right-wing populist parties is therefore seen as a 'healthy correction' to the over-representation of the higher educated, bringing the grievances of the lower educated back into the political process (ibid.: 86). Established political parties are recommended to adopt the agenda of right-wing populist parties in moderate form or risk the danger of anti-democratic mass movements, with reference to the doom scenario of the 1930s (Bovens & Wille 2011: 114).

This account is deeply problematic. The political dominance of the higher educated is not something new and there are no clear indications that the gap in participation is growing (Hakhverdian et al. 2011). In fact, as the authors of *Diplomademocracy* are forced to admit, the dominance of the higher educated has been the norm since the second half of the twentieth century (2009: 58). Similar things can be said about the political cleavage between highly educated 'culturally progressive' voters and lower-educated 'culturally conservative' voters: the cleavage has been there since the 1970s (Thomassen et al. 2000). Furthermore, while surveys reveal a correlation between the right-wing populist vote and anti-immigrant sentiments, they also show that attitudes towards multiculturalism and minorities have been remarkably constant (Uitermark 2010). *Diplomademocracy* provides no explanation of why dissatisfaction suddenly erupted in 2002, given that in 1998, under exactly the same government and with almost identical policies, confidence was at an all-time high (Aarts 2005).[8] The only logical conclusion would seem to be that Fortuyn actively fuelled discontent (van der Brug 2003, 2004, Bélanger & Aarts 2006), but that of course contradicts the pluralist conception of reflective representation, where things need to happen first among the electorate, and only then have an impact in the political field.

A further inconsistency is that the opinions of the lower educated are misrepresented, by ascribing them political meanings and interests which are not present in the data discussed. For example, the Dutch vote against the EU constitution is seen as an illustration of the revolt of lower-educated nationalists: 'the example of European unification illustrates how in a diploma democracy the "educated" opinions are included and the "non-educated" opinions are sometimes excluded from the participatory and political representative arenas' (Bovens & Wille 2009). Nonetheless, according to the exit polls cited in the study, 51 per cent of the higher educated voted against the constitution, showing that higher-educated opinions were equally excluded (ibid.).

---

[7] The report cites a 2006 Eurobarometer poll: '43% of the least educated think their country has not benefited from the EU (41% thinks it did), as opposed to 25% of the university educated (67% is positive)' (ibid.: 77).

[8] In fact, in April 2001, a new and very strict immigration law was introduced by the social democrat Secretary of State for Immigration, Job Cohen, complicating the reading of the Fortuyn vote as an appeal for a stricter immigration policy. Ironically, Job Cohen would later become the major figure-head of the multiculturalist tendency in Dutch politics, constantly criticized by the populist right, who at the same time built on his restrictive immigration policy.

Furthermore, opposition to EU unification cannot be simply explained as a form of nationalism. It is informed by a host of different issues, with loss of democratic voice being one of the more prominent concerns, as focus-group research commissioned by the Ministry of Foreign Affairs shows (Plasschaert Quality in Research 2005). This diversity is forcibly reduced into a framework of lower-educated nationalism versus higher-educated cosmopolitanism. It is also, by definition, not in the 'rational interest' of the lower educated to be nationalist: to question that view it suffices to think of the 350,000 workers in the key transportation sector (truck drivers, airport workers, dockworkers) that constitute almost literally the hands and feet of globalization, or the 400,000 workers in the tourist industry.

The pluralist conception of reflective representation leads to a description of the emergence of populism as the neutral reflection of long-term opinion changes among the electorate. These changes in opinion are portrayed as the spontaneous consequence of large, anonymous processes such as globalization, immigration and European unification. The reflective approach thus creates a distorted view of the rise of populism, a world in which political events, the media and political actors themselves have no influence on public opinion. The result is that the emergence of populism is naturalized, leading to the logical conclusion that if established parties want to remain representative they need to accept and accommodate the agenda of the populist Right.

Much of the analysis in *Diplomademocracy* is inspired by the work of the sociologists Houtman et al. (2008). Their research singles out cultural voting as the cause of the emergence of right-wing populism. The authors build on the framework of Lipset's classic study *Working Class Authoritarianism* that aimed to explain why workers vote against their economic interests by arguing that workers vote for the Right because of their conservative cultural values. Houtman and Achterberg claim cultural voting has further increased since then (hence the title of their book), and has led to the emergence of right-wing populism. But the problem of using such an explanatory framework in the Netherlands is that cultural voting has been the norm all along (Nieuwbeerta 1995). The authors admit so themselves:

> In the Nederlands, the relation between class position and voting behaviour was negligible, due to the influence of pillarisation. Within the pillarised relations, catholic workers, for example, would identify more with their Catholic employers than with their co-workers of other religions, as a consequence they would vote for the KVP (Catholic Party) rather than for the SDAP (Socialist), CPN (Communist), or PvdA (Social-Democrat). But why has it remained that way? Why has depillarisation and secularization in the Netherlands not lead to the emergence of a typical pattern of lower classes voting for the left and a middle class that votes for the right? In those other countries the arrival of a new cultural polarisation on authoritarianism has eroded the familiar pattern of lower classes voting for the left and middle classes voting for the right; in the Netherlands the same new polarisation has gradually taken over the 'buffering' role of confessional polarisation from the time of pillarisation. Despite depillarisation, lower educated Dutch as much as before, vote in contradiction with their class-based economic interests. (Houtman & Achterberg 2010: 21, author's translation)

What has replaced the old structures of pillarization,[9] in their view, is a new post-confessional culture with a new political cleavage: the opposition to authoritarianism between progressive and conservative cultural values (effectively Inglehart's post-materialism of the New Left versus Reagan's and Thatcher's conservatism of the New Right). This cleavage, with a delayed effect of 30 years, has led to the emergence of the New Right in the Netherlands: '[T]hat in the Netherlands the electoral breakthrough of the New Right only took place in 2002, shouldn't distract us from the fact that already from 1970 on, a new polarisation has taken place in the population, where above all immigration, integration and the multicultural society became the centre of the public and political debate' (ibid.: 31).

As a consequence of the pluralist preconceptions used in these studies, the rapid emergence of right-wing populism is necessarily reduced to long-term changes in voter opinions. What produces these changes in opinion is, however, clouded from view. It is rather surprising that, from behaviouralist science, a widely accepted reading of the emergence of Dutch populism has been produced that cannot explain rapid change, and in which the most important political actors and developments never even appear. On top of that, very little effort is being made to describe what populism is, how it functions or how it has managed to gain popular appeal. Populism seems to have no agency of its own.

Towards a constructivist reading of Dutch populism

In this second section, I will attempt to show how a constructivist perspective might address some of the shortcomings of the reflective approach: First of all, by showing that there is something inherent to the logic of populism that can only be explained through social construction. Secondly, a constructivist understanding of the nature of the Dutch consensus model can help to explain structural and rapid change as it has, in effect, happened before, in the 1960s. Thirdly, applying these insights helps to explain the breakthrough and success of right-wing populism.

Populism and the construction of the people

The label populism is often used in a derogatory sense, as an insult, meaning demagogy, simplicity, irrationality, loud-mouthing, etc. These common-sense notions of populism critique it for being an almost too literal expression of popular concerns and desires: making promises that are unrealistic, using language from the street that is not considered politically correct, etc. Hidden within these notions we find again a mimetic idea of populism, as a literal reflection of popular desires. It rhymes with how populist movements present themselves, as the ones that 'listen to the people' and 'say what the people think'. Informed by a similar perspective, there is the idea

---

[9] Pillarization refers to the religious and political segregation of Dutch society into four pillars: Protestant, Catholic, Socialist and Liberal (see next section for further explanation).

that populism somehow enacts a direct democratic form of politics (Taguieff 1995, Akkerman 2004).

The particularity of populist representation is however that it does not passively express popular demands; it is actively involved with the social construction of the subject that it represents (Laclau 2005a). Though there is no academic consensus on an exact definition of the word populism, there seems to be a general agreement that populism is a politics that appeals to the people, and opposes itself to the establishment (Canovan 1981, Taggart 2000, Laclau 2005b). This appeal to the people involves the image of a pure and undivided people, an essence, as in the True Finns, the Real America, Joe the Plumber, or the Dutch Henk and Ingrid. The result is that 'the people' in populist rhetoric is never equivalent to the entire political community, there are always groups that are excluded from it – starting with the establishment of course, but also other 'unpopular' elements, such as ethnic or religious minorities, are excluded. This division of the political community into different components is precisely where the essence of populism lies, according to Ernesto Laclau (2005b) in his book *On Populist Reason*:

> [A]n institutional discourse is one that attempts to make the limits of the discursive formation coincide with the limits of the community ... The opposite takes place in the case of populism: a frontier of exclusion divides society in two camps. The 'people', in that case, is something less than the totality of the members of the community: it is a partial component which nevertheless aspires to be conceived as the only legitimate totality. (81)

The same typically populist mechanism is at work in the appeal to virtual categories such as 'Henk and Ingrid' (a hypothetical couple invented by Wilders, the Dutch version of 'the average Joe'), 'the man on the street', 'ordinary people' and a core of hard-working, law-abiding and tax-paying people. They are symbolic elements that function as a stand-in for the community as a whole and are articulated in opposition to other elements (e.g. the left/liberal élite, Muslim migrants or the deserving poor) that are excluded from political legitimacy. An illustration of this front dynamic within Dutch populism is the 'Two Netherlands' speech of Geert Wilders at the Budget Review of 2009:

> The realm of Balkenende is a kingdom of two Netherlands ... On the one hand our elite, with their so-called ideals. Of a multicultural society, the mega-high taxes, the lunatic climate hysteria, the unstoppable islamisation, of the Brussels superstate and senseless development aid ... It is the left-wing canal elite and its smug friends. The other Netherlands consists of the people that have to pay the bill, literally and figuratively. Who are being threatened and robbed. Who are suffering from the havoc caused by the street-terrorists. Who are toiling under the height of the taxes and desire a more social Netherlands. These are the people that have built up our country.[10]

[10] Source: <www.pvv.nl> [accessed 15 February 2012].

Society is divided into two camps: the Netherlands of the left-wing élite and that of the 'ordinary' hard-working taxpaying citizens, the people. It is the 'plebs' – a relatively excluded and undervalued part of the community – that are declared to be the only legitimate 'populus'. The split that is produced between the élite and the people through this technique is what Laclau calls the 'internal frontier'.

What we can conclude from a reading of Laclau's work is that populism does not reflect or express the will of the people – because the will of the people is too heterogeneous to fit the populist presentation of the people-as-one. It symbolically constitutes 'the people' and the will of the people, and constructs an internal frontier primarily through negative identification: by placing certain groups outside the community, the 'constitutive outside'. 'The people' is formed by the disqualification of certain groups, by determining what it is not. Being opposed to the figure of the 'estranged élite', and to the Other (the enemy) – in the Dutch case usually Muslims (terrorists), or immigrants – provides a clear identity for an otherwise formless and very heterogeneous electorate that shares no clear ideology or policy preference in the positive sense.

In what follows, I will use these insights to explain how Dutch populism was able to construct an internal frontier on the basis of a series of dramatic events. However, let us first turn to the institutional context of the Netherlands.

The Dutch consensus model

Often described as a consociational democracy, the Netherlands has a tradition of consensus democracy commonly associated with dialogue and deliberation. It seems difficult to relate the present situation to that image. However, conflict and polarization are not something utterly alien to Dutch political history: there are similarities between the present period and that of the 1960s, when the New Left protest movements actively contested the existing institutional consensus. Examining that period might clarify how the present political situation came into existence.

Both in the Netherlands and internationally, Lijphart's (1968) classic work *The Politics of Accommodation* is the most famous analysis of the Dutch political system. Lijphart describes the birth of Dutch pillarization at the beginning of the twentieth century, and the downfall of this governmental logic in the 1960s with the arrival of the protest movements of the New Left. From 1917 to 1967, Dutch society is generally described as divided into three or four subgroups, the so-called zuilen (pillars): Protestant, Catholic, Socialist and Liberal.[11] The pillars functioned as societal subsystems, with their own political parties, newspapers, schools, trade unions, sports clubs and so forth. Though these pillars segregated Dutch society, overarching élite accommodation at the top connected them (thus providing the metaphorical roof uniting the pillars in a common structure). Due to the fragmented nature of the political field, where political power depended on the formation of changing multi-party coalitions, a political culture of moderation, consensus and pragmatism developed.

---

[11] There is disagreement about the exact status of the Liberal current, which is alternatively described as a 'universal pillar' (Schendelen 1984. In 1977, following rapid secularization, the Protestant and Catholic currents merged to become the Christian Democrat Party (CDA).

According to Lijphart, the key to keeping the system operable was the pacification of ideological differences, with a given set of techniques to maintain consensus: 1) a businesslike approach to politics: politics means governing, and is pragmatic and focused on results; 2) tolerance: the majority does not impose its interests, but strives to meet the concerns of minorities. Non-negotiable disagreement is resolved by agreeing to disagree; 3) summit diplomacy among the élites: the most important decisions are made in summits, behind closed doors if possible; 4) proportionality between the pillars: when distributing resources, subsidies are divided equally among factions; 5) depoliticization: depoliticizing and neutralizing ideological antagonism; 6) secrecy: during the negotiation and decision-making process, the public limelight is shunned; 7) the government's right to govern: in exchange for a docile position of the opposition, the government takes its interests into account.

This fairly paternalistic regime encountered a crisis in the 1960s under the pressure of the protest movements of the New Left. The result was that consensus started to give way to conflict, with a different set of techniques becoming prevalent (Daalder 1987): 1) exposure of the ideology of the establishment; 2) contestation and conflict; 3) appeal to the base; 4) polarization as a means to form an exclusive majority, on the basis of one's own programme; 5) politicization; 6) publicity; 7) dualism.

Critics of Lijphart pointed out that due to his insistence on a pluralist consensus based on generally accepted social norms (whereby deviance becomes anomy), he was not able to explain the breakdown of the consensus model into the polarized politics of the 1960s (Fennema 1976, Stuurman 1983).[12] This could be remedied by giving the model a constructivist Gramscian twist, replacing the pluralist conception of consensus by a Gramscian idea of consensus organized as hegemony. Stemming from Lijphart's own theory, there seems to be nothing natural about a consensus, as it is maintained by a series of political techniques. The benefit of a Gramscian idea of a constructed consensus is that it allows for the possibility that it might break down: periods of hegemony, of consensus and relative stability, are followed in a wave-like movement by periods of hegemonic crisis, conflict and turmoil (Gramsci 1971). The breakdown of the pillarization system in the 1960s could be described in terms of what Gramsci called an 'organic crisis': a deep hegemonic crisis, whereby the old consensus breaks down and the relation between the electorate and its traditional forms of political representation starts to slide, a process whereby, according to Gramsci, 'the great masses have become detached from their traditional ideologies, and no longer believe what they used to believe'. 'In this interregnum', he added, 'a great variety of morbid symptoms appear' (ibid.: 276).

The crisis in the 1960s ushered in a 15-year period of conflict and polarization which ended at the end of the 1970s, when it gave way to another period of consensus and depoliticization: the no-nonsense politics of the 1980s. In the new consensus, many of the progressive demands of the protest movements of the 1960s were accommodated.

---

[12] In a typical pluralist move, Lijphart describes the end of ideology as one of the main reasons for the downfall of the four pillars. While the main contention towards pillarization had an explicit ideological form – the political radicalism of the New Left – ideology did not disappear, it simply changed shape.

The legalization of abortion, soft drugs, euthanasia and prostitution became part of a progressive hegemony (Kennedy 2005), the cornerstone of the tolerant and liberal image of the Netherlands abroad. Of vital importance in terms of labour relations were the Wassenaar agreements of 1982,[13] the centrepiece of what became known and celebrated as the Dutch *poldermodel*. At this point, Lijphart was convinced that the old pacification politics had returned, this time for good (Lijphart 1989). But at the end of the 1990s, the meteoric rise of the charismatic right-wing populist Pim Fortuyn[14] and his dramatic assassination effectively undermined that consensus, heralding a new period of polarization.

The emergence of right-wing populism has occurred in a crisis of a similar nature and magnitude as that of the 1960s, with almost the entire political field experiencing major instability. The CDA, the dominant political power in the country since the Second World War, saw half of its electorate flee in the elections of 2010.[15] The party has been in crisis ever since. The Social Democrats (PvdA) face similar ordeals. Other parties are ideologically adrift. The right-wing Liberal Party has turned towards neo-conservatism. The Green Left (GroenLinks) is moving in a liberal direction, while the Socialist Party – once a marginal Maoist protest party and now classically social democratic – currently wins as many seats in the polls as the Christian Democrat and Social Democrat Parties taken together.[16] It is within this context of crisis and polarization that the 'morbid symptom' of right-wing populism manifests itself.

The rules of the conflict model, as formulated by Daalder, seem to be back in operation, this time centred on the 'unmasking of the multicultural ideology of the establishment'. Concurrently, the polarizing formation in 2010 of the most right-wing government in Dutch post-war history can fittingly be described as 'polarization as a means to form an exclusive majority'. Once the new government installed itself it became increasingly clear that the rules of the old consensus politics no longer applied. According to the official opening statement, the government aimed to 'give the country back to the hard-working Dutch people'. It was an echo of Fortuyn. The prime minister

---

[13] A historic agreement between employers and trade unions to restrain wage growth in exchange for working time reduction, which increased the competitiveness of the Dutch economy in the years that followed. Though originally referring to labour relations, the *poldermodel* was soon in use as a more general term; it became a latter-day variant of the consensus model of Lijphart.

[14] At the end of the 1990s, the charismatic media figure of Pim Fortuyn emerged as a political force in his own right. Fortuyn was able to gain widespread appeal on the basis of a populist platform that attacked state bureaucracy and immigration policy, while promoting entrepreneurship and aiming for a reassertion of Dutch national culture. Fortuyn was murdered by an animal-rights activist on 6 May 2002, nine days before the parliamentary elections, resulting in a national furore. In the elections that followed, the party of Fortuyn (LPF) won 26 seats (17% of the vote) out of nowhere, and was made part of the subsequent right-wing coalition government, Balkenende I. The party, a motley collection of nouveau riche businessmen, quickly fell apart due to internal strife and plain amateurism. But the political space created on the Right, and the political ideas of Fortuyn – which came to be accepted as legitimate after his murder – would remain available to subsequent populist right-wing parties to exploit.

[15] The elections of 2010 saw the CDA implode from 41 seats to 21. Many of these votes went to the Freedom Party (PVV) of Geert Wilders, which went from nine to 24 seats and became the third biggest party.

[16] From the weekly poll of peil.nl on 19 February 2012. <www.peil.nl/?3453> [accessed 20 February 2012].

went on to promise policies that those on the Right 'could lick their fingers too'. The austerity measures that followed have been implemented with atypical hostility towards the stricken sectors. All this is in flagrant contradiction of the consensus rules of proportionality and depoliticization. The consensus model of Lijphart also provides a clue for the wavering and accommodating attitude of the established parties and the opposition: instead of containment or counter-polarization there is a painstaking attempt to return to consensus through a politics of pacification and inclusion.

The breakthrough and success of right-wing populism

An important ingredient of Dutch consensus culture is moderation and thus prevention of antagonism (Lijphart 1968). Through the techniques mentioned before, some opinions and interests are included in the existing consensus, while those deemed to be too radical or divisive are excluded from the public sphere. Anti-immigrant sentiment was generally repressed and stigmatized in the Dutch public sphere, and it only became generally acceptable to voice concerns about immigration after Fortuyn.[17] Therefore, when Fortuyn started to become a successful media figure he had to deal with a political élite and a media establishment that were largely hostile to his views. He had to articulate and win a position in the political field that simply did not exist before.

The dramatic outcome of the 2002 elections, when the party of Pim Fortuyn was elected to power, is one of the recurring puzzles when explaining the rise of populism. It is generally portrayed in the Netherlands as a consequence of a long-lasting popular dissatisfaction with politics, resulting from a lack of attention to popular concerns around migration, integration and a multicultural society (Koopmans et al. 2005). However, in 1998, voter satisfaction with politics was still at an all-time high (Bélanger & Aarts 2006). In four years, with a similar coalition and similar policies, this changed into almost general dissatisfaction. The logical conclusion is that Pim Fortuyn himself must have played a defining role in articulating and fermenting this dissatisfaction. An important and underexplored ingredient for his success, besides his commonly cited charisma, is political innovation.

Fortuyn managed to create an altogether new form of right-wing political ideology. By critiquing Muslims for their supposedly 'backward' culture, not for their ethnic background or for being immigrants per se, Fortuyn formulated a new immigration critique that explicitly distanced itself from the traditional extreme right. From 2002 onwards, the Dutch integration debate changed from being about minorities to being about Muslims (Uitermark 2010). At the same time, Fortuyn started mobilizing the people against the consensus model as such: 'It is the culture of the polder model that we oppose. A closed culture that declares outsiders to be irrelevant and does not accept new interests . . . We want to give the country back to the people' (Wansink 2002). On the basis of a post-9/11 clash of civilizations imaginary, Pim Fortuyn was able to create

---

[17] Janmaat, the right-wing populist politician who from 1982 to 1998 served as the expression of extreme right anti-immigrant sentiment in Dutch politics, was publically ostracized and ridiculed for his views. His party never gained more than 2 to 3 per cent of the vote. When asked what made him different from Janmaat, Fortuyn said that 'everybody that is in, will stay in. I don't want to take people's civil rights away' (Wansink 2002).

an opposition between an enlightened nationalist Dutch identity, which prided itself on the emancipation of homosexuals and women, and the threat of an encroaching Islam that he described as a 'backward culture'. But perhaps even more importantly, he created an internal opposition, between the normal Dutch people to whom he promised to return the country, and the existing élites with their political correctness, multicultural relativism and technocratic *poldermodel*. This double frontier, the people on one side and the backward Islam and multicultural élite of the *poldermodel* on the other, would provide the basis for the politics of the populist Right in the years that followed, in particular that of Rita Verdonk and Geert Wilders.[18]

A second important ingredient to explain the success of right-wing populism is the cataclysmic effect of media events (Dayan & Katz 1992, Couldry et al. 2010). Two months before his murder and afraid of the death threats he had received in the run-up to the elections (he was at that moment still a very controversial figure), Pim Fortuyn declared on television that if something were to happen to him, the Dutch political élite would be responsible for helping to create the climate of 'demonization' that would have made it possible. When Fortuyn was indeed murdered, on 6 May 2002, it was blamed on 'the left-wing establishment' ('the bullet came from the Left', as the saying went), in particular the politicians and opinion-makers who had reputedly demonized Fortuyn for his views on immigration. The murder had a profound impact. It led to the election victory of Pim Fortuyn's party in the week after but it had important discursive effects as well. From that moment on, demonization became an effective code word for the populist Right to ward off criticism. The political élite and media establishment started accepting the ideas of the New Right as a legitimate political discourse in the Dutch public sphere. Yet another consequence was that the opposition Fortuyn created between the people and the multiculturalist élite became entrenched in the collective imaginary. From that moment on, this became the central antagonism in the Dutch public debate (Uitermark 2010). When the controversial filmmaker Theo van Gogh[19] was brutally assassinated in 2004 by a young Dutch Islamic fundamentalist for making

---

[18] Rita Verdonk attacked élite cultural relativism in the televised founding speech of her party Proud of the Netherlands: 'There is a strong "let's do away with us" current, that for years has been trying to make us believe that our culture does not exist and that finds our norms and values inferior to other cultures . . . We have been a hospitable people for centuries. But that we, the Dutch, have to make place in our own country and have to adapt ourselves to new cultures. To that I say: enough! There are borders.' Likewise, in his election programme of 2010–15, Geert Wilders promises to defend the interests of the common people (Henk and Ingrid) against Moslem immigrants (Fatima and Mohammed) and the cultural élite of the Amsterdam Canal Belt (PVV 2010).

[19] After the self-inflicted breakdown of the LPF in 2002, many assumed that things would soon return to normal. But in 2003 another political media celebrity was catapulted onto the public stage: Ayaan Hirsi Ali. Circumcized by her Somalian Islamic family when she was five and mistreated by a traditionalist upbringing, Hirsi Ali fled to the Netherlands in 1992. She joined the right-wing Liberal party (VVD) and was elected to Parliament in the 2003 elections. Her controversial anti-Islamism made her the most central figure in the public debate (Uitermark 2010: 80). In 2004, she started work on an anti-Islamic film entitled *Submission* together with Theo van Gogh, a filmmaker, controversial columnist and élitist *enfant terrible*. The 11-minute video pamphlet was aired in August 2004 on Dutch public television and led to widespread controversy. Six weeks later, Theo van Gogh was shot and stabbed to death on the streets of Amsterdam by the Dutch-Moroccan Islamic extremist Mohammed Bouyeri. In van Gogh's body, Bouyeri implanted a dagger with further death threats; Ayaan Hirsi Ali was one of the main addressees. The murder of van Gogh sent shockwaves through the country and it quickly became seen as the Dutch 9/11 (Demmers & Mehendale 2010).

the anti-Islam film *Submission*, this opposition was cemented even further in Dutch public consciousness (Buruma 2006, Hajer & Uitermark 2007). Due to unrelenting polemics by right-wing populists such as Rita Verdonk and Geert Wilders,[20] this internal frontier has continued to be at the centre of Dutch politics, and forms the basis of the restructuring of the Dutch political field at the moment.

Conclusion

There are important differences between approaches that consider populism merely as an expression of the long-term changes taking place in society and among the electorate, and a constructivist reading of populism that looks at how populism helps constitute the very identities that it represents. The aim of this article has been to critique the dominant reading of the emergence of populism in the Netherlands and to show that rapid change cannot be explained by a reflective approach. The existing political situation should be seen as both the culmination and consolidation of a ten-year period in which a discourse centred on national identity, Islam, law and order, terrorism and immigration came to dominate the Dutch public debate. This would not have been possible but for the dramatic impact of cataclysmic media events such as 9/11 and the subsequent political assassinations of Pim Fortuyn in 2002 and the filmmaker Theo van Gogh in 2004. Effectively building on these events and the political antagonisms these created, right-wing populist politicians such as Pim Fortuyn, Rita Verdonk and Geert Wilders, together with the broader current of New Right opinion-makers surrounding them, were able to articulate a new nationalist and anti-Islamic politics. They created a discourse that successfully framed the political debate in terms of a new double opposition: an enlightened tolerant Dutch culture (and in broader terms the Judeo-Christian West) was opposed to an encroaching backward Islam; and an assertive, nationalist and popular New Right was opposed to an out-of-touch multiculturalist left-wing élite.

If we are to develop a deeper understanding of the changes sweeping over Europe, we cannot limit ourselves to a nominalist or reflective reading of populism; we have to understand the wider context, the deeper structures and the inner logics explaining the success of right-wing populism. This implies a need to revisit thoroughly some of the old debates surrounding mass communication, audience reception and political ideology.

---

[20] In the tense climate following the murder of van Gogh, two right-leaning politicians in the VVD rose to prominence and would soon come to compete over the legacy of Fortuyn. Rita Verdonk, a former prison director, made a name for herself as the tough-handed Minister of Immigration and Integration from 2003 to 2006. After a failed attempt to become leader of the VVD in 2007, Verdonk started her own party, the right-wing nationalist Trots op Nederland (Proud of the Netherlands). The party quickly dwindled in the polls and Verdonk left the political scene after a humiliating defeat in the 2010 elections. Geert Wilders had a longstanding career in the VVD and collaborated closely with Ayaan Hirsi Ali, whose anti-Islamism he shared. In 2004 he moved to the Right and forced a break with the more moderate leadership of the VVD. By now a public figure due to his outspoken anti-Islamism and the death threats he received, Wilders left the VVD in September 2004 and continued as a one-man faction. In 2006, Wilders founded the anti-Islamist Freedom Party (PVV).

References

Aarts, C. (2005), *Dwarse Kiezers*, Oratie, Twente: Universiteit Twente.

Achterberg, P. and Houtman, D. (2006), 'Why Do So Many People Vote "Unnaturally"? A Cultural Explanation for Voting Behavior', *European Journal of Political Research*, 45(1): 75–92.

Akkerman, T. (2004), 'Alternatieven voor Populisme', *Socialisme en Democratie*, 61(1/2): 27–32.

Arditi, B. (2007), *Politics on the Edges of Liberalism: Difference, Populism, Revolution, Agitation*, Edinburgh: Edinburgh University Press.

Banning, C. (2002), 'De verwende kiezer en het jaloeziemodel', *NRC/Handelsblad*, 8 August 2002.

Bélanger, E. and Aarts, K. (2006), 'Explaining the Rise of the LPF: Issues, Discontent, and the 2002 Dutch Election', *Acta Politica*, 41: 4–20.

Bourdieu, P. (1984), *Distinction: A Social Critique of Judgment of Taste*, London: Routledge and Kegan Paul.

Bovens, M. and Wille, A. C. (2009), *Diplomademocracy. On the tensions between meritocracy and democracy*, Utrecht/Leiden: NWO.

— (2011), *Diplomademocratie: Over de spanning tussen meritocratie en democratie*, Amsterdam: Bert Bakker.

Buruma, I. (2006), *Murder in Amsterdam: The Death of Theo van Gogh and the Limits of Tolerance*, New York: Penguin Press.

Canovan, M. (1981), *Populism*, London: Junction Books.

Couldry, N., Hepp, A. and Krotz, F. (2010), *Media Events in a Global Age*. Oxford: Routledge.

Daalder, H. (1987), 'The Dutch Party System: From Segmentation to Polarization – and Then?' in H. Daalder (ed), *Party Systems in Denmark, Austria, Switzerland, The Netherlands and Belgium*, London: Frances Pinter, pp. 193–284.

Dayan, D. and Katz, E. (1992), *Media Events: The Live Broadcasting of History*. Cambridge, MA: Harvard University Press.

Demmers, J. and Mehendale, S. (2010), 'Neoliberal Xenophobia. The Dutch case'. *Alternatives: Global, Local, Political*, 35 (1): 53–70.

Durkheim, E. (2002/1897), *Suicide. A Study in Sociology* (trans. John A. Spaulding and George Simpson), London: Routledge.

Fennema, M. (1976), 'Professor Lijphart en de Nederlandse politiek', *Acta Politica* 11(1): 54–77.

Gramsci, A. (1971), *Selections from the Prison Notebooks*, trans. Quinton Hoare and Geoffrey Nowell Smith, London: Lawrence and Wishart.

Hajer, M. and Uitermark, J. (2007), 'Performing Authority: Discursive Politics after the Assassination of Theo van Gogh', *Public Administration*, 86(1): 1–15.

Hakhverdian, A., van der Brug, W. and de Vries, C. (2011), 'Geen bewijs voor toename "opleidingskloof"', *Beleid en Maatschappij*, 38(1): 98–105.

Hall, S. (2006), 'The rediscovery of ideology: Return of the repressed in media studies', in John Storey (ed.), *Cultural Theory and Popular Culture: A Reader*, Essex: Pearson, pp. 124–56.

Houtman, D., Achterberg, P. and Derks, A. (2008), *Farewell to the Leftist Working Class*, New Brunswick, NJ: Transaction.

Houtman, D. and Achterberg, P. (2010) 'Populisme in de polder: Stemmen en mopperen in een post-confessionele politieke cultuur', in *Kritiek Jaarboek voor socialistische discussie en analyse*, pp. 11–31.

Ionescu, G. and Gellner, E. (1969), *Populism, its Meaning and National Characteristics*, London: Weidenfeld and Nicolson.

Kennedy, J. (2005), *De Deugden van een Gidsland. Burgerschap en Democratie in Nederland*, Amsterdam: Bert Bakker.

Koopmans, R., Statham, P., Giugni, M. and Passy, F. (2005), *Contested Citizenship: Immigration and Ethnic Relation Politics in Europe*, Minneapolis: Minnesota University Press.

Laclau, E. (2005a), 'Populism: What's in a name', in F. Panizza (ed.), *Populism and the Mirror of Democracy*, London: Verso, pp. 32–49.

— (2005b), *On Populist Reason*, London: Verso.

Lijphart, A. (1968), *The Politics of Accommodation, Pluralism and Democracy in the Netherlands*, Berkeley: University of California Press.

— (1989), 'From the politics of accommodation to adversarial politics in the Netherlands: a reassessment', in H. Daalder and G. A. Irwin (eds), *Politics in the Netherlands: How Much Change*, London: Frank Cass, pp. 139–53.

Lukes, S. (2005/1974), *Power: A Radical View*, New York: Palgrave MacMillan.

Nieuwbeerta, P. (1995), *The Democratic Class Struggle in Twenty Countries (1945–1990)*, Amsterdam: Thesis Publishers.

Oosterbaan, W. (2002), 'Het onbehagen kan weer ondergronds', *Magazine NRC/ Handelsblad*, 2(November): 28–34.

Panizza, F. (2005), *Populism and the Mirror of Democracy*, London: Verso.

Plasschaert Quality in Research BV (2005), *Motivatie-onderzoek Europese Grondwet – een Kwalitatief Onderzoek*, Amsterdam: Plasschaert Quality in Research BV.

Praag, P. van (2001), '*De LPF-kiezer: rechts, cynisch of modaal?*', Jaarboek 2001 van het Documentatiecentrum Nederlandse Politieke partijen, pp. 96–116.

PVV (2010), *Verkiezingsprogramma PVV 2010–15. De Agenda van Hoop en Optimisme*, Den Haag: PVV.

Riemen, R. (2010), *De Eeuwige Terugkeer van Fascisme*, Amsterdam: Atlas.

Stokkom, B. van (2002) 'Boze kiezer is zorg van alle partijen', *De Volkskrant*, 13 September 2002.

Strinati, D. (1995), *Introduction to Theories of Popular Culture*, London: Routledge.

Stuurman, S. (1983), *Verzuiling, Kapitalisme en Patriarchaat: Aspecten van de Ontwikkeling van de Moderne Staat in Nederland*, Nijmegen: Sun.

Taggart, P. (2000), *Populism*, London: Open University Press.

Tagguief, P. (1995), 'Political Science Confronts Populism', *Telos* 103: 9–43.

Ter Braak, M. (1992/1937), *De Draagbare Ter Braak*, Amsterdam: Prometheus.

Thomassen, J., Aarts K. and van der Kolk H. (eds) (2000), *Politieke veranderingen in Nederland 1971–1998: Kiezers en de smalle marges van de politiek*, Den Haag: SDU.

Uitermark, J. (2010), 'Dynamics of Power in Dutch Integration Politics', PhD thesis, Universiteit van Amsterdam.

van der Brug, W. (2003), 'How the LPF Fuelled Discontent: Empirical Tests of Explanations of LPF Support', *Acta Politica*, 38: 89–106.

— (2004), Voting for the LPF: Some Clarifications, *Acta Politica*, 39: 84–91.

van der Waal, J., Achterberg, P. and Houtman, D. (2007), 'Class Is Not Dead—It Has Been Buried Alive: Class Voting and Cultural Voting in Postwar Western Societies (1956–1990)', *Politics & Society*, 35(3): 403–26.

van der Waal, J., Achterberg, P., Houtman, D., de Koster, W. and Manevska, K. (2010), '"Some Are More Equal than Others": Economic Egalitarianism and Welfare Chauvinism in the Netherlands', *Journal of European Social Policy*, 20(4): 350–63.

van Schendelen, M. (1984) 'Consociationalism, Pillarization and Conflict-Management in the Low Countries', *Acta Politica*, 19 (1), pp. 97–116.

Wansink, H. (2002), 'De Islam is een Achterlijke Cultuur', *De Volkskrant*, 9 February 2002.

14

The Stage as an Arena of Political Struggle: The Struggle between the Vlaams Blok/Belang and the Flemish City Theatres

Benjamin de Cleen

Since the early 1990s, the Flemish populist radical-right party VB (Vlaams Blok; renamed Vlaams Belang after a legal conviction for racism in 2004) has been an important player in Belgian politics. Founded after the split of the more radical nationalist and rightist wing from the nationalist Volksunie (People's Union) in the late 1970s, the VB became one of the most successful populist radical-right parties in Europe, although its heyday seems to have been from the early 1990s until the mid-2000s. This chapter discusses the VB by looking at the party's rhetoric about the Flemish city theatres in Antwerp, Ghent and Brussels. These are the three largest Dutch-speaking theatres in Belgium, which are funded by the Flemish Community and (to a lesser extent) by the respective cities. This choice is informed by the fact that these Flemish city theatres have been the cultural institutions most consistently criticized by the VB and have been among the most active opponents of the VB since the early 1990s. The VB's rhetoric about the theatres is characteristic of its views on the role of (subsidized) cultural institutions and of its ways of dealing with opposition from outside of political parties.

In order to lay bare the structure of the VB's rhetoric, a discourse-theoretical analysis (see Carpentier & De Cleen 2007) was carried out. Its main conceptual framework is drawn from the discourse theory of Ernesto Laclau and Chantal Mouffe (2001; Laclau 2005, Glynos & Howarth 2007). Discourses are defined as systems of meaning that establish relations between identities, objects and practices, and provide subject positions that people can identify with (Howarth 2000: 9, Howarth & Stavrakakis 2000: 3, Torfing 2005: 14). Every discursive practice builds on existing structures of meaning, for it would not make sense otherwise. In a concrete analysis, it is helpful to differentiate, analytically, the practice under study from the systems of meaning that existed before and that encompass much more than this practice under study (Jørgensen & Phillips 2002: 140–1). Therefore, a distinction is introduced in this chapter between rhetoric and discourse. *Rhetoric* refers to the structures of meaning produced through the discursive practices under study (the rhetoric of the VB, the rhetoric of the theatres). *Discourse* refers to the more encompassing and more stable structures of meaning on which rhetoric draws (and which are reproduced, contested or altered by rhetoric). Rhetoric is the result of the articulation of (elements of) discourses. The notion of *articulation* refers to the combination of (elements of) different discourses within a particular rhetoric (see Howarth & Stavrakakis 2000: 3, Laclau & Mouffe 2001: 105). The central question of this chapter is: on which discourses (and which elements from which discourses) does the VB's rhetoric draw and how does the party articulate (elements of) those discourses?

In order to answer this question, the chapter analyses texts using qualitative content analytical procedures of categorization, a process of sorting and organizing pieces of data and linking them together by grouping them into categories that are tied to the concepts used by the researcher (Coffey & Atkinson 1996, Titscher et al. 2000: 62). Three linguistic categories are of particular relevance to analysing how discourses are articulated in texts: vocabulary, semantic relations between words and sentences, and assumptions and presuppositions (Fairclough 2003: 129–33). Empirical material consists of written texts produced in the period between 2005 and 2006, during which the struggle between the VB and the city theatres reached a peak. The corpus consists of external communication by the VB (28 texts)[1] and the theatres (97 texts),[2] VB interventions in the Flemish Parliament (20 texts), the Brussels Flemish Community Commission (10 texts), and the Antwerp City Council (2 texts), coverage in the Dutch-speaking Belgian press (241 texts), on Flemish television[3] (2 texts) and in theatre magazines (34 texts).[4]

Each of the following sections discusses a discourse drawn on by the VB: nationalism, conservatism, populism and authoritarianism. With each successive section the picture becomes more complete, as the way the VB articulates these different discourses becomes clearer. The focus is on the VB, but in order to get a good understanding of the party's objections to the theatres, the chapter touches upon the rhetoric of the theatres as well.

Flemish nationalism versus the theatres' rhetoric of cultural diversity

As is the case for other populist radical-right parties, an exclusive and radical nationalism lies at the heart of VB rhetoric (Eatwell 2000, Spruyt 2000, Swyngedouw &

---

[1] Nine articles in the VB Magazine, 3 texts from the VB national website, 3 articles in the Antwerp VB magazine, 7 articles in the Brussels VB magazine, 3 articles in the Ghent VB magazine, 2 articles in the electronic newsletter of the Antwerp VB; 1 election propaganda booklet for the 2006 elections in Antwerp.

[2] Het Toneelhuis (Antwerp): 3 annual programme booklets, 11 monthly magazines, 7 promotional texts about plays; Koninklijke Vlaamse Schouwburg (Brussels): 3 annual programme booklets, the bi-monthly magazine from January 2005 to December 2006 (12 issues), 17 printed press/promotional texts, 3 speeches at a presentation for the season 2005–6; 10 KVS website blog posts; the KVS mission statement; a text about the history of the KVS; Publiekstheater/NTGent (Ghent): 14 monthly brochures, 3 press/promotional texts for an installation.

[3] The analysis is conducted on a literal transcript of the broadcast and does not take into account visual aspects.

[4] 16 articles in Rekto: Verso, 18 articles in Etcetera.

Ivaldi 2001, Mudde 2007). Nationalist discourse is built around the nodal point[5] nation, which is envisaged as a limited and sovereign community that exists through time and is tied to a certain space (e.g. Freeden 1998, Sutherland 2005, Anderson 2006). Because the nation has no positive identity – the members of a nation share no given essence that makes them a nation – it is constructed by opposing it to out-groups. These can be located outside the borders of the nation's territory (other nation states) and inside its borders but outside of the nation (foreigners) (Triandafyllidou 1998, Dyrberg 2003, Wodak et al. 2009: 27).

One of the main points of struggle between the VB and the Flemish city theatres is the theatres' Flemish character. The struggle revolves around the question of how strongly a Flemish city theatre should occupy itself with the boundary around the nation, how the boundary is defined and what this boundary implies for the relations between the nation and the outside. The struggle needs to be understood in light of the theatres' history. The establishment of the Flemish city theatres in the nineteenth century was rather closely tied to the history of the nationalist Flemish Movement – a label grouping the organizations and individuals striving for the emancipation and (later) autonomy of the Dutch-speaking population of the North of Belgium. In the first half of the twentieth century, the theatres were even more closely involved in Flemish nationalist politics, to the extent that they became involved in collaboration with the German occupier in two World Wars. After the Second World War, the city theatres were increasingly institutionalized within the developing autonomous political structures of the so-called Flemish Community. At the same time, however, the theatres' history was never Flemish nationalist alone. Of particular interest here is that, after the Second World War, the theatres moved away from and became increasingly critical of Flemish nationalism as a political project (Geerts 2009, Vanhaesebrouck 2010).

It should come as no surprise then that the theatres reacted very negatively to the electoral breakthrough of the VB in 1991. In a first stage, this mainly gave rise to reactions *against* the VB structured around a rejection of the VB's racism and a defence of democracy. In a later stage, the theatres also started to focus on positive strategies to increase cultural diversity in their personnel, productions and audience (Jans 2010). In the period under study, the theatres' position towards cultural diversity revolved around an opposition between their own openness and the closed character of the VB's nationalism. This openness has two aspects (that are often hard to disentangle): openness of the boundaries *around* the Flemish in-group and openness *of* the Flemish towards other groups. The VB's exclusive nationalism is contested by presenting immigrants and their descendents as part of Flanders, which is exemplified by plays that define minorities as part of Flanders and mix references to Flemish history with elements from minority cultures (see Vanhaesebrouck 2010). A vocabulary of dialogue, cross-fertilization and contact is also used to signify the open position towards those who are non-Flemish. The theatres oppose what they consider the VB's treatment of Flanders as an 'island'.[6] An open definition of Flanders is articulated with a city discourse.

---

[5] In Laclau and Mouffe's discourse theory, nodal points are 'privileged discursive points that partially fix meaning within signifying chains' (Torfing 1999: 98). Other signifiers within a discourse acquire their meaning through their relation to that (those) nodal point(s) (Laclau & Mouffe 2001: 112).

[6] Reyniers, J., *Brussel is de toekomst*, De Morgen, 14 March 2005.

Particularly the Brussels Koninklijke Vlaamse Schouwburg (Royal Flemish Theatre, KVS) takes the cultural and linguistic diversity of Brussels – the officially bilingual French and Dutch-speaking capital of Belgium and a city characterized by the strong presence of minorities – to mean that it should open its doors to French-speakers as well as to minorities.

The city theatres' position is not exactly applauded by the VB. To the city theatres' rhetoric of openness, contact and dialogue, the VB opposes a radical nationalism. The party will not settle for anything less than an independent Flemish state, and demands strict protection of the boundaries around the nation. At the heart of the VB's criticism of the theatres' relation with Flanders lies an essentialist conception of Flemish identity. The task of the Flemish theatres, for the VB, is to protect that Flemish identity. This is particularly pertinent in Brussels, which the party considers a frontier zone in the defence of Flemish identity. From this perspective, the Brussels KVS is treated as a weapon in the 'struggle for the preservation of the own identity'[7] in an environment that is defined by the 'hostility'[8] of the Francophone majority and the purported threats of a large immigrant population. This reveals the view of a Flanders engaged in a constant struggle with other cultures/nations for the preservation of its own identity. Within the VB's nationalism, the theatres' attention for and openness towards 'cultures' other than the Flemish is profoundly problematic. The VB sees this as an unacceptable diversion from the role of the Flemish theatre and a threat to the Flemish identity the theatres are supposed to defend. To the VB, the KVS should focus on producing Dutch spoken theatre for the Flemish population. Instead of being 'ashamed'[9] of their Flemish identity and Flemish nationalist history and embracing cultural diversity, the VB contends that the city theatres should be proud of and defend Flemish identity. As the VB's vocabulary of roots, history, threats and preservation already indicates its nationalism is profoundly conservative. But its conservatism goes beyond the defence of national identity. The next section looks at the VB's conservatism in more detail.

Conservatism versus cultural diversity and the avant-garde

A second discourse the VB draws upon is conservatism. This dimension of the struggle between the VB and the theatres revolves around the relation between past, present and future. Unlike most definitions of conservatism, the definition of conservatism used here does not characterize conservatism as an attitude towards objectively identifiable change (e.g. Wilson 1973, Jost et al. 2003) or as a particular set of demands (e.g. Scruton 1980, Nisbet 1986, Eccleshall 1994, 2000), but as a particular structure of meaning that can be used to formulate and support very different demands (see Huntington 1958, Vincent 1994: 210). Conservative discourse is built around conservation, envisaged as

[7] E. Arckens in *Bespreking van de beleidsnota Cultuur 2004–2009*, Vlaams parlement, stuk 15 (2004–5), nr. 7-D.
[8] Arckens in Bespreking van de beleidsnota.
[9] Arckens, E., Interpellatie tot de heer Bert Anciaux, Vlaams Minister van Cultuur, Jeugd, Sport en Brussel, over het problematisch karakter van het gentrificatieproces in Brussel op sociaal-cultureel vlak, Handelingen Commissie voor Brussel en de Vlaamse Rand, 29 June 2006.

a process of conserving into the future (part of) a present that has come to us from the past, and that is legitimated through reference to a desirable continuity between past, present, and future (see Narveson 2001: 10). It is the structure of the demand that counts, not its substance. Conservatism defines itself in opposition to what it presents as threats to the continuity between past, present and future (Huntington 1958: 461).

The VB draws on conservative discourse to formulate its nationalist demands as well as its rejection of avant-garde theatre. The party's nationalism is strongly articulated with conservatism, for its nationalism has at its core a Flemish identity rooted in the past. The division of the world into nations, each with their own state, is presented as natural. Flemish nationalism, to the VB, is about the defence and preservation of a pre-political identity, that is, an identity that has existed since long before any political party formulated nationalist demands. Against this, the theatres argue that their attention for cultural diversity is a matter of 'tuning the artistic project to the culturally diverse and plurilingual reality'.[10] They oppose this to the VB that 'turns its back on the challenges and continues to stare at an idealized Flemish past, as if it would be possible to turn back time'.[11] Using a conservative discourse, the VB opposes the (currently existing) multicultural society, which it blames for uprooting the natural and preferable state of things, as well as the multicultural politics of the theatre, which in the eyes of the VB is utopian. This strategy of delegitimizing opposition as utopian and of obfuscating its own profoundly political nature is characteristic of a conservatism that identifies itself as a 'political position opposed to ideological politics' (O'Sullivan 1999: 52, Eccleshall 2000: 281–2).

Conservatism also plays a role in the VB's resistance to avant-garde theatre. In Flemish theatre, innovation has taken up a central position since the 1980s (De Pauw 2006). Although this focus on innovation is being criticized from within the theatre by 2005, a taboo-breaking, innovation-centred tendency is still very prominent in the theatre. The VB rejects what it considers as provocations and insults of traditional values and long-standing identities (mocking Flanders, explicit sexuality, mocking religion). However, strongly voiced conservative arguments about the downfall of Western civilization and the crisis of society due to the morally, sexually and otherwise deviant nature of culture and media, which in earlier times could be heard regularly from the VB, have become far less prominent by 2005. The party's rejection of experimental theatre has become increasingly grounded in a populist discourse that criticizes avant-garde art because it is élitist.

Populism versus the artistic élite

The VB started out as an explicitly élitist party, but like other radical-right parties, it has become strongly populist (Rydgren 2005, Mudde 2007). Populism claims to speak for a powerless 'down' (the people), whose identity is constructed by opposing it to a

---

[10] KVS. *Terug van weggeweest.* KVS seizoen 2005–6, p. 1.
[11] Jans, E. and Janssens, I. *Een horizon van belangrijke vragen.* Etcetera 93, June 2005, 16.

powerful 'up' (the élite) (e.g. Mény & Surel 2000, Reinfeldt 2000: 51, Dyrberg 2003, Laclau 2005, Mudde 2007). The VB claims to be the party of the people, and seeks to delegitimize the so-called traditional parties (and especially the socialists) as an élite (Mudde 1995, Swyngedouw & Ivaldi 2001: 12–14, Jagers 2006: 219–52). The VB's populism also extends beyond its criticism of competing political parties.

The VB's nationalist and conservative objections to the city theatres' rhetoric of cultural diversity, as well as its conservative objection to their focus on experiment, are articulated with a populist criticism of the theatres as élitist. The city theatres, the VB argues, 'must per definition aim at the entirety of the population – so also at the common man'.[12] The programme of the city theatres is argued to be too experimental and too focused on a limited audience. The VB sometimes refers to the low attendance at the city theatres, but its objection against the élitism of the theatre is mostly a qualitative one: the '[t]heatre is full, that's right, but it is always the same little group of people that returns'.[13] This little group is presented as an élite and opposed to the people – 'the ordinary man',[14] or 'average Joe'.[15] The VB claims to defend the cultural needs of these ordinary people. Instead of focusing on 'avant-garde'[16] and experiment, the theatres should give more space to 'classic and popular repertoire theatre'[17] and 'lower the bar'.[18] Within this populist discourse, demands for more accessible theatre are a matter of democracy. The VB's resistance to what it considered experimental theatre is, by 2005, much more located in a populist rejection of high art as inaccessible to ordinary people than in a conservative protection of society against moral downfall. Still, populism and conservatism are articulated, for the definition of what is acceptable is situated in the taste and opinions of the majority of ordinary people, which the VB opposes to the progressive ideas of a small artistic élite.

The VB also draws on populism to delegitimize the city theatres' pro-diversity stance, as well as their explicit opposition to the VB. To the VB, it is their élitist position that explains why theatre-makers hold on to a positive view of cultural diversity and suffer from 'identity shame'. The Flemings that work for and are the audience of the theatre in Brussels, for example, are argued to accept the dominance of French (and other languages) in Brussels and multiculturalism because of 'a certain form of urban snobbism that has and creates an overly exaggerated idealistic image of city life'.[19] The party portrays them as 'people who do not have problems in Brussels. They live in a protected cultural milieu'.[20] The VB opposes this élite's purported idealistic view on

---

[12] Pas, F. (2005), 'Het moest gezegd', *Vlaams Belang Magazine*, 2(4): 12.
[13] F. Dewinter in a television interview in 'Ter Zake', Canvas, 12 March 2005.
[14] Ibid.
[15] 'Jan met de pet', literally 'Jan with the cap', ibid.
[16] Arckens in Beleidsnota Cultuur 2004–2009.
[17] Arkens, E., Actuele vraag tot de heer Bert Anciaux, Vlaams Minister van Cultuur, Jeugd, Sport en Brussel, over de verklaringen van de minister aangaande een Cultureel Pact tussen werkveld, overheid en samenleving, wat het aspect diversiteit betreft, Vlaams Parlement, Plenaire vergadering, 24–5 January 2006.
[18] Dewinter, 'Ter Zake'.
[19] Arckens, problematisch karakter van het gentrificatieproces in Brussel.
[20] F. Van den Eynde in Hillaert, W. 'Ik zou eens Shakespeare willen zien door Shakespeare', Rekto:verso 19, July-August 2006.

living in the city to the reality of living in a multicultural city for 'the large majority'.[21] The theatres' explicit resistance to the VB is dismissed in even stronger populist terms. In reaction to a number of initiatives on the part of the theatre and other artists in the run-up to the 2006 local elections, one of the party's leaders states:

> What more can I do than formulate the restrained complaint that the art world in Flanders one-sidedly and unanimously condemns the VB as heretic, with that in practice strengthening the cordon sanitaire[22] (that intellectual and democratic monstrosity) and de facto per definition and without nuance siding with the governing parties, so with the establishment. The Flemish art world is establishment. It marches out against the opposition and serves the powerful.[23]

Through a populist argument, artists and opposing political parties are presented as belonging to one and the same élite that is opposed to the party of the people and therefore also to the people. The VB also uses this populism to fend off the accusations of authoritarianism voiced against it. The final section looks at the VB's authoritarianism and its strategies to present itself as a democratic party in some more detail.

The VB, authoritarianism and democracy

The opposition of the theatres to the VB has always drawn strongly on the accusation that the VB is undemocratic (as has much of the opposition to the VB). This is no different in early 2005 when a Brussels VB representative ends his criticism of the KVS with the suggestion to 'turn off the subsidy faucet for a certain period as ultimate instrument if need be'.[24] The theatres' argument goes as follows: the VB's criticisms of the theatre (particularly when combined with demands to cut subsidies) are attacks on artistic freedom, and because artistic freedom is at the heart of democracy these impingements on artistic freedom prove the VB's authoritarian character. Authoritarianism can be defined as a discourse built around an authority, envisaged as an (individual or collective) actor who has the unquestionable right to take and enforce binding decisions. Authoritarianism is characterised by closedness in that it constructs and maintains a) a closed order governed by rules/norms that limit the liberty of the individual and in which the authority enforces the individual's compliance with the rules/norms if necessary, and b) closes the space for politics by treating this order, its rules/norms, and the authority within that order as fixed and unquestionable (see Stenner 2005, Kitschelt 2007: 1179). From this perspective, the VB's rhetoric about the theatre does indeed have authoritarian elements. The party's nationalism (the claim

---

[21] Ibid.

[22] The cordon sanitaire (literally quarantine line) is an agreement between the other parties not to enter into coalition or make political deals with the VB on any level.

[23] Annemans, G. (2006), 'Over kunst en politiek . . .', *Vlaams Belang Magazine*, 3(12): 3.

[24] Arckens, E. 'Interpellatie van de Minister voor Cultuur, jeugd, sport en Brussel Bert Anciaux in de Commissie voor Cultuur, media en sport van het Vlaams parlement over het beleid van de Koninklijke Vlaamse Schouwburg als Vlaamse culturele instelling in Brussel', Handelingen van de Commissie voor cultuur, jeugd, sport en media, 13 January 2005.

to speak for a pre-political nation), conservatism (the claim to defend unchangeable values, identities and ways of life) and populism (the claim to speak for a homogeneous people against an illegitimate élite) serve to limit the freedom of theatre-makers and to present their views as unacceptable and illegitimate.

However, the VB refuses the accusation of authoritarianism and presents itself as a democratic party. The party rejects the parallels between the VB and the Nazis that are regularly drawn by the party's critics in the theatre:[25]

> Of course no one has to 'shut up'. We continue to defend freedom of speech. That freedom should apply to everyone. And that freedom should also include freedom of artistic expression. We do not want to prohibit books or theatre plays, we do not want to throw abstract artists in jail, we do not want to have 'Entartete Kunst' burned, like the Nazis did.[26]

As this quote shows, the VB even presents itself as the defender of liberal democratic rights. At the same time, the party does limit the freedom of the theatres to do as they wish. The VB deals with this tension mainly through a populist argument. The party presents its demands not as a matter of impinging on artistic freedom but as a matter of using subsidies in a way that reflects taxpayers' wishes. This argument supports not only the demand that the theatres play more popular theatre but also (albeit more ambiguously) the demand that the theatres do not oppose the VB. Artists, according to the VB, have the right to speak out against the VB, but not when they are subsidized.[27] Culture that is produced with the help of subsidies paid by taxpayers that include VB voters should not speak out 'unanimously'[28] against the VB or should even *reflect* the political wishes of taxpayers. The first part of the following statement by Filip Dewinter, one of the electoral strongholds of the VB, exemplifies this:

> Political engagement in the theatre, evidently, but then not one-sidedly against us, not one-sidedly pro the multicul [a wordplay on multiculture, 'kul' means 'bollocks' in Dutch], not one-sidedly pro a certain inclination and only against the other. Then *everything* should be possible . . . 'where are the extreme right theatre makers?' I say: luckily there are none. I am happy there are none. Because theatre does not have as a primary goal to serve a political purpose, but to be itself, and the purpose of the theatre must indeed be itself'.[29]

As the second part of this quote shows, the VB cannot accuse the leftist theatres of pushing out right-wing artists because of a lack of (radical) right theatre-makers

---

[25] One example is the Antwerp city theatre playing Mefisto for ever – Tom Lanoye's play based on Klaus Mann's Mephisto. Roman einer Karriere, directed by Guy Cassiers – before the 2006 local elections in Antwerp.

[26] Vlaams belang, 'Geen censuur', 10 March 2005. <www.vlaamsbelang.org/0/381/>.[accessed 14 April 2012].

[27] Dewinter, F. *Eigen stad eerst?*, De Standaard, 26 February 2005, p. 30.

[28] Annemans, 'Over kunst en politiek. . .'.

[29] Dewinter, 'Ter Zake'.

who would *want* to speak out for the VB or its viewpoints. This might explain why Dewinter resorts to a *l'art pour l'art* discourse in arguing for a disconnection between theatre and politics. In doing so, the VB uses the idea of the autonomy of art from politics in an attempt to limit precisely that autonomy. Even if the argument is based on the VB being a democratically elected party, this argument has an authoritarian character, for it gives the VB the right to determine what artists can and cannot say. The party's definition of democracy is limited to elections and does not accept the legitimacy of the non-electoral politics of artists. These are dismissed as the strategies of a leftist élite opposing a party it cannot beat democratically. The party even turns the criticism of authoritarianism around by arguing that the theatres' opposition to the VB 'simply continue[s] a long tradition of abuse and manipulation of art for political goals and political indoctrination'.[30] This shows how populism does not merely serve to present the VB as the party of the people and to claim signifier democracy, but also to delegitimize political opponents as an élite that uses undemocratic tactics against the party of the people.

Conclusion

The aim of this chapter has been to shed light on the VB by analysing its rhetoric about the Flemish city theatres. In VB rhetoric about the theatre, nationalism, conservatism and populism reinforce each other. This results in the construction of a strong antagonism. On one side there is the VB, the party of the (ordinary) people, who wish to protect their own identity from changes caused to their environment by increasing immigration, and who are not interested in and/or are offended by the experimental high art produced by the theatres. On the other side are the city theatres and their audiences, who form an artistic élite that lives a protected life, is ashamed of its Flemish identity and embraces immigration, produces difficult art for a small élitist audience, aims to offend the feelings of the majority of ordinary people and supports the political establishment. In VB rhetoric, the two groups and what they stand for are almost completely opposed. This might explain the VB's strong criticism (and that of the theatres as well): there are many reasons to be displeased, and, in view of who the VB addresses as voters and how, the party has little to lose when it criticises the theatres. While the VB presents itself as a democratic party, its attempts to enforce what it considers unquestionable nationalist, conservative and populist demands, and the refusal to accept the legitimacy of opposing views and political opposition from outside of political parties, give VB rhetoric an authoritarian character.

References

Anderson, B. (2006), *Imagined Communities: Reflections on the Origin and Spread of Nationalism*, rev. edn, London: Verso.

---

[30] Vlaams Belang, 'Politieke Kunst', 24 February 2005. <www.vlaamsbelang.org/0/335/> [accessed 14 April 2012].

Carpentier, N. and De Cleen, B. (2007), 'Bringing Discourse Theory into Media Studies', *Journal of Language and Politics*, 6(2): 267–95.

Coffey, A. and Atkinson, P. (1996), *Making Sense of Qualitative Data*, London: Sage.

De Pauw, W. (2006), 'De nieuwe kleren van de keizer?', Unpublished PhD thesis, Brussels: Vrije Universiteit Brussels.

Dyrberg, T. B. (2003), 'Right/Left in Context of New Political Frontiers: What's Radical Politics Today?', *Journal of Language and Politics*, 2(2): 339–42.

Eatwell, R. (2000), 'The Rebirth of the 'Extreme Right' in Western Europe', *Parliamentary Affairs*, 53: 407–25.

Eccleshall, R. (1994), 'Conservatism', in R. Eccleshall, V. Geoghegan, R. Jay, M. Kenny, I. MacKenzie, and R. Wilford (eds), *Political Ideologies: An Introduction*, London, New York: Routledge, pp. 60–90.

Eccleshall, R. (2000), 'The Doing of Conservatism', *Journal of Political Ideologies*, 5(3): 275–87.

Fairclough, N. (2003), *Analysing Discourse. Textual Analysis for Social Research,* London: Routledge.

Freeden, M. (1998), 'Is Nationalism a Distinct Ideology?', *Political Studies*, 46(4): 748–65.

Geerts, R. (2009), 'De tachtigers schrijven', *Documenta*, 27(2/3): 193–208.

Glynos, J. and Howarth, D. (2007), *Logics of Critical Explanation in Social and Political Theory,* London: Routledge.

Howarth, D. (2000), *Discourse*, Buckingham and Philadelphia: Open University Press.

Howarth, D. and Stavrakakis, Y. (2000), 'Introducing discourse theory and political analysis', in D. Howarth, A. Norval and Y. Stavrakakis (eds), *Discourse Theory and Political Analysis. Identities, Hegemony and Social Change*, Manchester, New York: Manchester University Press, pp. 1–23.

Huntington, S. P. (1958), 'Conservatism as an Ideology', *American Political Science Review*, 51(2): 454–73.

Jagers, J. (2006), 'De stem van het volk! Populisme als concept getest bij Vlaamse politieke partijen', Unpublished Phd thesis, Antwerp: University of Antwerp.

Jans, E. (2010), 'Een regenboog boven het Vlaamse theater? Het multiculturele verhaal in de Vlaamse podiumkunsten', *Documenta*, 28(3/4).

Jørgensen, M. and Phillips, L. (2002), *Discourse Analysis as Theory and Method*, London: Sage.

Jost, J. T., Glaser, J., Kruglanski, A. W. and Sulloway, F. J. (2003), 'Political Conservatism as Motivated Social Cognition', *Psychological Bulletin*, 129(3): 339–75.

Kitschelt, H. (2007), 'Growth and Persistence of the Radical Right in Postindustrial Democracies: Advances and Challenges in Comparative Research', *West European Politics*, 30(5): 1176–1206.

Laclau, E. (2005), *On Populist Reason*, London: Verso.

Laclau, E. and Mouffe, C. (2001), *Hegemony and Socialist Strategy*, 2nd edn, London: Verso.

Mény, Y. and Surel, Y. (2000), *Par le peuple, pour le peuple: le populisme et les démocraties,* Paris: Fayard.

Mudde, C. (1995), 'One against of All, All against One! A Portrait of the Vlaams Blok', *Patterns of Prejudice*, 29: 5–28.

— (2007), *Populist Radical Right Parties in Europe*, Cambridge: Cambridge University Press.

Narveson, J. (2001), *The Libertarian Idea*, Peterborough, Ontario, Canada: Broadview Press.

Nisbet, R. (1986), *Conservatism: Dream and Reality*, Milton Keynes: Open University Press.

O'Sullivan, N.(1999) 'Conservatism', in: R. Eatwell and A. Wright (eds), *Contemporary Political Ideologies,* London & New York: Pinter.

Reinfeldt, S. (2000), *Nicht-wir und Die-da. Studien zum Rechten Populismus,* Wien: Braumüller.

Rydgren, J. (2005), 'Is Extreme Right-Wing Populism Contagious? Explaining the Emergence of a New Party Family', *European Journal of Political Research,* 44: 413–37.

Scruton, R. (1980), *The meaning of conservatism,* Harmondswood: Penguin.

Spruyt, M. (2000), *Wat het Vlaams blok verzwijgt,* Leuven: Van Halewijck.

Stenner, K. (2005), *The Authoritarian Dynamic,* Cambridge: Cambridge University Press.

Sutherland, C. (2005), 'Nation-building through Discourse Theory', *Nations and Nationalism,* 11(2): 185–202.

Swyngedouw, M. and Ivaldi, G. (2001), 'The Extreme Right Utopia in Belgium and France: The Ideology of the Flemish Vlaams Blok and the French Front National', *West European Politics,* 24(3): 1–22.

Titscher, S., Meyer, M., Wodak, R. and Vetter, E. (2000), *Methods of Text and Discourse Analysis,* London: Sage.

Torfing, J. (1999), *New Theories of Discourse.* Laclau, Mouffe and Žižek, Oxford: Blackwell.

— (2005), 'Discourse theory: achievements, arguments, and challenges', in D. Howarth and J. Torfing (eds), *Discourse Theory in European Politics,* London: Palgrave, pp. 1–32.

Triandafyllidou, A. (1998), 'National Identity and the "Other"', *Ethnic and Racial Studies,* 21(4): 593–612.

Vanhaesebrouck, K. (2010), 'The Hybridization of Flemish Identity: The Flemish National Heritage on the Contemporary Stage', *Contemporary Theatre Review,* 20(4): 465–74.

Vincent, A. (1994), 'British Conservatism and the Problem of Ideology', *Political Studies,* 17: 204–27.

Wilson, G. D. (ed.) (1973), *The Psychology of Conservatism,* Oxford: Academic Press.

Wodak, R., de Cillia, R., Reisigl, M. and Liebhart, K. (2009), *The Discursive Construction of National Identity* (2nd edn), Edinburgh: Edinburgh University Press.

Section III

Case Studies – Central and Eastern Europe

15

The Post-Communist Extreme Right: The Jobbik Party in Hungary

András Kovács

The Jobbik party: Short history, electoral results

Immediately after the fall of communism, far-right organizations and ideologies made an appearance in Hungary. In the initial stages these radical and overtly antisemitic groups appeared only on the margins of Hungarian political life. Most of them enjoyed foreign patronage, and became the local branches of Western fascist and neo-fascist organizations established by Hungarian fascists living abroad and Hungarian mutations of the skinhead movement. In mainstream politics, the first far-right party, the Magyar Igazság és Élet Pártja, Party of Hungarian Justice and Life (MIÉP), was founded in 1993 by the writer István Csurka, who had previously served as deputy chairman of the governing centre-right party, the Hungarian Democratic Forum (MDF). The standard discourse of the Hungarian far right had already taken its present form immediately after the expulsion of Csurka and his supporters from the governing party in 1993. Since then, the far-right ideologues have interpreted all conflicts and difficulties of the transition as a single process revolving around a struggle between a changing group of 'anti-Hungarians' who were governing the country before and after 1990 as well, and the 'national forces of resistance'. The tensions caused by economic and cultural globalization were portrayed as a conflict between cosmopolitan and national interests, joining international integration as a loss of national sovereignty, and the social consequences of the economic and political transition as the result of being at the mercy of colonial masters. The radical nationalist and antisemitic rhetoric of Csurka and his followers proved to be attractive to certain groups of the society: at the parliamentary election in 1994 the MIÉP got only 85,431 votes (1.58%); however, in 1998, MIÉP list got 248,901 votes (5.47%) which made it possible for the party to send 14 deputies to the Parliament. Although in 2002 MIÉP won nearly as many votes as four years earlier, due to the high turnout, its 245,326 votes (4.37%) were not enough to reach the 5 per cent threshold. This was the moment when Jobbik came on the scene.

Jobbik appeared in Hungarian political life as a generational organization. After MIÉP failed to reach the threshold needed to win seats in Parliament at the national elections in 2002, a group of radical right-wing students established an organization with the name Right-Wing Youth Association/Jobboldali Ifjúsági Közösség (JOBBIK). A year later, in October 2003, Jobbik was transformed into a political party and changed the meaning of its acronymic party name: from this moment on the official name of the party became Jobbik, The Movement for a Better Hungary.[1] In 2006, Jobbik entered an alliance with MIÉP. However, this coalition, called the MIÉP-Jobbik Third Way Alliance of Parties, won only 2.2 per cent (119,007 votes) of the popular vote and no seats. The alliance broke up shortly thereafter. Having successfully exploited the political and economic crisis after 2006, in 2009 the party received 427,773 votes (14.77%) and three seats in the European elections, and, finally, 855,436 votes (16.67%) and 17 seats (12.18%) in the 2010 parliamentary elections.

Structural causes of the rise of Jobbik

Research on elections and voter behaviour since 1990 has shown the inability of the Hungarian party system to integrate a substantial group of potential voters. Throughout the 20-year period after the collapse of communism, around one-third of voters have been characterized by uncertain party loyalties, weak political allegiances and significant voter volatility. This volatile group of voters, displaying strong anomic attitudes and a lack of any value priorities, has tended to migrate between the extremes on the political spectrum. Such attitudes and behaviour primarily characterized a section of society that was not the poorest but which contained many people who were the 'losers' in the transition, that is, people who lost out on chances of upward mobility and were threatened by losing their former status. Indicators suggest that for this shifting group, rejection and protest were the primary motives for voting. Moreover, the most important motive for choosing a party was its distance from the government in power (Kovács 2011: ch. 4).

The increasing distance between institutions and society and a steady decline in the authority of political institutions were the backdrop to this phenomenon. According to a 'confidence index' measuring the level of trust in ten different public institutions, Hungary achieved the third lowest score among 35 European countries, and these scores were extremely low in the case of the government, politicians and Parliament[2] (Tóth 2009: 19). Thus, over the last two decades, and especially during the recent economic crisis, a large amount of protest potential has accumulated in the country, creating a fertile ground for parties with an anti-establishment profile. Since, due to its reluctance to facing the communist past, the minuscule and hardly visible radical left wing was unable to exploit this potential, and a broad field opened up for the extreme right.

---

[1] The name Jobbik is actually a pun: the word 'jobb' means simultaneously 'better' and 'right(-wing)' in Hungarian.

[2] The index of confidence in institutions has been formed from the average confidence levels in political parties, Parliament, the government, the army, the police, public officials, trade unions, the press and television. The last four places are held by Parliament, the opposition, politicians and government.

The élitist attitude of the political class reinforced this alienation from the political institutions. Politicians of successive governments, in particular the leaders of the socialist-liberal coalition which governed the country between 2002 and 2010, made few efforts to convince citizens of the necessity of serious domestic reforms (requiring sacrifices from many), or of the long-term advantages of membership of such supranational organizations as the European Union (EU). Instead, when speaking about the necessary substantial and often painful changes, they used so-called reform-talk, a technocratic language that was incomprehensible to the majority but gradually became a marker of the political caste. At the same time, they tried to secure short-term political support by making promises concerning welfare and benefits, which they then failed to fulfil. Additionally, during these years, corruption became a systemic factor: owing to poor regulation of party financing, a large amount of 'black money' flowed to all mainstream parties (and sometimes to their politicians). Revelations of political corruption further eroded the authority of the political institutions and the political class.

The politicization of issues concerning the Roma population has doubtless been the most important factor in the rise of the extreme right. In Hungary, the various Roma groups make up between 5 and 8 per cent of the population. The majority of the Roma live in an 'underclass' status: they are unemployed, live in extreme poverty, are segregated from the majority, suffer from discrimination in everyday life and have few opportunities to change their situation (Szelényi & Ladányi 2006). Successive governments and the mainstream political élite have neglected the resulting economic and social tensions. Consequently, the 'Roma problem' has remained outside the political realm for two decades. The appearance of Jobbik has radically altered this state of affairs. Exploiting some local incidents and conflicts between Roma and non-Roma populations, Jobbik has succeeded in placing the issue at the heart of its political struggle, thereby establishing 'issue-ownership' and obtaining for the party a unique chance to appear as a substantial player in Hungarian political life (Karácsony & Róna 2010).

At the time of Jobbik's breakthrough in 2009, it became clear that both mainstream political actors – the socialist-liberal left and the national-conservative right – had followed a counterproductive strategy with regard to the extreme right: both of them had tried to exploit its appearance for their own political purposes. While the moderate right tended to neglect or downplay Jobbik's emergence and to split its constituency by appropriating certain parts of the party's agenda (radical anti-communism, support for Hungarian minorities abroad, etc.), the left – in an effort to keep its constituency mobilized and to discredit the 'collaborating' centre right – constantly employed an overexcited anti-fascist rhetoric, which enabled Jobbik to appear in the media as an agenda-setting political force.

The ideological and political framework of the extreme right

In the construction of the ideological and political profile of the party, the main purpose of Jobbik was to set clear and solid boundaries between the party and the political mainstream. While the parties of the left and centre right presented themselves as symbols and representatives of the new democratic order, Jobbik disputed the reality of the transition and claimed that, despite superficial changes, there existed a hidden continuity between the pre-1990 old regime and the post-1990 system. Though the party has presented itself as a supporter of parliamentary democracy and political pluralism, its ideologues claim that the transition was fake and that the old regime continues to exist within the new institutions. This continuity, they argue, is manifest in the continuity of the economic and political élite, which is a feature of the mainstream left and right. Consequently, the party's main declared political aim is to complete the transition by breaking the power monopoly of the old élite and establishing a real and just democracy. As the party leader, Gabor Vona, wrote in a programme article in the party outlet:

> Radicalism isn't an ideology, neither is it a conception, it's a perspective. If a person is struck by a car, and suffers serious injuries as a result, and two doctors arrive on the scene, one of whom slaps the injured fellow square in the face, while the other says, 'Here, have a paracetamol', the injured party would surely tell both of them to get lost. Hungary over the last decades hasn't merely been struck by a solitary automobile, it has been positively mown down by dozens of freight trains: and yet this is precisely what has been done. The Left just keeps slapping and kicking the patient regardless, while the Right just keeps stupefying them with all sorts of well-meaning sanctimony. Let's be straight about it for once: they have deliberately and completely destroyed the country. What we need here in the place of yet more slaps or painkillers is a radical – to continue the above analogy: a surgical – form of intervention. (Vona 2010, English translation of the original source)

By means of its argumentation, Jobbik has redefined traditional political cleavages. Instead of the traditional left-right divide, it set the new political frontline between the 'Old' and 'New', representing the 'Global' and the 'National'. With pseudo-revolutionary radicalism, Jobbik turned against the 'colonizing' global Other and its representatives, the old 'communist' and new 'post/neo-communist' élite. Jobbik's ideologues call for a new revolution in defence of the nation, whereby the party will form the young, new, revolutionary and national élite. As Krisztina Morvai, EP member of the party expressed in her introductory speech on the electoral programme of Jobbik:

> ... it is now also necessary to finally endeavour to apply those remedies, which politicians would like to have us believe simply do not exist, there being no alternative to the present system. This lie can now be maintained no longer. There is an alternative.... The moment has arrived when people yearning for both justice and self-determination no longer await the arrival of change from politics, but rather they themselves effect change! (Radical change 2010, English translation of the original source)

In confronting the global and the national, Jobbik's rhetoric has evoked the old antisemitic topos of a Jewish world conspiracy, with references – sometimes overt and sometimes coded – to the image of the cosmopolitan Jew who acts as the secret agent of globalization. A recurring formula in the present extremist discourse is the setting of 'our kind of people' (the in-group) against 'your kind' – outsiders that malign the country. It is because of these outsiders that '... we cannot feel at home in our own country'. The task is to reconquer Hungary from those who 'do not recognize common values and common principles' (Morvai 2008). This discourse, which is structurally very similar to Western anti-immigrant discourses, leaves little doubt about the identity of the 'Other', who is portrayed as a colonizing Israeli investor, as a media shark or as a former Jewish-communist functionary morphed into a Hungarian capitalist (see Kovács 2011: 200). However, so far, the anti-Semitism of the extreme right has not been transformed into a political ideology; it does not take the form of anti-Jewish political demands,[3] as it does in the case of the Roma, where Jobbik demands cutting and restricting welfare services and the legalization of segregation in schools. 'The Jew' in this rhetoric has become a symbol for the threatening 'Other'. The antisemitic language currently serves primarily as a medium for establishing extreme right-wing identity, which can then be used to reveal 'our kind' and 'your kind'. The language creates a collectivity: those who speak it belong to 'Us', to 'real Hungarians', as opposed to those who represent the continuity of the former communist and the present 'colonialist' exploitation:

> We Hungarians will not acknowledge without further ado that we have been sentenced to colonial status, and we shall not respond to the statement of your beloved boss, Shimon Peres, concerning the buying up of Hungary, by saying: Shalom, Shalom, just come and help yourself. Dear 'your kind', your impudence knows no bounds . . . If, after the fifty years of your communism, there had remained in us even a speck of the ancient Hungarian prowess, then after the so-called 'change of regime' your kind would not have unpacked your legendary suitcases, which were supposedly on standby. No. You would have left promptly with your suitcases! You would have voluntarily moved out of your stolen . . . villas, and . . . you would not have been able to put your grubby hands on the Hungarian people's property, our factories, our industrial plants, our hospitals . . . It would be nice if there were just a tiny little bit of truth to the supposed fear that the likes of you feel, owing to the alleged anti-Semitism and fascism etc. raging here . . . On the contrary, your kind visibly do not fear at all . . . We will not put up with this indefinitely. No and no! Because our kind have just this one home: Hungary. This is our country; we are at home here and it is here that we are at home. We shall take back our homeland from those who have taken it hostage! (Morvai 2008b)

In conjunction with a radically nationalistic and anti-globalist ideology, Jobbik's discourse strives to reposition the country in the East-West scheme. While the dominant discourse of the transition is organized around such subjects as 'returning to Europe' and 'becoming part of the West', Jobbik regularly uses radical anti-American, anti-Israel, pro-Russian, pro-Palestinian and pro-Iran rhetoric, such as Gabor Vona, the party leader:

> If we . . . profess that we are the descendents of Atilla, we would suddenly find hundreds of millions ready to form a common basis for alliance . . . if we take a

---

[3] "A first step into the direction of antisemitic political demands was the parliamentary question of a Jobbik MP on November 26, 2012, in which he demanded the listing of government members and MPs of Jewish origin 'representing security risk' for Hungary." See www.origo.hu/itthon/20121126-zsido-listat-keszitene-egy-jobbikos-kepviselo.html

look at the countries from Bulgaria to Turkey and all the way across to Eastern Asia, we realize that we, Hungarians, could have a lot of common political objectives with these countries. We come to realize that an alliance based and developed on the principles of Turanism instead of the Euro-Atlantic alliance would be more effective in serving the needs and interests of our nation ... We can safely say that a true Muslim believer ... is closer to God the Almighty, than the non-practising Christians inhabiting Europe today. If Hungary wants to regain its position as a strong player on the stage of international politics it should not head in the direction shown by Fidesz and MSZP ... but instead membership in a Turanic alliance or, if needed, its leading role and initiative in forming such an alliance. (Vona, 2011; English translation of the original source)

Additionally, in order to show their distance from 'the West', some ideologues close to the party have made serious efforts to establish a 'sacral alternative' to the universalistic Judeo-Christian heritage. They strive to reconstruct a neo-pagan, pre-Christian national mythology, similar to the one that served in the pre-war period as the religious foundation of an exclusivist ethno-nationalism (Hubbes 2011, Szilágyi 2011).

Jobbik's constituency

Since the party received the votes of more than 10 per cent of the Hungarian adult population, it is obvious that it appeals not only to a social fringe but also to large groups. In the ongoing debate on the composition of the Jobbik electorate, three characteristic positions have appeared. The first one identifies the largest group of Jobbik voters as the 'losers' in the transition, those who lost their former economic and social status immediately after the collapse of the communist system and became supporters of the extremist parties after 1994, and as those who were hit by the consequences of the 2008–9 economic crisis (Grajczjár & Tóth 2011: 78–9). The second position contradicts the first; it stresses, based on certain poll results, that students and people of relatively high social status are overrepresented among Jobbik voters. On the basis of these data, the analysis characterizes Jobbik's core electorate as an ideologically motivated – extreme nationalist, xenophobic and antisemitic – group, which clearly does not belong to the 'losers' camp (Rudas 2010). Finally, the third position, while not denying the importance of the presence of the higher status group, states that the party's substantial voter group – mostly independent of their social background – consists of those who proved to be receptive to the focus on the Roma problem and consider Jobbik to be the only party to have successfully turned it into a political issue (Karácsony & Róna 2010).

After the 2010 elections we conducted an empirical analysis of a large sample of Jobbik's voters.[4] The analysis provided a more refined picture of the constituency

---

[4] I am indebted to Ipsos Zrt. and the Medián Opinion and Market Research Institute (both in Budapest), which gave me access to the aggregated party preference research files for the period 2007–10. The Ipsos file contained the data of 1,057 Jobbik voters, and the Median file the data of 2,235 voters. I am grateful to Ildikó Barna (ELTE University, Budapest, Social Science Faculty) for her assistance in data analysis.

of the party than previous surveys. As in the case of several extreme rightist parties elsewhere, men are significantly more likely than women to vote for Jobbik. As regards education level, high school and vocational school graduates make up the largest group among Jobbik voters, and the group with at least a high school diploma increased throughout the period; and so, by 2010, its share was greater than in the case of the two major parliamentary parties. Though people aged over 50 represented a substantial proportion of Jobbik voters (27%), people aged 18–29 represented the largest age group (29%). Compared to other parties' constituencies, this age group (and also first-time voters) was the largest among Jobbik voters. The salience of the younger generation is reflected by the age composition of the parliamentary faction of the party: while the average age of Hungarian MP's is 47 years, the average for the Jobbik faction is 38 years. The employment structure of the Jobbik electorate also differs significantly from those of the larger parties: the proportions of the economically active group, of students and of the unemployed, are higher, while that of pensioners is lower. These data seem to verify the hypothesis according to which the most characteristic groups of Jobbik supporters do not belong to the deprived group of 'losers' but are mostly ideologically motivated voters (Rudas 2010).

However, a closer analysis of the aggregated party preference files resulted in a more complex picture. If we examine the regional distribution of the Jobbik vote, it is striking that while in certain areas the party achieved much higher results than the average, in other regions its score was much lower than its national result. In the north-eastern region of the country, where the impact of the economic crisis has been the most devastating and there is a large Roma population, the party received 23–27 per cent of the votes and was the second strongest political party. In the western regions, however, less than 15 per cent of voters supported Jobbik, while in Budapest, with 11 per cent of the votes, Jobbik was the weakest party to reach the 5 per cent threshold. Our data indicate that the electorate of the party was significantly different in the different regions. According to the results of our analysis, the constituency of the party consists of three larger groups. The distribution of one important electoral group, that of the students, did not show significant differences across the regions. This young, active and educated group, which constitutes the most dynamic part of the party (and its activists), certainly does not belong to the 'losers'. Qualitative research on university students who support the party indicated (Iterson 2011), however, that the main motive of their party choice was not extreme nationalism and xenophobia, but first of all the rejection of the whole political establishment, that is, a profound dislike of the whole political élite of the transition. Their distance from the establishment has been expressed by taking a radical stance on issues (irredentism, anti-Roma, opposition to supranational integration, etc.) that seem to be 'owned' by Jobbik.

Though anti-establishment sentiment can also motivate other supporter groups of the party, the fact that the second and third substantial groups in Jobbik's constituency appear in different regions is also indicative of the presence of special electoral motives. The common characteristic of both electoral groups seems to be a completed vocational school, that is, in terms of level of education, they belong to the skilled worker stratum. There are, however, substantial differences between them. In the economically more developed western regions of the country, where the Roma percentage of the population is low, unemployed people and low income groups tend to support Jobbik, whereas in the underdeveloped regions with a high Roma population percentage this is true of economically active, employed and better-off people. While the first group can be termed 'losers', the second group obviously does not belong to those most seriously affected by the transition and the crisis. The main motive for their party choice is probably status anxiety: they have experienced, in their region, a permanent deterioration in the economic situation. Consequently, their attained statuses are increasingly threatened. It is more and more difficult for them to find jobs corresponding to their educational level, to run businesses in a shrinking market, to face losses in the value of their property, to experience the declining quality of the local infrastructure (education, public health, transport, etc.) and to realize that they cannot expect effective support from the state. For this group – also identified in their research by Karácsony and Róna – the visible presence of a large Roma population serves as an explanation for the above problems and for the prejudiced rationalization of status anxiety. They perceive the Roma population as a competitor for scarce resources; the daily confrontations and conflicts that stem from the presence of this marginalized and deprived group in their towns and villages validate their conviction that only a 'solution to the Gypsy question' could fend off the perceived threats. However, in view of the paralysis of the state organs, they look for such a 'solution' outside the existing institutional system. Their specific problems lead them to take a strong anti-establishment stance. Therefore, they support the political programme of Jobbik, with its demands for drastic cuts in the welfare services for Roma, for the legalization of segregation in schools and in housing and for the organization or paramilitary units for 'self-defence'.

Thus, the results of the analysis indicate that the Jobbik constituency contains several electoral subgroups. A young and mainly student-dominated group is overrepresented among Jobbik voters in almost every region of the country. The group of 'losers' is significantly present in the Jobbik constituency in the economically prosperous regions. However, in poorer areas with large Roma populations, a relatively well-educated, economically active and better-off group constitutes the core electorate. Thus, on the 'demand side' the common denominator of the different electoral groups seems to be neither 'loser' status nor a purely ideologically motivated choice (extreme nationalism, racism, anti-Semitism, etc). Though all these elements are widespread among Jobbik voters, the binding element between the different groups of the constituency seems to be a strong anti-establishment attitude.[5] Consequently, a key factor to the party's success has necessarily been an ability to successfully unite these electoral groups with different motivations and expectations.

[5] On the impact and function of anti-establishment attitudes on the extreme right, see Bustikova 2009. In their study, Karácsony and Róna also identified the anti-establishment attitude as one of the most characteristic traits of the far-right constituency in Hungary (Karácsony & Róna 2010). Other research on the rise of the 'social demand' for right-wing extremism in Hungary showed that the proportion of those who do not have trust in the existing institutional system grew drastically between 2002 (12%) and 2009 (46%) (Krekó et al. 2011).

As the electoral successes of Jobbik indicate, these characteristics on the 'demand side' were correctly identified by the 'supply side': the party organized its programme declarations and campaigns around subjects that place Jobbik on one side of the political arena and all the other mainstream parties on the other. Demanding revision of the post-First World War Trianon Treaty, the exclusion of Roma, withdrawal from North Atlantic Treaty Organization (NATO) and European Union (EU) membership and the use of barely concealed antisemitic language for identity construction served this function. The 'ownership' of these subjects has positioned the party unambiguously in opposition to the 'establishment' parties – which, regardless of whether they are on the left or right, in government or in opposition, all accept the present European order and values (see Beichelt & Minkenberg 2001: 12, Karácsony & Róna 2010). The ideology of radical extreme ethnic nationalism proved to be an effective functioning frame for the expression of the anti-establishment attitudes stemming from different sources. The unification of the different anti-establishment groups into one constituency has been the achievement of a new political generation in the political sphere: people whose political socialization took place after the collapse of the old system. While the 'old' radical right – the Magyar Igazság és Élet Pártja (MIÉP) – was strongly traditionalist, anti-modern and supported by an ageing electorate, the core of Jobbik voters comprises younger age groups that are receptive to new methods of political marketing, skilled in the use of new social media and able to create their own political language and thus use new tools of outreach and mobilization.

The new extreme right: A post-communist phenomenon?

The post-communist extreme right in Hungary and in other countries in the region doubtless displays very similar features to the extreme right in the Western European countries, for example, by using anti-establishment, anti-élitist and xenophobic rhetoric. However, its appearance is not simply a consequence of the 'Europeanization' of the former communist countries, a sign of the formation of a Western-type party system. Most experts on the Eastern European extreme right agree that the emergence and character of these radical parties are sui generis consequences of the transition and, directly or indirectly, of the history of the countries in which they have emerged (Beichelt & Minkenberg 2001, Bustikova & Kitschelt 2009). There is an interesting and ongoing debate on the weight of the individual determinants in the emergence of the radical right, but according to a dominant consensus, a combination of pre- and post-Second World War legacies (especially the nature of the communist system) and the conflicts and cleavages of the transition period (especially the economic and social costs of the transition) determine the nature and strength of the radical right in individual post-communist countries. However, the forecasts made on the basis of these considerations in recent years appear to have been incorrect: particularly in Hungary the support for the radical right has been much stronger than expected (Beichelt & Minkenberg 2001: 16). Though much more research is needed to explain the latest developments, it seems that one factor explaining this failure is a tendency to 'depoliticize' the post-communist extreme right phenomenon by using mostly socio-psychological and/or historical-structural theories to explain the radical right party choice. The presence of large groups with authoritarian and social dominance-oriented attitudes as well as the existence of ethnocentric and nationalist legacies and socio-economic tensions have served as important preconditions for mobilizing the radical electorate, but the radical right's electoral success has ultimately depended on its ability to turn elements of people's 'life-world' that were not formerly part of the 'political' into political issues. In Hungary, an example of such an element has been the growing anti-establishment attitude. The extreme right is a political phenomenon per se, and the specificities of its Eastern European variants can be understood only by grasping the specificities of the political sphere in every singular post-communist country.

References

Beichelt, T. and Minkenberg, M. (2001), 'Explaining the radical right in transition. Theories of right-wing radicalism and opportunity structures in post-socialist Europe', Essay presented at the APSA 97th Annual Meeting in San Francisco, 2001.

Bustikova, L. (2009), 'The Extreme Right in Eastern Europe: EU Accession and the Quality of Governance', *Journal of Contemporary European Studies*, 17(2): 223–39.

Bustikova, L. and Kitschelt, H. (2009), 'The Radical Right in Post-communist Europe. Comparative Perspectives on Legacies and Party Competition', *Communist and Post-Communist Studies*, 42: 459–83.

Grajczjár, I. and Tóth, A. (2011), 'Válság, radikalizálódás és az újjászületés ígérete: a Jobbik útja a parlamentbe', in Enyedi, Z., Szabó, A. and Tardos, R. (eds), *Új képlet. Választások Magyarországon, 2010*, Budapest: Demokrácia Kutatások Magyar Központja Alapítvány, pp. 57–92.

Hubbes, L. A. (2011), 'Comparative investigation of Romanian and Hungarian ethno-pagan blogs'. <http://218.academia.edu/LaszloAttilaHubbes/Papers/1286539/Hungarian_and_Romanian_Ethno-pagan_Blogs> [accessed 11 February 2012].

Iterson van, S. (2011), 'Geloof in een beter Hongarije. Radicaal-rechts idealisme onder studenten in Boedapest', Unpublished dissertation, University of Amsterdam.

Karácsony, G. and Róna, D. (2010), 'A Jobbik titka. A szélsőjobb magyarországi megerősödésének lehetséges okairól', *Politikatudományi Szemle*, 2010(1). <www.valasztaskutatas.hu/eredmenyek/kutatas-jelentesek/rkkutjel/karacsony-gergely-rona-daniel-a-jobbik-titka-a/> [accessed 16 November 2011].

Krekó, P., Juhász A. and Molnár, C. (2011), 'A szélsőjobboldal iránti társadalmi kereslet növekedése Magyarországon', *Politikatudományi Szemle*, 2011(2): 53–82.

Kovács, A. (2011), *The Stranger at Hand. Antisemitic Prejudices in Post-Communist Hungary*, Boston, Leiden: Brill.

Morvai, K. (2008), 'Két emberkép között folyik a harc'. <www.barikád.hu> [accessed 1 November 2011].

— (2008b), 'A Magukfajták ideje lejárt'. <www.barikád.hu> [accessed 1 November 2011].

Radical change (2010), 'A guide to Jobbik's parliamentary electoral manifesto for national self-determination and social justice'. <http://jobbik.com/temp/Jobbik-RADICALCHANGE2010.pdf> [accessed 15 February 2012].

Rudas, T. (2010), 'A Jobbik törzsszavazóiról', in K. Tamás and T. I. György (eds), *Társadalmi riport*, Budapest: TÁRKI, pp. 512–26.

Szelényi, I. and Ladányi, J. (2006), *Patterns of Exclusion: Constructing Gypsy Ethnicity and the Making of an Underclass in Transitional Societies of Europe*, New York: Columbia University Press.

Szilágyi, T. (2011), 'Sacred Characteristics of the Nation: "Hungarianism" as Political Religion?' <www.revacern.eu/exchange-programme/EP-paper szilagyi.pdf > [accessed 11 February 2012].

Tóth, I. G. (2009), *Bizalomhiány, normazavarok, igazságtalanságérzet és paternalizmus a magyar társadalom értékszerkezetében*, Budapest: TÁRKI.

Vona, G. (2010), 'What do we mean by radicalism?' <www.jobbik.com/hungary/3138. html> [accessed 15 February 2012].

— (2011), 'Turanism instead of Euro-Atlantic alliance!' <www.jobbik.com/jobbik_news/europe/3198.html> [accessed 15 February 2012].

16

Comparing Radical-Right Populism in Estonia and Latvia

Daunis Auers and Andres Kasekamp

Introduction

2011 saw sharply contrasting parliamentary elections in neighbouring Estonia and Latvia. The 6 March 2011 poll in Estonia was the first election in post-communist Europe to feature an unchanged line-up of competing political parties, indicating a high level of political stability despite the financial and political turmoil that marked much of Europe in 2011 (Pettai et al. 2011). In contrast, the same year Latvia experienced its first early election, triggered by a referendum, on the recall of Parliament, called by the Latvian president in protest to a perceived 'privatization of democracy in Latvia' (Zatlers 2011). Moreover, the radical-right populist Visu Latvijai!/Tēvzemei un Brīvībai/LNNK (National Alliance of All for Latvia!/For Fatherland and Freedom/ Latvian National Independence Movement) almost doubled its share of the votes it won in the October 2010 regular election, and then subsequently took up government office in a new three-party coalition. In contrast, the Estonian Independence Party (Estonia's leading radical-right populist party) claimed just 0.4 per cent of the votes in March 2011.

This chapter examines and explains the contrasting fortunes of radical-right populist movements in Estonia and Latvia. We first analyse the status quo of radical-right populist parties in Estonia and Latvia and describe the recent emergence of the National Alliance as a credible and competitive party in Latvia.[1] We then compare political party rhetoric along three key radical-right populist dimensions – nativism, authoritarianism and populism (Mudde 2007, 2010). Finally, we argue that there are two key long-term explanations for the emergence of the National Alliance as a credible force in Latvia. First, the language of radical-right populists has long been

---

[1] There are no major *extreme* right parties (i.e. those rejecting the democratic system) in Estonia and Latvia.

a part of the Latvian political mainstream, but has only sporadically appeared in the Estonian discourse (see Auers & Kasekamp 2009). In this sense, radical-right populism can be seen as a 'pathologically normal' part of Latvian politics (Mudde 2010), and this *normalization* of radical-right populist rhetoric allowed the National Alliance to emerge as a credible political force without the negative stigma often attached to radical-right parties elsewhere in Europe. Second, the younger partner in the National Alliance (All for Latvia!), which has effectively taken control of the party alliance (following the merger of the two parties on 23 July 2011), is a genuine grassroots movement that has both an enthusiastic and active grassroots membership as well as a firm set of political principles that stand in sharp contrast to the 'thin' élite political constructions of the major Latvian parties, which are both ideologically weak and lacking a widespread membership. It has used this grassroots movement to mobilize young voters and to draw a sharp contrast between itself and the older, more élite parties, thus giving substance to its core populist rhetoric. As with other successful radical-right populists, the National Alliance also has a charismatic leader in Raivis Dzintars. In contrast, the Eesti Iseseisvuspartei (Estonian Independence Party, EI) lacks both a grassroots organization and charismatic leader and is politically marginalized because of its radical discourses.

The historical context

During their first periods of independence between the two world wars, radical-right proto-fascist movements were on the rise in the Baltic States, as elsewhere in Europe. The Estonian Vaps movement (The Estonian War of Independence Veterans' League) gained mass support and appeared to be on the verge of obtaining power through democratic elections when the incumbent government headed by Konstantin Päts declared a state of emergency in March 1934 and imprisoned the Vaps leadership. In Latvia, the Pērkonkrusts (Thunder Cross) movement gained adherents with its call for a 'Latvian Latvia', but shared the same fate as its Estonian comrades, when Prime Minister Kārlis Ulmanis established an authoritarian regime two months after Päts. Some members of these movements who managed to survive the Soviet occupation in 1940–1 re-emerged during the subsequent German occupation, and former members of Pērkonkrusts collaborated in the holocaust on Latvian territory (Kasekamp 1999).

During the re-establishment of independence in the early 1990s, Päts and Ulmanis were revered as the respective fathers of their nations and their mild authoritarian rule is recalled fondly by many. Indeed, the latter's great nephew, Guntis Ulmanis, an amiable, mid-ranking, Soviet-era bureaucrat, was elected the first president of post-Soviet Latvia (1993–9) largely on the strength of his surname. Although the extremist movements of the interwar era were revived by small groups of enthusiasts in the 1990s (notably Pērkonkrusts), they have had no electoral success or direct impact on the political system.

The first years of post-Soviet transition witnessed the emergence of a plethora of small, mainly marginal, new radical-right political parties. Only Eesti Kodanik (Estonian Citizen), led by the retired US colonel Jüri Toomepuu, made it into the

Estonian Parliament (receiving 7% of the vote in 1992). Nationalism was the driving force behind these movements. Soviet rule had brought about a dramatic demographic shift: at the end of the Second World War the population of Estonia was more than 90 per cent ethnically Estonian and nearly 80 per cent of the inhabitants of Latvia were ethnic Latvians. However, following large-scale immigration of Russian-speaking industrial workers and managers during the Soviet era, by the end of the 1980s, the Estonian share of the population had decreased to 63 per cent and the Latvian share to just 52 per cent (Kasekamp 2010: 155). Many of these parties sprang from the grass roots citizens' committees (the Congress of Estonia and the Citizens' Congress of Latvia) created in 1990 – independence movements which championed restitution and opposed the dominant and more moderate Popular Fronts which had gained control over Soviet institutions. Their emphasis was on restorationalism, that is, purging the country of its Soviet legacy and defending the principle of legal continuity with the first period of independence. This meant cleansing public institutions of the influence of former Communist Party members and 'decolonization' – encouraging Soviet-era migrants, mainly Russians, to return 'home'.

A catalyst for the reactivation of the Estonian radical right in the twenty-first century was the 'war of monuments' or battle over memory politics that erupted in the mid-2000s after accession to the European Union (EU) in 2004. The first triggering event was the Estonian government's removal of a monument to those who had fought in German uniform during the Second World War, which was erected by a veterans' group in the provincial town of Lihula in 2004. This incident in turn led to the relocation of a Soviet war memorial, the 'Bronze Soldier', in Tallinn in 2007, which occasioned rioting by mainly Russian youths and an international crisis with Russia (Brüggemann & Kasekamp 2008). In the same way, the first decade of the twenty-first century in Latvia has been marked by conflicts over the role and place of the Latvian and Russian languages in public schools as well as markedly differing interpretations of twentieth-century Latvian history, essentially revolving around the issue of whether Latvia was 'occupied' by the Soviet Union in 1940. These debates have kept ethnic tensions high and ensured that radical voices have a place in public discourse.

Indeed, Russia has continued to attempt to influence politics in the Baltic States. Russian politicians, officials and media have frequently contributed to stoking up ethnic tensions (Muižnieks 2008, Pelnēns 2009: 50, 138). Russian media typically utilize isolated cases of extremism to label the Baltic States hotbeds of neo-Nazism or to point to a 'revival of fascism'. Moreover, ethnic Russian extreme-right groups affiliated with opposition parties in Russia, such as the National Bolsheviks, were active in the Baltic States in the late 1990s, although they have been supplanted in recent years by newer, more sophisticated and networked Kremlin-backed groups such as Nashi or the Anti-Fascist Committee. Latvia has also seen the establishment of single-issue groups with close ties to Russian organizations. Thus the 'Russian School Defence Staff' flowered in 2003 and 2004 in opposition to new regulations on the teaching of Latvian in Russian-speaking schools, while in 2011 the 13 January Movement organized a successful signature gathering drive to force a referendum on the introduction of Russian as an official second language in Latvia. While these Russian nationalist groups are significant in terms of providing rhetorical opposition to titular radical Latvian and

Estonian nationalist organizations, our focus in this chapter is on ethnic Latvian and Estonian parties. We now turn to look first at radical-right populist movements and parties in Estonia and Latvia.

Radical-right movements and parties

Eesti Rahvuslik Liikumine (the Estonian National Movement) appeared at the time of the debates surrounding the removal of the Soviet war monument in Tallinn and in the past few years has been the most coherent and influential radical right populist political force, though it did not register itself as a political party. In March 2012 it merged with Eestimaa Rahvaliit (the Estonian People's Union), the party traditionally representing the rural population which lost its representation in Parliament following the March 2011 election, to form the new Eesti Konservatiivne Rahvaerakond (The Estonian Conservative People's Party). The only radical-right populist party to have contested national elections in Estonia in recent years is the Estonian Independence Party, but it has achieved paltry results: 0.4 per cent in the 2011 parliamentary election, 0.2 per cent in 2007 and 0.5 per cent in 2003. The 5 per cent threshold for obtaining seats in Parliament is an effective institutional barrier against the proliferation of small parties. A chronic impediment to the success of the radical right in Estonia has been the lack of a well-known and charismatic leader. Estonians tend to look to their northern neighbour and linguistically kin nation, Finland, for models. Most recently, after the triumph of the Eurosceptic populist True Finns in the 2011 Finnish election, an initiative group was set up for a Põliseestlased (True Estonians) party (Põliseestlased 2011), which, however, appears to have petered out.

In contrast, Latvia has a great number of radical and extreme right movements and organizations, including a small network of self-styled national socialist organizations. The internet, with its low start-up costs and relative anonymity, has seen a flowering of these radical organizations. Latvijas Republikas Tautas Tribunāls (the Latvian People's Tribunal) is one such case. It is run by veterans of the Latvian radical movement, which can trace its activities back to the independence movement of the 1980s. Its website consists of a list of people perceived to have betrayed the Latvian state. The accusations are often coloured with the claim that the facial features of the individuals show them to be members of some inferior caste (most frequently the accusation is that they are Jewish).[2] The 'Latvian' organization published an extremist newspaper, *Latvietis Latvijā* ('A Latvian in Latvia') between 1999 and 2001 and now hosts an internet site.[3] A higher profile organization is the Latvijas Nacionālā Fronte (Latvian National Front), which regularly publishes an antisemitic xenophobic newspaper that has serialized *The Protocols of the Elders of Zion* and is provocatively named DDD (standing for Deoccupation, Decolonization, Debolshevization) (Muižnieks 2005: 111). Anti-Semitism remains a key ideological position for the Latvian radical right.

---

[2] <http://tautastribunals.eu/> [accessed 5 December 2011].
[3] <http://home.parks.lv/latvietis/saturs.htm> [accessed 5 December 2011].

Nacionālā Spēka Savienība (National Power, NSS) is a younger and more publically active organization whose leader, Viktors Birze, has adopted a high profile at both nationalist and anti-homosexual gatherings. In April 2011, for example, NSS proposed repatriating the body of Herberts Cukurs, a Latvian aviator who perpetrated war crimes during the Second World War (and was assassinated by Israeli Mossad agents in Uruguay in 1965). Although these organizations are on the extreme fringes of the far-right movement in Latvia, and have little public support (NSS won just 0.13% of the vote when it competed in the 2006 parliamentary election), they do have ad-hoc contacts with mainstream Latvian parties and even appear in newspapers and mainstream television current affairs programmes (Auers & Kasekamp 2009).

In addition to far greater grass-roots activity, Latvia has also seen greater success for populist parties, although a successful and genuinely radical-right populist party only emerged in 2010. Indeed, Latvia has experienced three populist waves since 1991. The first phase in 1995 saw a disparate group of nationalists and populists win one-third of the seats in Parliament. Demokrātiskā Partija 'Saimnieks' (The Democratic Party 'Master') and Tautas Kustība Latvijai–Zīgerista Partija (The People's Movement for Latvia–Siegerists Party) combined an explicitly nationalist rhetoric with a direct appeal to the 'losers' in the first years of the economic transition (the elderly, rural dwellers, industrial workers and public sector employees), offering to imprison corrupt officials and businessmen as well as promising universal high levels of welfare. However, the populists had weak party organizations and significant internal differences between party leaders and thus quickly fragmented and collapsed.

The second phase came at the turn of the century, when political corruption had increasingly appeared on the public agenda following the publication of damning reports from the European Commission, the World Bank, Transparency International and other reputable organizations. Jaunais Laiks (New Era), a 'new centrist populist party' with a charismatic leader, flexible political ideology and central anti-corruption message, swept to victory in the 2002 election (Ucen 2007: 51). These first two party waves were clearly populist, but not radical-right populist. They were essentially 'orthodox' parties that supported 'the need for market reforms, a democratic form of government, Western integration' and had moderate nationalist appeal (Pop-Eleches 2002, Sikk 2006).

In contrast, the third and most recent wave of Latvian populism, from 2010 onwards, saw the emergence of a genuinely radical-right populist party – the National Alliance. The oldest part of the alliance is the Latvijas Nacionālās Neatkarības Kustība (Latvian National Independence Movement, LNNK) which can trace its roots back to 1988 and Tēvzemei un Brīvībai (For Fatherland and Freedom, TB) which developed from the Latvians Citizens' Committee (discussed above). These two parties enjoyed a successful alliance that lasted over a decade, spending only two years in opposition between 1998 and 2010. However, they became moderated by governmental responsibility and were losing their share of the nationalist Latvian vote to a new radical grassroots movement recently registered as a party – Visu Latvijai! (All for Latvia, VL!) – that had been building up its support through a series of high profile public demonstrations and an aggressive critique of the existing political élite. However, VL! failed to reach the 5 per cent threshold in the 2006 parliamentary election and was unlikely to do so in

2010, largely because it lacked the level of financing needed to successfully compete in Latvian elections. At the same time, TB/LNNK lacked support in the polls but had built up a substantial network of financial sponsors through its many years in national and municipal government coalitions. This made for a perfect political marriage. VL! brought youth, vigour and a legitimate radical-right populist message unsullied by years of government to the table, while TB/LNNK brought political experience and cash. The National Alliance won eight seats in 2010 and then 14 in the 2011 early parliamentary election.

The National Alliance ticks all the necessary boxes for a modern radical-right populist political party. It has followed the rhetorical master frame of the radical right and has a charismatic leader in Raivis Dzintars, the founder and driving force behind VL! Indeed, charismatic leadership, in the Weberian sense of a close bond between leader and followers, is one of the key internal factors to the success of the radical right, particularly in the early phase of party development as the party attempts to attract members and break through into the public's consciousness (Taggart 2000, Eatwell 2003, Mudde 2007). The Latvian electoral system uses an ordinal ballot with voters marking candidates on their preferred party list with a positive or negative mark. The final order of deputies is compiled according to these marks. In the 2010 election, Dzintars received twice as many positive marks as the second-placed candidate on the National Alliance candidate list. A year later, in the early 2011 parliamentary election, Dzintars received three times as many positive marks as the second-placed candidate (Latvian Central Election Commission 2011).

Radical-right populist discourses in Estonia and Latvia

The radical-right populist party family also shares a common successful 'master frame' of policies (Mudde 2007, 2010) that is communicated and diffused between related parties in different states (Rydgren 2005). This frame has three key components: nativism, authoritarianism and populism.

Nativism

Nativist discourse, which remains the central component of radical-right populism, is oriented around the belief that the state should be congruent with the titular nation. As a result, nativism has two core dimensions: 1) That the non-native population is a threat to the continued existence of the titular nation (xenophobia); and 2) that the titular nation should have privileges in order to ensure its continued existence (nationalism). However, this nativism is not framed as racism (as with interwar fascism), but rather focuses on ethnopluralism, which stresses the equality but incompatibility of different ethnicities living together (Rydgren 2005). As a result, radical-right populists are opposed 'to the social integration of marginalized groups' (Betz 1993: 413). Indeed, it is also claimed that the 'out groups' have also changed, with the anti-Semitism of the twenty-first century often being replaced with an Islamophobic message, although there is variation from country to country according to domestic historic and demographic factors (Hale Williams 2010).

The nature of radical-right populist nativism in post-communist Europe is fundamentally different to that in the Western European states. Lubomir Kopeček (2007) has pointed out that this is largely due to the virtual absence of third-world immigration in the region during the communist era, while comparatively low levels of economic development coupled with restrictive immigration policies have also limited immigration in the post-communist years. For example, between 2000 and 2007, just 10,326 persons immigrated to Estonia, equalling about 0.1 per cent of the population (Kovalenko et al. 2010: 10). Indeed, more than half of these were non-visible immigrants from neighbouring Finland and countries of the former Soviet Union. There are very few visible minorities in the Baltic States.

However, this does not mean that nativism has no salience in Estonia or Latvia. Rather than being aimed at Muslims or other visible minorities, it is primarily directed towards the Russian speakers that migrated to the Baltic States during the Soviet era. The independence movements in all three Baltic States were largely driven by these demographic concerns. Even the political mainstream used what would now be considered to be radical language – talk of decolonization and forced repatriation of Russian speakers – in order to 'cleanse' the Baltic States and return them to their interwar state. After independence, both Estonia and Latvia initiated restrictive citizenship laws that granted automatic citizenship only to those people, and their descendants, who had held citizenship before 1940. In 2011, approximately 8 per cent of permanent residents in Estonia and 20 per cent in Latvia were still classified as 'resident aliens' without any citizenship.

Andres Kasekamp (2003) has observed that during the first decade of independence, the first generation of Estonian radical-right populist parties were primarily concerned with combating the Soviet legacy, while in the twenty-first century their focus turned to opposing the EU. Thus the Estonian parliament is accused of 'treason' for having contravened the Estonian constitution by transferring Estonian sovereignty to Brussels (EIP 2007, Leito 2011). The alleged prostrate position of Estonia within the EU is equated to that of when it was in the Soviet Union. In contrast, Latvian radical-right populists continue to focus their ire on Russian speakers, only making oblique reference to Europe in exceptional circumstances, for example, following the Anders Breivik massacre in Norway in July 2011. Even then, the target was European immigration policy in the abstract rather than specific institutions or policies of the EU.

Indeed, Breivik's murderous rampage resulted in defensive comments that revealed the thinking of the radical right in the Baltic States. The leader of the Estonian Independence Party, Vello Leito, initially characterized Breivik's action as an 'international conspiracy' to blacken the reputation of European 'patriots' (Delfi 2011).[4] The Estonian National Movement likewise claimed that the beneficiaries of Breivik's insane act are the proponents of multiculturalism who seek to discredit nationalists and that the policy of multiculturalism is itself to blame (Põlluaas 2011). Jānis Iesalnieks, one of the Latvian National Alliance's most prominent board members

---

[4] Breivik's manifesto mentioned two Estonian groups: the Estonian Independence Party and the Estonian National Movement, though there is no evidence of any contact. The National Alliance in Latvia was also named.

and a prolific blogger, tweeted that Breivik's actions were quite understandable in light of the continuing high rates of immigration and the 'failed' policy of multiculturalism in Europe. His comments were quickly disowned by the party leadership and Iesalnieks stepped down from the board and announced that he would not stand in the September 2011 parliamentary election. Indeed, the threat of non-white immigration has sporadically appeared in Latvian discourses. In 2002, the newly formed Freedom Party aired a television advertisement of an African wearing the uniform of a Latvian soldier guarding the freedom monument and kissing a Latvian girl, which played on fears of mass immigration (Eglītis 2005). More recently, Latvian politics has seen an anti-Islam discourse enter the fringes of political debate. In the run-up to the 2011 Latvian parliamentary election, Jānis Ādamsons, a deputy from the pro-Russian Harmony Centre (which advertises tolerance as a core value), stated that he believed that the current Latvian government was planning on hosting 40–60,000 'Arabs'. Ādamsons went on to declare this a mistake, because while Latvians would always find a common dialogue with white Europeans, no such possibility existed for peaceful cooperation with non-Europeans (Diena 2011).

However, Russian speakers are the typical targets of both mainstream and radical-right parties in Latvia. Indeed, it is a feature of contemporary Latvian politics that even mainstream political parties contain individuals prone to outbursts of nationalist rhetoric (see Auers & Kasekamp 2009: 251–2). Moreover, there are enduring links between mainstream parties and the extremist fringes. For example, following the 2010 election, a Latvian WikiLeaks-type website published email correspondence between the new Minister of Foreign Affairs (Girts Valdis Kristovskis, one of the co-chairs of the governing Unity Alliance) and Aivars Slucis, a radically nationalist Latvian-American. Slucis, a medical doctor who has funded nationalist Latvian movements since the early 1990s (Muižnieks 2005), complained that he was unable to return to live and work in Latvia because he 'would not be able to treat Russians in the same way as Latvians', to which Kristovskis replied: 'I agree with your evaluation of the situation' (Lapsa 2010). While Slucis was quickly disowned by the Unity Alliance (which also returned his financial contribution), the National Alliance vigorously supported Slucis, both personally and his views on the Russian minority in general.

This reflects the more radical brand of Latvian nationalism represented by the National Alliance and particularly its youthful VL! wing. They are the only party publically to support the annual 16 March rally of Latvian Waffen SS veterans, with party members creating an 'alley' of Latvian flags to honour the veterans. VL! has previously also demonstrated against the signing of a border treaty with Russia. Its brief 4,000 figure election manifestos present a nativist vision of Latvia, declaring (in 2006) that Latvian citizenship should only be granted to 'loyal and trustworthy' people, while individuals with a 'hostile' attitude to the state would be deported. The 2011 manifesto began with a declaration that 'Latvians must feel at home in their ethnic homeland' (National Alliance Manifesto 2011).

Russian speakers remain the major 'out group' in Latvia, although there have also been occasional outbursts of nationalist language aimed at non-white groups. There is also a level of anti-Semitism in the political discourse. However, this is typically addressed indirectly. As a WikiLeaked cable from the US Ambassador stated, 'hidden below the surface in Latvian life [is] a strong current of intolerance, including anti-Semitism' (US Embassy Riga 2008). Only the radical-right populist VL! has addressed anti-Semitism directly, with the above-mentioned Iesalnieks causing a national scandal in the run-up to the 2010 election when he publically argued that 'intelligent anti-Semitism', a diffuse concept that he could not explicitly explain, had a place in public discourse (Marģēviča 2010). More typical is the indirect anti-Semitism that underlies criticism of American philanthropist George Soros and the Soros foundation, which stands accused of undermining Latvian identity and independence, and of supporting 'cosmopolitan' values.

Authoritarianism

Political and cultural authoritarianism is a key feature of the political right in general, but particularly the radical right (Kitschelt 1995, 2004). This authoritarianism entails belief in an ordered hierarchical society with a strong focus on state power as well as law and order issues. Essentially, the authoritarian dimension, which can be visualized as being on a libertarian–authoritarian axis, is measured by the extent to which parties advocate limits on individual freedom.

There is a strong strain of support for authoritarianism in the Baltic States that stretches back to the popular authoritarian regimes of the 1930s and which is evidenced by continuing high levels of public support (hovering between 30–40 per cent in Latvia between 1995 and 2004) for 'getting rid of parliament and elections and having a strong leader who can decide everything quickly' (see New Baltic Barometers 1995–2004). However, this is much less pronounced in Estonia. Initial Estonian admiration for Päts has largely been replaced by condemnation of his supine capitulation to the Soviets in 1939–40. In contrast, in 2003, Latvia erected a statue of the dictator Karlis Ulmanis in the centre of Riga, and in 2009 a complimentary new musical ('Leader') about Ulmanis debuted in Latvia's National Theatre.

Support for the Ulmanis regime remains central to the National Alliance's ideology. One of the key moments in the early development of VL! was a protest against art students staging an exhibition of works of art critical of Ulmanis. Moreover, Ulmanis is central to the National Alliance's ceremonial celebration of Latvia's Independence Day (18 November), with the party staging an evening torch rally from Ulmanis' statue to the Freedom Monument. VL! also has a strong militarist component. The pages of its party newspaper are adorned with pictures of leading party cadres posing in military uniforms, and the party advocates the expansion of the role and activities of the Zemessargi (home guard).

Populism

The third of the above-mentioned dimensions of the radical right, populism, divides society into two halves, envisaging a corrupt élite on one side and a pure 'common people' on the other. Populists argue that the established élites have betrayed the trust of the people (Canovan 1999). Jens Rydgren (2005) argued that radical-right parties have framed their populist rhetoric in this way because they cannot hope to be electorally successful by being anti-democratic in societies where the overwhelming majority of the public support democracy as the form of government, and are thus anti-élite rather than anti-systemic. They also argue that 'the people' should be given a greater role in politics through increased use of the tools of popular democracy, such as referendums and citizens' initiatives. Of the three components of the master frame, populism is the most established part of post-communist politics and populist rhetoric has not been a barrier to entry into governmental coalition (Mudde 2000). However, populism in the Baltic States is a disputed concept, with Sikk (2006) arguing that anti-corruption rhetoric is not necessarily populist when reputable comparative international research indicates that there are genuinely high levels of élite corruption (see, for example, the Transparency International Corruption Perceptions Index or World Bank Corruption in Transition reports). Moreover, Sikk argues, new parties will inevitably be anti-élite simply because of the fact that they are *new* and, as such, have to justify their formation and existence.

The most successful populist in Estonia has been an individual rather than a party. Astonishingly, in the 2009 European Parliament election, Indrek Tarand received one-quarter of the entire national vote, nearly equalling the total for the winning Estonian political party. His anti-party rhetoric helped him confound all predictions and achieve the extremely rare feat of an independent candidate being elected to the European Parliament (Ehin & Solvak 2012). However, it should be noted that Tarand's success came in a second-order election, allowing citizens to register their protest vote but continue supporting the mainstream parties in the March 2011 general election (in which Tarand did not participate). The charismatic and provocative Tarand once more employed his anti-establishment rhetoric as the unsuccessful opposition candidate for the presidency in 2011. In November 2011, a petition calling on Prime Minister Ansip to resign and for a new party to be formed by Tarand was circulated online (Avalik kiri 2011). Tarand enjoys being a loose cannon, and has not yet affiliated himself with any Estonian party (though he has previously been close to the mainstream anti-communist nationalists). Though he has aligned himself out of necessity with the Greens in the European Parliament, Tarand's main support comes from the same population segment that votes in general elections for the centre-right governing parties (Ehin & Solvak 2012). Another sign of the potential fertile ground for a new populist party was the NO99 theatre troupe's staging, in 2010, of a series of theatre performances imitating the process of the launching of a new populist political party ('United Estonia'). Their shows garnered record ticket sales and extensive media commentary, since many genuinely expected that a new political party would actually emerge from them.

In contrast, populist rhetoric is an established feature of both mainstream and radical-right populists in Latvia. Indeed, Latvia has long been marked by a powerful anti-corruption rhetoric, most recently in the early 2011 parliamentary election that saw a party formed a little over one month before the election surge to come second in the polls. The Zatlera Reformu Partija (Zatlers Reform Party) was formed by ex-president Valdis Zatlers, who had initiated the process that led to the recall of Parliament in protest at the influence of three 'oligarchs' on the democratic process in Latvia. The 2011 election was not about policies or ideologies but, as with the 1995, 2002 and 2010 elections, corruption. Indeed, together with nationalism, corruption is the central cleavage in contemporary Latvian politics (Auers 2012). On the one side, the anti-corruption parties blame Latvia's economic and social problems on distortions wrought by the oligarchs and the parties they control. On the other, the 'oligarch' parties counter that they defend Latvia's national interests from liberal internationalists, most particularly George Soros. Indeed, the Green-Farmers Union candidate for Prime Minister, Aivars Lembergs, stated that the Latvian parliament had been dissolved because of Soros' influence, repeatedly referring to a 2010 meeting between Zatlers and Soros in New York (Lembergs 2011). Soros has been a frequent target of the 'oligarch' parties, which identify their political opponents and critics as 'Sorosists', claiming that they have been bought off by Soros through the guise of grants from his philanthropic Soros Foundation. They claim that Soros' ultimate aim is to take power in Latvia. While the Jewish background of Soros himself is never directly addressed, it is presented through references to the 'cosmopolitanism' of the liberal internationalists.

The National Alliance was, unsurprisingly, on the side of the anti-corruption parties in this debate, emphasizing that it had consistently voted for strengthening state law and order. Moreover, it made much of the fact that it had introduced a new political culture into Parliament, allowing its deputies a free vote on all issues, regularly tweeting and blogging on what was happening behind the scenes in the corridors of power. Moreover, the National Alliance regularly uses the tools of popular democracy, most recently collecting signatures to trigger a referendum on the use of Latvian in public schools and on a directly elected presidency in Latvia.

Conclusions: Explaining the difference between Latvia and Estonia

Radical-right organizations and discourses are clearly far more prevalent in Latvia than in Estonia. Latvia has a greater number of grass roots movements, a more widespread rhetoric that encompasses both mainstream and more radical parties, and a parliamentary radical-right populist party that entered government in late 2011. Why this divergence between Estonia and Latvia? It has been argued that radical-right populism emerges in times of crisis, and is thus a form of protest against the existing political system (Betz 1994). However, both Latvia and Estonia went through severe economic crises during 2008–10, with GDP plummeting in 2009 in Latvia by 18 per cent and in Estonia by 14 per cent. Nevertheless, in both cases, the prime ministers, who were forced to make drastic cuts in public expenditure, were re-elected in 2011. Institutional as well as supply and demand arguments are more illuminating.

In institutional terms, the rules governing the registration of Estonian political parties were tightened in 1998, with the introduction of a requirement for a minimum 1,000 members, resulting in the elimination of several small parties and a higher hurdle for the creation of new political parties (Toomla 2011: 49). The law governing political parties in Latvia requires just 200 individual members to register a party, making it far easier for small, radical groups to become political parties. A further difference is that established Estonian political parties receive the lion's share of their funding from the state budget, which places start-up parties at a distinct disadvantage. Public financing for Latvian parties was only introduced in 2012 and parties are still permitted to receive private donations. Thus wealthy sponsors can contribute to a party's success in Latvia.

Supply and demand side perspectives also explain these differences. In supply side terms, the abundant weaknesses of the Estonian Independence Party have been highlighted above. The National Alliance in Latvia, on the other hand, is a 'thick' party that has adopted the radical-right populist master frame and has a charismatic young leader. It has successfully united the financial stability of the For Fatherland and Freedom/LNNK party with the energetically mobilized membership of VL!, and entered government in October 2011.

From a demand-side perspective, we can see that the economic and social situations in Latvia and Estonia began to diverge from the mid-1990s onwards. Estonia has generally been more successful in its state-building and European integration than Latvia (Norkus 2011: 30). Bustikova (2009: 224) has argued that the success of the extreme right in post-communist Europe is best understood as 'a reaction to corruption and the absence of political accountability . . . Extremists thrive in competitive democracies where the rule of law is weak'. To some extent this explains the variation between Latvia and Estonia. Estonia is perceived to have far lower rates of corruption, and international rankings place it in a higher category as regards its quality of democracy. Indeed, Estonians are significantly more satisfied and optimistic than Latvians (Lauristin & Vihalemm 2011: 19–21). This, naturally, means that the core message of the populists and radical-right populists – a drive the rascals out rhetoric – has far less impact. Moreover, the larger Russian minority in Latvia, combined with hitherto looser financing laws, has led to the development of a more strident Russian nationalist position (such as the February 2012 referendum on introducing Russian as a second official state language) that mobilizes Latvian nationalists.

References

Auers, D. (2012), 'Latvia', in S. Berglund, J. Ekman, F. Aarebrot and K. Deegan-Krause (eds), *The Handbook of Political Change in Eastern Europe*, 3rd edn, London: Edward Elgar (forthcoming).

Auers, D. and Kasekamp, A. (2009), 'Explaining the Electoral Failure of Extreme-right Parties in Estonia and Latvia', *Journal of Contemporary European Studies*, 17(2): 241–54.

Avalik kiri Eesti Vabariigi peaministrile (2011), [Public letter to the Prime Minister of Estonia]. <http://www.petitsioon.com/avalik_kirI_eestI_vabariigI_peaministrile> [accessed 30 November 2011].

Betz H. G. (1993), 'The New Politics of Resentment. Radical Right-Wing Populist Parties in Western Europe', *Comparative Politics* 25(4).

— (1994), *Radical Right-Wing Populism in Western Europe*, Basingstoke: Macmillan.

Brüggemann, K. and Kasekamp, A. (2008), 'The Politics of History and the "War of Monuments" in Estonia', *Nationalities Papers*, 36(2): 425–48.

Bustikova, L. (2009), 'The Extreme Right in Eastern Europe: EU Accession and the Quality of Governance', *Journal of Contemporary European Studies*, 17(2): 223–39.

Canovan, M. (1999), 'Trust the people! Populism and the Two Faces of Democracy', *Political Studies*, 47: 2–16.

Delfi (2011), 'Eesti Iseseisvuspartei juht: Breivik oli pisike ettur [Leader of the Estonian Independence Party: Breivik was a pawn]', 26 July 2011. <www.delfi.ee/news/paevauudised/eesti/eesti-iseseisvuspartei-juht-breivik-oli-pisike-ettur.d?id=50177715> [accessed 1 September 2011].

Diena (2011), 'SC norobežojas no Ādamsona teiktā, ka viņš labāk saprastos ar baltās rases cilvēkiem' [Harmony Centre Distances Itself from Adamsons, who would better get on with white people], 2 September 2011. <www.diena.lv/latvija/zinas/sc-norobezoja s-no-adamsona-teikta-ka-vins-labak-saprastos-ar-baltas-rases-cilvekiem-13901332> [accessed 5 September 2011].

Eatwell, R. (2003), 'Ten Theories of the Extreme Right', in P. Merkl and L. Weinberg (eds), *Right Wing Extremism in the Twenty-first Century*, London: Frank Cass, pp. 45–69.

Eglītis, A. (2005), 'Racism Rears its Ugly Head', *Baltic Times*, 13 April 2005.

Ehin, P. and Solvak, M. (2012), 'Party Voters Gone Astray: Explaining Independent Candidate Success in the 2009 European Elections in Estonia', *Journal of Elections, Public Opinion and Parties*, 22(3): 269–91.

EIP (2007), Estonian Independence Party programme. <www.iseseisvuspartei.ee/test/index.php/program-40english41.html> [accessed 25 November 2011].

Hale Williams, M. (2010), 'Can Leopards Change Their Spots? Between Xenophobia and Trans-ethnic Populism among West European Parties', *Nationalism and Ethnic Politics*, 16: 111–34.

Kasekamp, A. (1999), 'Radical Right-Wing Movements in the North-East Baltic', *Journal of Contemporary History*, 34(4): 587–600.

— (2003), 'Extreme-right Parties in Contemporary Estonia', *Patterns of Prejudice*, 37(4): 401–14.

— (2010), *A History of the Baltic States*, Basingstoke: Palgrave Macmillan.

Kitschelt, H. (1995), *The Radical Right in Western Europe. A Comparative Analysis*, Ann Arbor, MI: University of Michigan Press.

Kitschelt, H. (2004), *Diversification and Reconfiguration of Party Systems in Post-Industrial Democracies*, Bonn: Friedrich Ebert Stiftung.

Kopeček, L. (2007), 'The Far Right in Europe. A Summary of Attempts to Define the Concept, Analyze its Identity, and Compare the Western European and Central European Far Right', *Central European Political Studies Review*, 9(4): 280–93.

Kovalenko, J., Mensah, P., Leoncikas, T. and Zibas, K. (2010), *New Immigrants in Estonia, Latvia and Lithuania*, Tallinn: Legal Information Centre for Human Rights.

Lapsa, L. (2010), 'Meli iegāž Kristovski: "īstā" Sluča vēstule izrādās vēl briesmīgāka', 8 November 2010. <www.pietiek.com> [accessed 18 October 2011].

Latvian Central Election Commission (2011), 'Elections and Referendums'. <http://web.cvk.lv/pub/public/28334.html> [accessed 28 November 2011].

Lauristin, M. and Vihalemm, P. (2011), 'Satisfaction with outcomes of Baltic transition in spring 2011', in M. Lauristin (ed.), *Estonian Human Development Report 2010/2011. Baltic Way(s) of Human Development: Twenty Years On*, Tallinn: Eesti Koostöö Kogu, pp. 19–21.

Leito, V. (2011), *Vello Leito poliitiline manifest* [Vello Leito's political manifesto]. <www.iseseisvuspartei.ee/test/index.php/pressiteated-avatud/items/vello-leito-poliitiline-manifest.html> [accessed 27 November 2011].

Lembergs, A. (2011), 'Jus nevarat mani salauzt, Zatlera kungs!' [You cannot break me, Mr Zatlers], 30 May 2011. <www.apollo.lv> [accessed 19 October 2011].

Margēviča, A. (2010), 'Premjers un Vienotība gatavi izstumt Visu Latvijai!' [Prime Minister and Unity prepared to reject All for Latvia!]. <www.pietiek.com/raksti/premjers_un_vienotiba_gatavI_izstumt_visu_latvijai!> [accessed 29 October 2011].

Mudde, C. (2000), 'In the Name of the Peasantry, the Proletariat, and the People: Populisms in Eastern Europe', *East European Politics and Societies*, 14(2): 33–53.
— (2007), *Populist Radical Right Parties in Europe*, Cambridge: Cambridge University Press.
— (2010), 'The Populist Radical Right: A Pathological Normalcy', *West European Politics*, 33(6): 1167–86.
Muižnieks, N. (2005), 'Latvia', in Cas Mudde (ed.), *Racist Extremism in Central and Eastern Europe*, London: Routledge, pp. 101–28.
Muižnieks, N. (ed.) (2008), *Manufacturing Enemy Images? Russian Media Portrayal of Latvia*, Riga: University of Latvia Academic Press.
National Alliance Manifesto (2011) <http://cvk.lv> [accessed 11 October 2012].
New Baltic Barometers (1995–2004). <www.balticvoices.org/nbb/surveys.php> [accessed 28 November 2011].
Norkus, Z. (2011), 'Estonian, Latvian and Lithuanian post-communist development in the comparative perspective', in M. Lauristin (ed.), *Estonian Human Development Report 2010/2011. Baltic Way(s) of Human Development: Twenty Years On*, Tallinn: Eesti Koostöö Kogu, pp. 22–30.
Pelnēns, G. (ed.) (2009), *The 'Humanitarian Dimension' of Russian Foreign Policy toward Georgia, Moldova, Ukraine, and the Baltic States*, Riga: Centre for East European Policy Studies.
Pettai, V., Auers, D. and Ramonaite, A. (2011), 'Political development', in M. Lauristin (ed.), *Estonian Human Development Report: Baltic Way(s) of Human Development: Twenty Years On*, Tallinn: Eesti Koostöö Kogu, pp. 144–64.
Põliseestlased (2011), 'True Estonians'. <http://poliseestlased.org/> [accessed 2 October 2011].
Põlluaas, H. (2011), 'Oodates multikultirühmlaste öist koputust' [Waiting for the night-time knock on the door by multiculturalists], *Delfi*, 2 August 2011. <www.delfi.ee/news/paevauudised/arvamus/henn-polluaas-oodates-multikultiruhmlaste-oist-koputust.d?id=50526603> [accessed 2 August 2011].
Pop-Eleches, G. (2002), 'Radicalization or protest vote? Explaining the success of unorthodox parties in Eastern Europe', paper presented at the 2002 Annual Meeting of the American Association for the Advancement of Slavic Studies, Pittsburgh, 21–4 November 2002.
Rydgren, J. (2005), 'Is Extreme Right-Wing Populism Contagious? Explaining the Emergence of a New Party Family', *European Journal of Political Research*, 44: 413–37.
Sikk, A. (2006), *Highways to Power: New Party Success in Three Young Democracies*. Tartu: Tartu University Press.
Taggart, P. (2000), *Populism*, Buckingham: Open University Press.
Toomla, R. (2011), *Eesti erakonnad 2000–2010* [Estonian political parties 2000–10], Tartu: Tartu University Press.
Ucen, P. (2007), 'Parties, Populism, and Anti-Establishment Politics in East Central Europe', *SAIS Review* XXVII(1): 49–62.
US Embassy Riga (2008), 'Andris Grutups and the Jewish community of Latvia'. <http://leaks.hohesc.us/?view=08RIGA87> [accessed 9 December 2011].
Zatlers, V. (2011), 'Speech Calling For Referendum on Recalling Parliament'. <www.youtube.com/watch?v=mT6944am6IY> [accessed 18 July 2011].

17

From Para-Militarism to Radical Right-Wing Populism: The Rise of the Ukrainian Far-Right Party Svoboda[1]

Anton Shekhovtsov

Introduction

This chapter seeks to give an overview of the far-right scene in contemporary Ukraine, to consider the organizational and ideological nature of the Vseukrains'ke Ob'yednannya 'Svoboda' (All-Ukrainian 'Freedom' Union, Svoboda) and, most importantly, to highlight the determinants of the current rise of popular support for this party.

Today, genuinely independent radical right-wing parties, which pursue an anti-democratic agenda, may function only in liberal countries that tend 'to tolerate the intolerant'. Initially, far-right parties had electoral success in advanced industrial European countries, where such parties as the Front National (France), Lega Nord (Italy), Freiheitliche Partei Österreichs (Austria), Fremskrittspartiet (Norway), Dansk Folkeparti (Denmark) and some others challenged the democratic order by their promotion of ethnocratic liberalism (Betz 1994, Kitschelt & McGann 1995, Ignazi 2003, Carter 2005, Mudde 2007). During the 1980s, when Western Europe saw the rise of the radical right, states on the other side of the 'Iron Curtain' experienced different political and social change, namely the spread of pro-democratic social movements that opposed socialist regimes. Although the pro-democratic trend in opposition to socialism was dominant at those times, in some Central and East European countries small far-right groups were already emerging. Socialist regimes tried to suppress all opposition, but eventually lost – in the majority of cases – to pro-democratic movements. However, the transition to democracy that followed a series of revolutions in the Warsaw Pact member states at the end of the 1980s and the collapse of the Soviet

---

[1] This chapter is based on a paper presented at the Seventh Annual Danyliw Research Seminar on Contemporary Ukraine held at the University of Ottawa, 20–2 October 2011.

Union and Yugoslavia opened the gate to the far right as well (Ramet 1999, Minkenberg 2010). The history of the far right in post-socialist Europe is wide-ranging: some radical right-wing parties, like Narodowe Odrodzenie Polski (Poland), followed interwar fascist traditions, while others, like Partidul România Mare (Romania), involved former communists. Although radical right-wing parties did and do exist in post-1989 semi-authoritarian regimes, such as Serbia under Slobodan Milošević (e.g. Srpska radikalna stranka) and Vladimir Putin's Russia (e.g. Liberal'no-demokraticheskaya partiya Rossii); they can be considered instruments of the ruling parties rather than independent political phenomena (Shekhovtsov & Umland 2011: 14–16). Thus, a democratic system of government seems to be a prerequisite for active participation of the far right in electoral politics today.

Far-right parties pose a threat to established democratic societies, but it may be assumed that the radical right poses a greater threat to developing democracies, such as Ukraine. Hence the paradox: the presence of far-right parties is an indication of the largely – or still – democratic nature of Ukraine, but at the same time the far right impedes the country's democratic development.

Main actors on the Ukrainian far-right scene

Contemporary far-right organizations and movements in Ukraine can be divided into two groups: Ukrainian and pro-Russian/Slavic ultra-nationalists. Each of these groups, in turn, can be divided into two subgroups: registered political parties and social movements. Basic information on registered radical right-wing parties that are more or less active in the current political and social life of Ukraine is given in Table 17.1, in accordance with the aforementioned ideological criteria.[2]

It should be noted that Ukrainian ultra-nationalists are principally based in Western and Central Ukraine, while the bulwark of pro-Russian/Slavic ultra-nationalists is in the Crimea, as well as Eastern and Southern Ukraine. In his study on anti-Semitism in contemporary Ukraine, Per Rudling offers a similar regional division and distinguishes two political traditions of anti-Semitism: the legacy of 'anti-Russian, anti-Semitic and anti-Polish sentiments' that 'has its strongest support in Western Ukraine' and 'the xenophobic Eurasian nationalism, steeped in the Soviet "anti-Zionist" tradition' that is 'stronger in the southern and eastern parts of the country' (2012: 198).

As this chapter focuses, in particular, on the rise of Svoboda, pro-Russian/Slavic ultra-nationalists will not be discussed here, due to space restrictions. Indeed, they would require a separate analysis and will thus be mentioned only in passing in this chapter.

Ideologically, all Ukrainian ultra-nationalist parties, except for the All-Ukrainian Political Party 'Brotherhood' (Bratstvo), promote Ukrainian ethnic nationalism, social conservatism, anti-communist and anti-immigrant sentiments. According to the

---

[2]   On the Ukrainian radical right in the 1990s, see: Kuzio 1997, Wilson 1997, Kubicek 1999, Solchanyk 1999.

Table 17.1 Registered far-right parties in contemporary Ukraine.

Party	Founded	Registered	Current leader
Ukrainian ultra-nationalists			
Ukrains'ka Natsional'na Asambleya (Ukrainian National Assembly, UNA)	1990	1994/1997[1]	Yuriy Shukhevych
Vseukrains'ke Ob'yednannya 'Svoboda' (All-Ukrainian 'Freedom' Union, Svoboda)	1991	1995	Oleh Tyahnybok
Konhres Ukrains'kykh Natsionalistiv (Congress of Ukrainian Nationalists, KUN)	1992	1993	Stepan Bratsyun
Vseukrains'ka Partiya 'Nova Syla' (All-Ukrainian Party 'New Force', Nova Syla)	1999	1999	Yuriy Zbitnyev
Vseukrains'ka Politychna Partiya 'Bratstvo' (All-Ukrainian Political Party 'Brotherhood', Bratstvo)	2002	2004	Dmytro Korchyns'ky
Pro-Russian/Slavic ultra-nationalists			
Prohresyvna Sotsialistychna Partiya Ukrainy (Progressive Socialist Party of Ukraine, PSPU)[2]	1996	1996	Nataliya Vitrenko
Partiya 'Rodyna' ('Motherland' Party)	2008	1999[3]	Ihor Markov

[1] The party was banned in 1995 but managed to reregister in 1997.

[2] Due to its socialist economic position, the party is sometimes considered left wing, but in political terms it is radical right wing.

[3] The party was founded in 2008 on the basis of the Progressive Democratic Party of Ukraine which was registered in 1999.

Congress of Ukrainian Nationalists (KUN), 'a nation is the highest form of organization of human community, organically bound by a common ethnic origin, language, territory, history, culture, historical mission and national idea' (KUN 2011). The Ukrainian National Assembly's (UNA) conception of a nation is similar, but the party also holds that a nation conforms to a hierarchical order and is a system comprising four 'Varnas' (in the terms of 'our Aryan ancestors', as UNA states): 'Brahmins (people of spirit, wise men), Kshatriya (statesmen, warriors), businessmen (managers, economists) and specialists (professionals)' (UNA-UNSO 2007). Ukrainian ultra-nationalists reject the idea of a political nation: as the ideologists of the KUN argue, they 'stand against the attempts by liberal and cosmopolitan forces to create a "new" pseudo-Ukrainian idea of "a new political Ukrainian or Slavic nation"' (KUN 2011).

The UNA, KUN and Svoboda are also Russophobic and antisemitic. Moreover, 'white racism'[3] is overtly or covertly inherent in the doctrines of the UNA, Svoboda and All-Ukrainian Party 'New Force' (*Nova Syla*), and most evidently manifests itself

[3] 'White racism' is a type of racism that glorifies the 'white race' and simultaneously justifies discrimination towards other 'races'.

through the parties' anti-immigrant positions. Thus, speculating on the degree of desirability of the various categories of migrants to Ukraine, Nova Syla's Yuriy Zbitnyev distinguishes four types of migrants: 1) ethnic Ukrainians who are the most desirable migrants; 2) representatives of genetically and culturally close peoples (Slavs, Balts, Celts, Germans, Scandinavians) who are considered desirable migrants during the period of demographic crisis in Ukraine; 3) representatives of remote white peoples (Romans, Finno-Ugrians, Georgians) who are neither desirable nor undesirable migrants and 4) representatives of other racial groups (Semites, Mongoloids, Negroids) who are unwelcome in the country (Zbitnyev & Shcherbyna 2011: 196). It is worth mentioning that a number of Zbitnyev's texts imply that Russians are Finno-Ugrians rather than Slavs.

Although the KUN holds that Ukrainian nationalism is a revolutionary movement that will, under no circumstances, desist from achieving its primary objective (KUN 2011), this party is the most moderate far-right organization in the Ukrainian ultra-nationalist camp. The UNA, with its militarism and thrust for Ukraine's new 'civilizational and racial level of development', is the most extreme. At the same time, Nova Syla's Yuriy Zbitnyev is one of the leaders of the neo-Nazi group Social-National Assembly, an organization that is also close to the younger members of Svoboda, but Nova Syla itself, while remaining on the fringes of Ukrainian politics, is not much influenced by these relations.

Bratstvo is an exceptional case on the Ukrainian far-right scene and its inclusion in the 'Ukrainian ultra-nationalists' category is tentative. Despite the fact that Dmytro Korchyns'ky was once a prominent leader of the UNA and commander of its paramilitary unit, Bratstvo is far less radical than the UNA. Its official ideology is 'Christian Orthodox national-anarchism' and the activities of Bratstvo – flamboyant protests and extravagant acts[4] – suggest that this party is a provocative art project in the political sphere ('politics is fun', 'the place of politics is between literature and music' (Korchyns'ky 2004)), rather than a conventional political party. Besides that, Bratstvo opposes globalization, NATO and financialism – the ideological position that aligns the party with pro-Russian/Slavic ultra-nationalists. On many occasions, Bratstvo has joined the Progressive Socialist Party of Ukraine (PSPU) for anti-NATO protests.

International connections corroborate the degree of radicalism of the Ukrainian ultra-nationalists: the KUN was a member of the now defunct pan-European far-right party Alliance for Europe of the Nations that united national-conservative and radical right-wing parties, Svoboda is a member of the radical right-wing Alliance of European National Movements, the UNA cooperated with the neo-Nazi National Democratic Party of Germany, while Bratstvo maintained close relationships with the Russian National-Bolshevik Party whose ideology evolved from neo-fascism in the 1990s to a mix of moderate nationalism and liberalism in the 2000s (Sokolov 2006).

Since the reinstatement of Ukraine's independence in 1991, up to the present day, no radical right-wing party, except for the PSPU, has been able to enter the

---

[4] For example, in 2004, Bratstvo gathered signatures to qualify John Herbst, the current Ambassador of the United States of America to Ukraine, to run for Ukrainian President instead of Viktor Yushchenko.

Verkhovna Rada as a party. A few members of far-right parties did manage to enter Parliament, but they had been elected in single-member constituencies or as members of national-democratic electoral blocs. However, the number of elected far-right politicians was never enough for them to form a parliamentary group. The main reasons for the Ukrainian far right's political fiasco in the past were the lack of unity, virulent Russophobia, the absence of a suitable niche in the highly polarized Ukrainian sociopolitical sphere and the limited, if any, access to mainstream national media.[5]

History of Svoboda

Contemporary Svoboda is a relatively new political phenomenon but, in terms of organization, its history dates back to 1991 when the 5,000-strong paramilitary ultra-nationalists group Guard of the Movement, created in 1987 and led by Yaroslav Andrushkiv and Yuriy Kryvoruchko, decided to form a party (Musafirova 2011). This decision was implemented in Lviv on 13 October 1991, almost three months after the August 1991 Soviet coup d'état attempt and the adoption of the Act of Declaration of Independence of Ukraine. Andrushkiv was appointed head of the Social-National Party of Ukraine (SNPU), while Kryvoruchko was engaged in ideological matters. Later, the SNPU was joined by the Lviv Student Fellowship and the Organization of Ukrainian Youth, 'Legacy'; the leaders of these groups, Oleh Tyahnybok and Andriy Parubiy respectively, became responsible for organizational issues and matters concerning young persons.

In November 1994, the SNPU launched its weekly newspaper, *Social-Nationalist*, edited by Nestor Pronyuk, who was also the author of the party symbol – a modified *Wolfsangel* (wolf's hook), a symbol of many post-war European neo-Nazi organizations. In 1993, the SNPU formed paramilitary 'popular guard units' consisting of two subunits that comprised workers and students; these 'popular guard units' became the basis of the Society of Assistance to the Armed Forces and Navy of Ukraine, 'Patriot of Ukraine', formed in 1996 and headed by Parubiy. On 16 October 1995, the party was officially registered with the Ministry of Justice of Ukraine.

Already, in 1991, Andrushkiv and Kryvoruchko had drafted the party's political programme which differed from the one submitted to the Ministry of Justice in 1995. The earlier programme reflected the esoteric ideological appeal of the party. The document stated that the official ideology of the SNPU was social-nationalism. 'One of the principal missions of the SNPU' was to 'allow the Ukrainian to see the world through Ukrainian eyes, to give him [sic] back the national character', while 'one of the high-priority tasks' of the party was 'the struggle against the pro-Moscow attitudes and Moscow's impact upon Ukraine' (SNPU 2008). The programme was, as such, emphatically Russophobic, and point 6 of the document bluntly called Russia 'the cause of all the troubles in Ukraine' (ibid.). The document saw Ukraine as a state whose citizens would enjoy the same rights and privileges, regardless of ethnic or religious origin. The SNPU was loyal to the multi-party system, although the programme

---

[5] For a more detailed analysis of the consistent electoral failure of the Ukrainian far right, see Umland 2008a, b, Shekhovtsov 2011.

argued against communist parties and social movements. The party also anticipated 'an unprecedented political and economic crisis, [and] catastrophic decline in production'. To save Ukraine, and build a new state and a new society, the SNPU was going to take the lead in the Ukrainian revolution (ibid.). The programme submitted to the Ministry of Justice did not include many of the aforementioned radical points and was considered a ploy by the leaders of the SNPU: after the party was officially registered, its members used the older version of the programme (Zelyk 2008: 64).

Although the original programme of the SNPU ruled out the possibility of siding with other parties (SNPU 2008), in 1998 the social-nationalists established an electoral bloc, called 'Less Words', with another far-right party, the Vseukrains'ke ob'yednannya or 'Derzhavna samostiynist' Ukrainy' (All-Ukrainian Union 'State Independence of Ukraine'). Although the bloc won only 0.16 per cent of the votes in the 1998 parliamentary elections, Tyahnybok won a parliamentary seat in one of the Lviv region single-member districts. Tyahnybok's incumbency was the beginning of his personal rise in the SNPU, and later that year he was nominated head of the SNPU's Kyiv local organization.

The very limited success of the SNPU stimulated the party's publishing activities. At the end of 1998, the SNPU published a collection of selected articles from *Social-Nationalist* that ceased to exist in 1996 (Radoms'ky 1998). The following year, Parubiy published a collection of his own articles (1999), while the SNPU published a book by Valentyn Moroz, *In Search of a Ukrainian Pinochet?* (1999), and launched a journal entitled *Reference Points*, edited by Andrushkiv and Parubiy.

In 2000, the party established contacts with Euronat, an association of radical European right-wing parties. Jean-Marie Le Pen, then leader of the Front National, participated in the SNPU's sixth party convention, held on 21 May 2000 (Zelyk 2008: 67).

However, at that time, the party was in decline. It chose to contest the 2002 parliamentary elections only in single-member districts, and again only Tyahnybok won a seat. Interestingly, he did not run as a member of the SNPU, but as a non-party candidate nominated by the electoral alliance Our Ukraine, led by Viktor Yushchenko whom the SNPU, however, actively supported. Tyahnybok's 2002 electoral programme featured almost nothing from the SNPU's 1991 and 1995 political programmes and cannot be considered ultra-nationalist (Tyahnybok 2002).

In 2004, the SNPU adopted a new political programme. It did not mention social-nationalism at all and was not Russophobic, although it did refer to the inadmissibility of economic and political dependence on Russia because of the latter's monopoly over energy supplies to Ukraine (SNPU 2006). Unlike previous programmes, which defended the *same* rights and privileges for all citizens of Ukraine, the new document supported the adoption of a law that would determine *different* rights and privileges for the titular ethnic group and ethnic minorities. The SNPU also argued that the core values of Ukrainian society should be 'the fundamental values of the Ukrainian people: Ukrainian language, national symbols, Ukrainian folk customs and traditions, as well as such universal values as heroism, honour, conscience, nobility, dignity, self-respect, honesty, freedom [and] justice' (ibid.). In a populist style, the party also promoted the idea of transition from indirect democracy to direct rule by the people. Interestingly, the SNPU seemed to be in favour of Ukraine joining NATO and the European Union (EU), as well as being willing to resume the country's membership of the nuclear club.

On 14 February 2004, the SNPU held its ninth convention, which became crucial to the party's political future. Tyahnybok became head of the party, now called Svoboda, and consolidated power into his hands. The convention also disbanded the 'Patriot of Ukraine', as this paramilitary organization posed a threat to the new 'respectable' image of Svoboda, although the 'Patriot of Ukraine' was revived as an independent group and continued to cooperate closely with Svoboda until 2007. The moderated programme of the SNPU was taken as a blueprint for the Svoboda programme. Although Tyahnybok portrayed Svoboda as a successor to the SNPU, Andrushkiv rejected this claim and called Svoboda 'a different political phenomenon' (Kolodrubets 2004). Moreover, Andrushkiv did not embrace the SNPU's transformation, and neither he nor Parubiy remained in the 'new' party.

Svoboda took part in the 2006 and 2007 parliamentary elections, but the party's results were far from any political relevance: 0.36 per cent of the votes in 2006 and 0.76 per cent in 2007. Although Svoboda doubled its vote, the overall result was still relatively insignificant.

Before the 2007 early parliamentary elections, Svoboda announced its 'Programme for the Protection of Ukrainians', which was partly integrated into the new political programme adopted in 2009 (Svoboda 2009). The document proposed: implementing lustration policies to purge the Ukrainian political system and administrative machine of communists, former KGB agents and adherents of former semi-authoritarian President Leonid Kuchma; the introduction of polygraph testing for government employees and candidates for elective office; the introduction of criminal responsibility for any manifestation of Ukrainophobia; a return to the Soviet policy of registering citizens' ethnicity in internal passports and birth certificates. The latter was required in order to realize another of Svoboda's ideas: the ethnic composition of government office-holders at all levels should conform to the ethnic composition of a given region. The 2009 programme calls for Ukraine's withdrawal from the Commonwealth of Independent States and the Eurasian Economic Community.[6] Although Svoboda is still in favour of the country joining NATO, its attitude to the EU has changed. The programme no longer mentions the EU, but does promote the workings of GUAM, the Organization for Democracy and Economic Development (a regional organization that unites Georgia, Ukraine, Azerbaijan and Moldova), as well as a call to build close political and economic links with 'the countries of the Baltic-Black Sea geopolitical axis' (Svoboda 2009). Vitaliy Atanasov analyzes this particular political programme of Svoboda in more detail (2011b).

Despite the fact that Svoboda's ideology is primarily based on ethnic Ukrainian nationalism, since 2005 the party has been also focusing on the issue of illegal migration from Asian countries to Ukraine and indirectly promoting 'white racism'. A gradual departure from narrow ethnocentrism, or perhaps supplementing it with 'white racism', has allowed Svoboda to attract those Ukrainians who may not support the

---

[6]   In fact, Ukraine only has observer status in the Eurasian Economic Community.

party's Ukrainian ultra-nationalism but still favour 'white racism'. Here, Tyahnybok's party is an obvious choice, as no other major political force addresses the issue of Asian immigration officially.

In 2009, the party declared a membership of 15,000. Although it seems to be an exaggeration, there is no doubt that the party has grown steadily in numbers since 2004. Svoboda also seems to benefit from the increasing popularity of extreme-right youth movements and organizations like the Social-National Assembly (SNA), 'Patriot of Ukraine' and Autonomous Resistance, whose aim is to create 'a uniracial and uninational society'. The activities of these groups are not limited to physical or symbolic violence against ethnic and social minorities, as they also take an active part in numerous social campaigns – generally along with representatives of Svoboda – ranging from mass protests against price rises to leafleting against alcohol and drug use. Needless to say, members of these extreme-right movements are often members of Tyahnybok's party. Interestingly, 'street combat youth movements' like the SNA no longer focus on ethnic issues: in contrast to the older Ukrainian far right, the new groups are, first and foremost, racist movements. Their disregard for the perceived 'Ukrainian versus Russian' ethno-cultural cleavage allows them to gain support from many 'white' ultra-nationalists. Once drawn to these movements, 'white racists' also contribute to the organizational efficiency of the Svoboda party, which is, to reiterate, considered the only representative of 'white racism' in the Ukrainian electoral sphere.

On 15 March 2009, Svoboda won the early regional elections in the Ternopil region: it obtained 34.69 per cent of the votes and 50 seats out of 120 on the Ternopil regional council, while its nearest competitor, the United Centre, gained only 14.20 per cent of the vote. Svoboda's result at the Ternopil regional elections was the best electoral outcome – either at regional or national level – for a far-right party in Ukraine's history. Oleksiy Kayda, head of the secretariat of Svoboda, was nominated chairman of the council. Jean-Marie Le Pen and Bruno Gollnisch of the National Front congratulated Tyahnybok on his victory in the regional elections during the latter's visit to Strasbourg in March 2009.

The results of the 2010 regional elections were another success story for Svoboda. It won the elections in Lviv and Ivano-Frankivs'k regions; in total, Svoboda obtained 2,279 seats on councils at all levels across Ukraine. Figure 17.1 displays the distribution of the votes for Svoboda across Ukraine.

Thus, in the course of 20 years, Svoboda had developed from being a paramilitary social movement to a successful regional party. Under the leadership of the relatively young and charismatic Tyahnybok, the SNPU/Svoboda's only member who managed to enter the Verkhovna Rada, the party, to a certain degree, moderated its political programme and did its best to model itself on European radical right-wing parties such as the Front National or the Freedom Party of Austria. The next section analyses the current rise of popular support for Svoboda in Ukraine.

Svoboda gaining momentum

Svoboda's stunning victory in the 2009 Ternopil regional elections, where it obtained 34.69 per cent of the votes, became a crucial watershed for the party. The backdrop

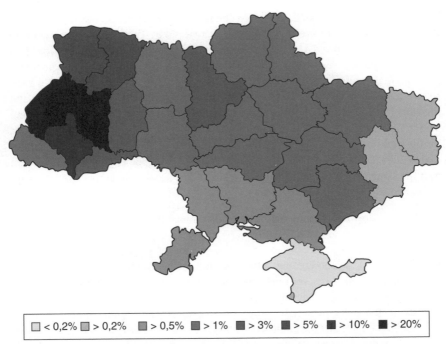

□ < 0,2% □ > 0,2%   ■ > 0,5%   ■ > 1%   ■ > 3%   ■ > 5%   ■ > 10%   ■ > 20%

Figure 17.1 Distribution of the votes for Svoboda at the 2010 regional elections.

against which Tyahnybok's party won the elections in the Ternopil region is both ambiguous and complex. This background entails regional and national aspects.

At regional level, there was a conflict between the Head of the Ternopil regional council, Mykhaylo Mykolenko from the Blok Yulii Tymoshenko (Bloc of Yuliya Tymoshenko, BYuT) and the Head of the Ternopil regional state administration, Yuriy Chizhmar from Nasha Ukraina (Our Ukraine, NU). Moreover, the mainstream right-wing political forces, namely the BYuT and NU, whose leaders were the main heroes of the 2004 'Orange revolution', were in opposition to each other on the council. NU was particularly displeased because the members of the KUN who were elected to the council on the NU list eventually joined the governing majority led by the BYuT, so NU was left in the minority. Because of the conflict between the BYuT and NU, Chizhmar addressed the Verkhovna Rada and asked for early elections. When the Verkhovna Rada announced the early elections in the Ternopil region, the BYuT and Arseniy Yatsenyuk's Front Zmin (Front for Change), another relatively popular political party, abstained from campaigning in protest at the supposedly illegitimate decision.

At national level, these developments were very similar but more complex. In September 2008, two coalition parliamentary groups, Nasha Ukraina – Narodna Samooborona (Our Ukraine – People's Self-Defence) and the BYuT, started to clash with each other over the scope of presidential powers, and Prime Minister Yuliya Tymoshenko was accused of colluding with the opposition Party of Regions, whose leader lost the 2004 presidential elections. In Western Ukraine in general, and in the

Ternopil region in particular, the alleged collusion between the BYuT and the Party of Regions, and the controversial gas agreements reached by Tymoshenko in Moscow in 2009, which were perceived by some as a betrayal of Ukraine's national interest, resulted in a loss of public trust in the BYuT, which had won the 2007 early parliamentary elections in the majority of the Western Ukrainian regions. Furthermore, by March 2009, against a backdrop of the political conflicts inside the governing 'Orange' coalition and the global financial crisis, public support for the Verkhovna Rada and then President Viktor Yushchenko had fallen dramatically: according to public opinion polls, support for the Verkhovna Rada dropped from 50.6 per cent in May 2008 to 27.4 per cent in March 2009, while support for Yushchenko dropped from 50 per cent to 25.2 per cent over the same period (Tsentr Razumkova 2011). It is possible to emphasize two main reasons for the Svoboda party's victory.

• The breakdown of the national-democratic 'Orange' political camp and the absence of relevant political rivals.
  Because of the conflict between two main 'Orange' political forces, namely the BYuT and NU, Svoboda found a large political niche. To some extent, Tyahnybok's organization filled the void that the main 'Orange' forces left empty, due to their conflicts and public disillusionment. Moreover, by March 2009, Svoboda became virtually the only radical right-wing party to contest the Ternopil regional elections. The KUN largely lost the public's trust because of their disloyalty to NU. As a result, the KUN gained only 1.21 per cent of the vote and lost the ten seats they previously held on the council.
• Organizational and ideological efficacy.
  Svoboda reinterpreted the controversial gas agreements reached by Prime Minister Tymoshenko in Moscow in terms of the national liberation struggle against Russia, which presumably wanted to gain control over Ukraine's economy. Furthermore, Svoboda started campaigning immediately after the early elections were announced in December 2008. The party also took full advantage of the BYuT's and Front for Change's boycott of the elections. Therefore, Svoboda enjoyed its fair share of the media spotlight.

Svoboda and the role of the national media

The national mainstream media played an important role in promoting Svoboda after the 2009 regional elections, in the way suggested by Herbert Kitschelt in his 1995 study of the radical right. He argued:

> Once maverick parties have succeeded in local secondary elections, their accomplishment is amplified and disseminated by the selective attention of the mass media . . . In this window of opportunity, the new party must quickly act to broaden its challenge to the political system and keep the attention of the mass media and the voters. This is most easily achieved by a chain of secondary elections that draw in ever wider electoral constituencies and eventually climax in a national election bout. (Kitschelt & McGann 1995: 99)

The next 'chain of secondary elections', which was lucky for Svoboda, were held a year after the victory in the Ternopil region.

More media attention for Svoboda followed the regional elections. Political commentator Serhiy Shcherbyna, from the newspaper *Ukrains'ka pravda*, noted the disproportionate presence of Svoboda on the two most popular Ukrainian political TV talk-shows, namely Yevhen Kyselyov's 'Velyka polityka' and Savik Shuster's 'Shuster Live' (Shcherbyna 2011; see also Atanasov 2011a, Umland 2011). Shcherbyna argues that between January and June 2011, representatives of Svoboda were invited to take part in 11 out of 19 'Velyka polityka' programmes. These representatives included controversial figures such as Yuriy Mykhal'chyshyn, who in January 2011 threatened the current government with the (largely imaginary) ultra-nationalist army named after the notorious Ukrainian fascist Stepan Bandera (Kabachiy 2011). In turn, 'Shuster Live' invited representatives of Svoboda onto 10 out of 20 programmes. This means that Tyahnybok's associates were invited to every second 'Velyka polityka' or 'Shuster Live' programme, and these statistics are indeed striking given the fact that Svoboda was not represented in the Verkhovna Rada at that time.

The puzzle of Svoboda's increased representation in the national mainstream media can, at least partially, be solved by highlighting the owners of the TV channels that feature the aforementioned political talk shows. 'Velyka polityka' appears on the Inter TV Channel, the majority of whose shares are owned by the U.A. Inter Media Group that belongs to Valeriy Khoroshkovs'ky. In spring 2010, President Viktor Yanukovych appointed Khoroshkovs'ky Head of the Security Service of Ukraine (he replaced Valentyn Nalyvaychenko who was favoured by former President Yushchenko) and a staff member of the National Bank of Ukraine. 'Shuster Live' is featured on the First National, the major state TV channel operated by the National Television Company of Ukraine, which is controlled by the Cabinet of Ministers. Since Khoroshkovsky is close to the present government, while the Cabinet is under the control of the Verkhovna Rada, there are justified suspicions that the Party of Regions, which is now in power, is actually promoting Tyahnybok's party in order to weaken the national-democratic opposition, or what is left of the 'Orange' camp. Practices like these are nothing new in European politics. Roger Eatwell, commenting on the initial rise of the Front National in the early 1980s, argued:

> Television in France was still heavily controlled by the state . . . Possibly in an attempt to weaken the mainstream right, [François] Mitterand seems to have played a part in instructing the state television network to give the fringe parties more access. Le Pen quickly began to exploit his limited opportunities, proving himself to be an excellent speaker on television as well as at mass rallies . . . Given the importance of television to modern political campaigning and legitimacy, this was a major breakthrough. It also suited a party whose leader had a strong charismatic appeal, for Le Pen's image tended to affect people more than his policy statements. (1996: 319–20)

Andreas Umland believes that Tyahnybok's organization is at least partly indebted to its increased representation in the mass media for its rise at national level, and reminds us that 'even the most respected Ukrainian media, such as TV Channel 5, or the leading Internet publication *Ukrains'ka pravda*, have regularly provided Tyahnybok and his fellow party members with forums to disseminate their views and popularize their party' (Umland 2011).

Although the presence of Svoboda in the national media indeed played an important role in its promotion (while lack of access to national media was one of the reasons for the failure of the radical right in previous years), it would be unreasonable to ascribe the rise of the party to media coverage alone. Moreover, if President Yanukovych and/ or the Party of Regions have indeed been trying to weaken the national democrats and 'cultivate' Tyahnybok's party as a convenient 'sparring partner', which can easily be discredited if and when required, the role of Yanukovych's regime in the breakup of the 'Orange' camp should not be exaggerated. The conflicts inside the 'Orange' coalition began to emerge as early as 2005 and resulted in the dismissal of then Prime Minister Tymoshenko's government by then President Yushchenko.

Conclusion

The rise of Tyahnybok's Svoboda is conditioned by: 1) efficient strategies aimed at aggregating societal demands in the social, economic and educational spheres; 2) the growing legitimacy of Svoboda determined by its ideological modernization, its process of 'respectabilization', the breakup of the national-democratic ('Orange') political camp, the absence of rival far-right political parties, its massive presence in the national media and 3) the growing organizational efficiency of the party conditioned by the increase in funding after the 2009 and 2010 regional elections, the increase in membership and the recruitment of young activists from extreme-right movements.

On 17 November 2011, the Verkhovna Rada adopted a law that implies the election of Members of Parliament under a mixed system (50% will be elected from party lists and 50% will be elected from single-member constituencies) and introduced a 5 per cent electoral threshold. It is not yet clear whether Svoboda will be able to reach the 5 per cent threshold, as Tyahnybok assumes, but it is obvious that this far-right party, for the aforementioned reasons, is now gaining momentum.

Given the geopolitical significance of Ukraine, the risks associated with the Ukrainian far right should not be underestimated. Although it is unlikely that Svoboda will be able to seize power, at least five major points should be mentioned with regard to the domestic and international threat it poses:

- Svoboda contributes significantly to the political polarization of Ukrainian society. The perceived rise of this party and its likely entrance to the Verkhovna Rada (Ukrainian Parliament) after the forthcoming 2012 general election will spark negative feelings on the part of the Russian minority and contribute to the activization of pro-Russian nationalist movements that can garner support from Russia and advance separatist activities in the largely Russian-speaking regions, such as the Crimea.

- The rise in popular support for Svoboda takes place at the expense of support for national democrats. Thus, Svoboda erodes the Ukrainian democratic camp and makes it difficult for it to oppose the accumulation of power by Ukrainian President Viktor Yanukovych and the now dominant Party of Regions, of which Yanukovych is honorary leader.
- As Svoboda is highly critical of the Eastern and Southern regions of Ukraine, which are largely supportive of Svoboda's major political antagonist, the Party of Regions, and where the Russian language is more common than the Ukrainian language (Tsentr Razumkova 2008), this far-right party may trigger a process of separation by Western Ukraine, pre-eminently the regions in Galicia and partly Volhynia, from the rest of the country (Voznyak 2011).
- The virulently anti-Russian position of Svoboda may sour Ukraine's relations with Russia, and given the country's dependence on Russia for energy supplies, the EU's energy security and Ukraine's economic development might be put at risk.
- Svoboda's negative stance towards European integration, and in particular the policies aimed at the country's rapprochement with the EU (e.g. readmission of illegal immigrants), may hinder this process to the disadvantage of EU-Ukraine cooperation, which is already affected by the regression of democracy and 'selective justice' for opposition leaders in Ukraine under President Yanukovych (European Parliament 2011).

References

Atanasov, V. (2011a), 'Osoblyvosti natsional-radyka'lnoi dzhynsy', *Mediagramotnost*, 11 May 2011. <www.osvita.mediasapiens.kiev.ua/material/2505> [accessed 13 January 2012].

— (2011b), 'Stydka utopiya "Svobody"', *Politychna krytyka*, 2: 36–50.

Betz, H.-G. (1994), *Radical Right-Wing Populism in Western Europe*, New York: St. Martin's Press.

Carter, E. L. (2005), *The Extreme Right in Western Europe: Success or Failure?* Manchester: Manchester University Press.

Eatwell, R. (1996), *Fascism: A History*, New York: Allen Lane.

European Parliament (2011), 'Joint Motion for a Resolution on the Current Developments in Ukraine', RC-B7–0543/2011. <www.europarl.europa.eu/sides/getDoc. do?type=MOTION&reference=P7-RC-2011–0543&language=EN> [accessed 13 January 2012].

Ignazi, P. (2003), *Extreme Right Parties in Western Europe*, Oxford: Oxford University Press.

Kabachiy, R. (2011), 'Ukrainian Nationalism: Are Russian Strategies at Work?', *Open Democracy*, 18 January 2011. <www.opendemocracy.net/od-russia/roman-kabachiy/uk rainian-nationalism-are-russian-strategies-at-work> [accessed 13 January 2012].

Kitschelt, H. with McGann, A. (1995), *The Radical Right in Western Europe: A Comparative Analysis*, Ann Arbor: University of Michigan Press.

Kolodrubets, O. (2004), 'Yaroslav Andrushkiv: SNPU ta VO "Svoboda" – rizni politychni yavishcha', *Vgolos*, 27 April 2004. <http://vgolos.com.ua/politic/5536.html> [accessed 13 January 2012].

Korchyns'ky, D. (2004), 'Peredvyborna prohrama kandydata na post Prezydenta Ukrainy Korchyns'koho Dmytra Oleksandrovycha'. <www.cvk.gov.ua/pls/vp2004/WP009?PT021F01=68&PT001F01=500> [accessed 13 January 2012].

Kubicek, P. (1999), 'What Happened to the Nationalists in Ukraine?', *Nationalism and Ethnic Politics*, 5: 29–30.

KUN (2011), 'Prohrama Konhresu Ukrains'kykh Natsionalistiv'. <http://cun.org.ua/pro-partiyu/programa> [accessed 13 January 2012].

Kuzio, T. (1997), 'Radical Nationalist Parties and Movements in Contemporary Ukraine before and after Independence: the Right and its Politics, 1989–1994', *Nationalities Papers*, 25: 211–42.

Minkenberg, M. (ed.) (2010), *Historical Legacies and the Radical Right in Post-Cold War Central and Eastern Europe*, Stuttgart: ibidem-Verlag.

Moroz, V. (1999), *U poshukakh ukrains'koho Pinocheta*? Lviv: Surma.

Mudde, C. (2007), *Populist Radical Right Parties in Europe*, Cambridge: Cambridge University Press.

Musafirova, O. (2011), 'Osnovatel' Sotsial-Natsional'noy partii Yaroslav Andrushkiv: "Esli vyyavili seksota, to luchshe ne trogat"', *Glavkom*, 26 July 2011. <http://glavcom.ua/articles/4295.html> [accessed 13 January 2012].

Parubiy, A. (1999), *Pohlyad sprava*, Lviv: Orientyry.

Radoms'ky, A. (ed.) (1998), *Pravy napryam*, Lviv: Vydavnytstvo 'TzOV Liga-pres'.

Ramet, S. P. (ed.) (1999), *The Radical Right in Central and Eastern Europe since 1989*, University Park: Pennsylvania State University Press.

Rudling, P. A. (2012), 'Anti-Semitism and the extreme right in contemporary Ukraine', in A. Mammone, E. Godin and B. Jenkins (eds), *Mapping the Extreme Right in Contemporary Europe: From Local to Transnational*, London: Routledge, pp. 189–205.

Shcherbyna, S. (2011), 'Politychni tok-shou. Yak vony tse roblyat'?', *Ukrains'ka pravda*, 7 June 2011. <www.pravda.com.ua/articles/2011/06/7/6275793/> [accessed 13 January 2012].

Shekhovtsov, A. (2011), 'The Creeping Resurgence of the Ukrainian Radical Right? The Case of the Freedom Party', *Europe-Asia Studies*, 63: 203–28.

Shekhovtsov, A. and Umland, A. (2011), 'Vladimir Zhirinovsky and the LDPR', *Russian Analytical Digest*, 102: 14–6.

SNPU (2006), 'Prohrama Sotsial-Natsional'noi Partii Ukrainy [2004]', *Radykal'ny Ukrains'ky Natsionalizm*. <http://web.archive.org/web/20060715130656/http://www.run.org.ua/content/view/531/33/> [accessed 13 January 2012].

— (2008), 'Prohrama Sotsial-Natsional'noi Partii Ukrainy', in *Kurs I. Osnovy natsionalizmu*, Ivano-Frankivs'k: Instytut politychnoi osvity VO 'Svoboda', pp. 88–91.

Sokolov, M. (2006), 'Natsional-bol'shevistskaya partiya: ideologicheskaya evolyutsiya i politicheskiy stil'', in A. Verkhovsky (ed.), *Russkiy natsionalizm: ideologiya i nastroenie*, Moscow: Tsentr 'Sova', pp. 139–64.

Solchanyk, R. (1999), 'The Radical Right in Ukraine', in S. P. Ramet (ed.), *The Radical Right in Central and Eastern Europe*, University Park: Pennsylvania State University Press, pp. 279–96.

Svoboda (2009), 'Prohrama VO "Svoboda" (chynna)'. <www.svoboda.org.ua/pro_partiyu/prohrama> [accessed 13 January 2012].

Tsentr Razumkova (2008), 'Yaka mova ye dlya Vas ridnoyu? (rehional'ny rozpodil, dynamika 2006–8)'. <www.uceps.org/ukr/poll.php?poll_id=436> [accessed 13 January 2012].

— (2011), 'Chi pidtrymuyete Vy diyal'nist' Verkhovnoi Rady Ukrainy? (dynamika, 2000–11)'. <www.uceps.org/ukr/poll.php?poll_id=68> [accessed 13 January 2012].

Tyahnybok, O. (2002), 'Peredvyborna prohrama kandydata u narodni deputaty Ukrainy vid vyborchoho bloku "Blok Viktora Yushchenko Nasha Ukraina"'. <www.cvk.gov.ua/pls/vd2002/printblob?pf7341=3380&kodvib=400> [accessed 13 January 2012].

Umland, A. (2008a), 'Die andere Anomalie der Ukraine: ein Parlament ohne rechtsradikale Fraktionen', *Ukraine-Analysen*, 41: 7–10.

— (2008b), 'Kraine slabye', *Korrespondent*, 23: 34.

— (2011), 'Ukraine Right-Wing Politics: Is the Genie Out of the Bottle?', *Open Democracy*, 3 January 2011. <www.opendemocracy.net/od-russia/andreas-umland/ukraine-right-wing-politics-is-genie-out-of-bottle> [accessed 13 January 2012].

UNA-UNSO (2007), 'Svitohlyadna doktryna UNA'. <http://una-unso.in.ua/?p=10909> [accessed 13 January 2012].

Voznyak, T. (2011), 'Prizraki galitskogo separatizma i ul'tranatsionalizma', *Zerkalo nedeli*, 41. <http://zn.ua/POLITICS/prizrakI_galitskogo_separatizma_I_ultranatsionalizma-91378.html> [accessed 13 January 2012].

Wilson, A. (1997), *Ukrainian Nationalism in the 1990s: A Minority Faith*, Cambridge: Cambridge University Press.

Zbitnyev, Y. and Shcherbyna, V. (2011), 'Yevhenika dlya Ukrainy: tezy do kontseptsii demohrafichnoi polityky', in Y. Zbitnyev (ed.), *Kontsitutsiyna asambleya, abo pravo na povstannya*, Kyiv: Sammit-knyha, pp. 189–98.

Zelyk, R. (2008), 'Istoriya SNPU – VO "Svoboda"', in *Kurs I. Osnovy natsionalizmu*, Ivano-Frankivs'k: Instytut politychnoi osvity VO 'Svoboda', pp. 56–71.

Section IV

Case Studies – Scandinavian Context

18

Populism – Changes over Time and Space: A Comparative and Retrospective Analysis of Populist Parties in the Nordic Countries from 1965 to 2012

Björn Fryklund

Denmark belongs to the Danes . . . A multiethnic Denmark would mean the breaking down of our stable homogeneous society by anti-development and reactionary cultures.

(Danish People's Party Work Programme 2007)

Together with similar parties in the Nordic countries and in Europe, the Danish People's Party belongs to the group of populist parties that has secured a greater footing in recent decades and become a permanent feature on the political stage (2007). It is clear that parties with a right-wing populist profile have been gaining in strength in Europe since the end of the 1990s. Indeed, the years 1999–2000 can be regarded as a turning point with regard to the participation of these parties in the political arena. During these years the Front National enjoyed considerable success in France; Jean-Marie Le Pen even challenged Chirac in the presidential election in 2002. During the same period, Jörg Haider´s FPÖ (Freiheitliche Partei Österreichs or Freedom Party of Austria) made significant gains in Austria, to the extent that the party became influential in the government. In Denmark, the Danish People's Party also gained influence – so much so that the party played a crucial political role in the Danish Parliament. Many right-wing populist parties also made significant headway in the European parliamentary elections held in 1999. Since then, these parties have increased their representation in the European Parliament, despite the general trend of parties losing seats due to European Union (EU) expansion. Since 2005 the Danish People's Party has strengthened its position and increased its electoral support. The Fremskrittspartiet (Progress Party) has done the same in Norway. In Finland, the party known as the True Finns, the successor to the Finnish Rural Party, developed and greatly increased its electoral support in the respective municipal European elections

Table 18.1 General election results (per cent and mandates) for RRP-parties in the Nordic countries during the twenty-first century

Elec./ Country	2001	2002	2003	2004	2005	2006	2007	2008	2009	2010	2011
Sweden		1.4				2.9				5.7	
		(—)				(—)				(20)	
Norway	14.6				22.1				22.9		
	(26)				(38)				(41)		
Denmark	12.0				13.3	13.8					12.3
	(22)				(24)	(25)					(22)
Finland			1.6				4.1				19.1
			(3)				(5)				(39)

of 2008 and 2009. In the general election in 2007, the True Finns gained 4.1 per cent of the votes and five seats in Parliament. In the elections in 2010, the party obtained 19.1 per cent of the votes and 39 seats. This means that currently, in 2012, populist parties in Norway and Finland attract about a quarter of all voters. These are significant figures. The challenge is to decide how to analyse and understand these parties. In Sweden, the Sverigedemokraterna (Sweden Democrats) attracted almost 3 per cent of the vote in the 2006 parliamentary election and, at the same time, acquired a large number of seats in the municipal elections, especially in the southern part of Sweden, for example, Skåne (Scania) and Blekinge. In the 2010 election, Sverigedemokraterna obtained national representation in the Swedish Parliament for the first time, with 20 seats and 5.7 per cent of the votes (see Table 18.1).

The presence of populist parties gives rise to a democratic dilemma of which society, with its various institutions, is forced to take account. This dilemma can be regarded as having two dimensions. The first dimension is that, according to a strict definition of the concept of democracy, populist parties ought to be regarded as democratic. The parties have taken part in free and democratic elections and have gained so much support for their politics that they have been able to gain a number of seats in decision-making assemblies. The challenge, and also the second dimension of the dilemma, occurs when these parties establish themselves and, in their policies and rhetoric, advocate a society based on ethnic and cultural homogeneity. This leads to certain groups, especially people with a foreign background, being excluded from participating in society, having their freedom and rights limited and to exclusion and inclusion mechanisms in society being strengthened – a development that runs the risk of challenging central principles in today's liberal democracies (Kiiskinen et al. 2007; Kiiskinen & Saveljeff 2010).

The history of Nordic populism – a brief overview

The history of Nordic populism can be described as a wave-like process, a process that moves from political dissatisfaction based on populist appeal, related to the tax issue during the 1970s, to those concerning refugee and immigrant issues in the 1980s, the 1990s and the early part of the twenty-first century. Although in the Nordic countries the populist parties – Mogens Glistrup's Fremskridtsparti (The Progress Party) in Denmark, Anders Lange's Fremskrittsparti (The Progress Party) in Norway and Veikko Vennamo's Rural Party in Finland – found themselves close to extinction in the latter part of the 1970s, they experienced a second wave of popularity in the 1980s. A third wave of popularity then helped to keep these parties buoyant during the late 1990s and into the twenty-first century. In Denmark, Pia Kjærsgaard's Danish People's Party took over from the Progress Party and saw a significant electoral breakthrough in the 2001 election. The party won a number of victories, partly through its marked balance-of-power role in the Parliament, and partly through being a driving, supportive partner for both the previous and present liberal-conservative governments. In Norway, Carl I. Hagen's Progress Party, now under the leadership of Siv Jensen, continues to harvest political success and is Norway´s second largest party, with 22.9 per cent of the vote and 41 seats in the Norwegian Parliament in the general election in 2009. Although in Finland the Rural Party has now played out its political role, it has been replaced by a similar party, known as the True Finns. In the municipal elections held in November 2008, support for the party increased to the extent that they gained 5.4 per cent of the vote, which was a marked increase in relation to the election results of 2004. As previously indicated, in the parliamentary elections of 2007 and 2011, the True Finns increased their vote from 4.1 per cent and five seats to 19.1 per cent and 39 seats (Betz 1994, Björklund & Andersen 2002, 2008, Rydgren & Widfeldt 2004, Wold 2005, Banks & Grinrich 2006; Ringsmose & Pedersen 2006, Marsdal 2007).

As this description indicates, populist parties have been part of the Nordic political scene for several decades and constitute a real challenge to the other parties. A better understanding of how these parties and their successors have developed and changed over time, in combination with factors that benefit or obstruct populism, also leads to new opportunities to address and deal with the challenge that populist parties can be said to represent (Kiiskinen et al. 2007).

Attempting to capture the changes in Nordic populism through time and space is best done from a comparative perspective. Including the Swedish societal context in this overarching Nordic framework is also important, since here the development of populism appears to differ from that of the other Nordic countries. In this sense, Sweden can be regarded as 'a straggler' (see also Ch. 19 by Oja and Mral in this volume). How is it, for example, that only now, at the beginning of the second decade of the twenty-first century and after the developments that have taken place in many other European and Nordic countries, do we also begin to see a markedly populist party on the increase in the Swedish context? Analysing this development could reveal why Sweden increasingly resembles the other Nordic countries and large parts of Europe, and be an important key to gaining an understanding of which political, social and economic factors counteract or support populism. An overall perspective of the political, social and economic changes that have taken place in the Nordic countries over a 50-year time span is necessary if we are to fully understand the Nordic development of populist parties.

Survey of the research field concerning the Nordic countries

Research on populist parties has, thus far, focused on three main areas. **The first** has been concerned with an exploration of the general and social structural changes that might explain the growth of populist parties (Betz 1994, Taggart 1996, Kitschelt 1997, Betz & Immerfall 1998). **In the second**, research has focused on charting the ideology of populist parties (Canovan 1981, Mudde 2000, Taggart 2000, Ignazi 2003, Mudde 2007, Davies & Jackson 2008). **In the third**, the emphasis has been on doing case studies in the countries in which populist parties have been successful (Mény & Surel 2002, Rydgren 2002, Rydgren & Widfeldt 2004). From a Nordic viewpoint, the research has highlighted a problem that was discussed as early as 1981 in the study *Populism och missnöjespartier i Norden* (Populism and Protest Parties in the Nordic Countries), carried out by myself and my research colleague Tomas Peterson. This related to why no party based on popular discontent had emerged in Sweden during the early 1970s. In Sweden at that time, no political party could be likened to those that were developing in the other Nordic countries. However, during the 1980s and the beginning of the 1990s, and more specifically in the general elections of 1988 and 1991, a process developed in Sweden that resulted in the growth of two completely new parties, namely the Green Party and New Democracy. On the traditional political scale, the Green Party was positioned to the left and New Democracy to the right (Taggart 1996). To some extent New Democracy adopted a populist appeal, and in 1991 won parliamentary seats; however, unlike its Nordic counterparts, it did not manage to maintain its parliamentary successes.

In connection with the 1994 elections, New Democracy disappeared from the political scene altogether and ceased to exist. The tide has again turned, however, and in the general election of 2010 the Sweden Democrats succeeded in holding the balance of power in the Swedish Parliament. If the Nordic development of populist parties is compared with that which took place in many other European countries, it is clear that the Swedish case is something of an anomaly. A number of attempts have been made to explain this Swedish exception. With regard to the success of the Sweden Democrats at the municipal level in 2006, and then at the national level in 2010, it would appear that the previous Swedish immunity to populism is now on the wane. Against this background, a greater focus on the factors that support or counteract populism is needed in order to contribute to a further understanding of this complex field. Why has it taken so long for a manifestly populist party to gain a foothold in Sweden?

Up to now, research has mainly focused on a number of explanatory factors. The strong historical position of the Social Democrats has led to a unique political and ideological hegemony in Sweden, this takes the form of a far-reaching consensus on the Swedish democracy and welfare model. The lack of any decisive political or ideological social issue to unite or split the population has also played a role. The Swedish economy has generally been in good shape too, and social welfare worked well until the beginning of the 1990s. These relations are considered to have made Swedish society and its political culture almost immune to populism during the period in which it took shape in neighbouring Nordic countries and in a number of other countries in Europe (Taggart 1996, Kitschelt 1997, Rydgren 2002, 2006, Bennich-Björkman & Blomqvist 2008).

When social relations are changed this specific immunity is also nullified, which can in turn open the door to populism. In Denmark and Norway, the referendums relating to membership of the EC (now the EU) in the early 1970s became a watershed that polarized the political system, the political parties and popular and electoral opinion for a long time. In Sweden, people had to wait until the 1990s to vote on membership of the EU, which was then followed by a referendum in 2003 about participation in the EU's monetary union. The referendum in Sweden could have had as lasting an effect on politics and public opinion as it did in Norway and Denmark. Research also shows that neither xenophobic tendencies nor an emphasis on issues related to immigration are sufficient grounds for the growth of, or sympathy for, populist parties. If such issues are to affect how citizens decide to vote, then they need to be politicized and linked to political dissatisfaction in other social fields, which in turn means that the immigrant issue becomes the organizing principle for political dissatisfaction. Research shows that, so far, the immigration question has not influenced how the Swedish electorate votes (Holmberg & Weibull 2001, 2005). In addition, immigration has not been politicized in Sweden to the same extent as in other Nordic and European countries in which populist parties have won victories (Rydgren 2002). According to the Swedish official analysis of the general elections in 2006 and 2010, only minor changes could be observed during the period with regard to these tendencies. Both the importance and politicization of the immigrant question are still rather low-key in Sweden compared to other political issues, even though a minor increase can be observed over time.

Populism's different forms of expression in the Nordic countries – a comparative analysis

Populism's forms of expression in the Nordic countries vary and change with the national and social context. Although this might seem obvious, it is unfortunately often forgotten or neglected in analyses and social debates. Political, social and economic change processes can be broken down into a number of variables that I regard as central to the analysis of populist parties, namely **class, popularity, political culture and ethnic nationalism**. The concept of class is basically decided by professional affiliation (Esping Andersen 1993, Olin Wright 1997, Goldthorpe 2007). *Populist parties have a tendency to describe themselves as not belonging to any specific class* and instead see themselves as the representatives of 'ordinary people' and their interests. These parties also level strong criticism at other parties that they claim contribute to the creation of a society based on class affinity and, where the special interests of different classes are prioritized, at the expense of those of 'ordinary people'.

Populism is given the opportunity to develop from the contexts in which sections of the population feel slighted by the political élite and perception that this élite does not look after people's interests. Populist parties have a capacity to encapsulate these tendencies and create populist appeal based on experience of class differences. The significance of the class concept thus becomes an important variable to relate to (Fryklund & Peterson 1981, Kiiskinen et al. 2007).

The concept of **popularity**, or **popularism**, consisting of popular traditions, popular appeal and popular dimensions, is regarded as part of an ongoing struggle between the people and the powers that be, a struggle that has found expression in the history of every nation. It is a common heritage that outlives different social systems and remains in the political and ideological domains as complete traditions or parts of them, or as experiences in institutional or thought forms. Traditions of a political, ideological or cultural nature, as well as of thought and action, are woven into the opposition between the people and those in power. Such traditions have been developed around themes relating to nation, ethnicity, culture, religion, polity, democracy, work, family, morals and social solidarity. *Popularity/popularism and popular appeal have been and remain important components of the Nordic countries' political development.* They have presumably had greater significance in Denmark and Norway, and to a certain extent also in Finland, than they have in Sweden. Popularity thus constitutes another central variable in the study of populism, since populism is about popular appeal (the people versus the élite) that is regarded as being deeply rooted in every nation. When the popular appeal of the established parties wavers, it is given opportunity to compete in the struggle to attract voters (Fryklund & Peterson 1981, Kiiskinen et al. 2007).

With regard to the third central variable of the analysis, **political culture**, this can be exemplified by the different constructions and bases of the welfare states in the Nordic countries (Bennich-Björkman & Blomqvist 2008). Here my main thrust is that *a nation's political culture is popularity's concrete form(s) of expression in the political arena.* The shape that political culture takes in a nation has, in my opinion, its origins in the definition of the concept of popularity. Different and selective interpretations of the popularity theme give rise to a limited number of meaningful and consistent political cultures with a specific content. Political culture is the cornerstone on which politics rests and from which it is enacted, it gives meaning to politics by justifying material, cultural, social and political institutions. It is not enough simply to analyse political, social and economic structures in order to understand how a political system is supported or dissolved. That would be to disregard the foundation on which the system, the national political culture and its traditions rest. How people judge politics is important for a system's legitimacy and serviceability (Edgerton et al. 1994). Even if similarities exist in the Nordic countries with regard to their democratic and social welfare models, there are also important differences between them. These are central factors to keep in mind.

In simple terms one could talk about a *petit bourgeois*-popular liberal Denmark, a popular-national Norway, a Swedish 'People's Home' (welfare state) and a strongly class-polarized Finland. These differences are matched by disparities in the political system, which also affect the articulation of popular appeal and the populism that results. When talking about a Nordic welfare model, Sweden tends to stand out as a typical textbook example. In other Nordic countries the development of the political system has characteristic features, for example, (*petit bourgeois*) popular-liberal Denmark with its personality votes, collaboration and diffusion of class conflicts, Norway with its emphasis on decentralization and district politics as well as a mistrust of central power and central control and Finland which, due to its special history, did not acquire any comparable political system until after the Second World War. When we talk about Swedish social development as a typical case for the formation of a modern welfare state, this mainly refers to efficient and smooth economic growth and its structural effects on societal development. What is of importance here is long-standing social democratic governance and a tradition of agreements between parts of the labour market (without government interference) – that which is usually called the Swedish labour market model (Fryklund & Peterson 1983, Taggart 1996, Kitschelt 1997, Rydgren 2002). Populist parties have a tendency to take over parts of the popular political culture and, in the struggle for votes, use these as tools with which to undermine the political establishment. Analysing the national political cultures in the Nordic countries, with a focus on origin and (new) reproduction over time, is therefore important when explaining and understanding the different forms of populism.

Nationalism can be politically or ethnically based (Kohn 1944, Smith 1986). With regard to (a lack of) democracy, there is an inbuilt ethnic national dimension in the populist appeal that relates to the struggle between the people and the powers that be and, within that, concerning how social welfare should be distributed. In the former case, people with an ethnic background other than that of the national majority population are not included in popular democracy, and in the latter case social welfare is only regarded as being available to the majority population (ethno-national welfare chauvinism) (Kitschelt 1997, Taggart 2000, Mény & Surel 2002, Kiiskinen et al. 2007). In the analysis of populist parties, ethnicity-based nationalism is central, in that the experience of Danishness, Norwegianness, Swedishness or Finnishness forms the basis on which refugee and immigrant issues are used as *organizing principles* for these parties' social critique of other political issues. Suspicion of foreigners, xenophobia and racism are most deep-seated in nationalism formed on ethno-cultural grounds, and can differ between the Nordic countries and how they have been articulated over time and space. How nationalism, on the basis of ethnic and/or political preferences, is used in populist appeals in the various Nordic countries is therefore important when explaining and understanding the different specific forms of populism. The choice of 1965 as a starting date for the analysis refers to the point where the first indication of populist parties in the Nordic countries (Veikko Vennamo's Rural Party in Finland) could be observed. The period 2009–12, is of special interest because it is for this period that we have been able to follow and analyse national election proceedings in all four countries at a time when populist parties appear to be gaining an increasingly prominent political role.

Is populism a threat to democracy or a functional natural feature of democracy?

The political landscape has changed (Mény & Surel 2002). Populism has returned both as an empirical reality and as an important research topic. Populism is increasingly used to describe political phenomena that do not fit into the traditional political system, as a description of unusual political events and forms of expression, and as a challenger that questions the basis of liberal democracy, liberal institutions, values and laws/rules (Hainsworth 2000, Schain et al. 2002, Eatwell & Mudde 2004, Panizza 2005, Kiiskinen et al. 2007). A key issue, discussed in recent years, is whether the presence of populism constitutes a natural functional strand of liberal democracy or a threat to it, or whether it should rather be seen as a challenge to it. The first approach sees populism as a natural feature of today's democratic social systems (Canovan 1999, 2002). In order to understand populism and its relation to democracy, populism is regarded as a side effect that democracy might give rise to, rather than as an intractable and temporary flare-up reaction to the system itself. The relation between populism and democracy can thus be described as a constant shadow relation (Canovan 1999). A second approach is that, since populist parties de facto constitute a threat to democracy, they should be resisted with moral weapons, rather than be regarded as worthy political opponents to be addressed using political resources within the framework of the democratic process (Eatwell & Mudde 2004, Mouffe 2008). A third approach that has dominated the discourse surrounding populism in recent years is to regard these parties as a challenge to democracy. This has mainly focused on which aspects of democracy are challenged and, subsequently, why populist parties are an important research object for politically oriented sociologists to take note of (Capoccia 2001, Bale 2003, Meguid 2008, Mudde 2007, Kiiskinen et al. 2007, van Spanje & van der Brug 2007, de Lange 2008, Kiiskinen & Saveljeff 2010, Saveljeff 2011). A fourth approach concerns the emergence of new parties, such as populist parties, as an indication that voters have demands that have not been sufficiently considered by the established parties. If the established parties are less sensitive and not open to the electorate's demands, then the possibility of a new party profiling itself on the basis of these demands, and thereby winning political influence, is greater.

The established parties find it difficult to provide answers to the question of how to solve the democratic dilemma, although they do signal that a strategic approach towards radical right-wing populist (RRP) parties needs to be formed in a way that gives the established parties an opportunity to *handle* this democratic dilemma. In this sense, the presence of the democratic dilemma causes a *strategic dilemma*, in relation to which the established parties need to weigh the goals they are striving towards with the strategic approach of the RRP party at the same time as they relate to the strongly value-charged issue that has been politicized by the RRP party and the democratic dilemma that the presence of the RRP party gives rise to. As a result of this, the character of the democratic dilemma is somewhat changed, and the goal of not losing votes becomes paramount. This also leads to *the democratic dilemma becoming subordinated to the strategic dilemma* that the presence of the RRP parties also gives rise to (Kiiskinen & Saveljeff 2010: 229ff., Saveljeff 2011).

Taking the results of the Swedish general election on 19 September 2010 as a point of departure – when the Swedish RRP party known as the Sweden Democrats won parliamentary representation for the first time – it becomes clear that the presence of RRP parties represented at a national level is now also a tangible part of the Swedish political context. In the aftermath of the election results in September 2010, much of the debate focused on how the presence of the Sweden Democrats in Parliament should be dealt with and what kind of influence the party could expect in Swedish politics in relation to its electoral support. It is therefore possible to conclude that, in the current Swedish political climate, the topicality of research related to the presence of RRP parties in the democratic institutions is high. The same goes for the political situation in the other Nordic countries, and probably for many other European countries too. It also reveals the need for future research into what affects the content of the strategic approaches used by the established parties to deal with parties perceived as *the ugly ducklings of politics.*

References

Bale, D. (2003), 'Cinderella and Her Ugly Sisters: The Mainstream and Extreme Right in Europe's Bipolarising Party Systems', *West European Politics*, 26(3): 67–90.

Banks, M. and Grinrich, A. (eds) (2006), *Neo-nationalism in Europe and Beyond: Perspectives from Social Anthropology*, New York: Berghahn Books.

Bennich-Björkman, L. and Blomqvist, P. (eds) (2008), *Mellan folkhem och Europa – svensk politik i brytningstid*, Malmö: Liber.

Betz, H.-G. (1994), *Radical Right-wing Populism in Western Europe*, London: Macmillan Press.

Betz, H.-G. and Immerfall, S. (eds) (1998), *The New Politics of the RIGHT – Neo-populist Parties and Movements in Established Democracies*, London: Macmillan.

Björklund, T. and Andersen, J. G. (2002), "Anti-immigration parties in Denmark and Norway: The progress parties and the Danish peoples party" in M. Schain, A. Zolberg and P. Hossay (eds) *Shadows over Europe: The development and impact of the extreme right in Western Europe*, New York: Palgrave Macmillian.

Björklund, T. and Andersen, J. G. (2008), "The Far Right Parties in Scandinavia" in P. Davies and P. Jackson (eds), *The Far Right in Europe: An Encyclopedia*, Oxford: Grennwood World Press.

Canovan, M. (1981), *Populism*, New York: Harcourt Brace Jovanovich.

— (1999), 'Trust the People! Populism and the Two Faces of Democracy', *Political Studies*, 47: 2–16.

— (2002), 'Taking politics to the people: Populism as the ideology of democracy', in Y. Mény and Y. Surel (eds), *Democracies and the Populist Challenge*, Basingstoke: Palgrave Macmillan, pp. 25–44.

Capoccia, G. (2001), 'Defending democracy: Reactions to political extremism in inter-war Europe', *European Journal of Political Research*, 39: 431–60.

de Lange, S. (2008), *From Pariah to Power: The Government Participation of Radical Right-Wing Populist Parties in West European Democracies,* Zelzate: DCL Print & Design.

Davies, P. and Jackson, P. (eds) (2008), *The Far Right in Europe: An Encyclopedia*, Oxford: Grennwood World Press

Eatwell, R. and Mudde, C. (eds) (2004), *Western Democracies and the New Extreme Right Challenge*, London, New York: Routledge.

Edgerton, D., Fryklund, B. and Peterson, T. (1994). '*Until the Lamb of God Appears . . .' The 1991 Parliamentary Election: Sweden Chooses a New Political System*, Lund: Lund University Press.

Esping-Andersen, G. (1993), *Changing Classes,* London: Sage.

Fryklund, B. and Peterson, T. (1981), *Populism och missnöjespartier i Norden*, Lund: Arkiv.

— (1983), 'Klass och folklighet', *Sociologisk Forskning*, 1983: 2.

Goldthorpe, J. (2007) *On Sociology*, 2nd edn, Vol. 1, Stanford: Stanford University Press.

Hainsworth, P. (ed.) (2000), *The Politics of the Extreme Right – From the Margins to the Mainstream*, London, New York: Pinter.

Holmberg, S. and Weibull, L. (eds) (2001), *Land du välsignade. SOM-undersökningen 2000*, Göteborg: SOM-institutet.

— (2005), *Lyckan kommer, lyckan går. Trettio kapitel om politik, medier och samhälle. SOM-undersökningen 2004*, Göteborg: SOM-institutet.

Ignazi, P. (2003), *Extreme Right Parties in Western Europe*, New York: Oxford University Press.

Kiiskinen, J. and Saveljeff, S. (2010), *ATT DANSA I OTAKT MED VÄLJARNA – Socialdemokraternas och Moderaternas strategiska bemötande av Sverigedemokraterna*, Malmö: Malmö Studies in International Migration and Ethnic Relations, No. 9 (2010).

Kiiskinen, J., Saveljeff, S. and Fryklund, B. (2007), *Populism and Mistrust of Foreigners: Sweden in Europe*, Integrationsverkets Skriftserie VI.

Kitschelt, H. (1997), *The Radical Right in Western Europe – A Comparative Analysis*, Michigan: The University of Michigan Press.

Kohn, H. (1944), *The Idea of Nationalism. A Study in Its Origins and Background*, New York: Macmillan.

Marsdal, M. (2007), *Frp-koden*, Oslo: Forlaget Manifest.

Meguid, B. (2008), *Party Competition between Unequals: Strategies and Electoral Fortunes in Western Europe*, Cambridge: Cambridge University Press.

Mény, Y. and Surel, Y. (eds) (2002), *Democracies and the Populist Challenge*, Basingstoke: Palgrave Macmillan.

Mudde, C. (2000), *The Ideology of the Extreme Right*, Manchester, NY: Manchester University Press.

— (2007), *Populist Radical Right Parties in Europe*, New York: Cambridge University Press.

— (2008), *Om det politiska*, Hägersten: Tankekraft förlag.

Panizza, F. (ed.) (2005), *Populism and the Mirror of Democracy*, London/New York: Verso.

Ringsmose, J. and Pedersen, K. (2006), 'Fra protest til indflydelse: Organisatoriske forskelle mellem Fremskridtpartiet og Dansk Folkeparti', i *Tidskriftet Politik*, 8(3): 68–78.

Rydgren, J. (2002), *Radical Right Populism in Sweden: Still a Failure, but for How Long?* Stockholm: Sociologiska Institutionen Stockholms Universitet.

— (2006), *From Tax Populism to Ethnic Nationalism: Radical Right-wing Populism in Sweden*, New York, Oxford: Berghahn Books.

Rydgren, J. and Widfeldt, A. (eds) (2004), *Från Le Pen till Pim Fortuyn – populism och parlamentarisk högerextremism i dagens Europa*, Malmö: Liber.

Saveljeff, S. (2011), *New questions and new answers – Strategies towards parties with a radical right-wing populist profile*, Current Themes in IMER Research No. 11, Malmö: MIM, Malmö University.

Schain, M., Zolberg, A. and Hossay, P. (eds) (2002), *Shadows over Europe: The Development and Impact of the Extreme Right in Western Europe*, New York: Palgrave Macmillan.

Smith, A. D. (1986), *The Ethnic Origins of Nations*, Oxford: Oxford University Press.

Taggart, P. (1996), *The New Populism and the New Politics. New Protest Parties in Sweden in a Comparative Perspective*, London: Macmillan Press.

— (2000), *Populism*, Buckingham: Open University Press.

van Spanje, J. and van der Brug, W. (2007), 'The Party as Pariah: The Exclusion of Anti-Immigration Parties and its Effect on their Ideological Positions', *West European Politics*, 30(5): 1022–40.

Wold, S. O. (2005), *Folk mot elite. Dansk Folkeparti og det norske Fremskrittspartiets populistiske diskurs*, Oslo: hovedoppgave ved Institutt for statsvitenskap, Universitetet i Oslo.

Wright, O. E. (1997), *Class Counts*, Cambridge: Cambridge University Press.

19

The Sweden Democrats Came In from the Cold: How the Debate about Allowing the SD into Media Arenas Shifted between 2002 and 2010

Simon Oja and Brigitte Mral

This chapter explores some problems experienced by the Swedish media and the political establishment in relation to media exposure of *Sverigedemokraterna* (SD), the Sweden Democrats, a nationalist populist party. Since the SD was founded in 1988 the party has had an upward trajectory in its number of votes in parliamentary elections. They did not even experience a setback in 1991 when another right-wing populist party, *Ny Demokrati* (NyD), the New Democracy, came more or less out of the blue, winning 6.7 per cent of the vote and securing 25 seats in parliament. In 2010 SD reached its long-time goal when they gathered 5.7 per cent of the votes and thereby managed to exceed the threshold of 4 per cent representation for the first time, resulting in 20 seats in the parliament.

The SD has a different background than other right-wing populist parties in Scandinavia. The party did not emerge from criticism of high taxes and bureaucracy. Instead, its historical heritage is racism and neo-Nazism, and the party has links to fascist and Nazi ideology through individuals and personal relationships. These affiliations are especially evident in the party's early years. The SD has moved away from this complex background over the past few years, and in many respects has become a different and 'cleaner' party than when it was first founded. So even if SD has been a right-wing populist party in the past, we believe that the term 'national xenophobic party' is a more accurate description of the current party. Additionally, the SD's Nazi history has also led most politicians and the media to consider it, to a greater or lesser degree, to be a threat to democracy. In this chapter, we will present a brief history of the SD and discuss some arguments *pro et contra* allowing the SD into the media and various debate arenas.[1] We will especially focus on the debate about allowing the SD to buy advertising space in newspapers and on TV.[2]

---

[1] The debate concerning access to media and debate arenas is not unique to Sweden. In 2009 there was, for example, a lengthy debate in Great Britain concerning whether the British National Party (BNP) should be allowed to appear on the prime time show *Question Time*. See: http://news.bbc.co.uk/2/hi/8321683.stm [accessed 17 February 2012].

[2] This text summarizes some of the results from a larger project in which both themes are studied during the pre-election periods of 2002, 2006 and 2010.

The Sweden Democrats: An overview

The history of the SD is complicated and the origin of the party is subject to different historiographies. The SD's jubilee publication, *20 röster om 20 år: Sverigedemokraterna 1988–2008* (20 voices about 20 years: the Sweden Democrats 1988–2008), states that the party was formed by approximately 20 people in an apartment in Stockholm on 6 February 1988 (page 194). A book by Stieg Larsson and Mikael Ekman, *Sverigedemokraterna: Den nationella rörelsen* (The Sweden Democrats: The National Movement), presents a slightly different picture. According to Larsson and Ekman, only 7 people were present when the SD was formed (2001: 108). The discussion at that meeting about how to name the party (both 'Sweden Democrats' and 'Swedish Fatherland Party' were proposed) is described in the SD's jubilee publication but not the party's historical links. That there are two different versions of the same story is not unusual per se, but this disparity highlights the complicated relationship that the SD have with their history.

The SD was formed from the openly racist organization *Bevara Sverige Svenskt* (BSS), Keep Sweden Swedish, and a central figure behind the formation of both BSS and the SD was Leif Zeilon who had a background in *Demokratisk Allians*, Democratic Alliance, a relatively unsuccessful extreme right-wing organization (Larsson & Ekman 2001: 56, 108). Another central figure was Sven Davidsson who began his political career in the *Nysvenska Rörelsen*, the New Swedish Movement.[3] Davidsson was the first chairperson of BSS (ibid.: 62). Ekman and Larsson maintain that BSS had a solid background in what they call the 'national movement' (ibid.: 66). The national movement can be described as a heterogeneous, extreme, right-wing, ideological and political movement centred on the ideas of both a strong national state and opposition to a multicultural society. The BSS was not a traditional party but rather like a campaign organization that lobbied for a more restrictive immigration policy and the repatriation of immigrants who were already in Sweden. In a historical perspective, BSS constitutes a kind of bridge between the nationalistic ideas and opinions of the post-war period's national movement, and the nationalistic populism of the SD today. BSS was supposedly an attempt to think innovatively. The goal was to create an organization without becoming a party. The SD is the result of the same persons' attempts to transform the new strategies into a political party. The party has been significantly shaped by the agenda of the party leaders. This makes the history of the party very much a history about its different leaders.

The first leader of the SD was Anders Klarström, who led the party between 1992 and 1995. Klarström came from a background in the national movement and began his political career in the Nazi party *Nordiska Rikspartiet*, the Nordic National Party, and its *Riksaktionsgrupp*, National Action Group (ibid.: 125). The next leader of the SD was Mikael Jansson, who led the party between 1995 and 2005. Unlike Klarström, Jansson received his political schooling in an established party, *Centerpartiet*, the Centre Party, and was therefore familiar with running an election campaign and with the significance

---

[3]   Sweden's only pure ideological fascist party according to Lodenius and Larsson.

of a media image. It was Jansson who began weeding out visible symbols that linked the SD with Nazism (ibid.: 163). The measure that probably attracted most public attention was the ban on uniforms, which was one of Mikael Jansson's first initiatives as party leader. The uniform ban message was repeated in a number of internal bulletins over a period of three years (ibid.: 168–9). Mikael Jansson mentions in his jubilee publication text that the 'ban on uniforms' was an initiative that managed to solve a problem with skinheads who were not welcome at meetings (Jansson 2008: 50). On the other hand, the party chose to retain the torch as party symbol, which strongly resembles the symbol of the Neo-Nazi BNP (Larsson & Ekman 2001: 170).

The third and current leader of the SD is Jimmie Åkesson, who has held the position since spring 2005. Jimmie Åkesson is the first leader who was politically schooled in the SD. Just like Mikael Jansson, the image of the SD is important for Jimmie Åkesson. For a brief period after the SD was formed, the party's symbol was a forget-me-not, but this flower was quickly replaced by the torch (Mattsson 2009: 24). During the spring of 2006, the party executive decided to let members vote on whether the party symbol should be changed; the outcome was to replace the torch with a blue anemone (2008: 204).[4]

Although Jimmie Åkesson was born in 1979, he is a party veteran who joined the SD when he was 15 years old, just when Jansson replaced Klarström as the party leader. Regarding the party's ideology Åkesson sees an unbroken line from when the party was formed until the present day (Lodenius 2009: 22). According to Åkesson, the party took a giant step forward in 1999 when its programme was rewritten. This revision eradicated the 'remains of the party's worst years' (Åkesson 2008: 10). Demands for reinstatement of capital punishment and nationalization of the banking and insurance sectors were abandoned. The party's immigration policy agenda became 'more aligned with reality' which, according to Åkesson, probably was the most significant change. In the same year, 1999, three of the perhaps most notoriously violent crimes connected to the Swedish ultra-right movement took place. An organized syndicalist[5] was murdered by three activists with connections to *Nationell Ungdom* (NU), National Youth. Additionally, two policemen were murdered in Malexander by bank robbers with connections to Nazi movements including the *Nationalsocialistisk Front* (NSF), National Socialist Front. Two journalists in Nacka were also the targets of a car bomb attack (Larsson & Ekman 2001: 172). In a joint article on 30 November 1999, Sweden's four largest newspapers published the names and photos of 62 Nazis and motorcycle gang members who threatened democracy (AB 30 November 1999, DN 30 November 1999, Exp. 30 November 1999, SvD 30 November 1999).[6] This unique co-publication was a direct response to the escalating violence. The initiative created a major political problem for the SD, especially when Aftonbladet published an article in which the SD was described as a forum for people with Nazi sympathies (Gustafsson 1999).

---

[4] The symbols can be found in the SD's jubilee publication, *20 röster om 20 år*, page 213. The former party symbol the torch and the current blue anemone can both be found on the official website for the Sweden Democrats, the forget-me-not is only mentioned in the text. https://sverigedemokra-terna.se/vart-parti/partihistorik/ [accessed 7 June 2012].

[5] A labour movement that advocates a form of socialist economic corporatism.

[6] Aftonbladet (AB), Dagens Nyheter (DN), Expressen (Exp.) and Svenska Dagbladet (SvD).

These acts of violence led to Mikael Jansson distancing himself and the party from Nazism at the beginning of 2000 with an article headlined *Vår avsky för nazismen*, Our loathing of Nazism, in which he wrote that it is 'the democratic parties' responsibility not to sanction or harbour anti-democratic forces' and that: 'As a SD I can ascertain that the sanitation of Nazism is working well'(Jansson 2000).[7] The article is complicated and not explicitly related to the headline, but at the same time this disassociation from Nazism had never been articulated before (Larsson & Ekman 2001: 170–2). One and a half years later, the SD split into two groups – although this seemed due to personal rather than ideological differences the breakaway group claimed that the SD was in the process of being liberalized (ibid.: 183–5). According to Åkesson, the splitting of the SD in 2001 when the breakaway group formed *Nationaldemokraterna* (ND), the National Democrats, was to be seen as one of the most significant events in the party's history. It meant that 'the fools who were still in our party could now leave and join the others' (Åkesson 2008: 11). The advantages of the party split – part of the so-called normalization of SD – can be described as 'radical flank effects' (Rydgren 2005: 129). The radical breakaway group, because of its new stance as a more radical alternative – in this case the ND – normalizes the original party. It is now possible for the moderate group to gain more acceptance for the same position that it previously held because of the breakaway group's more radical stand. Another possible effect is that as the more radical group becomes marginalized, the more moderate group becomes a potential actor for other parties' to open communication with because of the new dynamics.

The SD have continued to win more votes in every election since 1988, when they won a modest 1,118 votes. In the 2002 elections the SD gathered 1.4 per cent of the votes nationally. This big success put them on the national political map. In the 2006 elections, the SD was about one percentage point from entering the Swedish parliament. The party's numbers of votes had more than doubled since the last election, and it received 162,463 votes (or 2.9%). In municipal elections, the party won an entire 281 mandates across 144 municipalities (Expo). The 2006 election signified the passing of yet another important perimeter, specifically the 2.5 per cent mark, which means that the SD qualified for government party support (SCB 2006: 198). In Skåne County[8] the SD was represented in 32 of 33 municipalities after the 2006 election (Mattsson 2009: 118). In the lead up to the 2010 election, there was no doubt that the SD intended to win seats in the parliament. They had reached well over the 4 per cent threshold in several polls (DN, 19 October 2009). By the election 2010 they managed to get 339,610 votes (or 5.7%), which was a number large enough that the party gained representation. They also managed to get seats in the last municipality in Skåne and are now represented in all 33 municipalities.

The election figures for the SD are not remarkable; there are right-wing populist parties across Europe that have achieved far better election results. The success of the SD, however, is an obvious trend (see Figures 19.1 and 19.2).

---

[7]   Translations from Swedish by the writers.
[8]   Skåne County is the most southern administrative county of Sweden.

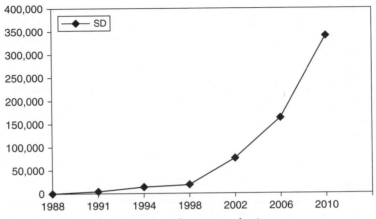

Figure 19.1 Number of votes in parliamentary elections.

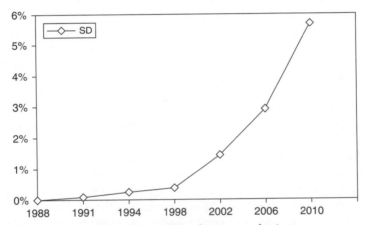

Figure 19.2 Percentage of votes in parliamentary elections.

Media treatment of the Sweden Democrats

The established parties and society at large have distanced themselves from the SD. Up until the 2006 election, the media tried to restrict the SD's media exposure. The parties in parliament also had a joint strategy of avoiding debating with them (Lodenius 2009: 17). Swedish parties have also sought to maintain a *cordon sanitaire*, which means that they have not collaborated with the SD in any way or accepted their anti-immigrant rhetoric or political programmes (Rydgren 2005: 115). But since the SD has continued to gain popularity, there is reason to question this strategy. *Publicistklubbens årsbok*, The Publicists Yearbook for 2007, asked whether the time had come to take the SD seriously (Lodenius 2007). *Expo*, an organization that studies and maps anti-democratic, ultra-right and racist trends in society, has published study material on the SD together with Arbetarnas Bildningsförbund (ABF), the Workers' Educational Association. For example, a guide to handling debates with the SD (ABF and Expo 2007, Bengtsson 2008). In the afterword to *The Sweden Democrats – a national movement*, Larsson and Ekman write: 'The Sweden Democrats cannot be fended off with boycotts, scorn or social welfare initiatives. They can definitely not be fought with knuckle-dusters or violent attacks. This is a political movement and must be addressed as such, with a political opposition that upholds democratic values and freedom of expression' (2001: 327).

The SD today comply with democratic principles and seemingly act within the framework of democracy. For example, they have no obvious, hidden agenda for introducing a dictatorship, according to Lodenius (2009: 35). It could be argued, however, that a party can be democratic in form but not in content. The UN Declaration on Human Rights contains a list of rights that the party does not acknowledge, such as the right of asylum and freedom of religion (ibid.: 35). Expo's Alexander Bengtsson makes a similar analysis and maintains that there are no grounds for calling the SD an anti-democratic party. 'Their views of how democracy should function could be questioned though,' he says (Bengtsson 2008: 14).

The established parties began to take the SD's successes seriously after the 2002 election – particularly the *Socialdemokraterna* (the Social Democrats). In March 2003, the party secretary, Lars Stjernkvist, presented a programme that explained that the Social Democrats would not take part in debates with the SD in a public arena, but that their party politics would be addressed in other forums like municipalities. The Social Democrats also introduced training programmes for municipal politicians to equip them with arguments (Åkervall 2009: 123). After the 2006 election, a certain degree of self-criticism was expressed by the established parties. The Social Democrats, probably one of the most driving parties in this cause, formed a working group for democratic debate where one of the topics would be how to address the SD (ibid.: 131).

The success of the established parties' strategies should be debated. Studies show that the party was successful in the 2006 elections in municipalities where, after the 2002 election, new party coalitions were formed in an attempt to exclude the SD. In fact, the party was more successful in these municipalities than in those where no similar initiatives were taken (Bengtsson 2009b: 149). This same pattern is also reported by Ulla Ekström von Essen in DN after the 2006 election (24 September 2006). In hindsight it is easy to make judgements about different choices that were made, but at the time the reasons might have been good and relevant. But choices of strategy are not final and irreversible, and in this case there were probably good reasons to rethink the strategy. The political parties have, however, never really reversed any strategy decisions; instead, they have gradually changed them. Before the 2002 election, for example, none of the established parties were of the opinion that the SD should be debated. In August 2006, a little over a month before the election day, Erik Ullenhag, representative for Folkpartiet, the Liberal Party, set out a new strategy: the SD should be debated where they were active (Exp., 10 August 2006). And after the election in 2006 the position changed again. Sven-Otto Littorin, representative for Moderaterna, the Conservative Party, declared that the SD should be debated. By this time the Social Democrats had the same strategy as in 2002, but during 2007 they also changed their position. The established parties have not really reversed any strategy, but rather have tried to adapt to the new situation. The same cannot be said for the publicists in the advertising debate. We will now focus on the advertising debate and look at the argumentation as well as the different positions publicists have taken over the years and the reasons given for these stances.

The advertising debate

This analysis is part of a larger study of the public debate about allowing the SD access to the media and political arenas. The analyses of different themes are based on a method that is inspired by and founded on classical pro et contra theory and that also relies on modern argumentation theory (Govier 2001, van Eemeren & Grootendorst 2004, Kock, 2011). Classical pro et contra theory here means Protagoras' theoretical understanding of argumentation. This theory is built on the concept of *dissoi logoi*, that is that any topic of argumentation has at least two sides, one for and one against. (Mendelson 2002) The pro et contra theory has its strength in that it is generated from the practice of debate and highlights the polarization of public debate as a concept. For this reason it makes for an excellent method for structuring modern public debate, as politicians and the media tend to polarize opinions and arguments. However, it is not sufficient to understand and explain the individual arguments in a merely descriptive way. In order to deepen the analysis the method has to be combined with modern argumentation theory. The theory that we found most useful for this is Stephen Toulmin's argumentation model and related terminology. The terms included in the model are data, warrant, backing, claim, qualifier and rebuttal (Toulmin 1958). Data is the information regarded as the base for the argument and claim is the position to which the arguer wants to move the recipient. Warrant is information that gives a reason to move from data to conclusion and in order to make the warrant stronger there can be a backing to the warrant, that is, additional information to support the warrant. Qualifier signals how confident the claim is perceived to be and the rebuttal states conditions in which the claim is no longer valid. Here the Toulmin model will only be used in a modified basic construction concerning data, claim, warrant and backing. By employing the terms it is possible to not only structure what is said but also to determine what is inferred and relevant for the arguments.

The argumentation analysis has a normative part and for that we apply a model for evaluating argumentation used by informal logics. This model for evaluating argumentation functions as a method for making conclusions about the relevance and validity for the various arguments.[9] The argumentation will be analysed in three steps:

---

[9] This methodology is still under development as it is a part of the thesis work of Simon Oja.

1.   Acceptability of the argument;
2.   Relevance of the argument;
3.   Value of the argument.

The first question about the acceptability of an argument aims to investigate if the foundation of the argument is solid, and its meaning based on grounds that we can accept and acknowledge. If we find that the argument is solid we move on to the second question: whether the argument is of any relevance to the issue in question. If we find the argument acceptable in terms of construction and relevant to the issue that is being debated, the third and final step is to evaluate the argument. To analyse argumentation is in itself an argumentative act and it is therefore especially important to disclose the process of the work so that it is clear how and why a specific conclusion is reached. Arguments are not absolute, they can be stronger or weaker and they can shift position. This perhaps makes the third step the most difficult but also the most important. As decisions are made, arguments are evaluated and weighed against one another. Rhetorical argumentation analysis has to include this step as well in order to move beyond a mainly descriptive approach.

In this chapter we present arguments that were given for and against a specific issue in the public debate. We have chosen to focus on the national election campaigns of 2002, 2006 and 2010 and the theme of allowing the SD to buy advertising space in newspapers and on television.[10]

The debate regarding the SD flares up in connection to every election. This trend has been proven throughout the 2000s regardless of whether the issue has been if the SD should be allowed to buy advertising or if the other parties should debate them. Our first example of this is the advertising debate from 2002, which started when the newspaper *Dagens Nyheter* (*DN*) refused to publish an ad from the SD in the early summer (Bergström, DN, 7 July 2002).[11]

Other newspapers continued to make the same decision as *Dagens Nyheter* during the course of the summer, and just ten days before the parliamentary election, *Svenska Dagbladet* also decided to boycott election ads from the SD. All major newspapers had now taken a clear position against publication (*Journalisten*, 6 September 2002). There was a consensus among legally responsible publishers to not allow the party access to their advertisement spaces. What arguments did this group make for boycotting election ads from the SD in 2002? To start with the publisher of the liberal morning paper *Dagens Nyheter*, Hans Bergström, gave two arguments. His first claim was that 'The party has a strong racist streak' which was supported by the warrant that '[the SD's] standpoint is that adopting children from non-European countries should be prohibited.' This warrant was backed up by an example: 'A two-month old baby from North Korea has not been culturally influenced. The notion must be based on racism.' Further, Hans Bergström maintained, as a second argument, that '[the SD's] democratic credentials cannot be trusted' (TT, Göteborgsposten, 8 August 2002), a claim for

---

[10]   The data is collected through searches in media archives to identify occasions when the debate arises in media and then manually locating relevant articles in connection to the debate.
[11]   All articles can be found in Appendix I.

which he gave no warrant or backing. In an article in *Journalisten* (6 September 2002), Bergström gave another reason for his decision: '... I felt extremely uneasy about the idea that DN would be taking the fore and giving legitimacy to the Sweden Democrats in the election campaign.'

When *Svenska Dagbladet* decided to boycott ads from the SD at the end of August, the argument was: 'If we were the only Swedish newspaper that accepted an ad from them [SD], our readers would find that even more offensive' (TT, DN, 23 August 2002). Here one interpretation could be that *Svenska Dagbladet* relied on the same data as those *Dagens Nyheter* had put forward as a claim, namely that SD are racists. Then *Svenska Dagbladet's* claim that ads would be offensive is supported by a warrant grounded in doxa that racism is offensive in Sweden.

The only pro argument that could be found for publishing ads on this occasion was in a letter to the editor in *Dagens Nyheter* where a reader writes: '... boycotting their (or any other party's) ads is a serious move against democracy and freedom of expression in Sweden.' The editor-in-chief of *Dagens Nyheter*, Hans Bergström, responds to this with a counter argument: 'DN has no obligation to give space to Nazi parties, violence-prone parties to the right or the left, or parties with a racist streak' and '[DN] is a free newspaper.' (Bergström, DN, 16 August 2002). The argument pro is based in the data that Sweden has freedom of expression with the implicit claim that SD should be allowed to buy advertising space. The warrant for this could be that Sweden is a democracy with the implicit backing that democracies should allow all parties to buy advertising space. The counter argument uses the fact that the newspaper is independent and not obliged to publish any ads as their data. The claim is that they do not publish ads from Nazi parties, violence-prone parties or racist parties with the implicit warrant that they regard the SD as a racist party.

If we summarize the topics, the justification for refusing to sell advertising space was that the newspapers did not want to support Nazi, violence-prone or racist political parties, that they did not want to give the SD legitimacy, that the SD's democratic credentials could not be trusted, that readers may consider the ads offensive, and that editors in chief were entitled to refuse advertising. This makes the arguments a combination of principles, facts and emotional reasons. On the other hand the advocates for allowing the SD to buy advertising space find their justification in abstract arguments about democracy and freedom of expression.

A similar discussion took place around the same time concerning ads for the SD on Malmö's metropolitan buses. Ads for the party were boycotted and the Managing Director of the bus company Skånetrafiken, Gösta Ahlberg, told the newspaper *Sydsvenskan* that his company did not want to be associated with 'these kinds of parties': 'It's not good for our reputation' (Orrenius, *Sydsvenskan*, 2 June 2002).

Two years later, in 2004, a similar debate about advertising on buses in the Skåne region flared up again. Metropolitan buses in Malmö had agreed to accept ads from the SD. This time, Ahlberg says that Skånetrafiken cannot 'act as a kind of jury' and decide who can and cannot advertise. 'The Sweden Democrats are allowed to take part in Swedish elections. It would be very strange if we decided that they couldn't make their voices heard'. And the manager of metropolitan buses in Malmö, Göran Lundblad, said: 'We consider the message, not the sender. According to our agreement with advertising company Clear Channel, we are not entitled to refuse ads unless the message is derogatory or offensive' (Ivarsson, Sydsvenskan, 4 June 2004). Two years after dismissing the SD with ethical and ethos-arguments in 2002, the only grounds for refusal were now offensive messages because the party now was considered democratically legitimate. The change here was not a shift in the SD politics, as one might assume. Instead, the change from 2002 was that the SD had gathered more votes in the elections in 2002 than they had before. The legitimization therefore lies not in the party's political opinions but in its acceptance in the public sphere and its political support as measured in voters and mandates.

In the lead-up to the 2006 elections, *Dagens Nyheter*, *Svenska Dagbladet* and several other newspapers choose to accept advertising from the SD. The new editor-in-chief for *Dagens Nyheter*, Jan Wifstrand, motivated the decision as follows:

> There is no justification today, in my opinion, for boycotting ads from the Sweden Democrats. They should be judged on each individual message and the design of each ad. A newspaper like DN should have a broad framework for freedom of expression. As long as advertisers do not blatantly violate the constitution or human rights or commit gross ethical errors, they can advertise in DN. (DN 16 June 2006)

This approach in 2006 was new, but soon constituted the journalistic approach towards the SD from most Swedish newspapers. The argumentation has some similarities with the one in Malmö in 2004, most notably in regard to the message being in focus rather then the sender.

Since the election in 2002, the SD had increased from 8 mandates in 5 municipalities to 49 mandates in 29 municipalities. *Svenska Dagbladets* editor-in-chief Lena K. Samuelsson argued that the SD now was so well legitimized that an advertising boycott could no longer be justified. 'The party has simply become more established in our democratic system'. Several ads had already appeared in the local press, including *Sydsvenska Dagbladet*. *Sydsvenskan's* editor-in-chief Peter Melin says, 'We have problems with the Freedom of the Press Act as it is. My task is not to restrict it any further' (Letmark, DN, 16 June 2006). Lena K. Samuelsson's argument is very similar to the arguments from the debate in Malmö in 2002. However the argument Peter Melin makes is quite difficult to understand. According to Melin there is a problem with the freedom of press act, but the nature of this problem is not explained.

On 11 August 2006, *Svenska Dagbladet's* editor-in-chief Lena K. Samuelsson wrote:

> A xenophobic cloud hangs over the SD. This is a marginal party whose values are shared by very few thinking people. Even so, the SD became an established party within our political system after the last elections and won seats in a number of democratic assemblies. Boycotting ads from this party does not seem to be the right approach. As a publicist, standing up for freedom of expression is vital. /.../ And for that reason, any new ad requests from the SD will be judged on the same basis as always: the contents must not be illegal or grossly offensive/violating. (SvD, 11 August 2006)

Samuelsson concludes by making a relatively illogical interconnection between defending democratic values and advertising: 'Svenska Dagbladet and Sweden's other major newspapers stand for strong democratic values, freedom, diversity and openness. Values that conflict directly with the SD's concept of reality. /. . ./ To claim that we and other newspapers are helping a xenophobic party is absurd'. Lena K. Samuelsson tries to argue that strong democratic values, support for freedom, diversity and openness counterbalance the power of xenophobic parties. It is as if ads from the SD would work less well in *Svenska Dagbladet* because of the paper's liberal profile. On the editorial pages this might be correct, but the connection between the newspapers editorial texts and ads are much harder to see. Especially when part of being legitimized comes through being accepted in public arenas as newspapers and their ads. Another interesting aspect of Samuelsson's argumentation is that she still viewed the SD as a party whose ideology was structured around conflicts but that the language and categorization had changed. In 2002 the SD were racists but in 2006 they were xenophobic.

Of all the national newspapers, only *Expressen* retained its general advertising boycott from the previous election campaign.[12] *Expressen's* editor-in-chief Otto Sjöberg says, 'I have made a publishing decision: Last year's decision concerning a general boycott remains intact'. His assessment is that the party represents anti-democratic values, regardless of any messages in its ads. In editorial spaces '. . . *Expressen* reports on issues that are journalistically motivated' and 'The party will be reviewed in terms of size and content' according to Sjöberg (Letmark, DN, 16 June 2006). This shows that *Expressen* still viewed the SD in the same way as in 2002, but when it comes to news reporting the paper will treat them as any other party. This statement might be a response to the critique of giving the SD too much coverage in relation to the size of the party and its possibility of influencing politics.

In a leading article in *Expressen* 6 August 2011, Richard Slätt writes that the party's politics have not changed over the past four years.

> The party itself has never initiated the removal of racist formulations in its programs or other official documents. Racist points were only removed after confrontation with the media or political opponents. Before 2002, their program stated that Sweden should be both ethnically and culturally homogeneous. After the National Annual Meeting in 2005, the wording became 'a demographically homogeneous society has better prerequisites . . .' So what is the difference? Nothing. The Sweden Democrats still dream about a White Sweden. Free from 'foreign' influence. (Exp., 6 August 2011)

Richard Slätt targets the problem with the editors' new approach to the SD and that is that nothing has changed when it comes to ideology and politics. Slätt only goes back four years, but as we have mentioned before Jimmie Åkesson regards it as much longer.

---

12 Aftonbladet would also allow ads from the SD if the content was not illegal. Response from the editor-in-chief Anders Gerdin in a reader's question. Published on the same day as the election in 2006.

The argument here is that the editors' cannot justify their change in standpoint as they do. If they viewed the SD as racist in 2002, they still are racists in 2006; that has not changed. So if ads from the SD were dismissed in 2002 based on the party's ideology that policy should stand in 2006 as well, given that the tolerance for the party's opinions and ideology had not developed.

Slätt argues that advertising in newspapers you do not own is not a legal right and concludes with a historic parallel: 'Did the National Socialist German Workers' Party (NSDAP) become more legitimate because they came into power in Germany after 1933?'

In this round, the advocates based their arguments on the principle of the freedom of the press and how the SD now had become more 'legitimate' and how advertising should be based on the content, not the sender; while opponents claimed that the SD represented anti-democratic values, regardless of the content in their ads and – in the long-term – regardless of whether they were democratically elected into municipal or any other kind of assembly.

The lead-up to the parliamentary election in 2010 was the first occasion that the commercial station TV4 was allowed to broadcast political ads in connection with national elections, and the channel immediately agreed to sell advertising space to the SD. The managing director of the TV4 Group, Jan Scherman, commented on the decision in *Dagens Nyheter*,

> We have looked into all the rules and regulations and decided to offer space to all parties who support a democratic constitution in their party programs and comply with the democratic principles described in the Radio and Television Act. We cannot choose advertisers because of how much we value their individual appearances. The Sweden Democrats have won seats in a number of democratic assemblies – and if we say no, they could take the case to the European Court of Justice. (TT, DN, 1 July 2009)

All newspapers except for *Aftonbladet* and to a certain extent the free newspaper, *Metro*, were now willing to accept ads from the SD. The responsible publisher for *Dagens Nyheter*, Torbjörn Larsson, says, 'We have freedom of expression in Sweden and we make a decision about each individual ad. Whether we publish or not depends on the content' (DN, 17 September 2009). *Expressen's* editor-in-chief Thomas Mattson says:

> If they [the ads] fall within the framework of the Freedom of the Press Act and are not offensive or violating, then the principled approach should be to publish. Expressen is a liberal newspaper, we believe in free speech, the power of debate and democratic discourse. I do not therefore support a general boycott. An SD ad that claimed that all crime is carried out by immigrants would be stopped but an SD ad that claimed that child benefits should be raised by 75 SEK would be accepted. (DN, 17 September 2009)

On the same day, *Aftonbladet* published an explanation of its negative attitude under the heading 'Why we stop the SD's election ads'. The newspaper stated that 'A populist, xenophobic movement is taking hold of the public discourse and in the long-term, politicians. As publicists, we have no desire to sit on the sidelines and watch this happen' (Helin & Mellin, AB, 17 September 2009).

Aftonbladet also addressed the argument that there was no reason to boycott the SD if their ad texts did not break the law. *Aftonbladet* called this a 'passive and convenient journalistically-correct line' and that it 'dodges an important debate and paves the way for a xenophobic agenda in Sweden's public discourse'. *Aftonbladet* also speculated that the factual content of SD's ads will, in all probability, be harmless: 'A child in an idyllic setting ("Bullerbyn" – Noisy Village) under the word "freedom", type of thing'. But, they wrote, 'the emotions that the Sweden Democrats are appealing to are not harmless. The emotional rhetoric of the Sweden Democrats has a double agenda that we do not want to convey. The core is always to define the unknown as a threat, that immigrants are a problem'.

Aftonbladet's argumentation for boycotting ads from the SD even though they might not break the law shows obvious similarities with *Expressen's* argumentation from the previous election campaign in 2006. There is also another similarity to *Expressen's* argumentation in the article. Like Richard Slätt four years earlier – although less explicitly and more generally – *Aftonbladet* makes a connection to the situation prior to the Second World War by stating that '[the SD has] the same ideologies that the National Movement has held since the 1920s'.

As a small point of interest, *Metro*, the free commuter newspaper that survives on advertising revenue, circumvented issues related to both freedom of the press and politics by rejecting the SD with a marketing argument. Swedish Metro's managing director, Andreas Ohlson, said on 19 October 2009, 'We want to offer an attractive advertising space to our advertisers and must therefore reserve the right to refuse advertising space at our own discretion' (Schori, Dagens Media). Consideration for other advertisers was the reason given – in other words: they did not want to risk losing customers.

The main lines of argument are thus fairly obvious. The actors who advocate accepting ads from the SD quote freedom of press and freedom of expression arguments and that they judge the content of the ads, not the sender. Neither of these arguments are particularly sustainable because the immediate objection is that the newspapers would hardly publish advertising from explicit Nazi or left-wing radical groups even though the message were supposedly harmless. Freedom of press and freedom of expression are important and central in a democracy, but that alone does not make them sustainable arguments in this debate. The possibility to advertise in media is not the same thing as an absolute right to have ads published. Advertising is a business deal and it is up to each newspaper and TV channel to make its own choices. This is not to be confused with the freedom to express opinions. Freedom of the press is not just the freedom to publish without governmental oversight, it is also the freedom to choose to not publish.

Critics and others who refuse to sell advertising space to the SD do so because of the party's ideology, which they maintain is xenophobic and right-wing populist even though the advertisers' messages seem harmless. An example of how ads from the SD look like is a poster/ad used in the election to the European parliament in 2009. The poster shows a gravelled road on the countryside with tall grass on the sides and a lake in the background. On the road there are two blond children walking, a girl with a basket in one hand and flowers in the other and a boy with a fishing rod in one hand and box for his fishing equipment in the other. Above them there is a text that reads: *Ge oss Sverige tillbaka!* (Give us Sweden back!). On a white banner below them it reads: *Sverigedemokraterna. Trygghet & tradition* (Sweden Democrats. Security & tradition).

This shift towards a softer public image has created a problem for the advocates for boycotting the SD ads on grounds that they are anti-democratic. The party has worked hard to exonerate itself and during the process won representation in municipals, gathered more votes on the national level and become an alternative for a larger group of voters.

Worth noting, however, is how fast most newspapers have changed their policies and how the reasons for publication that were considered weak in 2002 – arguments for democracy and freedom of expression – are now relied upon by most newspapers. This is particularly evident in the case of *Expressen* and *Dagens Nyheter* where the opinions of the editors-in-chief in both 2002 and 2006 are diametrically opposed to those of the current editors-in-chief. As a consequence *Dagens Nyheter* and *Expressen* accepted political campaign ads from the SD in the 2010 election campaign. *Aftonbladet* on the other hand had a new editor-in-chief and went back to their previous position as of 2002 and refused to print political campaign ads from the SD, regardless of how harmless the message might have been.

The SD are now represented on all levels in the Swedish democratic system and still remain a controversial party. There are valid reasons and arguments to be made for both sides in the debate on the publishing of political campaign ads. As we have illustrated, valid arguments are not exclusive to one side or the other. And the answer of how to handle the situation of political campaign ads from controversial parties is not in any way a given. The decisions in Swedish media are not final. This is a debate that will probably rise again, if not before, then in connection with the election in 2014. And as these decisions have become a topic for public debate, the argumentation should be made as clear as possible and the arguments should be well-founded, because exposure within the media implies legitimization of a party. If the media have doubts about the politics of the SD it is not enough to say, for example, that the newspaper has a liberal view and embodies democratic values. That response represents a mixed argument and is not constructive in forming an opinion as to the appropriateness of publishing ads. The main objective for public debate should be to make it easier for the public to form an opinion. If that can be achieved, then it is perhaps also more likely that we as a society make decisions that we are satisfied with, even in retrospect.

Appendix I

Aftonbladet

Aftonbladet, 'De vill störta demokratin – Unik kartläggning: 62 av Sveriges värsta nazister och MC-kriminella', *Aftonbladet,* 30 November 1999.

Gustavsson, M. 'Ett nätverk för nazister – Sverigedemokraterna pekas ut av avhoppare', *Aftonbladet,* 2 December 1999.

Helin, J. and Mellin, L. 'Därför stoppar vi SD:s valannonser', *Aftonbladet*, 17 September 2009.
Linderborg, Å., 'Stoppad av Sverigedemokraterna', *Aftonbladet*, 20 October 2009.

Dagens Nyheter

Bergström H., 'Brev till utgivaren', *Dagens Nyheter*, 16 August 2002.
— 'Den råa högerpopulismen', *Dagens Nyheter*, 7 July 2002.
Dagens Nyheter, 'Aftonbladet ensam om konsekvent SD-bojkott', *Dagens Nyheter*, 17 September 2009.
— 'Hotet mot demokratin: Våldet skrämmer till tystnad', *Dagens Nyheter*, 30 November 1999.
— 'I en enkel värld', *Dagens Nyheter*, 19 October 2009.
Ekström von Essen, U. 'Sverigedemokraterna har kommit för att stanna', *Dagens Nyheter*, 24 September 2006.
Letmark, P., 'Fritt fram för Sverigedemokraterna att annonsera', *Dagens Nyheter*, 16 June 2006.
TT, 'Svd stoppar också rasistisk annons', *Dagens Nyheter*, 23 August 2002.
TT, 'Fritt fram för Sd-reklam i Tv4' *Dagens Nyheter*, 1 July 2009.

Dagens Media

Schori, M., 'Metro: Vårt beslut ligger fast', *Dagens Media*, 19 October 2009.

Expressen

Expressen, 'Hotet mot rättvisan. De vill skrämma alla till tystnad', *Expressen*, 30 November 1999.
Slätt, R., 'Gå inte på Sd:s trick', *Expressen*, 11 August 2006.
Ullhagen, E., 'Svenska tidningar gör Sd rumsrena', *Expressen*, 10 August 2006.

Göteborgsposten

TT, 'DN stoppar annons', *Göteborgsposten*, 8 August 2002.

Journalisten

Journalisten, 'Totalt annonsstopp för Sd' *Journalisten*, 6 September 2002.

Svenska Dagbladet

Dunér, H., 'TV4 säger ja till SD' *Svenska Dagbladet*, 18 September 2009.
Samuelsson, L., 'Yttrandefriheten är också viktig, Ullenhag', *Svenska Dagbladet*, 11 August 2006.
Svenska Dagbladet, 'Hotet mot rättsstaten. Nazistgrupper och MC-gäng sätter lagen ur spel', *Svenska Dagbladet*, 30 November 1999.

Sydsvenskan

Ivarsson, D., 'Region Skåne stoppar sd:s bussreklam', *Sydsvenskan*, 4 June 2004.

Orrenius, N., 'Sd-reklam okej på Skånebussar', *Sydsvenskan*, 3 June 2004.

References

20 röster om 20 år: Sverigedemokraterna 1988–2008 (2008), Helsingborg: Blåsippans förlag.

Åkesson, J. (2008), 'Främst var det EU-frågan som drog mig till politiken', in *20 röster om 20 år: Sverigedemokraterna 1988–2008*, Helsingborg: Blåsippans förlag, pp. 5–16.

Åkervall, J. (2009), 'Ett delikat dilemma', in *Högerpopulismen – En antologi om Sverigedemokraterna*, Stockholm: Premiss, pp. 119–42.

Arbetarnas bildningsförbund & Expo (2007), *Sverigedemokraterna – ett parti som andra? Ett studiematerial om Sveriges största parti utanför riksdagen*, Stockholm: ABF.

Bengtsson, A. (2008), *Sverigedemokraterna har fel. Så tar du debatten*, Stockholm: Stiftelsen Expo.

Bengtsson, H. (2009a), *Högerpopulismen – En antologi om Sverigedemokraterna*, Stockholm: Premiss.

— (2009b), 'Bekämpa rädslan!', in *Högerpopulismen – En antologi om Sverigedemokraterna*, Stockholm: Premiss, 11, pp. 143–53.

Govier, T. (2001), *A Practical Study of Argument*, Belmont, CA: Wadsworth Thompson Learning.

Jansson, M. (2008), 'Nästan 20 år nu, Sverigevänner!', in *20 röster om 20 år: Sverigedemokraterna 1988–2008*, Helsingborg: Blåsippans förlag, pp. 47–80.

— (2000), *Vår avsky för nazismen* SD-Bulletin, February.

Kock, C. (2011), 'Kvalitet I offentlig debat – hvad er det?' *Fred og Frihed*, 89(29): 4–7.

Larsson, S. and Ekman, M. (2001), *Sverigedemokraterna: Den nationella rörelsen*, Stockholm: Ordfront.

Lodenius, A.-L. (2009), 'Sverigedemokraternas historia', in *Högerpopulismen – En antologi om Sverigedemokraterna*, Stockholm: Premiss, 31, pp. 11–41.

Lodenius, A.-L. (ed.) (2007), *Publicistklubbens årsbok 2007* Journalister & extremister.

Mattsson, P. (2009), *Sverigedemokraterna in på bara skinnet: reportage*, Stockholm: Natur & Kultur.

Mendelson, M. (2002), *Many Sides. A Protagorean Apporach to the Theory, Practice and Pedagogy of Argument*, Dordrecht: Kluwer Academic.

Poohl, D., 'Fakta: Sverigedemokraterna' Expo. <http://expo.se/2010/fakta-sverigedemokraterna_3530.html> [accessed 20 February 2012].

Rydgren, J. (2005), *Från skattemissnöje till etnisk nationalism: högerpopulism och parlamentarisk högerextremism i Sverige*, Lund: Studentlitteratur.

Statistiska centralbyrån (2008), *Allmänna valen 2006. Del 4. Specialundersökningar*, Stockholm: Statistiska centralbyrån.

The Sweden Democrats official website <https://sverigedemokraterna.se/vart-parti/partihistorik/> [accessed 7 June 2012].

Toulmin, S. (1958), *The Uses of Argument*, London: Cambridge University Press.

van Eemeren F. and Grootendorst, R. (2004), *A Systematic Theory of Argumentation. The Pragma-dialectical Approach*, Cambridge: Cambridge University Press.

20

Nationalism and Discursive Discrimination against Immigrants in Austria, Denmark and Sweden

Kristina Boréus

In a TV debate prior to the 2006 general election in Austria, the leader of the BZÖ, one of two parties on the far right in that election campaign, stated in reference to people receiving social assistance in Vienna that: '. . . 25% are foreigners . . . I think that's unfair. In my opinion social spending should be for Austrians and not for foreigners'.[1]

This statement is clearly discriminatory against people living in the city who are considered to be 'foreign', most likely including people who immigrated long ago as well as their children who were born in the country. First, it is discriminatory since exclusion from social rights is proposed for a particular group of citizens of Vienna. Second, the statement is discriminatory since it is an example of how 'foreigners' were constantly presented in a negative light (in this case, as living on welfare) by the party. Proposals for unfavourable treatment and negative other-presentation are two kinds of discrimination that can be performed linguistically. The quote also expresses a kind of nationalism in which native Austrians are seen as rightful receivers of benefits that non-natives should not be entitled to.

Discrimination against immigrants by native populations is a serious problem in Europe. The rise of populist parties on the far right – such as the BZÖ – in several European countries (Merkl & Weinberg 2003, Mudde 2007) increases the risk of immigrants being discriminated against. So do certain kinds of nationalism. This chapter is about how different aspects of nationalism might contribute to a specific kind of discrimination against immigrants, that is, discursive discrimination (DD), both by making a more fertile breeding ground for parties like the BZÖ and by creating general discursive frames that permit DD. This chapter is a contribution to an empirically based understanding of how different forms of nationalism might be related to discursive discrimination.

---

[1] In *Wahlkonfrontation 06*, 6 September 2006. All quotes from election propaganda in this chapter are my translations from German, Danish or Swedish.

The argument of the chapter proceeds in three steps. First, I clarify some connections between certain aspects of nationalism and DD at the conceptual level. Second, I reveal some similarities and differences in relation to DD in corpora from three countries that have witnessed varying degrees of success for far-right parties: Austria, Denmark and Sweden. Third, the empirical findings regarding DD are discussed in the light of scholarly literature on nationalism in these countries.

Discursive discrimination and nationalism

Discrimination is defined here as the unfavourable treatment of people due to their (alleged) belonging to a particular group. Discrimination can be carried out by different means (e.g. by violence and force, by economic means or by the use of language, as in the quote above) and in different contexts. *Discursive* discrimination is unfavourable treatment through the use of language; it is discrimination manifested in discourse.

The term 'discourse' refers to patterns of language use, the more or less strict rules that regulate what categories are used and what tends to be stated about a subject in a particular context. Thus, a discourse is a kind of social practice (see Reisigl & Wodak 2001: 36). DD is normally entangled with other forms of discriminatory social practice in a society: the BZÖ and other parties do not only *propose* infringements of immigrants' social rights, they also support social practices that actually disfavour non-natives economically by means other than the merely discursive. DD and racism in discourse have been studied by means of different analytical concepts (e.g. Blommaert & Verschueren 1998, van Dijk 1993, 2002, Reisgl and Wodak 2001, Boréus 2006a). Two concepts, referring to different kinds of DD, are used here: proposals for unfavourable treatment and negative other-presentation.

Proposals for unfavourable treatment are claims to the effect that a group of people should be denied the rights that others in society have as well as the defence of ongoing treatment of this kind. In the case of immigrants, the right of abode, political rights, social rights and cultural rights are often at stake. Of importance in the empirical results presented below are issues having to do with the right of abode and cultural rights. People have a *right of abode* when they have the right to live in a certain territory. *Cultural rights* include the rights to engage in cultural practices that are customary within the group that an individual identifies with. Attempts at forced assimilation conflict with cultural rights.

Negative other-presentation is often a focal point in studies on discursive discrimination (e.g. van Dijk 1993) and is expressed when one group portrays another group as inferior. This can be done in several more or less explicit linguistic ways. In this chapter I exemplify negative other-presentation with *presumptions*, that is, information for which it is taken for granted that receivers of a message delivered in a particular context will know and accept (Chilton 2004: 64–5, 80). An example of this is when a party demands, as part of its election campaign, that 'foreigners' that commit crimes be deported. Presumed knowledge here could mean that the demands that a party chooses to present in its election campaigns are justified by what the party wants to portray as serious problems, hence that the criminality of foreign residents is a serious problem. In this way 'foreigners' are presented by that party as causing a serious problem through their criminal activities, but without explicit statements being made to that effect.

Nationalism might be related to DD, since it involves drawing borders between 'us' and 'them', thus allowing for differential treatment of groups. My starting point is theories on nationalism according to which nations are anything but natural entities: they are *constructed* through social practice, ranging from physical border controls to the patterns of what is said and written. Nations are *imagined communities* (Anderson 1991), to a large extent discursively constructed (Wodak et al. 2009). An imagined national community rests on the idea that we belong together with people that we do not know but who share our nation, including people of other generations, even those not yet born.

Nationalism changes over time (Hall 1998) and is often diffuse. It is also context-bound (see Suszycki 2007 for a study of how different kinds of Swedish nationalism are expressed in different contexts). Despite this, there is a certain stability in the way a particular imagined community constructs itself. The construction of people and country can vary between imagined communities in at least three ways which are of relevance to DD.

The first important way in which imagined communities differ is in accordance with the strength of *ethnic nationalism*. Members might, in principle, see themselves as united only by certain political principles and include everyone living in a territory in the imagined community, what is referred to in the literature as civic or state nationalism (see, for example, Hall 1998: 23–4, Wodak et al. 2009: 18–21). Most or perhaps all imagined communities, however, display more or less strong elements of ethnic nationalism, sometimes used as the only definition of nationalism, such as that by Gellner (1983: 1), according to whom nationalism is a political principle which holds that political and national units should be congruent. Despite such definitions, the criteria for inclusion that accompany civic nationalism are also at work in discourses having to do with the nation. Commonly, criteria for inclusion based on civic and ethnic nationalism are expressed in different discursive contexts within the same country, and even the same speaker might express both kinds of nationalism (see Reisigl 2007 for examples of this).

The strength of ethnic nationalism in the national cocktail of self-definition has consequences for attitudes to immigrants. A very strong form of ethnic nationalism is *nativism*, defined by Mudde (2007: 19) as an ideology that 'holds that states should be inhabited exclusively by members of the native group ("the nation") and that nonnative elements (persons and ideas) are fundamentally threatening to the homogenous nation-state'. Strong ethnic nationalism makes it difficult for immigrants to become insiders; the imagined community is more closed if ethnic nationalism is strong than if it is weak. The linguistic categories chosen for the separating of outsiders from insiders and how they are discursively related can emphasize the otherness of immigrants if ethnic nationalism is strong.

Being an outsider is not the same as being discriminated against: immigrants *might* be treated as honoured guests. The outsider position is, however, seldom safe: hospitality can easily be exhausted. For that reason, the ease or difficulty with which one can be accepted as a member is relevant for discrimination. Furthermore, strong ethnic nationalism might motivate assimilation politics – if they want to be here they have to adapt – and other treatment based on the understanding that the presence of non-natives is a threat, such as keeping them out in the first place or trying to get rid of them. Strong ethnic nationalism is thus commonly expressed as discursive discrimination either in the form of negative other-presentation (outsiders are presented as threats) or as proposals for unfavorable treatment, such as pushing for assimilation or keeping threatening outsiders at bay by other means.

The second and third ways in which imagined communities might differ in terms of importance regarding the attitudes towards immigrants, and thus DD, are related to the cultural and political traits considered important in the self-construction of the community. How does an imagined community construct its members in relation to outsiders – what is its '*homo nationalis*' (Wodak et al. 2009: 4) like? The *construction of the nation-state* that the members inhabit also matters. Some constructions of the members of an imagined community and their country are more compatible with DD than others. Again, both negative other-presentation and proposals for unfavourable treatment are at stake here. The former might be expressed when outsiders are compared to the 'we'-construction. The two kinds of construction will also affect what

Table 20.1 Connections between the characteristics of imagined communities, treatment of immigrants and discursive expressions

Character of imagined community	Relation to treatment of immigrants	Discursive expressions
strength of ethnic nationalism	strong ethnic nationalism: (1) makes it difficult to become a member, which increases the risk of discrimination (2) justifies attempts to keep immigrants out, to assimilate or to get rid of them	strong ethnic nationalism: (1) the categories separating outsiders from insiders that emphasize outsiders' otherness are chosen (2) DD as negative other-presentation: immigrants as threatening (3) DD as proposals for unfavourable treatment in line with attempts to assimilate or get rid of immigrants
characteristics of the *homo nationalis*	different self-constructions compatible with different ways of conceptualizing and treating immigrants	(1) other-presentation in relation to construction of the self (2) proposals for treatment in accordance with the characteristics of *homo nationalis*
characteristics of the nation-state/ country	different constructions compatible with different ways of treating immigrants	proposals for treatment in accordance with the characteristics of the nation-state

'we' consider as legitimate treatment of 'them'. Table 20.1 summarizes the discussion. Before I turn to the second step of the argument, I will briefly present the study from which the empirical examples of DD are drawn.

An analysis of discursive discrimination in election campaigns

The results presented below are drawn from a discourse analysis of texts from general election campaigns in Austria, Denmark and Sweden after 1985.[2] The corpora were analysed using coding instructions designed to identify ways in which people are categorized and the expressions of DD. The rhetoric of all parliamentarian parties was analysed. The choice of these particular countries was motivated by a research design according to which discourses in countries that have seen varying degrees of success of populist radical-right parties could be compared. As shown in Figure 20.1, radical-right parties have, comparatively, been very strong in Austria, fairly strong in Denmark and weak in Sweden.

Nationalism of certain kinds may provide a good breeding ground for radical-right parties, as well as being conducive to DD: the modern radical-right parties have generally been ethnic nationalist and highly critical of both immigration and immigrants. These

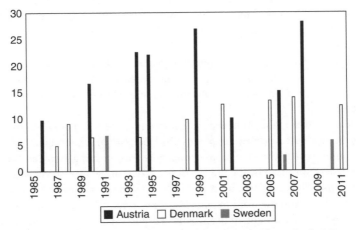

Figure 20.1 Percentage of votes in general elections for radical-right parties since 1985 (when receiving more than 2% of the vote)[3]

---

[2] The general election campaigns in Austria 1986, 1994 and 2006, the Danish campaigns in 1987, 1994, 2007 and 2011, and the Swedish campaigns in 1988, 1991, 1994, 1998, 2002, 2006 and 2010 were analysed. The corpora include transcripts from interviews with party representatives and debates between them arranged by the leading public service TV channels, election platforms, programmes on immigration and immigrant politics, etc.

[3] The parties represented in Figure 20.1 are the Austrian Freedom Party (*Freiheitliche Partei Österreichs*), FPÖ and BZÖ (*Bündnis Zukunft Österreich*) in Austria, Denmark's Progress Party (*Fremskridtspartiet*), the Danish People's Party (*Dansk Folkeparti*) and, in Sweden, New Democracy (*Ny Demokrati*) and the Sweden Democrats (*Sverigedemokraterna*).

aspects of the parties' policies have been well studied (e.g. for Austria Reisigl & Wodak 2001, Heinisch 2002, Wodak & Pelinka 2002, Krzyżanowski & Wodak 2009, Meret 2009; for Denmark Trads 2002, Ringsmose 2003, Meret 2009; for Sweden Westlind 1996, Rydgren 2005, von Essen & Fleischer 2006 and several others). However, the European radical-right parties do not stand alone in formulating policies that curb immigration and affect immigrants negatively. Examples of such policies are on the agendas of several of the mainstream parties, as will be shown below.

The discourse analysis shows that DD was expressed in the election campaigns in all three countries. In general, this was more explicit and more common in the countries with stronger radical-right parties (see Boréus 2010 for a comparison of proposals for the exclusion of immigrants from various rights and of negative other-presentation in four Danish and Swedish election campaigns). There are differences between the Austrian and Danish discourses. The results reported here reveal differences, in particular between Austria and Denmark on the one hand, and Sweden on the other.

Insiders and outsiders in the imagined community

Although there are also references in all the corpora to particular ethnic or religious groups among immigrants (not least to Muslims in the later election campaigns), a much more common way to separate people is into categories that lump together national outsiders. These categories are basically of two kinds:

1.   Categories that highlight the migration process or the sorting criteria used by authorities. 'Immigrant', 'refugee', 'asylum-seeker' and many different subcategories of 'refugee' (e.g. 'convention refugee') were used in all three countries.
2.   Categories that highlight how people sorted into them *do not belong* to the nation. In all the Austrian campaigns, the label *Ausländer*, 'foreigner', was commonly used, while the more strongly distance-creating *Fremden*, 'aliens'/ 'foreigners', was used by the radical-right parties. In the Danish corpus, *udlænding*, 'foreigner', was used, particularly by the parties most critical of immigration, and the word *fremmede* (corresponding to *Fremden*) was regularly used by the radical right. In the Swedish corpus, categories of this kind were not used, not even by the radical-right parties.

Thus, the acceptance of expressions that highlight the 'otherness' of non-natives in the Austrian and Danish public debates might indicate that the imagined communities in Austria and Denmark are more closed than the Swedish one, and thus that the presence of ethnic nationalism is stronger in the former countries.

The way groups are related to each other in all three countries indicates however that it might not be an easy task to become a member of the imagined community in any of them. All the corpora include examples of those who have immigrated being related to original insiders in a way that shows that the groups are non-overlapping – that the immigrants are not insiders – even when they have lived in the country for a long time. An example from the Austrian Social Democrats, the SPÖ, is: '. . . to contribute to a coexistence of *natives /Inländer/* and *foreigners /Ausländer/* based on understanding'.[4] A Danish example is '. . . some of the *foreigners /udlændinge/* that there is so much talk about, there are actually some that contribute . . . to *Danes* being able to get work at Danish enterprises, to workplaces not moving out but staying in this country'.[5]

An example from the Swedish campaigns is a party leader claiming that '. . . the *immigrant* group. They're incredibly enterprising and they're much more enterprising than *Swedes* are'.[6] Even more telling is: 'A group of *Swedish citizens with a foreign background* have worked actively in the Czech Republic, Poland and in the Baltic republics together with *Swedish workmates*'.[7] Here, Swedish citizens 'with a foreign background' are not among the Swedish workmates: apparently it takes more than citizenship to become Swedish.

None of the quotes above express DD: they are neither proposals for unfavourable treatment nor negative other-presentations. However, discrimination against immigrants is made possible by the sorting mechanism at work: discursive discrimination against immigrants as immigrants would be impossible were they not conceptually separated from the rest of the population, as in the examples. In the following sections I provide several examples of how those including themselves among the national 'we' discriminate discursively against immigrants. Here, the differences between the countries are more salient. Central themes in the Austrian and Danish – but not Swedish – election campaigns were the importance of keeping immigrants out and assimilating those living in the country, as well as claims to the effect that 'foreigners' should be thrown out.

Keep them out!

The radical-right parties in all three countries campaigned on policies of reduced immigration. In Austria and Denmark, though not in Sweden, immigrants, particularly refugees, were clearly talked about as being *unwanted*, even by mainstream parties. It was made clear that keeping them out is good. Where they have managed to get in, it is a good thing if they do not get the chance to stay permanently.

The Austrian 2006 campaign provides clear examples. The Austrian People's Party, ÖVP, the dominating right-wing party, described the good achievements of the government they had been leading. Under the heading 'Austria. It is going well for us here', it was claimed that the number of asylum applicants had decreased between 2005 and 2006, that the number of naturalized persons had decreased and that the number of residence permits was decreasing. In other words, the right-wing government had managed to keep 'them' out, or at least keep them in a position where they were easy to get rid of, as is the case with non-citizens and even more so with those lacking permanent residence permits.[8] The Social Democrats in opposition did not agree. According to them, the proportion of foreigners was very high in Austria, compared to that in other countries, and the influx had

---

[4] *Das Wahlprogramm der Sozialdemokratischen Partei Österreichs. Es geht um viel. Es geht um Öster-reich*, 1994. All italics in quotes have been added by me.
[5] Representative of the Left Liberal Party (*Radikale Venstre*) in the TV interview *Mød partierne*, 28 August 2011.
[6] Leader of the Centre Party in the final TV debate, *Slutdebatten*, 17 September 2010.
[7] The programme *En offensiv mot diskrimineringen i arbetslivet*, the Liberal Party, 1994.
[8] In *Kursbuch. Zukunft.*

been higher under the right-wing government than during the previous SPÖ government. 'Immigration must serve Austrian interests', it was stated.[9] (See also Figure 20.2.)

The radical right in all of the countries campaigned on limiting immigration. Here, asylum applicants and refugees who have obtained asylum are presented as a threat if the presumptions are interpreted as stating that (a) the asylum process and the reception of refugees in Austria is very costly, which (b) threatens the possibility for Austrian society to pay out (old-age) pensions, entailing (c) a threat to the security of the pensioners. Another presumption is that the economic security of Austrian pensioners should be privileged over spending millions of Euros on asylum seekers.

As Michał Krzyżanowski shows in his chapter in this volume, the FPÖ rhetoric has shifted to targeting Muslims since 2005. The transition from the phase when 'the political elite' was portrayed as the main enemy of the Austrian people to one during which labour immigrants, refugees and asylum applicants were constructed as the most important enemies (Heinisch 2002: 113ff) is clearly visible when the election campaigns of 1986 and 1994 are compared. The change towards targeting Muslims is apparent in the 2006 campaign. Immigrants were still made main targets in 2006, however. The two posters depicted in this chapter were part of a series of three 'statt' ('instead of') posters,

Figure 20.2 FPÖ poster in Vienna in September 2006: 'Secure pensions instead of millions for asylum'.

---

[9] In the folder *AUS VERANTWORTUNG FÜR ÖSTERREICH: Integration beschleunigen. Zuwanderung steuern. Illegalität stoppen.*

of which a variety of the poster *Daham statt Islam* described in Krzyżanowski's chapter (in that case as used in the 2008 election campaign), was the third.

The preference for policies intended to 'keep them out' is also visible in the Danish 2007 campaign. The leader of the Social Democrats was criticized by the right-wing parties for having proposed that refugees from Iraq, residing in asylum centres and who could not be sent back due to the situation in the country they had fled from, should be allowed to live and work outside the centres until they could be sent back. The accusation, repeated throughout the campaign, was that such policies would turn Denmark into a 'magnet' for immigrants, clearly an unwanted effect.[10]

Although the 'keep them out' rhetoric does not explicitly express a negative other-presentation, it rests on presumptions that are derogative. Even if we are not told why, 'they' are presumably problematic and threatening.

'Keep them out' rhetoric is not expressed by mainstream parties anywhere in the Swedish corpus.[11] Thus, these results also indicate stronger ethnic nationalism in Austria and Denmark than in Sweden, as do the results presented in the next section.

Assimilate them!

The radical-right parties in all three countries called for the assimilation of immigrants. In Austria and Denmark, though not in Sweden, assimilation (under the label of 'integration') was demanded of immigrants, even by mainstream parties, especially in the later campaigns. In the Austrian 2006 campaign, the ÖVP, in particular, focused on integration. A central slogan of theirs was 'Promote and require integration'.[12] What then were immigrants obliged to do? A central claim was that they should learn German, but the demands did not end there: 'This includes for us, however, also assuming the historic and cultural background of our country and accepting the fundamental social order that is based on freedom, tolerance and equality in chances for all people…'.[13] The SPÖ stated that '[w]e expect that immigrants accept their own responsibility to learn German and to learn and accept common values, equal citizen rights and the rights of women'.[14] (See also Figure 20.3.)

During Denmark's 2007 elections, similarly vague calls for 'integration' were made by the mainstream parties. The leading right-wing party, *Venstre*, expressed that 'Danes with [an] immigrant background should not only speak Danish and work or educate themselves. They should also know and respect the principles that the Danish democracy rests upon.'[15]

---

[10] In *Duellen Valg 07*, the TV debate between the right-wing prime minister and the leader of the Social Democrats, 4 November 2007 and in the final TV debate, *Afslutningsdebat*, 11 November.

[11] Although the Social Democrats were against a proposal by some right-wing parties in the campaign of 2002 to permit labour immigration from outside the EU, refugee immigration has not been contested by any of the mainstream parties, and parties in government have not taken credit for measures that keep immigration down in their propaganda material.

[12] In *Kursbuch. Zukunft*, the folder *Wolfgang Schüssel*, at www.oevp.at in September 2006 and in other material.

[13] www.oevp.at in September 2006.

[14] *AUS VERANTWORTUNG FÜR ÖSTERREICH: Integration beschleunigen. Zuwanderung steuern. Illegalität stoppen*, 2006.

[15] www.venstre.dk in November 2007.

Figure 20.3 FPÖ poster in Vienna in September 2006: 'German instead of "nix understand".

The radical right parties made explicit demands for assimilation. Several things could be interpreted as presumed with regard to this vague demand for knowledge of German to replace answers to the effect that someone does not understand German at all, for example, that many immigrants either know very little German or refuse to learn or to communicate in German, all of which could be interpreted as negative other-presentation in a discourse where it is taken for granted that all immigrants have an obligation to learn the language. How this replacement should be realized is not indicated, however the demand is in line with explicit FPÖ proposals in the campaign, such as the possibility of repealing citizenship due to poor knowledge of German (*FPÖ Wahlprogramm*).

Since there were no explicit policy proposals made in this context, these were not proposals for assimilation proper. This rhetoric is best analysed as a kind of non-explicit negative other-presentation. First, for these to be central points in election campaigns (as they were in Austria in 2006) the presumption is that there is a problem, namely that immigrants resist integration, something clearly seen as negative. Second, statements regarding the things that immigrants should learn to respect – freedom, tolerance, women's rights, democracy – presume that these highly respected values are threatened by the presence of immigrants who might not respect them.

Throw them out!

Another way to cope with the threat of ethnic others is to get rid of them and restrict their right of abode. The Austrian 2006 campaign stands out for its particularly strong calls for limitations on the right of abode. The FPÖ had split the year before, the splinter party, the BZÖ, was still in government and both parties were in parliament. Thus there were two far-right parties with similar programmes competing on the same ground, most of all over immigration and immigrant policy. A salient call made by both parties in the campaign was: Throw them out! Among particular proposals were the following: expel 30 per cent of the foreigners in Austria (BZÖ); make it possible to expel foreigners who have committed a serious crime (BZÖ); expel foreign criminals (FPÖ); recall residence permits for unemployed guest workers (FPÖ); expel people without residence permits (FPÖ); expel foreigners that work illegally (FPÖ); make abuse of the social system grounds for expulsion (FPÖ).[16]

Make use of them!

The Swedish corpus differs from those of the other two countries in terms of a certain representation often being made, that of immigrants as national assets:

> One could also consider the utility aspect. When our international contacts multiply, there is an increasing need in our country for more well-educated people with good language skills. With immigrant children we get these skills. The Centre Party holds that immigrant children constitute a resource for our society that we ought to make better use of.[17]

This rhetoric is certainly another example of the unwillingness or incapacity to let new members of society into the imagined community – 'immigrant children' might even refer to people who were born and raised in Sweden by parents who once immigrated – and it is objectifying. It is, however, not discriminatory in the sense used here: no proposal for unfavourable treatment is made, and it is a case of positive rather than negative other-presentation. 'Immigrants as an asset to the nation' is not found in the corpora from the other countries.[18] The construction of immigrants as a resource for the nation was a discursive pattern in neither case.

Different nationalisms – different discrimination?

The differences relating to DD in the three corpora indicate that there are also differences in the broader discursive frames relating to nationalism. In the third and concluding step of the argument, I will discuss the empirical findings in relation to the

---

[16] The calls were made in different propaganda materials, for example, *FPÖ Wahlprogramm* and *Freiheitlicher Parlamentsklub-BZÖ. Zukunftsprogramm 2010. Unser Beitrag für eine bürgerliche Regierung*.
[17] *Invandrarpolitiskt program*, the Centre Party, 1994.
[18] Although it was sometimes stated that labour immigration was needed, immigrants in the countries are not described as resources for society.

literature on nationalism. Since what was focused on above was certain ways in which Sweden seemingly differs from the other countries, this section will focus particularly on Swedish nationalism.

The empirical examples showed how the imagined community produces outsiders and insiders in three countries, which points to the presence of ethnic nationalism in all of them. In Austria and Denmark labels for outsiders that emphasize their otherness were used, but not in Sweden. From all three corpora, however, it is clear that even immigrants who had lived in the country for a long time were not always part of the in-group. DD was documented in the corpora in several ways. 'Keep them out' rhetoric was produced by Austrian and Danish mainstream parties but not by the Swedish ones. Such rhetoric was interpreted as resting on negative other-presentation. Vague assimilation demands were expressed by the mainstream parties in Austria and Denmark, but not in Sweden, and were also interpreted as negative other-presentation. The blunt demands to throw 'them' out expressed by the radical right in Austria were clearly proposals for unfavourable treatment. A representation found only in the Swedish corpus was that of immigrants as a national asset, which is objectifying but not discriminatory.

If Table 20.1 makes sense, the differences with regard to DD indicate that ethnic nationalism might be weaker in Sweden. These findings are in line with the literature. Wodak et al. (2009) report, based on a review of the literature on Austrian nationalism, strong feelings for the German language to be part of the 'we'-construction. Pride in being an Austrian was often brought up in the focus groups they themselves conducted. In his study of political speeches, Reisigl (2007) points to the presence of ethnic nationalism (politicians referring to Austria as a *Kulturnation*) alongside expressions of Austria as a civic nation, in the 1990s. According to Hedetoft (2006), Danes have long felt proud of being Danes and have strengthened this feeling by differentiating themselves from various 'others' over time: the Germans, the Swedes and, more recently, immigrants within the country. Underlying Danish political debates among the mainstream parties is the understanding that a common national culture is necessary in order to maintain democracy, freedom and security, while Danish culture is seen as being particularly vulnerable to heterogeneity (Mouritsen 2006: 124).

In contrast to the signs of fairly strong ethnic nationalism pointed to in the literature on Austria and Denmark, Swedish nationalism has been characterized as taking pride in opposing the kind of nationalism that is ethnocentric and oppressive of minorities (Edquist 2008: 4). Swedes in the post-war period are described as considering themselves to have 'overcome the ills of nationalism once and for all' (Johansson 2004: 180). Swedes can even believe themselves not to have a particular culture but only values, such as democracy, rationality and modernity (Daun 2005: 17–18; see also Boréus 2006b). Swedish interest in ethnic Swedes in other countries has been limited; 'blood has not been a significant tie' in that context (Berggren 2004: 72). Swedes are described as easily provoked by the question of what they feel proud of as Swedes – as they tend to see themselves as people who have overcome that kind of nationalism (Johansson 2001: 8). This is also a part of the self-identity that arises in focus groups (Jansson et al. 2011).

The Swedish *homo nationalis* and construction of the nation state may also have characteristics that check assimilation and 'keep them out' rhetoric to some extent, and that are difficult to reconcile with blunt demands to throw immigrants out. The characteristics of the Swedish *homo nationalis* are, according to recurrent descriptions, *modern* and *equality-loving* (Hall 2000: 277, Johansson 2001: 8). It can be difficult to combine that kind of self-identity with ethnic nationalism, often seen as atavistic and causing inequality. Sweden is described in official documentation as a positive example for the world with regard to refugee policy, and as generous, with strong respect for human rights and with a policy that expresses international solidarity (Johansson 2008: 117). If this construction of the nation is felt to be important enough, it will be difficult to reconcile it with a 'keep them out' or 'throw them out' rhetoric but compatible with the positive other-presentation inherent in the construction of immigrants as a national asset.

Yet, Swedish nationalism is hardly purely civic and free of ethnic aspects. The Swedish *homo nationalis* also has its 'others'. Several studies indicate a tendency to polarize Swedes, understood to be modern, sexually liberated and in favour of women's emancipation, with immigrants, seen as lacking in these respects (Runcis 2001: chs 4, 5, Towns 2002, Brune 2004: part III). And after all, the Sweden Democrats, a radical-right party that expresses a far more explicit ethnic nationalism than the mainstream parties, were voted into Parliament in 2010. Ethnic nationalism is seldom explicit or strong in Swedish public debate, but it is there for the radical-right parties to exploit.

The full picture of the conditions for radical-right parties to grow and for discursive discrimination to be expressed is, of course, much more complex than has been presented here. The research literature on radical-right parties offers a considerable number of explanations for the differences in success of these parties (for a review see Mudde 2007: chs 9–11). There are also conditions that influence the kind and level of DD against immigrants not related to nationalism. A further complication involves the relationship between nationalism on the one hand, and the growth of radical-right parties and DD on the other, being dialectic rather than one way.

These complexities should not be disregarded. However, when trying to understand why and how immigrants are discursively discriminated against and why the radical-right parties meet with greater or less success, it is wise to look at wider discursive frames, especially the extent to which ethnic nationalism is expressed and which characteristics of *homo nationalis* and the nation state are at play.

Note: I want to thank Maria Jansson, Ulf Mörkenstam and Cecilia Åse for their very valuable comments on earlier drafts of this text.

References

Anderson, B. (1991), *Imagined Communities: Reflections on the Origin and Spread of Nationalism*, London: Verso.

Berggren, H. (2004), 'The forward-looking angel: Nationalism and modernity in Sweden in the twentieth century', in K. Almqvist and K. Glans (eds), *The Swedish Success Story?* Stockholm: Axel and Margaret Ax:son Johnson Foundation.

Blommaert, J. and Verschueren, J. (1998), *Debating Diversity: Analysing the Discourse of Tolerance*, London, New York: Routledge.

Boréus, K. (2006a), 'Discursive Discrimination: A Typology', *European Journal of Social Theory*, 9(3): 405–24.

— (2006b), 'En analys av kulturbegreppet i debatten om "det mångkulturella samhället"', in L. Roxell and E. Tiby (eds), *Frågor, fält och filter. Kriminologisk metodbok*, Lund: Studentlitteratur, pp. 207–30.

— (2010), 'Including or excluding immigrants? The impact of right-wing populism in Denmark and Sweden', in B. Bengtsson, P. Strömblad and A-H Bay (eds), *Diversity, Inclusion and Citizenship in Scandinavia*, Newcastle upon Tyne: Cambridge Scholars Publishing, pp. 127–57.

Brune, Y. (2004), *Nyheter från gränsen: tre studier i journalistik om 'invandrare', flyktingar och rasism*, Stockholm: Carlssons.

Chilton, P. (2004), *Analysing Political Discourse. Theory and Practice*, London, New York: Routledge.

Daun, Å. (2005), *En stuga på sjätte våningen. Svensk mentalitet i en mångkulturell värld*, Stockholm: Symposion.

Edquist, S. (2008), 'En folklig svenskhet? Nationalismen och folkrörelserna i vår tid', in U. Lundberg and M. Tydén (eds), *Sverigebilder. Det nationellas betydelser i politik och vardag*, Stockholm: Institute for Futures Studies, pp. 29–48.

Ekström von Essen, U. and Fleischer, R. (2006), *Sverigedemokraterna i de svenska kommunerna 2002–2006. En studie av politisk aktivitet, strategi och mobilisering*, Norrköping: Integrationsverket.

Gellner, E. (1983), *Nations and Nationalism*, Malden, Oxford, Carlton: Blackwell.

Hall, P. (1998), *The Social Construction of Nationalism: Sweden as an Example*, Lund: Lund University Press.

— (2000), *Den svenskaste historien. Nationalism i Sverige under sex sekler*, Stockholm: Carlsson Bokförlag.

Hedetoft, U. (2006), 'Divergens eller konvergens', in U. Hedetoft, B. Petterson and L. Sturfelt (eds), *Bortom stereotyperna? Invandrare och integration i Danmark och Sverige*, Malmö: Centrum för Danmarksstudier, pp. 390–407.

Heinisch, R. (2002), *Populism, Proporz, Pariah: Austria Turns Right. Austrian Political Change, Its Causes and Repercussions*, New York: Nova Science Publishers.

Jansson, M., Wendt, M. and Åse, C. (2011), 'Tre nyanser av Sverige', in D. Sainsbury and M. Soininen (eds), *Kön makt nation*, Stockholm: Stockholm University, pp. 122–43.

Johansson, A. W. (2001), 'Inledning. Svensk nationalism och identitet efter andra världskriget', in A. W. Johansson (ed.), *Vad är Sverige? Röster om svensk nationell identitet*, Stockholm: Prisma, pp. 7–17.

— (2004), 'If you seek his monument, look around! Reflections on national identity and collective memory in Sweden after the Second World War', in K. Almqvist and K. Glans (eds), *The Swedish Success Story?* Stockholm: Axel and Margaret Ax:son Johnson Foundation, pp. 175–86.

Johansson, C. (2008), 'Svenska flyktingpolitiska visioner. Självbild eller verklighet?', in U. Lundberg and M. Tydén (eds), *Sverigebilder. Det nationellas betydelser i politik och vardag*, Stockholm: Institute for Futures Studies, pp. 113–29.

Krzyżanowski, M. and Wodak, R. (2009), *The Politics of Exclusion. Debating Migration in Austria*, New Brunswick, NJ: Transaction Publishers.

Meret, S. (2009), *The Danish People's Party, the Italian Northern League and the Austrian Freedom Party in a Comparative Perspective: Party Ideology and Electoral Support*, Aalborg: Aalborg University.

Merkl, P. H. and Weinberg, L. (2003), *Right-wing Extremism in the Twenty-first Century*, London, New York: Routledge.

Mouritsen, P. (2006), 'Fælles værdier, statsreligion og islam i dansk politisk kultur', in U. Hedetoft, B. Petterson and L. Sturfelt (eds), *Bortom stereotyperna? Invandrare och integration i Danmark och Sverige*, Malmö: Centrum för Danmarksstudier, pp. 109–47.

Mudde, C. (2007), *Populist Radical Right Parties in Europe*, Cambridge: Cambridge University Press.

Reisigl, M. (2007), *Nationale Rhetorik in Fest- und Gedenkreden. Eine diskursanalytische Studie zum 'österreichischen Millennium' in den Jahren 1946 und 1996*, Tübingen: Stauffenburg Verlag.

Reisigl, M. and Wodak, R. (2001), *Discourse and Discrimination. Rhetorics of racism and antisemitism*, London, New York: Routledge.

Ringsmose, J. (2003), *'Kedeligt har det i hvert fald ikke været . . .' Fremskridtspartiet 1989–1995*, Odense: Syddansk Universitetsforlag.

Runcis, M. (2001), *'Sverige är inte hela världen'. Folkbildning för och om invandrare i utbildningsprogrammen*, Stiftelsen etermedierna i Sverige.

Rydgren, J. (2005), *Från skattemissnöje till etnisk nationalism. Högerpopulism och parlamentarisk högerextremism i Sverige*, Lund: Studentlitteratur.

Suszycki, A. M. (2007), 'Nationalism in Sweden and the EU Membership', in I. P. Karolewski and A. M. Suszycki (eds), *Nationalism and European Integration. The Need for New Theoretical and Empirical Insights*, New York, London: Continuum, pp. 85–100.

Towns, A. (2002), 'Paradoxes of (In)Equality: Something is Rotten in the Gender Equal State of Sweden', *Cooperation and Conflict*, 37(2): 157–79.

Trads, D. (2002), *Danskerne først! En historie om Dansk Folkeparti*, Copenhagen: Gyldendal.

van Dijk, T. A. (1993), *Elite Discourse and Racism*, Newbury Park, London, New Delhi: Sage.

— (2002), 'Discourse and Racism', in D. T. Goldberg and J. Solomos (eds), *A Companion to Racial and Ethnic Studies*, Malden, Oxford: Blackwell, pp. 191–205.

Westlind, D. (1996), *Politics and Popular Identity. Understanding Recent Populist Movements in Sweden and the United States*, Lund: Lund University Press.

Wodak, R., de Cillia, R., Reisigl, M. and Liebhart, K. (2009), *The Discursive Construction of National Identity*, Edinburgh: Edinburgh University Press.

Wodak, R. and Pelinka, A. (eds) (2002), *The Haider Phenomenon in Austria*, New Brunswick, London: Transaction Publishers.

21

Mediatization as an Echo-Chamber for Xenophobic Discourses in the Threat Society: The Muhammad Cartoons in Denmark and Sweden

Stig A. Nohrstedt

Introduction

This chapter reflects on the role of mainstream journalism in the proliferation of Islamophobia in late modern society, by analysing two cases where newspapers in Denmark and Sweden published cartoons of the prophet Muhammad. Both are instances of mediated perceptions of Muslims, symbolized by the Prophet, as a threat to freedom of speech, but in rather different ways. However, together they illustrate discursive processes and opinion-building strategies used by right-wing populism in which journalism becomes both amplifier and echo-chamber due to media logic. The first case, where the Danish newspaper *Jyllands-Posten* printed a series of Muhammad cartoons in 2005, has been intensively discussed both by journalists and media researchers (e.g. Eide et al. 2008, Sundström 2009). The second case, in 2007 where the Swedish newspaper *Nerikes-Allehanda* published a cartoon portraying Muhammad as a toy dog, has also been studied by media researchers (Camauër 2011, Camauër (ed.) forthcoming). In both instances, the publication of the caricatures resulted in protests, violent demonstrations and death threats against the cartoonists and editors, but led to varying editorial conclusions.

I will focus on certain aspects of these two cases that relate to the spin of threat perceptions as driving factors behind the publishing of the cartoons. I will argue that these cases are examples of mediatized crisis spirals typical of a new phase of late-modern society, which I label the 'threat society'. The dual perspective elaborated is related to two analytical levels – macro and micro – which are necessary for an understanding of the media-related mechanisms that can partly explain these two cases, and also more recently, the Oslo and Toulouse mass murders in July 2011 and March 2012, respectively. Of course, the importance of the media is indirect in the sense that 1) the operative 'rationale' for the terrible crimes is to get the attention of the media, as explicitly expressed in Brevik's so-called manifest, and would not have been conducted without the media, and 2) because of the nationalized framing and tendency in the media to depict some foreigners as a potential risk to the national community.

The media's role

Studies of the media have shown that they play an important role in the facilitation of xenophobic attitudes and opinion-building. In the 1970s and 1980s, several analysts concluded that news reporting on immigration and refugees was constructed from a basic distinction between 'Us' and 'Them' – where immigrants, refugees and asylum-seekers were depicted as risk phenomena for the national society and population. The alleged dangers included, for example, new arrivals bringing diseases, criminal behaviour, economic burdens, foreign social and moral norms; in short, 'They' threatened 'Our' way of life and cultural identity (e.g. Hartman & Husband 1974, Hall et al. 1978, van Dijk 1993, European Dilemma 2005, Nohrstedt & Camauër 2006, KhosraviNik 2009, 2010, KhosraviNik et al. 2012; see also chapters by Wodak (Ch. 2), Kovács (Ch. 15) and Kallis (Ch. 4) in this volume). In some studies, a dual-media construction of immigrants has been identified with distant 'Others' outside national borders; for example, asylum-seekers are depicted in negative and stigmatizing terms, whereas close 'Others', already living in the country with neighbours and school personnel supporting them when applying for residence permits, are positively described as assimilated and grateful for the hospitality they have received in their new country (Brune 2004, Camauër 2011).

Mainstream media operate within national horizons or frames, what Billig has called 'banal nationalism' (1995). They are institutions in the domain of the nation state, and their audience, almost without exception, is limited by territorial borders. They address their readers, listeners or viewers as citizens with an implicit national identity.

In several ways this has consequences for the media as facilitators of right-wing populism (RWP) and extremism. The implied implicit 'We' in the media's addresses to their audience makes every problem, risk and danger a threat to 'Us'. If a pandemic breaks out or refugees are gathering at the borders, the media logic tends to describe this as something that 'We' must protect ourselves from. The inclination and incitement to focus on the problems, risks and dangers that people in other countries face, perhaps equal to our own, is far less prominent compared with this in-group perspective. These 'Others' are secondary in importance or even irrelevant for the direction of media attention. There are organizational and economic mechanisms behind this – the media live by attracting people's attention, the main success factor for commercial media (see van Dijk 1993, Triandafyllidou et al. 2009, Krzyżanowski & Wodak 2009).

For the 'hot' nationalism, for example, RWP that Billig (1995) juxtaposes with the 'banal' variant, the media provide a discursive environment that fertilizes their impact on the general public. As the main carrier of 'banal' nationalism, the media prepare and give resonance to right-wing propaganda when they point to the 'Other' as the problem. In this way, RWP propaganda simply makes explicit and echoes what the media logic implicitly and 'banally' implies. Further, the media's 'banal' nationalism helps to cover up the RWP movement's international character, which comes out so clearly in the contributions to this volume. The narrow national frames of media logic are obstacles to journalism that could reveal the collaboration and transnational, 'foreign', elements in the propaganda that pretend to protect and defend 'Danishness', 'Swedishness' and 'Britishness'. The general lack of global, or at least transnational, news perspectives in the mainstream media, in this instance, helps the RWP to avoid being exposed before the general public in their 'nudity' as promoters of the national interest.

The inherent 'banal' nationalism of the media further leaves journalists off guard when they are accused, from the RWP side, of being 'politically correct' and hiding the 'truth' about all the allegedly negative consequences of immigration and 'multicultural' influences. This lack of defence against RWP propaganda seems to come from a naive and superficial understanding of its strategy and rhetorical methods that this volume hopefully will contribute to remedying (see also the chapters by Andersson (Ch. 22), Pelinka (Ch. 1), Oja & Mral (Ch. 19) and Wodak (Ch. 2) in this volume). However, the institutional roots behind this professional shortcoming are first, journalists' instinctive opposition to all kinds of censorship, and second, the accord between RWP propaganda and a media logic built on the distinction between the imagined national community and the external dangers that are threatening 'Us' (see also Wodak et al. 2009).

Here is not the place to elaborate upon the argument above in relation to the extensive globalization literature. Suffice it to note that although the theoretical speculations about the media as a globalizing agent are frequent (e.g. Volkmer 2001, Beck 2006, Reese 2007, Eide et al. 2008, Chouliaraki 2009), others are more sceptical (e.g. Riegert 1998, Biltereyest 2001, Nohrstedt & Ottosen 2001, Hafez 2007, Kunelius & Eide 2007). Empirically based research in the field remains rare, but existing studies generally confirm that media content disseminates and promotes national frames (e.g. Olausson 2005, Östman 2009).

The media's role in connection with the cartoon cases must however also be discussed with regard to the question concerning the relationship between media content and social processes, including crises and intercultural communication processes, as well as how democratic values such as freedom of speech and religion are contested from various perspectives.

The media as constitutive of the threat society

Elsewhere I have described the threat society as a stage of late modernity, drawing upon the analyses of Beck, Furedi, Bauman, Cottle and Atheide (for references see Nohrstedt 2011). A threat society is marked by the expansion of a culture of fear, and of politics focusing on the management of various threats. The role of the media is central to the theory of a threat society. Mediatization explains the special role of the media in the development of a threat society. Media logic and the staging of spectacular 'media events' contribute to a symbolic reality which functions as a habitat where threats, crises and conflicts are broadly constructed and gain ontological, epistemological and identity-political existence. In a threat society, these processes do not occur in isolation from other institutions and actors. On the contrary, there are different threat exploiters who play a promotional role in these processes, which are largely displayed in the media. In that problems and dangers in a threat society are constructed as 'threats', they are broadly connected with 'otherism', that is, with the construction of an opposition between 'Us' and 'Them'. The discourse of threat politics constantly constructs recurrent threats, which dominate social life and produce crises and conflicts, with the common characteristic of a staged situation in which 'We' are exposed to dangers caused by 'Them'; therefore, to maintain and preserve our safe and secure life, 'We' have to protect ourselves from 'Them'. A threat society may thus run the risk of becoming a 'hate society'. Even though it does not go that far, it seems that a threat society does harbour strong endogenous tendencies towards discrimination and xenophobia, with mediatization also neglecting to construct threats as a result of the media audience's (our) actions, or lack thereof.

To sum up the macro-level argument: First, the 'banal' nationalism of the media proliferates as 'hot' nationalism, for example, RWP, due to reasons related to media logic. Second, in a late modern threat society, politics is marked by at least the three following features, which are also reinforced by the current media logic (for further details, see Nohrstedt 2011):

1. *Threats and dangers dominate in the political rhetoric.*
2. *Political changes are driven by worst-case scenarios.*
3. *Political and social identity increasingly takes on the shape of a vulnerable and exposed individual who does not dare to trust his/her fellow citizens.*

In the following I will show that this macro-level analysis is necessary for explaining – at the micro-level – why the two cartoon cases became media events in the first place.

Empirical cases: The Muhammad cartoons in Jyllands-Posten and Nerikes Allehanda

In 2005, the Danish newspaper *Jyllands-Posten* (JP) published 12 cartoons of the Prophet Muhammad to counteract an allegedly growing self-censorship in the country of expressions that might offend the Muslim minority, as declared by the editorial that accompanied the cartoons. To some, these cartoons were offensive, for example, the one that depicted Muhammad as a terrorist (with a burning fuse bomb in his turban). A crisis emerged in the relations between Denmark and several Muslim countries when additional Danish newspapers published the cartoons, and because of the refusal of the Danish Prime Minister to meet with the countries' diplomats. Violent demonstrations in several Muslim countries led to attempts to burn down the Danish embassy in Islamabad and to boycott Danish products.

Two years later, the Swedish provincial newspaper *Nerikes-Allehanda* also printed a cartoon of Muhammad, but this time the Prophet was depicted as a toy dog. The cartoon, drawn by Lars Vilks, had already been published in several other Swedish newspapers. When *Nerikes-Allehanda* (NA) published the cartoon, local Muslim organizations responded by organizing demonstrations. The editor-in-chief of NA expressed great surprise when publication of the cartoon resulted in worldwide media attention, a public burning of the Swedish flag in Pakistan, and death threats against both the artist and himself. In spite of the crisis in Denmark only two years earlier, he had not expected this reaction as the cartoon had been published earlier in the Swedish media (Camauër (ed.) forthcoming).

I will not discuss the two cases in detail here as each has initiated various studies, by both academic scholars and journalists (e.g. Eide et al. 2008, Sundström 2009, ter Wal et al. 2009). My analysis will concentrate first on the declared motives for publishing the caricatures, and second on the broad shift that marked both cases. I will emphasize the threat spirals that publication of the cartoons triggered, and particularly how the ill-founded reasons for publishing the cartoons unleashed dramatic reactions worldwide. This is important since, even if only in one of the cases, the JP, the explanation could be the newspaper's recent history as a promoter of xenophobic views in, for example, editorials, which is not possible in the NA case, with its clear position against RWP propaganda.

Consequences

The dramatic consequences that followed publication of the Muhammad cartoons in Denmark and Sweden have been mentioned. There were local protests and demonstrations and violent reactions internationally in some Muslim countries, including burning of the Danish flag, a boycott of Danish products, death threats against artists and editors, demolition of Danish property and attacks on the Danish embassy in Islamabad. Even a lethal bomb blast outside the same embassy three years after publication was attributed to the JP's publication of the Muhammad cartoons. In all, more than 130 people were killed in events relating to the Danish case (Hervik et al. 2008). No known deaths were reported in the Swedish case, however a 'fatwa' (here an Islamic death sentence) was declared against the artist, as well as the NA's editor-in-chief, and two years after the Swedish publication, suspected assassins relating to this case were arrested in Ireland and the United States of America.

Motives for publishing the cartoons

The editorials that accompanied the cartoons were, in both cases, remarkably similar. Both argued that freedom of speech implies that people may be offended by others' opinions, critical and ironic art, and that there is no right to be protected from being insulted in public debates and discussions. It is 'incompatible with contemporary democracy and freedom of speech' to insist on 'special consideration of /one's own/ religious feelings' (article published in JP 30 September 2005, together with the cartoons: translated in Eide et al. 2008: 31). Furthermore, as the editor-in-chief of NA argued, there is 'a right to ridicule a religion' (editorial headline, NA 19 August 2007). In JP, the argument seeking to justify the decision to publish the cartoons was explicit in its manifestation against the threat of increased self-censorship:'... we are approaching a slippery slope where no one can tell where self-censorship will end. That is why *Morgenavisen Jyllands-Posten* has invited members of the Danish Editorial Cartoonists Union to draw Muhammad as they see him ...' (JP 30 September 2005).

In NA, however, the argument was somewhat unclear, as no explicit motive for 'publishing' the cartoon was mentioned. Implicitly, however, one can reconstruct the argument from the attached editorial. The editorial began by stating that Vilks had drawn some caricatures that ridiculed the Prophet Muhammad, and that 'so far three exhibitors have refused to display his pictures'. After naming the exhibitors, the editor concluded:'This is unacceptable self-censorship'. This sentence is followed by a principled declaration that a liberal society must manage to do two things simultaneously: 1) protect Muslims' right to religious freedom and build mosques, and 2) 'it is also allowed to ridicule the foremost symbols of Islam – like all other religions' symbols'.

Further, in the NA article, the editor expressed another principle, namely that 'The right to freedom of religion – and the right to blaspheme religions go together. They presuppose each other'. The editorial's final sentences concluded that this was also important for Muslims, and he argued that a 'fundamentalist Muslim', who would like to express his beliefs through visual art, 'could be stopped because obviously galleries can easily be convinced that the pictures are inappropriate, that they may result in rumpus. Hence the restrictions on Lars Vilks' possibilities to express himself, may also affect the right of Muslims to express themselves' (editorial, NA 1 September 2007).

Critique of the motives expressed for publishing the cartoons

In the JP case, Peter Hervik analysed the spin involved with the act of publishing. This act was declared by the newspaper's editor-in-chief to be a protest and a symbolic counterstroke against an alleged trend of increasing self-censorship in Denmark. However, the factual evidence for this alleged 'slippery slope' was suspect, to say the least. The concrete background was the author Kåre Bluitgen's complaints that he had had trouble finding illustrators to work on a children's book about the Quran and the life of the Prophet Muhammad, in combination with his explanation of these illustrators being afraid of Muslim reaction. This was given as the explicit reason for JP to invite cartoonists to 'draw Muhammad as they see him' (JP 30 September 2005, Hervik et al. 2008: 31). However, Bluitgen's story was far from watertight, as many illustrators may have refused to work with him because of his being a well-known Islamophobic figure in Denmark, with very few outside the right wing wanting to be associated with him (Sundström 2009). Furthermore, the fact that JP managed to recruit a number of cartoonists at short notice seems to falsify the alleged common fear of Muslim reactions and self-censorship (ibid.). JP's motives were also questionable, given their track record as a newspaper with 'provocations and Islamophobic news items, which might explain why, initially, so few other Danish media took notice of the cartoons' (Hervik 2008: 64).

The media hype came a month later when eleven ambassadors from Muslim countries wrote a letter to the Danish Prime Minister expressing their concerns about Islamophobic tendencies in Denmark and the eruption of political violence following publication of the cartoons. The letter requested a meeting between the ambassadors and the Prime Minster – a meeting which he refused – explaining that it was not possible under the Constitution for the Danish Government to interfere with the freedom of the press. But that was something that the ambassadors denied they had ever asked for, and which experts who analysed the letter concluded was not implicated by the text except as a biased interpretation. Despite further attempts from the ambassadors to assure the Danish authorities that they had not asked for any legal interference but rather for consultation concerning the alarming situation, the Prime Minister continued, publically, to describe their request as a demand for government restrictions on the free media in Denmark, for example, in an interview on 7 January 2006 (Sundström 2009: 227).

Consequently, this transformed the self-censorship discourse into a discourse of freedom of speech. When the JP case escalated, it was covered extensively in both the national and international media. The reaction to the JP case in Muslim countries was triggered not only by publication of the cartoons, but also by the arrogant behaviour of the Danish Prime Minister (Hervik et al. 2008: 33). The spin on the alleged freedom of speech issue, which was probably initiated as part of a damage control strategy, now became significant to transnational Islamophobic movements and 'highly successful' (Hervik 2008: 65).

A more recent JP editorial, on 27 February 2010, illustrated this; the editor denounced the argument by another Danish newspaper that had made a public apology to Muslims that were offended by the cartoons and requested dialogue. The JP editor scorned this argument: 'Dialogue is positive as a point of departure, but we see no ground for entering a dialogue about for example the reasonableness of stoning of women that have been raped, or hanging homosexuals from building cranes'. The total lack of self-criticism, as well as the refusal of any dialogue, amounted to an extreme variant of 'otherism'.

The NA case followed a similar shift, but in contradistinction to the JP case, the provincial Swedish paper had no track record of Islamophobic reporting. When the editors of NA received the news that Vilks' Muhammad sketches had been removed from an exhibition in a small village museum, and when Vilks himself relayed that two other exhibitors had refused to display his cartoons because of fear of Muslim protests, the NA editors decided to publish Vilk's caricature of the Prophet Muhammad. In the attached editorial it was implied, as already mentioned, that the motive was to demonstrate the right to freedom of speech, including the right to ridicule. In a private conversation, the editor-in-chief later explained that the decision was – at least partly – based on the assumption that by publishing the caricature they would show that the fears expressed by exhibitors were exaggerated and unfounded. So by implication, the NA editors expected the act of publishing to prove that Muslims would not object or take action against institutions that reproduced the Muhammad cartoon, that is, that there was no conflict between 'civilizations' involved. As the cartoon had already been published by other Swedish newspapers, they did not foresee that a newspaper with a local circulation would trigger such global attention and reaction.

As in the JP case, the editors' interpretation of earlier events and Vilks' own statement, that the exhibitors did not display his drawings because of fear of harsh Muslim reaction, are questionable. As mentioned above, the NA editor described three exhibitors having refused to show Vilks drawings as acts of 'unacceptable self-censorship' (NA 19 August 2007). At a seminar several months later, the editors admitted that they did not know for sure whether all three exhibitors had actually refused to show Vilks' cartoons because of fear of Muslim reaction. As one of the exhibitors involved was the Modern Museum in Stockholm – a national scene for contemporary art – it is more than plausible that the decision was based on other motives, for example, aesthetic quality.

Similar to the JP case, and in spite of the editors' intentions, publication of the cartoon in NA grew from a demonstration of the wide scope of freedom of speech, tolerance of deviant opinions and absence of clashes between religions and cultures in Sweden into a discourse of violent conflict between a democratic and free society and threatening fundamentalist Muslims. This was mainly driven by subjective news journalism and headlines. Death threats against the cartoonists and the editors received paramount exposure in NA and other Swedish media, although by comparison, Middle Eastern media paid less attention to these reports – probably because the sources were known within the region to be of low reliability (Camauër (ed.) forthcoming, El Din forthcoming, Tahir forthcoming). In 2007, when Iranian President Ahmadinejad was asked about the case of the NA cartoon at a press conference, he said that it was typical Zionist provocation, but that the Iranian people had no reason whatsoever to feel offended or to take action. Only the first part of his response about the Zionist conspiracy was relayed by the AFP news agency and the Swedish press (Tahir forthcoming). Instead of news reports of the moderate coverage in the Middle-Eastern media, the Swedish media and NA reproduced a discourse about freedom of speech under threat, and its brave defenders, with the front page of the NA showing a photograph of the editor-in-chief in front of the main entrance to the NA office under the main headline: 'Productive dialogue at the gate of freedom of the press' (NA 1 September 2007).

All in all, the enduring impression of the Swedish press coverage, both in NA and in other Swedish media, seems to be of a growing threat against Swedish democracy and freedom of the press. The manner in which distant Muslims' reactions were depicted resonated with a narrative of 'clashing civilizations' (Huntington 1996).

The crux

What then is the crux of these two cases? I argue that it remains a mystery as to why these media events ever happened in the first place. In both cases, the declared motives for publishing are, on closer inspection, questionable from a purely factual point of view. It was not substantiated that self-censorship, due to fear of Muslim reaction, had been important when illustrators (in the JP case) and exhibitors (in the NA case) declined to produce or display the Muhammad cartoons. The editors of the two newspapers drew these conclusions, but evidently with no firm ground in the form of factual evidence. In both cases, however, mediatized threat spirals emerged. In the end, the image of a growing threat from the Muslim world against Nordic democracy and freedom was disseminated to the general public. In the JP case, this was confirmation of its previous Islamophobic reporting; and in the NA case, ironically, it was falsification of its editors' assumption that publishing the cartoon would prove the fear of Muslim reaction to be exaggerated or even false. Considering that the NA editors assumed that they could falsify the belief in an imminent Muslim threat, the common denominator and remaining impact of the two cartoon cases equate to the proliferation of an image of an acute Muslim threat against the 'homeland', that is, a kind of 'culture of fear' (Furedi 2006).

The striking result of these two cases is that both JP and NA, in spite of the latter's intention to do the opposite, caused threat spirals, the promotion of threat-politics and the proliferation of a culture of fear, consciously (JP) or unconsciously (NA), because of the nationalistic outlook within media framing (see also Oberhuber et al. 2005). And that is almost by definition the index of a dominant cultural pattern, when discursive and ideological outcomes are led in a certain direction, irrespective of the content and/or intention of the actual publication. Without the backdrop of Islamophobic propaganda of 'European soil being invaded by Muslims with a programme for elimination of democracy and freedom of speech', *the interpretation* of rumours about illustrators and exhibitors that had refused to produce or display the Muhammad cartoons as evidence of self-censorship would never have occurred. Whether the editors acted intentionally or not is not the issue here. The fact that in both instances the statements of self-censorship were uncritically accepted constitutes evidence for the existence of 'otherism', of a kind related to a threat society, in collective perceptions in the Nordic countries and in other parts of Europe.

The 'manifest', more than 1,500 pages in length, that the Norwegian terrorist Breivik published on the internet, just before the mass murders in Oslo and on Utøya, with its Islamophobic conspiracy theory of, for example, demographic warfare against the Christian-Western civilization, including Israel, is another extreme exponent of the 'otherism' and culture of fear that is growing in the threat society. He is obviously a typical exponent of the extremism that displays 'accusation in a mirror' (Hamelink 2011: 29), that is, he argues that mass-murder, even the use of weapons of mass destruction, is necessary as a form of self-defence against Muslim 'demographic warfare' (Breivik 2011: 824).

Finally, the lack of global journalism is a complementary factor that explains why, in these cases, the media initiated the threat spirals. Initially, narrow national horizons were important for the decision to publish, both at JP and NA. Both newspapers were occupied by the alleged intercultural problems in their respective countries. Because of their narrow perspectives they could not foresee what transnational implications their decisions would have – they were only considering the local/national situation. This is especially remarkable in the NA case, as they should have drawn on the experience of the JP case two years earlier. The only lesson they did seem to learn was not to display the cartoon in the online version of the newspaper.

The implications for intercultural communication of these threat spirals differ between the Danish and Swedish cases. In retrospect, NA's editor-in-chief expressed a lesson learnt from the cartoon incident – that even a provincial newspaper can have global reach – and declared his wish for improved dialogue with moderate and 'close

Muslims'. In the JP case, the lesson seems to be even more hard-necked resistance to dialogue in any practical sense (see JP editorial 27 February 2010).

References

Bauman, Z. (2006), *Liquid Fear*, Cambridge: Polity Press.

Beck, U. (2006), *Cosmopolitan Vision*, Cambridge: Polity Press.

Billig, M. (1995), *Banal Nationalism*, London: SAGE Publications.

Biltereyest, D. (2001), 'Global news research and complex citizenship: Towards an agenda for research on foreign/international news and audiences', in S. Hjarvard (ed.), *News in a Globalized Society*, Gothenburg: NORDICOM., pp. 41–62.

Breivik, A. B. (2011) '2083. A European Declaration of Independence', <http://publicintelligence.net/anders-behring-breiviks-complete-manifesto-2083-a-european-declaration-of-independence/> [accessed 24 March 2012].

Brune, Y. (2004), *Nyheter från gränsen. Tre studier i journalistik om 'invandrare', flyktingar och rasistiskt våld. [News from the border. Three studies in journalism on 'immigrants', refugees and racist violence.]* Gothenburg: Institutionen för journalistik, och masskommunikation [Department for Journalism and Mass Communication], Gothenburg University.

Camauër, L. (2011), 'Constructing "close" and "distant" Muslim identities: The Mohammed cartoon in the Swedish newspaper *Nerikes Allehanda*', in S. A. Nohrstedt (ed.), *Communicating Risks: Towards the Threat Society?* Gothenburg: NORDICOM., pp. 137–60.

Camauër, L. (ed.) (forthcoming), *Rondellhunden och tryckfriheten. En studie av rapporteringen om en karikatyrpublicering i Sverige [Roundabout Dogs and Freedom of the Press. A study of reporting on a cartoon published in Sweden]*, Stockholm: Stiftelsen för mediestudier [Foundation for Media Studies].

Camauër, L. and Nohrstedt, S. A. (eds) (2006), *Mediernas vi och dom. Mediernas betydelse för den strukturella diskrimineringen [The Media's Us and Them: The media's impact on structural discrimination]*, Stockholm: SOU, 21.

Chouliaraki, L. (2009), 'Global divides in transnational media: Managing the visibility of suffering', *NORDICOM Review*, 30(June), pp. 73–89. Jubilee Issue, Media and Global Divides, IAMCR World Congress, Stockholm 20–5 July 2008.

Cottle, S. (2009), *Global Crisis Reporting: Journalism in the Global Age*, Maidenhead: Open University Press.

Eide, E., Kunelius, R. and Phillips, A. (eds) (2008), *Transnational Media Events: The Mohammed Cartoons and the Imagined Clash of Civilisations*, Gothenburg: NORDICOM.

Ezz El Din, M. (forthcoming), 'The coverage of the *Nerikes Allehanda (NA)* caricatures in Egyptian newspapers and Pan Arab online news from Al Jazeera and Al Arabiya', in L. Camauër (ed.) *Rondellhunden och tryckfriheten. En studie av rapporteringen om en karikatyrpublicering i Sverige [Roundabout Dogs and Freedom of the Press. A study of reporting on a cartoon published in Sweden]*, Stockholm: Stiftelsen för mediestudier [Foundation for Media Studies].

European Dilemma: Institutional Patterns and Politics of 'Racial' Discrimination (Research Project Xenophob), EU Fifth Framework Programme 2002–5, <www.multietn.uu.se/research/eu_dilemma/project_overview.pdf> [accessed 25 October 2005].

Furedi, F. (2006), *Culture of Fear Revisited,* London: Continuum.

Hafez, K. (2007), *The Myth of Media Globalization,* Cambridge: Polity Press.

Hall, S., Critcher, C., Jefferson, T., Clarke, J. and Roberts, B. (1978), *Policing the Crisis: Mugging, the State and Law and Order,* London: Macmillan.

Hamelink, C. (2011), *Media and Conflict. Escalating Evil,* London: Paradigm Publishers.

Hartmann, P. and Husband, C. (1974), *Racism and the Mass Media,* London: Rowman & Littlefield.

Hervik, P. (2008), 'Original spin and its side effects: Freedom of speech as Danish news management', in E. Eide, R. Kunelius and A. Phillips (eds), *Transnational Media Events. The Mohammed Cartoons and the Imagined Clash of Civilizations,* Gothenburg: NORDICOM., pp. 59–80.

Hervik, P., Eide, E. and Kunelius, R. (2008), 'A long and messy event', in E. Eide, R. Kunelius and A. Phillips (eds), *Transnational Media Events. The Mohammed Cartoons and the Imagined Clash of Civilizations,* Gothenburg: NORDICOM., pp. 29–38.

Huntington, S. P. (1996), *The Clash of Civilizations and the Remaking of World.* New York: Simon & Schuster.

KhosraviNik, M. (2009), 'The Representation of Refugees, Asylum Seekers and Immigrants in British Newspapers during the Balkan Conflict (1999) and the British General Election (2005)', *Discourse & Society,* 20(4): 477–98.

— (2010), 'The Representation of Refugees, Asylum Seekers and Immigrants in British Newspapers: A Critical Discourse Analysis', *Journal of Language and Politics,* 9(1): 1–28.

KhosraviNik, M., Krzyżanowski, M. and Wodak, R. (2012), 'Dynamics of discursive representations of refugees and asylum seekers in the British press 1996–2006', in M. Messer, R. Schroeder and R. Wodak (eds), *Migrations: Interdisciplinary Perspectives,* Springer-Verlag.

Krzyżanowski, M. and Wodak, R. (2009), *The Politics of Exclusion: Debating Migration in Austria,* New Brunswick, NJ: Transaction Publishers.

Kunelius, R. and Eide, E. (2007), 'The Mohammed cartoons, journalism, free speech and globalization', in R. Kunelius, E. Eide, O. Hahn Oliver and R. Schröder (eds), *Reading the Mohammed Cartoons Controversy: An International Analysis of Press Discourses on Free Speech and Political Spin,* Working Papers in International Journalism, Bochum, Freiburg: Projekt Verlag, pp. 9–23.

Nohrstedt, S. A. (2011), 'Threat-society and the media', in S. A. Nohrstedt (ed.), *Communicating Risks: Towards the Threat Society?* Gothenburg: NORDICOM., pp. 17–51.

Nohrstedt, S. A. and Camauër, L. (2006), 'Introduktion' [Introduction], in L. Camauër and S. A. Nohrstedt (eds), *Mediernas vi och dom. Mediernas betydelse för den strukturella diskrimineringen [The Media's Us and Them: The Media's Impact on Structural Discrimination],* Stockholm: SOU. 21, pp. 9–34.

Nohrstedt, S. A. and Ottosen, R. (eds) (2001), *Journalism in the New World Order. Gulf War, National News Discourses and Globalization,* Vol. 1, Gothenburg: NORDICOM.

Olausson, U. (2005), *Medborgarskap och globalisering: Den diskursiva konstruktionen av politisk identitet [Citizenship and globalization: The discursive construction of political identity]* (PhD dissertation), Örebro Studies in Media and Communication 3, Örebro: Örebro University.

Östman, J. (2009), *Journalism at the borders. The constitution of nationalist closure in news decoding* (PhD dissertation), Örebro Studies in Media and Communication 8, Örebro: Örebro University.

Reese, S. (2007), 'Theorizing a globalized journalism', in M. Löffelholz and D. Weaver (eds), *Global Journalism Research. Theories, Methods, Findings, Future*, London: Blackwell Publishing., pp. 240–52.

Riegert, K. (1998), '"*Nationalising*" *Foreign Conflict*', Stockholm: Department of Political Science, Stockholm University.

Sundström, L. (2009), *Världens lyckligaste folk. En bok om Danmark [The Happiest People in the World. A Book about Denmark]*, Stockholm: Leopards förlag.

Tahir, K. (forthcoming), 'Kränkning eller yttrandefrihet: Muhammedteckningen i den muslimska världen' [Violation or Expression: The Muhammad cartoons in the Muslim world], in L. Camauër (ed.) *Rondellhunden och tryckfriheten. En studie av rapporteringen om en karikatyrpublicering i Sverige [Roundabout Dogs and Freedom of the Press. A study of reporting on a cartoon published in Sweden]*, Stockholm: Stiftelsen för mediestudier [Foundation for Media Studies].

ter Wal, J., Triandafyllidou, A., Steindler, C. and Kontochristou, M. (2009), 'The Muhammed cartoons crisis 2006: The role of Islam in the European public sphere', in A. Triandafyllidou, R. Wodak and M. Krzyżanowski (eds), *The European Public Sphere and the Media. Europe in Crisis*, London: Palgrave-Macmillan., pp. 239–60.

van Dijk, T. (1993), *Elite Discourse and Racism*. London: SAGE Publications.

Volkmer, I. (2001), 'International communication theory in transition. Parameters of the new global sphere of mediation', in S. Hjarvard (ed.), *News in a Globalized Society*. Gothenburg: NORDICOM, pp. 65–76.

Wodak, R., de Cillia, R., Reisigl, M., and Liebhart, K. (2009), *The Discursive Construction of National Identity* (2nd edn), Edinburgh: Edinburgh University Press.

22

Dealing with the Extreme Right

Christoph Andersson

Reporting on right-wing extremists and parties is risky; journalists are often harassed and threatened. It is imperative, however, to continuously report on the extreme right – and how it tries to gain political power. The question is how journalists should conduct themselves when entering an extreme environment.

Gelsenkirchen, in western Germany, Saturday, 27 March 2010. A crew from the television company ZDF suddenly came under attack during an anti-Islam meeting arranged by the regional right-wing party PRO NRW, that is, Pro Nordrhein-Westphalia.

The crowd was screaming 'Nazis *raus*, Nazis out' and 'go and pee on yourselves, fascist horde' to the crew.

Around 250 people were participating in the meeting, held inside a fifteenth-century castle, Schloss Horst. Highly ranked politicians from all parts of Europe were present, some representing the Belgian Vlaams Belang, and some the Freiheitliche Partei Österreichs or Freedom Party of Austria (FPÖ). One person was there for the very first time, Kent Ekeroth from the Swedish Democrats, a party that emerged from the Swedish Nazi movement (Jansson & Schmid 2004).

He, however, was acting differently from all the other representatives, he stood and tried to calm the crowd down. Among the crowd was another Swede, millionaire and businessman Patrik Brinkmann. He was very red in the face from screaming: 'Nazis *raus*, Nazis raus!'

Brinkmann had recently promised to support the PRO NRW's election campaign with five million euros. The party would be running for the State parliamentary elections in May 2010.

The ZDF team was present to report on how PRO NRW representatives were connected to the far-right-wing party NPD, The National Democrats. Beside Brinkman, who made a fortune from buying and selling on the stock market, at least two other participants who had former close connections with the NPD were present.

In August 2008, Brinkman arranged a conference with the NPD, trying to get nationalistic hardliners to change their anti-Jewish view to a more anti-Islamic one (Andersson, Swedish radio 2010c). In interviews and speeches Brinkmann claimed that a nationalistic party criticizing Islam ('a religion that treats women like shit') would be accepted more easily by the German public than a party still stigmatizing the Jews, 63 years after the fall of the Third Reich (Andersson, Swedish radio 2010b).

When the NPD refused to shift its focus onto Islam, Brinkmann found a new ally – the PRO NRW – which readily opened its doors to former NPD members and others struggling to 'create a right-wing party, without anti-Semitism'. To become accepted by the German public, the PRO party needed to redefine the word 'Nazi'. This four-letter word is currently used by the PRO as a derogatory term for all those considered political opponents, be they scholars or representatives from other parties, regardless of whether they are from the Left or Right, or journalists. The aim is to give an impression that the FPÖ, Vlaams Belang, PRO NRW and the Swedish Democrats do not have any extreme right-wing views. Contrary to that notion, they pose as good democrats, representing society's mainstream, while it is their opponents who are the extremists. The ZDF is included in the extreme category.

The incident finally ended with that the reporter and his crew, as well as a professor accompanying the team as an expert on right-wing extremism, being violently forced to leave the premises. One of the politicians from PRO NRW, Manfred Rouhs, a former NPD member, tried to stab his finger into the face of a reporter and was screaming straight into his ear: 'Nazis *raus*, Nazis get out.'

Usually, German police are present when the extreme right holds its meetings. The police are very well aware that reporters and camera crews frequently come under attack. But this time neither the state police, nor the German 'feds', die Bundespolizei, were present. From a police perspective, highly ranked politicians – MPs from Flanders and Austria – and a Swedish millionaire, Brinkmann, all dressed in fine expensive suits, would not be expected to become aggressive. This, however, is exactly what happened.

Why do some journalists come under attack and not others?

I was watching, and recording the incident on audio tape, and was just a few metres away from the incident. My brief was to collect material for a Swedish radio documentary on how the various extreme right-wing parties were cooperating across borders. As a matter of fact, nationalism was becoming more and more internationalized, which the Gelsenkirchen meeting clearly demonstrated. One of the walls was covered with a huge poster showing the FPÖ, Vlaams Belang and PRO NRW logos. The message was 'Stop Islam'. An illustration showed a Muslim woman in a niqab, and behind her were black minarets, drawn like missiles, ready for launch.

The anger, stated on the poster and voiced at the meeting, was also focused on the ZDF crew. The question is why this was not focused on me as a radio reporter. Actually, the ZDF crew and I were partly covering the same issues. So why was the television team thrown out when I and other reporters, working on our own, were not? I recall a personal experience similar to the one my German colleagues were having that day, but in Sweden in August 2005, just outside the city of Nyköping, 100 km south of Stockholm. At a Swedish-German gathering a young neo-Nazi threatened to kill me, there and then, on the spot, in front of all his Nazi friends – as well as in front of the Swedish police (Andersson 2010a: 108–13). But none of the hardliners laid a hand on me. The attack was only verbal. On the day described above, however, ZDF crew members in Gelsenkirchen did not experience any death threats; nevertheless, people from the PRO NRW did use physical force on them. Another difference is that the police were present in Nyköping, even though Swedish law enforcement did not react or do anything. The only conclusion to be drawn from the two incidents is that reporters need to be very well prepared to deal with such situations on their own. They cannot really depend on help from the police, whether present or not.

One option would be for the media companies to hire their own security guards. On the one hand it might create a feeling of being protected, on the other it does not really avoid being thrown out. Worse is if the use of private security guards gives the impression that the journalists are afraid, that they are 'cowards' and dare not meet 'nationalists' on their own. Furthermore, bringing in additional people can lead to reduced journalistic success. Who would like to be interviewed by a journalist accompanied by a group of hired bodyguards? What affect would a number of people surrounding a journalist have on interviews?

Good journalism is generally the result of a meeting between two persons, an honestly interested reporter asking questions and an interviewee willing to answer, in a climate of at least some mutual respect. Anyone else introduced to this situation might disturb the quality of the interview. Of particular importance is that an interview can only take place if journalists are on the premises. Otherwise they will have to rely on secondary sources, such as what parties themselves make public on the Net, or what others are publishing.

One might argue that undercover journalism, using hidden cameras and microphones, is an option. I reject this, apart from exceptional situations, when all open methods have been tried but absolutely nothing else works, and the subject is of great public interest. Otherwise, such methods are unjustifiable. It is important to be aware that undercover methods might not only be illegal or unethical, they also open up strong criticism of journalists, who might be viewed as trying to provoke situations that would otherwise not take place. It is, besides, very dangerous. The journalist using such methods may later be looked upon as a traitor, which might lead to the very people who once considered him or her to be a sincere political friend taking their revenge. Therefore, the bottom line must always be to use overt rather than covert methods and not get thrown out of meetings.

Moreover, a consequence of being thrown out will be that the public are deprived of important information on extreme right-wing parties or activists, who have ambitions to run for local, regional or national governments, and finally rule the country. Questions, therefore, need to be asked and observations made on how democratic these parties really are – and if they do in fact have a hidden racist agenda. The issue is therefore: are there any journalistic strategies for achieving this goal?

Ways to act in an extreme environment

Let us go back to that Saturday in Gelsenkirchen, in March 2010, and analyse what caused the expulsion of the ZDF crew – and if something could have been done to avoid it. Before the main meeting started, a press conference was held in Schloss Horst.

We were probably around 30 journalists, including cameramen, sound engineers and photographers.

What usually happens when established political parties are invited to conferences such as this is that reporters shake hands with participating politicians, or at least the press officer running the meeting. But this did not happen in this case. I hardly saw anyone shaking hands with any of the right-wing representatives present. I nevertheless took the initiative to greet Mr Brinkmann, on whom I had recently made a radio documentary, broadcast just a week before, on 'Sveriges Radio' station P1, 'Patriot i frack, Patriot in tuxedo' (Andersson 2010d). The programme narrated the story of how, during a two-year period from 2008 to 2010, he had tried to influence the German extreme right towards becoming more anti-Islamic. I also greeted the press officer, general secretary Markus Wiener of PRO NRW, and the party's chairman, the lawyer Markus Beisicht. I even greeted a former party-leader candidate of the NPD. He is one of Brinkmann's best friends and had switched from the NPD to the PRO. His name is Andreas Molau. I interviewed him in 2008 for the Brinkmann documentary.

Some German colleagues found my behaviour strange. One expressed himself very clearly, 'We do not greet Nazis'. I see this very differently; nothing in the Swedish or German press code states that people with extreme views should not be greeted, or should be treated in a hostile manner. People have a right to be treated respectfully, regardless of their political or religious beliefs – even if the reporter is opposed to those beliefs. Interviewing people is moreover built on obtaining their cooperation.

A very good example of this is the work of the reporter Gitta Sereny. After the war she interviewed highly ranked former Nazis, people responsible for the Holocaust and war crimes. Among them was Fritz Stangl, former Commander of the Treblinka death camp from 1942 to 1943. Her contribution to our understanding of the mechanisms leading to a society as extreme as that of Nazi Germany cannot be underestimated. But she could achieve such great reporting only after getting Stangl to cooperate, by convincing him of her genuine journalistic interest (Sereny 2000: 110–58). For her, growing up under Nazi suppression, this was surely an extremely difficult task. Still, Gitta Sereny managed to keep her integrity by acting as a journalist, and by not taking on the role of prosecutor. Gitta Sereny taught us a great deal about what kind of attitude should be adopted when dealing with extreme right-wing individuals.

Reacting to them with hate or disregard would not only be to play their game, inadvertently placing them in the victim's position, it would even make interviews impossible.

Journalism is about asking questions and getting answers to those questions; it is not about starting unnecessary arguments. It is certainly not about getting into a debate with extremists, and trying to win it. That will usually lead to confrontation, with very negative results for reporting.

All these factors were in play at the press conference in Schloss Horst: As soon the conference opened for questions the ZDF reporter took the initiative. He read out long quotes from a report presented by the Verfassungsschutz, the secret police of Westphalia. I recorded it all on tape. Finally he stated:

'The PRO party is described as racist, hostile to immigrants, and right wing in the extreme.'

The PRO leader, Beisicht, responded 'most willingly', but since he was not asked any real questions he made a statement himself:

'It's like story time, with the Minister of the Interior telling fairy tales,' he claimed, and used the opportunity to deny and reject all forms of racism. The turn went back to the ZDF reporter. He now drew a conclusion, based on a report by the secret state police, that the PRO party says one thing in public but actually has a completely different agenda.

'You are very welcome to use this hour to tell fairy tales,' Beisicht responded, and returned to his message: 'Racism once led Germany to a catastrophe so that cannot be the answer. We reject all kinds of racism!' The ZDF reporter and Beisicht interrupted one another several times. It caused tension, which became heightened as the conference proceeded.

The escalation process

Beisicht wanted to make sure that every reporter understood that the PRO party did not want to proscribe Islam. He claimed that freedom of religion was not at stake, it was only the construction of new mosques, with '*prozige*, boastful minarets', which should be banned. The statement provoked a female colleague of the ZDF reporter. She is a TV reporter of Turkish descent.

'I am anxious to hear how you would define the word boastful?' she asked.

The PRO press officer, Markus Wiener, replied:

'For decades we have not had any huge or boastful Mosques or minarets.'

He was interrupted by the female reporter, now making a statement herself. In contrast to the ZDF reporter, she became very personal; she told how her Turkish father, now 65 years old, once came to Germany as one of many guest workers. At that time, he and the other Turkish migrants did not have any appropriate mosques to pray in. She claimed that religion in those days had to be practised in the most primitive circumstances, in cold chilly buildings. She said that she was very happy that her parents now had the opportunity to go and pray in real decent mosques:

'That will certainly not threaten your Western European culture!' she said.

'Thanks for bringing that up', Wiener responded, 'we do not have anything against modernizing mosques, with the very best kind of heating and sanitation, but we are definitely against minarets, fifty-five metres tall'. 'You know the expression, "The minarets are our bayonets and the believers are our soldiers", the architecture is used to demonstrate Islamic dominance, that's why we are against it'.

Now the female reporter became angry:

'I don't think you have any idea of what Islam is and how diverse and how colourful the religion actually is! Open your eyes and try to see the German kind of Islam, it's practised by many young, well-educated and dedicated Turks and Arabs!'

On the one hand, her reaction was understandable, being of Turkish descent and feeling targeted herself. On the other hand, debating in this forum would later contribute to getting her ZDF colleague into trouble. She finally stated that the PRO Party was 'stigmatizing Muslims'. Beisicht countered that he himself had been 'stigmatized' and needed to live under police protection. He asked the reporter when a Christian church was last built in Turkey. The reporter countered by screaming that 'This discussion is about Germany!'

Until this point, the right-wing politicians from other countries had not said a word, but a FPÖ representative became extremely provoked by the female reporter, even though she was dressed in modern fashion and was not covering her hair. He confronted her with: 'You are a disgrace to your profession, your task is to ask questions and not to act as if you are in a courtroom!'

The two German reporters took up a lot of the conference time, arguing and making statements. It was only at the very end of the conference that I saw an opportunity to ask my questions. I was very interested in what the whole Gelsenkirchen gathering was actually about. According to the invitation it was to stop the building of mosques, by arguing that a law be proposed at European Union (EU) level.

To be able to do so the present parties must use the Lisbon Treaty, forcing the European Commission to draft a legal proposal for a new EU directive. This could only be done if they got enough signatures from EU citizens in favour of such a directive. If they managed to do that, the matter could later be brought before the European Parliament. I was most interested in following up this process and reporting it in my radio documentary. Therefore, I needed all the politicians on the podium to answer my question about how many signatures they would be able to get in each country.

'Finally we get a real question', one said, relieved.

Everyone on the podium claimed that they would get extremely high numbers, as they saw themselves as representing the mainstream, the majority in each country. My plan was, later, to compare the figures mentioned with the actual numbers of signatures.

What the politicians could not see was their propaganda-like answers from a long-term perspective. These would help me to measure how strong they actually were politically, in comparison to what they claimed to be. In other words, the question was a bit trickier than it first appeared. Still, it did not cause any tension or aggressive behaviour, towards me or Swedish radio.

What I did not know at this time was that the whole idea of getting signatures would, politically, be more or less dead within about 16 months. This was because one of the strongest supporters of the parties present was a young Norwegian named Anders Behring Breivik. On 22 July 2011 he would blow up government buildings in central Oslo and massacre many young people on Utøya Island. The number of deaths that day was over 70 men and women. Breivik's actions resulted in a decline in public support for right-wing populist parties, at least temporarily.

The final throwing-out process

After the press conference the meeting commenced in the main hall of the castle. Markus Beisicht began his welcome speech by greeting participants. From the back I observed something very strange, a new participant arrived and checked in at the conference reception desk. It was a young man wearing a jacket with the letters LONSDALE. The brand is often used by NPD followers. The name LONSDALE includes the letters

NSDA, only a P is required to create the abbreviation NSDAP, short for Adolf Hitler's Nazi party, Nazionalsozialistische Deutsche Arbeiterpartei (Andersson 2010a: 74).

I could also see that the man had an SS motto tattooed on his body. The remarkable thing was that, in spite of his obvious and visual political leanings, the PRO people let him join the meeting – even though the message presented at the press conference was quite the opposite, that they did not want to have anything to do with racists or Nazis.

Simultaneously, the ZDF crew and I moved forward to document this man, who was about to enter the meeting. This was immediately noticed by Markus Beisicht. He interrupted his speech, saying that the ZDF team was disturbing the proceedings. Meanwhile some PRO politicians decided to stop the man entering the hall in his Lonsdale outfit. In a friendly and non-hostile way, the man was asked to leave, in front of the running ZDF camera. He accepted and went away calmly.

Now Beisicht, highly irritated, saw a chance finally to get rid of the entire ZDF crew, including the professor, brought in as an expert on the extreme right. He blamed the ZDF reporter for trying to question why the man was allowed to join the meeting – and how this complied with all the previous statements made at the press conference. I in fact asked the very same type of question, but only the ZDF reporter and his crew were urged to 'Sit down – or leave!' (Kolenvideo 2010). Within a few seconds PRO politicians and activists were trying to push the ZDF crew out of the hall while the crowd screamed 'Nazis *raus*, Nazis *raus*'.

Naturally, the ZDF team recorded the violence it was subjected to and broadcasted the scene later, on 1 April (Frank ZDF 2010). The question now is whether this scene could make up for everything the crew missed by getting thrown out of the meeting. The issue is what impact did that crew, comprising four people, huge cameras and broadcast equipment, have on the confrontation that was building from the very beginning of the press conference.

To Beisicht it was all a demonstration of media power, to which he needed to respond. It was imperative that he show all those present, politicians, participants and journalists, that he was strong enough to meet the challenge of a huge and important media company like ZDF.

Maybe all this might have been avoided if the ZDF reporter had adopted a different strategy. He should not have started by making statements and bringing a big crew to the press conference. It would, perhaps, have been enough for ZDF to be represented by just one reporter and a lightly equipped cameraman.

Regarding what happened in Nyköping in August 2005, as mentioned earlier, I also demonstrated far too much power by using a microphone with a huge windshield and headphones that were far too large. I was one of three radio reporters on the spot. We were all from public Swedish radio, backing one another up and each with a car at our disposal – two with the symbols SR, Swedish Radio.

One of the SR vehicles was built for live broadcasting, with antennas on its roof. Together, we signalled considerable media power, such that the right-wingers probably felt provoked (Andersson 2006, Swedish Radio). I remember getting into an argument with the right-wingers, not about any security police report, but whether the car park we were on was a public one or not. The argument caused the situation to escalate further, resulting in death threats.

There are no general guidelines

Still, there are never solid working guidelines. Sometimes a demonstration of media power will actually prevent reporters being attacked. I experienced this on the very same day that the Nyköping incident took place. One of my two colleagues and I were stopped at a roadblock, about 60 kilometres south of the city. Heavies from the extreme right were actually blocking a public road. The reason was that the road lay next to a nearby country house, in which hundreds of right-wingers from all over Northern Europe and the United States of America were preparing for a rally. I and my radio colleague were completely outnumbered. Neither the police nor any other colleagues were present. Fortunately our two cars, especially the one with the huge antennas, helped to create some kind of status.

Another important factor was that I, some weeks before, had arranged to hold an interview with a German NPD politician representing the party in the State Parliament of Saxony. He was one of the main speakers at the rally. As we were not let in, he came out and gave an interview just beyond the roadblock. I treated him no differently from any other politician. We shook hands, made small talk and did not argue or debate, which might have made him either defensive or aggressive. By treating him respectfully, and getting the same respect back, the situation never escalated. Still, it was a failure, as neither I nor my fellow reporter was able to attend or monitor the rally itself.

This is similar to the situation in which the ZDF crew found itself in Gelsenkirchen. Actually, the really interesting speeches and statements were yet to come – in the absence of the ZDF. These began with a speech by the scholar Alfred Merchtesheimer, once active in the German peace movement during the 1980s and a former member of the Green faction in the Bundestag.

In his speech, Merchtesheimer urged 'that the participants not only should hold protest meetings outside mosques, but also outside Christian churches'. This was recorded on my tape. He considered Catholic and Protestant clergy leaders to be far too tolerant of Islam. During his speech, church bells suddenly started ringing outside, which is customary in Germany on Saturday afternoons. 'What is this? Some sort of attack (on us)!?' Merchetsheimer said.

The next speaker was the leader of Vlaams Belang, Filip Dewinter. He described Islam as a 'wild beast', ready to attack its 'weakest victim'. He even went as far as comparing the spreading of Islam with the spreading of AIDS. His final conclusion was that it was everyone's duty to be 'Islamophobic', in the struggle to defend Western values. Dewinter was followed by the Swedish Democrat Kent Ekeroth, running for a seat in the Swedish Parliament in the autumn elections. Ekeroth told everyone about his home country and the city of Malmö:

'The Islamization of Sweden has led, as it always does, to violence and unrest,' he said. He continued with: 'The Jewish population of Malmö is fleeing due to anti-Semitic attacks from the Muslim population.'

He was indeed right in that there had been attacks on Jews in Malmö, but his statement that all Muslims in Malmö were attacking all Jews, making them leave town, was incorrect. Finally, Ekeroth urged all Muslims to leave Sweden and 'go home'.

What was actually said at the conference itself was far more radical than what was said earlier, during the press conference. Being present to record events was therefore most important in order to get a true picture of what the parties present actually represented. The recordings open up many questions that may be put, not only to present politicians but to the Muslim Community, the Church and established political parties.

Conclusion: Do not get into the position of being thrown out

It is very important that journalistic methods should never be questioned; the recordings were made overtly, and with the consent of the PRO party and others. Quite different from Swedish radio, ZDF, in November 2011, still suffers from what happened that day. On various sites on the internet, accusations are made that the incident with the Lonsdale man was staged by the ZDF, although I personally have seen no evidence to support that statement (PRO NRW 2010: anonymous video). The ZDF reporter (Frank, Udo) also strongly rejects those accusations The incident, however, is used for an ongoing never-ending defamation of the ZDF, as well as an ongoing campaign in which the PRO party portrays itself as the victim, that it is haunted by the media in general and ZDF in particular. Even if untrue it probably causes a lot of damage for further ZDF reporting on the far right and its aims. Sometimes there is no way to avoid situations such as this, though sometimes there is, simply by being aware of how to act as a reporter in a hostile environment. This will impact on how we journalists are treated, and positively affect our ability to provide adequate and important information about what is going on within the right-wing movements and parties, all over Europe.

References

Andersson, C. (2006), 'Kampen om gatorna, skallarna och parlamenten – om polisen och extremhögern', Stockholm: radio documentary for Swedish Radio, station P1, broadcast 25 February, 2:03 p.m.
— (2010a), *Från gatan in i parlamenten – om extremhögerns väg mot politisk makt*, Stockholm: Norstedts förlag.
— (2010b), *Lissabonfördraget testas av Europas ultrahöger*, Stockholm: Radio report on Människor och tro, Swedish Radio, station P1, broadcast 26 February, 2:03 p.m.
— (2010c), Original broadcast recording for the Swedish Radio P1 made on 27 March 2010 in Gelsenkirchen.
— (2010d), *Patriot i frack*, Stockholm: Radio Documentary for Swedish Radio, station P1, broadcast 20 March, 2:03 p.m.
Anonymous on Youtube (2010), 'ZDF Desinformation Teil 3 von 6.avi'. <www.youtube.com/watch?v=St2LdaTIj1E&feature=related> [accessed 14 November 2011].

Frank, U. (2010), 'Wölfe im Schafspelz – Wie Rechtspopulisten als angebliche Bürgerbewegung auftreten', Mainz: ZDF reporter, broadcast 1 April 2010, 9 p.m. <www.youtube.com/watch?NR=1&v=340lWp71aqg> [accessed 14 November 2011].

Jansson, K.-A. and Schmid, I. (2004), *Blågul Nazism*, Stockholm: Forum för levande historia.

Kolelnvideos chanal on Youtube (2010), 'Ein ZDF-Team und Alexander Häuser bei der Anti-Moschee-Konferenz von pro NRW'. <www.youtube.com/watch?v=qtYwG_kk_bc&feature=player_embedded> [accessed 14 November 2011].

Sereny, G. (2000), *Tyskt trauma*, Stockholm: Ordfront.

Telephone call, Udo Frank, 14 November 2011.

Index

Hiking the

The

IMPORTANT NOTICE

Due to a combination of successive, severe storms and a major fire in the Ventana Wilderness since 1997—the year the data was collected for the 1998 update—trail conditions have deteriorated dramatically. Certain trails, because of their popularity and their proximity to major roads, are still passable, but a great many of the more remote trails that traverse the heart of the Ventana are heavily overgrown, washed out, and littered with fallen trees. The USFS has said that budgetary constraints preclude them from restoring most of these trails in the foreseeable future. Therefore Wilderness Press cannot confirm the usability of any of the trails listed in this guide. Anyone wishing to take a hike here should call the USFS office in King City first for information regarding specific trail conditions. That phone number is (831) 385-5434. You may also call the USFS branch office in Big Sur at (831) 677-2315.

Also, please refer to page 167 in this guide (following the Index) for the 1998 Update.

(compiled by Jeffrey Van Middlebrook)